COND	NAME IN FULL	FORM	YEAR
A	Bernie Belanger	2DA	76
A	Rick Miller	2HA	76

Automotive Mechanics
and Technology

Tillmann Steckner, B.A.
Technical Department
A. B. Lucas Secondary School
London, Ontario

A Completely Revised Edition of

*Automotive Mechanics:
Principles and Operation*

by **Mervin J. McGuffin**
Area Superintendent
Board of Education
London, Ontario

Automotive Mechanics and Technology

Macmillan of Canada

©1975 The Macmillan Company of Canada Limited, 70 Bond Street, Toronto M5B 1X3. Affiliated with Maclean-Hunter Learning Materials Company.

ISBN 0-7705-1195-3

Artwork by Ed Alton, J. Gardisch, Antony Bradshaw, and W. Mohr.

Grateful acknowledgment is made to the many companies in the automotive industry and allied fields who have kindly assisted in the preparation of the text by supplying illustrative material. Appropriate credit has been given with each illustration, even where the original illustration has served only as the basis for a revised diagram or where minor changes have been made by the publisher.

Cover photo : Wheel courtesy of Green and Ross Tire Company ; photograph by Peter Paterson / Photo Design.

Printed in Canada

Preface

What makes writing an automotive text such a challenge is not only technological change, which seems to accelerate at an ever-increasing pace, but also modern trends in education. While the teaching of automotive courses still plays an important role in apprenticeship training, we now see more and more students who take these courses either to prepare themselves for more advanced studies or simply to lay the foundation for a meaningful avocation.

Probably more technological changes have taken place since the first edition of this book appeared in 1962 than during the thirty years preceding it. Unfortunately, we are in a transition stage where both new and old systems are with us—disc brakes and drum brakes, radial and bias-ply tires, electronic and conventional ignition systems, A.C. and D.C. generators, standard and sealed cooling systems, revised tire ratings and new lubricant classifications, as well as old ones. The time has not yet arrived when one can safely omit what one day might be considered outdated material. This applies equally to the English standard of measurement, even though metrication is being quickly introduced within the industry in North America.

Nor can we ignore any longer the increasing role of imported vehicles employing such systems as fuel injection, independent rear suspension, overhead camshafts, and rack and pinion steering. While the future of the Wankel engine is still uncertain, the great curiosity that it has aroused has had to be satisfied. Chapters on gaskets, seals, and sealers, and on emission controls have also been added.

To treat these topics thoroughly it has been necessary to expand the original text considerably, and to assist in the understanding of many of the illustrations a second colour has been used in the new edition. Since all automotive texts deal with the same basic technical information, the difference between them must lie to a large extent in their general approach and the manner in which information is given. Every attempt has been made to present the material here in an easy-to-follow manner for the student. The engine chapter, for example, follows closely the logical order of assembly. The chapters themselves are tightly interrelated so that knowledge acquired in one chapter can readily be applied in the next.

Other new features of this edition are an emphasis on service, maintenance tips, assignments involving the identification of tools and parts, first-aid instructions, a discussion of carbon monoxide, metric conversion tables, decimal equivalents, and "Trouble-Shooting" sections at the end of several chapters. It is to be hoped that this last feature will help to overcome the most frequently heard complaint of service managers, shop foremen, and garage operators, namely that most mechanics lack the ability to think for themselves and to diagnose problems. This is also one reason why this text goes deeply into the "hows" and "whys" of things. Everyday experiences are widely used to illustrate the basic principles. Safety is not treated as a separate topic but rather is introduced throughout the text, wherever it is relevant to the material being discussed.

I very much wish to express my thanks to all those who assisted me in this project— manufacturers, fellow teachers, mechanics, engineers, students, and friends. I am also deeply grateful to Mr. M. J. McGuffin, the author of the first edition of the text, without whose encouragement this book would never have been written.

T.S.

Contents

It should be noted that, with the change to the metric system in this country, some metric units and symbols that have been in common use will be replaced with others that conform to the SI system. A list of the various units, entitled Metric SI Units for the Canadian Automotive Industry, is available from the Automotive Parts Manufacturers Association, Suite 402, 55 York Street, Toronto, Ontario. Also, in the tables of Weights and Measures on pages 305-6 of this book, mention is made of such changes, where they are applicable.

1

Automotive Service Tools

Study Guide

That proper maintenance of the modern automobile requires a thorough understanding of its operating principles is stating the obvious but workmanship can only be as good as the tools employed and the skill with which they are used.

Most trade terms are very descriptive, and can be quickly added to your vocabulary. For example, the names of tools are usually derived from the principle, purpose, or shape involved.

Hand Tools

The first technician was probably born when man first picked up a branch to move a boulder or a fallen tree from his path. By doing this, he discovered the principle of leverage, or mechanical advantage. Most automotive hand tools are an application of this basic principle.

The twisting force we apply when tightening or loosening nuts, bolts, and screws involves another very important concept: the idea of torque.

Let us apply these two principles to an actual working problem. If you study Fig. 1:1, you can learn a great deal about the proper use of hand tools and the principles involved:
1. The leverage of the wrench is 1 foot.
2. The applied force (the pull of the hand) is 30 pounds.
3. Since Torque (twisting force) = Force × Leverage, the torque applied to the fastener is 30 pounds × 1 foot or 30 lb.-ft. (pound-feet).[1]
4. Nuts, screws, and bolts, with very few exceptions, are tightened in a clockwise direction.
5. If conditions allow, the wrench should be pulled rather than pushed. This avoids hand injuries if the tool should slip.

Wrenches

Good wrenches are manufactured from forged, high-quality, heat-treated, carbon alloy-steels[2] and are carefully proportioned to withstand normal working loads applied by hand.

The following "tips" will help you to avoid

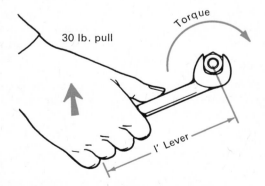

Fig. 1:1   Leverage, Force, and Torque

[1]Some texts and manuals refer to foot-pounds (ft.-lb.) rather than pound-feet (lb.-ft.). While using either method doesn't affect calculations, torque should be expressed in pound-feet; the units of foot-pounds measure work and power. (See Chapter 7.) The metric unit for measuring torque has been the kilogram metre (kg·m); the new unit is the newton metre (N·m).
[2]An alloy is a mixture of metals, usually heat-treated to obtain such desired qualities as strength and hardness.

injury, spoilage, and much frustration:

1. Never increase the leverage of a wrench by means of pipes or other aids.
2. Never hammer a wrench.
3. Heating a tool will permanently weaken it.
4. Don't magnetize a wrench. This will not only weaken the tool, but it will also magnetize other sensitive parts with which it comes into contact.
5. Using a tool of the wrong size not only damages the tool and the fastener; it is also dangerous for the mechanic.
6. Do not attach any wrenches to power tools unless they are specifically designed for this purpose.
7. Avoid obvious abuses, such as using wrenches as prying tools or as a means to complete electrical circuits.
8. Keep the tools clean; avoid contact with acids and do not place them on batteries or running machinery.
9. Shine and polish alone do not necessarily mean high quality. Well-known brand names usually carry a guarantee for replacement of broken tools. A clumsy and heavy design is probably a sign of poor quality.

The size of a wrench is determined by the distance between the parallel flats of the nut or bolt for which it is designed (Fig. 1:2).

Wrenches are available both in inch sizes and in metric sizes (used on most imported cars and some domestic models) (Fig. 1:3). The most common inch sizes range from ³⁄₁₆" to 1½". Within this range, sizes generally increase or decrease in ¹⁄₁₆" steps (³⁄₁₆", ¼", ⁵⁄₁₆", ⅜", ⁷⁄₁₆", etc.). There are, however, some exceptions where sizes are given in thirty-seconds and even sixty-fourths of an inch. The sizes of metric wrenches, on the other hand, are indicated in whole numbers such as 6 mm, 7 mm, 8 mm, etc.

Open-end Wrenches

The open-end wrench (Fig. 1:3) grips only two sides of the fastener's head. If the applied torque is high, the wrench should only be used if no other wrench will work.

The open-end wrench is usually made with a 15° jaw angle, as shown in Fig. 1:4. If you turn this wrench over on its other side, you will notice that the jaws point 15° in the opposite direction. The "swing angle" is therefore 30°. This feature allows the wrench to be used in close or obstructed areas.

Another important feature of open-end wrenches is the combination of two sizes in one wrench. Typical combinations are ½" with ⁹⁄₁₆" and ⁹⁄₁₆" with ⅝".

Another kind of open-end wrench, usually called an ignition wrench, ranges in size from ¹³⁄₆₄" to ⁹⁄₁₆". It has a very short, more manageable handle for work on electrical and fuel systems. This tool is listed in catalogues as an ignition wrench, short open-end wrench, or midget open-end wrench. Some have jaw angles of 15° and 60° to reach around obstructions.

Box Wrenches

Box wrenches (Figs. 1:5-1:7) completely enclose, or box in, the head of the fastener. This prevents slippage, even with the higher torque loads that the increased leverage of their long handles permit. Box wrenches are slanted at 15°, and can reach into very tight places (see Fig. 1:7). Most box wrenches are of the double hexagon type, i.e., their heads are twelve-pointed. The swing angle of the double hexagon wrench is therefore 360° divided by 12 points or 30°.

Some box wrenches have a curved handle to reach hard-to-get-at places. They are known as obstruction wrenches.

Offset Box Wrenches or Box Socket Wrenches

This wrench (Fig. 1:8) is basically a box wrench with its head offset by 45°. This allows the

Snap-on Tools of Canada, Ltd.

Fig. 1:2   Wrench Size

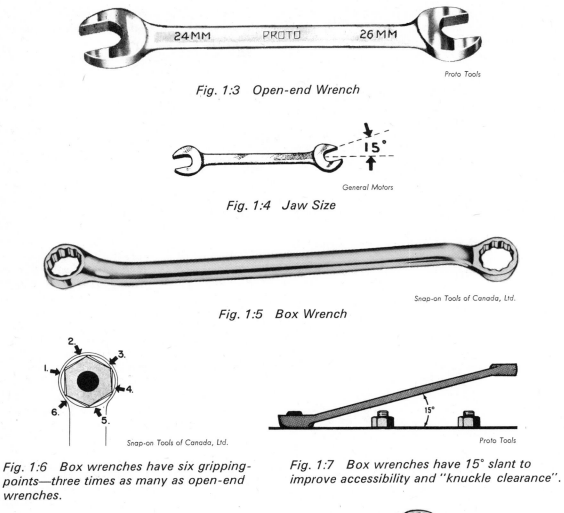

Fig. 1:3 Open-end Wrench

Proto Tools

Fig. 1:4 Jaw Size

General Motors

Fig. 1:5 Box Wrench

Snap-on Tools of Canada, Ltd.

Snap-on Tools of Canada, Ltd.

Proto Tools

Fig. 1:6 Box wrenches have six gripping-points—three times as many as open-end wrenches.

Fig. 1:7 Box wrenches have 15° slant to improve accessibility and "knuckle clearance".

Proto Tools

Fig. 1:8 Offset Box Wrench. The head is offset by 45°.

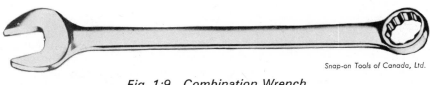

Snap-on Tools of Canada, Ltd.

Fig. 1:9 Combination Wrench

mechanic to reach into recesses and depressions or to increase "knuckle clearance".

Combination Wrenches

The combination wrench (Fig. 1:9) combines the open-end wrench and the box wrench in one tool. The head or wrench size is the same at both ends. The box end can be used when torque requirements are high, and the open end when little force but more speed is required.

Line Wrenches or Flare Nut Wrenches

This extra-wide, slotted, box-type wrench (Fig. 1:10) is designed to slip over tubing to tighten or loosen line fittings. Hydraulic fittings are very easily damaged with ordinary tools because they have very thin walls and they are often made of brass. Since the lines carry brake fluid, fuel, or oil, the hazards involved are obvious.

Hex-head Wrenches or Allen Wrenches

These wrenches fit fasteners with an internal hexagon (see Fig. 1:11). Since it is very important that the corners are sharp to ensure a good grip, worn tips should be ground down.

Adjustable Wrenches or Crescent Wrenches

The adjustable wrench (Fig. 1:12) fits any size of fastener within its jaw range. As a rule of thumb, the maximum jaw opening is roughly the length of the wrench divided by eight, or somewhat less. For example, an 8" adjustable will usually fit sizes up to 1".

Note well: Anyone who takes pride in good workmanship uses adjustables only in emergencies. The jaws of adjustables are simply too clumsy and inaccurate for precision work. The results are hand injuries and rounded hexagons that will no longer fit any type of wrench properly.

Socket Wrenches

These wrenches, often simply called "sockets" (Fig. 1:13), make the mechanic's work both easier and faster. In obstructed or recessed areas, they are often the only tools that will do the job. Since sockets can be attached to a great variety of handles and extensions, it is possible to make up whatever combination the situation calls for.

The most common socket profiles are shown in Fig. 1:14. Socket sets, each comprising a wide range of wrench sizes, are divided into drive sizes. (The drive is the square adapter hole.)

Drive sizes available are 1/4", 3/8", 1/2", 5/8", and 3/4". The 5/8" and 3/4" drive sizes are used mostly on heavy equipment. The more common sizes are used as follows:
1. The 1/4" drive, or "midget" set, is for small, light work such as that required on small fuel, electrical, and trim components.
2. The 3/8" drive, or "Ferret" set, is for fast, low to medium torque applications such as those encountered during tune-ups.
3. The 1/2" drive set can handle as much as 350 lb.-ft. in the larger socket sizes needed for work on engines, transmissions, rear axles, and suspensions.

Many mechanics prefer single hexagon sockets to double hexagon sockets because they last longer, are less likely to slip (even on worn fasteners), and are easy to keep clean. The wider swing-angle of single hexagon sockets (60°) is rarely a disadvantage since most ratchets (Fig. 1:21) and ratchet adapters (Fig. 1:18) have swing angles of 18° or less.

Deep Sockets

Deep sockets (Fig. 1:15) are designed to reach less accessible hexagons. Threaded linkage rods with adjusting nuts, "U"-bolts, and spark plugs are typical examples.

Spark-plug Sockets

Spark-plug sockets (Fig. 1:16) are deep sockets equipped with an inner rubber liner that holds the spark plug and protects its insulator. Some spark-plug sockets have, in addition to the square internal drive, an external hexagon drive for work in very crowded areas.

Flexible Sockets

Flexible sockets (Fig. 1:17) are very helpful in obstructed areas. Because their angular drive often causes them to tip, some mechanics prefer "flex sockets" to be of the more stable single hexagon type. *Caution:* The angular

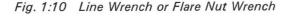

Snap-on Tools of Canada, Ltd.

Fig. 1:10   Line Wrench or Flare Nut Wrench

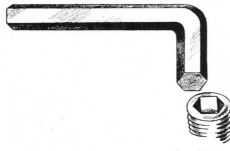

General Motors

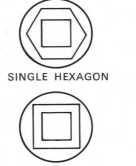

Snap-on Tools of Canada, Ltd.

Fig. 1:11   Hex-head Wrench or Allen Wrench (shown with a set screw)

Fig. 1:12   Adjustable Wrench

SINGLE HEXAGON   DOUBLE HEXAGON

Snap-on Tools of Canada, Ltd.

Fig. 1:13   Socket Wrenches

SINGLE HEXAGON   DOUBLE HEXAGON

SINGLE SQUARE   DOUBLE SQUARE

Fig. 1:14   Common Socket Profiles

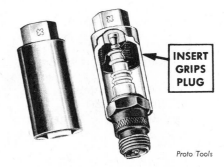

INSERT
GRIPS
PLUG

Proto Tools

Fig. 1:16   Spark-plug Socket. Note the external hexagon drive in addition to the square internal drive.

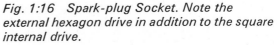

Snap-on Tools of Canada, Ltd.

Fig. 1:15   Single Hexagon Deep Socket

Proto Tools

Fig. 1:17   Flexible Socket

Proto Tools

Fig. 1:18   Reversible Ratchet Adapter

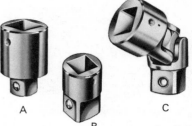

A   B   C

Proto Tools

Fig. 1:19   (a) ½" to ⅜" Adapter; (b) ⅜" to ½" Adapter; (c) Universal Joint.

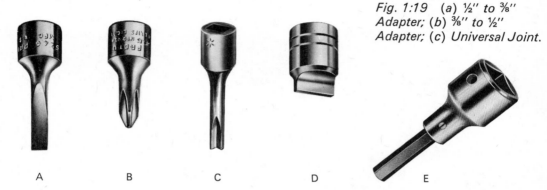

A   B   C   D   E

Proto Tools

Fig. 1:20   (a) Screwdriver Adapter; (b) Phillips Screwdriver Adapter; (c) Clutch Screwdriver Adapter; (d) Screwdriver Adapter; (e) Allen Wrench Adapter.

drive of flex sockets results in inaccurate (higher) torque-wrench readings!

Adapters

The adapters shown in Figs. 1:18-1:20 are the most common types. Their purposes are self-evident.

Socket Handles

The most common socket handles are shown in Figs. 1:21-1:25. The descriptive names require little comment, but two important rules apply to all of these handles:
1. The longer the handle leverage, the greater is the torque and the slower the tool.
2. To avoid damage to tools and fasteners, select the drive size of the handle extension or socket which comes closest to the stem or thread size of the fastener.
Reversible Ratchet Handles, or simply *Ratch-*

ets (Fig. 1:21) usually have a swing angle of 18° or less. A small lever at the ratchet head permits the mechanic to select the direction in which torque is applied and in which the ratchet "free-wheels". Do not wash ratchets in solvents except when they are completely dismantled for occasional cleaning and lubrication.

The *Flex-Ratchet* (Fig. 1:22) is particularly useful for removing spark plugs in some less accessible engine locations.

Hinge Handles or *Power Bars* (Fig. 1:23) give excellent leverage and torque when the hinge is at right angles; but, when the handle is raised, torque decreases as speed increases. Fully straightened, the hinge handle can be used as a "spinner". This flexible tool is ideal for spark-plug removal, especially if a ratchet adapter (Fig. 1:18) is attached to it.

The *Speed Handle* (Fig. 1:24) is typically a fast, low-torque tool used on cover screws or freely spinning fasteners.

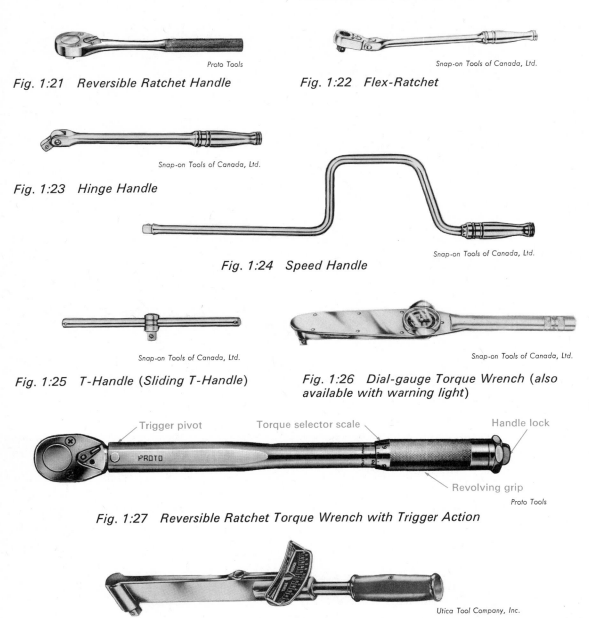

Proto Tools

Fig. 1:21   Reversible Ratchet Handle

Snap-on Tools of Canada, Ltd.

Fig. 1:22   Flex-Ratchet

Snap-on Tools of Canada, Ltd.

Fig. 1:23   Hinge Handle

Snap-on Tools of Canada, Ltd.

Fig. 1:24   Speed Handle

Snap-on Tools of Canada, Ltd.

Fig. 1:25   T-Handle (Sliding T-Handle)

Snap-on Tools of Canada, Ltd.

Fig. 1:26   Dial-gauge Torque Wrench (also available with warning light)

Trigger pivot   Torque selector scale   Handle lock

PROTO

Revolving grip

Proto Tools

Fig. 1:27   Reversible Ratchet Torque Wrench with Trigger Action

Utica Tool Company, Inc.

Fig. 1:28   Beam-type Torque Wrench

Torque Handles or *Torque Wrenches* or *Torque Meters* indicate the torque applied to a fastener. The torque wrench, usually calibrated in lb.-ft. (see page 1), is one of the most important tools in the automotive trade. No mechanic should be without one. Torque wrenches calibrated in lb.-in. (pound-inches) and metric units are available.[3]

Some dial-gauge types (Fig. 1:26) have a signal light to indicate when the desired torque is reached. The type in Fig. 1:27 is very popular

[3]To convert lb.-ft. to lb.-in., N·m, or kg·m, see under "Weights and Measures" on pages 305-6.

because it has a built-in trigger action that indicates to the hand and to the ear that the torque limit selected at the handle grip has been reached. This torque wrench also serves as a reversible ratchet.

Note : Do not use universal sockets or other flexible drives on torque wrenches for they will cause inaccurate torque readings. Special torque wrench adapters are available to torque inaccessible fasteners.

Extension Bars

Extension bars, or simply extensions (Fig. 1:29) can be used singly or in combination to extend the length of the tool from the drive part of the handle to the socket.

Snap-on Tools of Canada, Ltd.

Fig. 1:29   Extension Bar

Flexible Extensions

These are designed for very low torque applications in obstructed areas.

Note well: The proper use of sockets requires that one hand does the pulling at the handle while the other counteracts this pull by supporting the drive side of the handle directly above the socket. If this method is not used, damage and injury will probably follow. Broken spark-plug insulators and bruised knuckles due to slippage are the most common "casualties".

Screwdrivers

A screwdriver should not be used as a chisel, punch, or pry bar. To avoid damage to either the screwdriver or the fastener, hold the screwdriver straight and make certain that the blade tip fits the screw head exactly (Fig. 1:30). Regrind worn screwdriver tips as illustrated in Fig. 1:31.

A typical set of standard blade or slot screwdrivers is shown in Fig. 1:32. Over-all length ranges from under 2" to 20". The tip size is not related to the length of the screwdriver. The very short, compact type is also known as a "stubby" screwdriver. Note that the blade

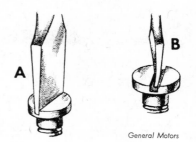

General Motors

Fig. 1:30   (a) Screwdriver should fit the screw slot as shown here. (b) A poor fit damages the screwdriver and the screw slot.

shank may have a hexagon just below the handle. By applying a wrench, torque may be increased within reason.

The most common types of screwdriver tips are shown in Fig. 1:33. The advantages of tips B, C, and D are that they can apply greater torque to the screw head and that they are also self-centring (an important feature for fast assembly work using power tools). Tip sizes of Phillips screwdrivers (Fig. 1:33b) increase from No. 1 through to No. 4.

Offset Screwdriver or Angle Screwdriver

The offset screwdriver has two blades at right angles to each other (i.e. the swing angle is 90°). Since this is not necessary with the Phillips type, it has two different tip sizes instead. The angle screwdriver not only enables the mechanic to turn screws in tight spaces but it gives good leverage (torque) as well.

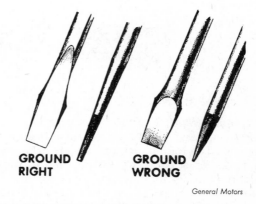

GROUND RIGHT   **GROUND WRONG**

General Motors

Fig. 1:31   How to Regrind Worn Tips

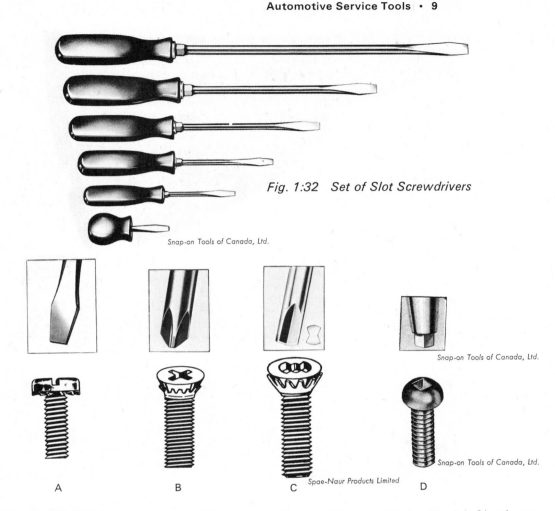

Fig. 1:32 Set of Slot Screwdrivers

Snap-on Tools of Canada, Ltd.

Snap-on Tools of Canada, Ltd.

Snap-on Tools of Canada, Ltd.

A   B   C   D

Spae-Naur Products Limited

Fig. 1:33 Common Types of Screwdriver Tips: (a) Standard Tip; (b) Phillips Tip; (c) Clutch-type Tip; (d) Robertson Tip.

Proto Tools

Fig. 1:34 Offset Screwdriver

The Screw Starter

The screw starter (Fig. 1:35) can hold a screw so that it can be started in some inaccessible area, for example, inside a distributor or behind an instrument panel. The upper end of the screw starter may have a magnetic tip to "fish" for lost screws. *Warning:* Do not touch any bearings with it! It will magnetize them.

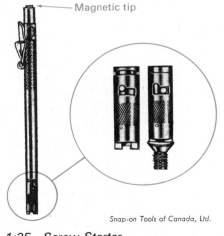

Magnetic tip

Snap-on Tools of Canada, Ltd.

Fig. 1:35 Screw Starter

Pliers

There is such a great variety of pliers that only some of the most common ones are covered here.

Note: Never use pliers as a substitute wrench to turn any type of fastener, and particularly not with hydraulic lines and fittings!

Duck-bill Pliers

These hold or bend small parts (electrical and fuel systems).

Proto Tools

Fig. 1:36 Duck-bill Pliers

Side-cutting or Diagonal Pliers

These cut small parts, especially wires, and remove, shorten, and spread cotter pins.

Proto Tools

Fig. 1:37 Side-cutting Pliers or Diagonal Pliers

Combination Pliers

These pliers combine the functions of duck-bill and side-cutting pliers but perform neither of them very well. They are popular pliers in emergency kits.

Snap-on Tools of Canada, Ltd.

Fig. 1:38 Combination Pliers

Lock-channel Pliers and Slip-joint Pliers

These two types hold parts of various sizes and shapes. Note the parallel jaw action. The slip-joint type is not shown but differs only in the locking mechanism.

Snap-on Tools of Canada, Ltd.

Fig. 1:39 Lock-channel Pliers

Needle-nose Pliers

These pliers are used to hold, bend, or loop wires, and to install, pick up, and hold small parts such as clips and small cotter pins (electrical and fuel systems). Offset needle-nose pliers (Fig. 1:40b) have angled jaws. Both types have limited jaw pressure and they are easily damaged.

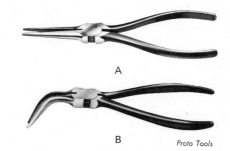

A

B

Proto Tools

Fig. 1:40 Needle-nose Pliers

Battery Pliers

Battery pliers are used to remove worn or corroded fasteners, especially on batteries.

Owatonna Tool Company

Fig. 1:41 Battery Pliers

Vise Grips

Vise grips are available in a variety of sizes and jaw shapes. Their main feature is very high jaw pressure, which can be held after the hand is removed. They are good holding or clamping tools, but improperly used they can cause great damage. They come with curved jaws (for rods and pipes), with jaw blades (for bending and clamping sheet metal), or with a jaw chain (to turn or hold parts not easily damaged).

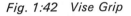

Proto Tools

Fig. 1:42   Vise Grip

Hose-clamp Pliers

These are used to remove wire clamps on hoses (cooling and fuel systems).

K-D Tools

Fig. 1:43   Hose-clamp Pliers

Lock-ring Pliers

Lock-ring pliers are available in many styles, and are sometimes equipped with interchangeable tips. They are used to remove and install lock rings.

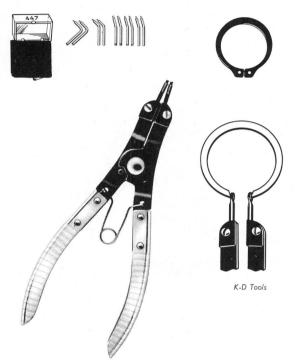

K-D Tools

Fig. 1:44   Lock-ring Pliers (expanding type with interchangeable tips)

Door-handle-clip Pliers

Door-handle-clip pliers may be of various designs to hold different types of clips. The most common design is shown in Fig. 1:45.

K-D Tools

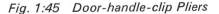

Fig. 1:45   Door-handle-clip Pliers

Hammers

The Ball Peen Hammer

The ball peen hammer (Fig. 1:46) (so named because its ball-shaped side is used to peen, or spread, rivets) is the most popular type of hammer in the automotive trade. Its size is usually determined by the weight of its head. Common sizes range from 2 oz. to 3 lb. Be sure the handle is securely attached to the hammer

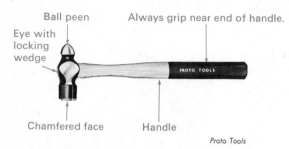

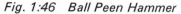

Fig. 1:46 Ball Peen Hammer

Proto Tools

Fig. 1:47   Plastic Tip Hammer with Interchangeable Tips

Proto Tools

Fig. 1:48   Rubber Mallet

Proto Tools

Fig. 1:49   Brass Hammer

head. Never use the end of the handle as a tapping tool.

Soft-faced Hammers

These hammers (Figs. 1:47-1:49) are used for striking surfaces that are easily marred or damaged. In some cases an ordinary hammer can be used if the workpiece is protected by soft material, e.g., rubber, wood, or lead.

Punches

The Starting Punch and the Pin Punch

The purposes and uses of the starting punch and the pin punch are illustrated in Fig. 1:50. The pin punch, which is also known as a drift punch, bends or breaks too easily to be used as a starting punch. Punches are frequently employed to align parts with screw holes during assembly.

The Centre Punch

The centre punch (Fig. 1:51) is used to mark the centre of a hole to be drilled and also to

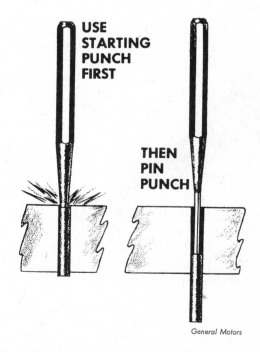

General Motors

Fig. 1:50   Starting Punch and Pin Punch

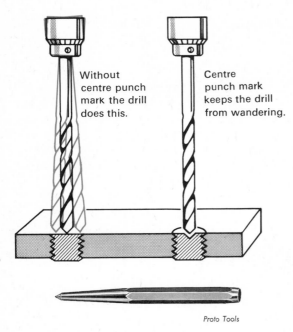

Without centre punch mark the drill does this.

Centre punch mark keeps the drill from wandering.

Proto Tools

Fig. 1:51 Centre Punch

make corresponding identification or locating marks when dismantling two or more parts that are attached to each other. This ensures that matching parts or slightly worn parts can be reassembled in their original positions (Figs. 5:11 and 5:24a).

Belt or Hole Punches

These are hollow punches used to cut holes in soft materials such as gaskets and weather stripping (see Fig. 1:52).

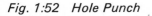

C. S. Osborne & Co.

Fig. 1:52 Hole Punch

Chisels

Chisels (Fig. 1:53) are cutting tools designed to remove rivets, burrs, and split nuts, and to cut sheet metal. The cutting edge can be flat, rounded, or diamond-shaped to suit the job.

Note well: To avoid injury, especially to the eyes, the striking face of punches and chisels should be slightly curved and the edges must be rounded to prevent "mushrooming" and chipping. Safety glasses should always be worn when working with punches and chisels!

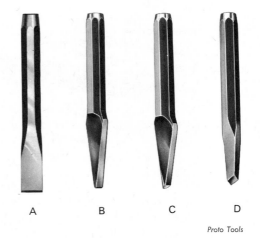

A   B   C   D

Proto Tools

Fig. 1:53 Chisels: (a) Cold Chisel; (b) Cape Chisel; (c) Round-nosed Cape Chisel; (d) Diamond Point Chisel.

Pry Bars or Line-up Bars

The pry or line-up bars shown in Fig. 1:54 require little comment. They are used to position parts during assembly (for example, overlapping bolt holes) or to pry parts during removal.

Caution: The latter can be dangerous and cause damage to the parts!

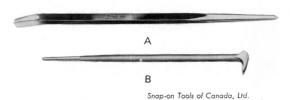

A

B

Snap-on Tools of Canada, Ltd.

Fig. 1:54 Pry and Line-up Bars: (a) Pry Bar; (b) Rolling-head Bar.

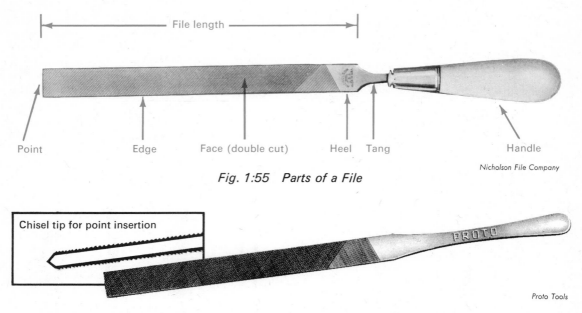

Fig. 1:55   Parts of a File

Nicholson File Company

Chisel tip for point insertion

Proto Tools

Fig. 1:56   Ignition Point File 5"—a Fine Tungsten Point File for Spark Plugs, Distributor Points, and Other Electrical Contact Points, with Chisel Tip for Entering Gaps and Slots.

Files

Files (Fig. 1:55) are available in a wide range of sizes, shapes, and degrees of coarseness. They may be as small as a nail file or 1½ feet long; they can be flat, square, triangular, or round; they can be thick, or as thin as the blade of a knife; they can be single cut to produce a smooth finish and for use with hard metals, or double cut (crisscross) to remove such metals as cast iron or mild steel more quickly. The cutting edges of the *Body File* are curved to help eject the cuttings of softer materials (body solder, paint, plastic filler, and fibreglass). The most common file in automotive maintenance is the *Point File* (Fig. 1:56). Made of very hard tungsten steel and double cut to prevent side slipping, point files can remove tough oxide layers on contact points (e.g., breaker points in regulators, distributors, and switches). The point file is ideal to file the centre electrode on used spark plugs.

Note the following important points:
1. A file with a loose handle can be very dangerous.
2. A file cuts only on the forward stroke.
3. Don't dull a new file on a hard surface (rust, scale, or hardened steel).

Hacksaws

Hacksaws (Fig. 1:57) are usually made with an adjustable frame designed to take blades 8, 10, or 12 inches long. Hacksaw blades may have 14, 18, 24, or 32 teeth per inch. For general use,

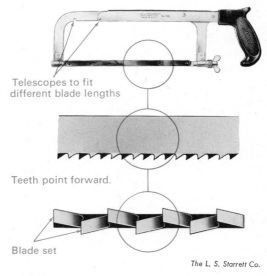

Telescopes to fit different blade lengths

Teeth point forward.

Blade set

The L. S. Starrett Co.

Fig. 1:57   Hacksaw

a high-speed blade with 24 teeth per inch is recommended. The coarser and faster blades (14 and 18 teeth per inch), while giving better "chip clearance" on softer materials, are useless when cutting harder materials and small wall sections such as those found on exhaust pipes.

High-Speed Hole Saws

High-speed hole saws (Fig. 1:58) that can be attached to an electric drill are available in sizes from ⁹⁄₁₆″ to over 4″ in diameter. They are very convenient for cutting panel holes for aerials, hoses, and cables.

Proto Tools

Fig. 1:58 Hole saw

Threading Tools

Taps

Taps (Fig. 1:59) are made in several styles and are used for cutting inside threads.

The *Taper Tap* is used for starting a thread and threading completely through a piece of metal.

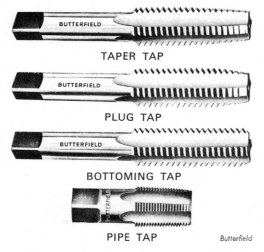

TAPER TAP

PLUG TAP

BOTTOMING TAP

PIPE TAP

Butterfield

Fig. 1:59 Standard Hand Taps of Carbon Steel and High-speed Steel

The *Plug Tap* is used for cutting threads part way to the bottom of a hole after they have been started with the taper tap.

The *Bottoming Tap* is used to cut a thread to the bottom of a blind hole.

The *Pipe Tap* is used for cutting pipe threads such as those found on some oil- and fuel-line connections.

There are various styles of tap handles to suit the location of the work and the size of the tap (Fig. 1:60).

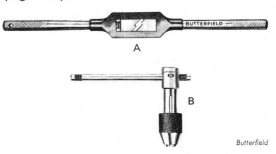

A

B

Butterfield

Fig. 1:60 (a) Tap Handle; (b) T-Handle Tap Wrench.

Dies

Dies (Fig. 1:61a) are used to cut outside threads. The die is held in a diestock (Fig. 1:61b) for the threading operation. The ad-

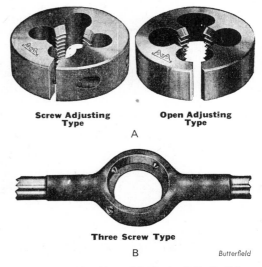

Screw Adjusting Type   Open Adjusting Type

A

Three Screw Type

B

Butterfield

Fig. 1:61 (a) Adjustable Round Split Dies of Carbon Steel; (b) Diestock for Use with Adjustable Round Split Dies.

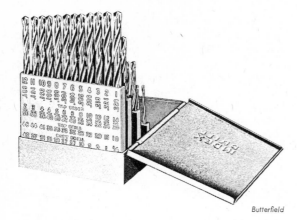

Butterfield

Proto Tools

Fig. 1:62 Twist Drills with Index Box. Holes in panels are individually drilled. Drill sizes, decimal equivalents, and tap sizes are plainly marked on panels. Panels are hinged and fold into box.

Fig. 1:63 Screw Extractor

serves as a drill-bit holder and makes it easy to identify drill sizes.

justing screw or screws make it possible to select the type of thread fit desired.

Twist Drills or Drill Bits

Twist drills (Fig. 1:62) are made of either carbon steel or high-speed steel. While drill bits made of the latter are more expensive, they are usually a much better buy, both in terms of long life and toughness when drilling harder alloys. Whole sets with the most common sizes are available in handy index boxes. The drill index

Screw Extractors

Screw extractors (Fig. 1:63) are used to remove broken screws or studs. In order for this to be done, a hole must be drilled into the broken piece. The extractor is then driven into the hole and turned with a wrench. Screw extractors are available for all common thread sizes.

The purpose of the items shown in Figs. 1:64-1:82 is more or less self-evident if you study their names and design.

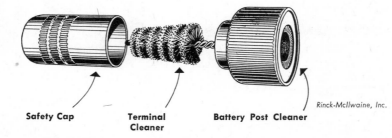

Safety Cap   **Terminal Cleaner**   **Battery Post Cleaner**   *Rinck-McIlwaine, Inc.*

Fig. 1:64 Battery Post and Terminal Cleaner

Proto Tools

Fig. 1:65 Flexible Carbon Scraper

K-D Tools

Fig. 1:66 "Shark Tooth" Radiator Hose Pliers (for hose removal)

K-D Tools

Fig. 1:67   Battery Carrier Strap

Proto Tools

Fig. 1:68   Putty Knife and Gasket Scraper

Ken-Tool

Fig. 1:69   Strap Wrench for Oil Filter Removal (Caution: To prevent overtorquing and leakage, do not use for oil filter installation. Use your hands instead!)

Snap-on Tools of Canada, Ltd.

Fig. 1:70   Telescoping Magnetic Pick-up Tool (Caution: This tool will magnetize all steel parts. Failure is often the result!)

Telescoping scale ←

KENNEDY A-120

Deflator nipple

Adapter valve

Fig. 1:71   Tire Pressure Gauge

Ken-Tool

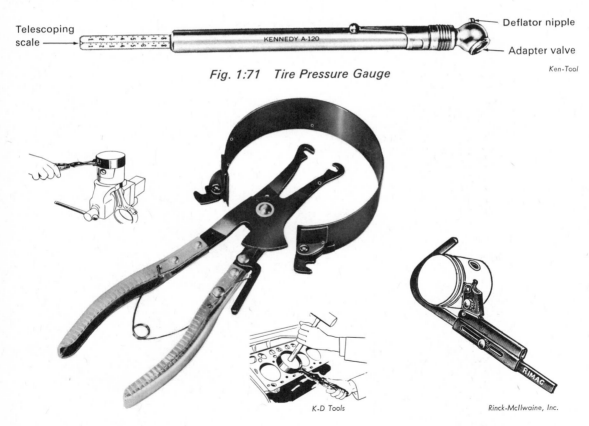

K-D Tools

Fig. 1:72   Piston-ring Compressor

Rinck-McIlwaine, Inc.

Fig. 1:73   Ring-groove Cleaner

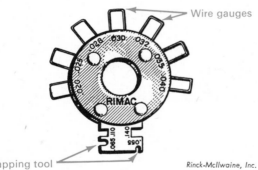

K-D Tools

Fig. 1:74 Piston-ring Expander Set (This type prevents ring distortion.)

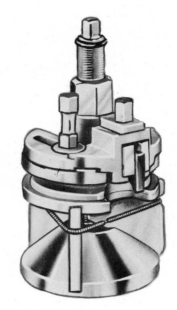

Snap-on Tools of Canada, Ltd.

Fig. 1:75 Cylinder Ridge Reamer

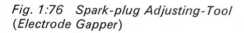

Wire gauges

Gapping tool

Rinck-McIlwaine, Inc.

Fig. 1:76 Spark-plug Adjusting-Tool (Electrode Gapper)

K-D Tools

Fig. 1:77 High-voltage Pliers for Tune-ups

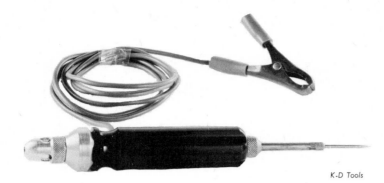

K-D Tools

Fig. 1:78   Test Light

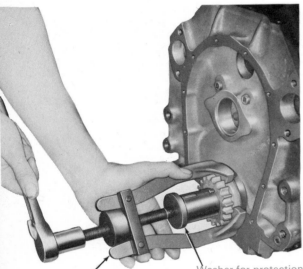

Puller with interchangeable legs

Washer for protection

General Motors

Fig. 1:79   Puller Being Used to Remove a
Steel Gear (Caution: Do not apply this method
to fibre gears.)

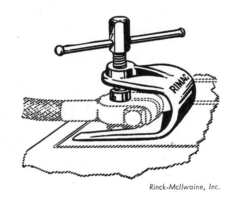

Rinck-McIlwaine, Inc.

Fig. 1:80   Puller Being Used to Remove a
Seized Battery Terminal

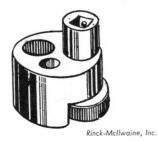

Rinck-McIlwaine, Inc.

Fig. 1:81   Stud-Puller

Proto Tools

Fig. 1:82   Wheel Wrench

Measuring Devices

In almost every phase of automotive service, measurements are taken to determine size, fit, clearance, or wear; and unless this is done accurately, workmanship is bound to suffer. These measurements may be based on the English standard of measurement (feet, inches, pounds, ounces, degrees Fahrenheit, etc.) or on the metric system (metres, centimetres, millimetres, kilograms, degrees Celsius, etc.). A conversion table is provided on pages 305-6.

If we measure in inches, we can express parts of an inch either in common fractions (½", ¼", ⅛", 1/16", 1/32", or 1/64") or in decimal fractions (0.1", 0.01", 0.001", etc.).

The Depth Gauge

A depth gauge (Fig. 1:83) is a small steel rule equipped with a sliding cross-bar, or head, graduated in inches and common fractions of inches. It is often used for carburetor adjustments.

The Pocket Slide Caliper

This caliper (Fig. 1:84), also divided in common fractions, is designed for quick inside and outside measurements of such parts as bearings, seals, fittings, housings, and fasteners.

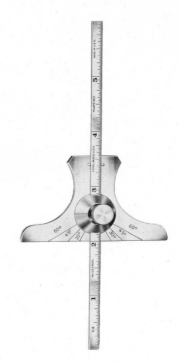

The L. S. Starrett Co.

Fig. 1:83   Depth Gauge (combination depth and angle type)

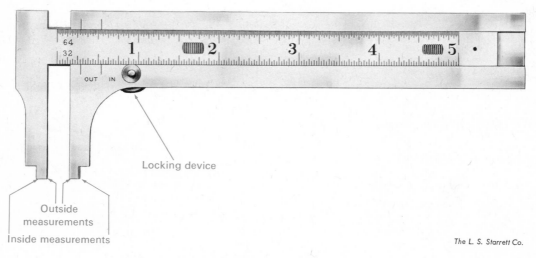

Locking device

Outside measurements

Inside measurements

The L. S. Starrett Co.

Fig. 1:84   Pocket Slide-Caliper

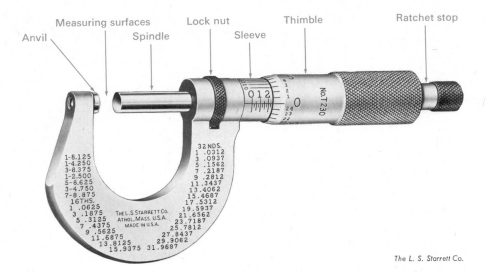

Fig. 1:85   Micrometer

The L. S. Starrett Co.

The Micrometer

The micrometer (Fig. 1:85) is the most frequently used type of caliper in the automotive
shop for measuring parts or their degree of
wear. It is an indispensable device for making
precision fits, and you should know how to
handle it properly.

Micrometers are made in a variety of sizes but
each size usually has a variable range of only
one inch, e.g., 0-1″, 1-2″, and 2-3″. The range
is, in most cases, stamped on the micrometer
frame. Some types have interchangeable anvil
extensions to increase their measuring range by
several inches.

The *Inside Micrometer* (Fig. 1:86) often
requires the attachment of calibrated extension
pieces to vary its measuring range. Fig. 1:87
shows a *Micrometer Depth Gauge*.

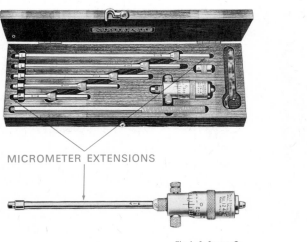

The L. S. Starrett Co.

Fig. 1:86   Inside Micrometer

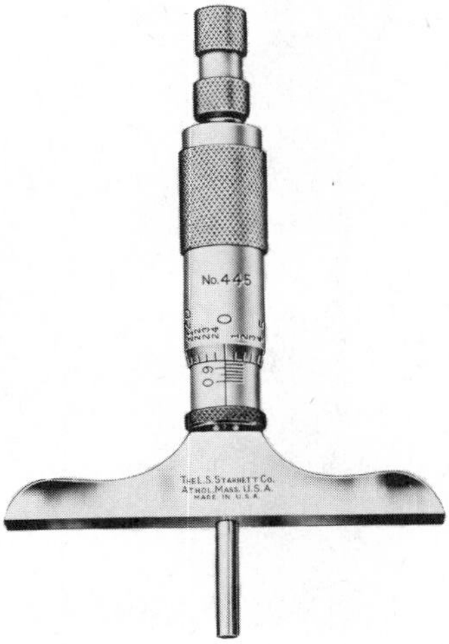

The L. S. Starrett Co.

Fig. 1:87   Micrometer Depth Gauge

Reading a Micrometer

When measuring a part with a micrometer, be sure there is no dirt either on the micrometer or on the part being measured. Support the micrometer by holding the frame with one hand, and turn the thimble between the thumb and index finger of the other hand (Fig. 1:88). Never go beyond the first indication of resistance. (If you were to measure a piece of smooth paper, it should not tear when pulled out.)

Most modern micrometers include a friction ratchet or ratchet stop to prevent overtightening. Don't tilt or sway the micrometer while measuring.

Since the thimble moves on a special thread with 40 turns per inch, one complete turn of the thimble increases (or decreases) the measuring distance between the anvil and the spindle tip by 0.025" (or 25/1000"). Two complete turns therefore change the distance by 0.050", three turns by 0.075", four turns by 0.100", etc., as indicated by each division on the datum or reference line. The full 40 turns (Don't go beyond!) represent 1.000" (because 40 × 0.025" = 1.000"). If, however, the thimble can be moved only part of a complete turn, then simply add that number on the thimble scale, which is in line with the datum line on the sleeve or hub. If no number on the thimble scale, which represents thousandths of an inch (or 0.001"), lines up with the datum line, choose the one closest. Some more refined models have an added Vernier scale on the thimble to measure ten-thousandths of an inch (0.0001"). You should, however, always add the whole inch number inscribed on the frame to the reading obtained. With some practice you will learn to read a micrometer quickly and accurately. Let's start with a typical example in Fig. 1:89.

The last number visible on the datum line is 2, therefore	= 0.200"
One full datum line division beyond the 2 (i.e. one more thimble turn), therefore	= 0.025"
The twenty-fourth division on the thimble scale lines up with the datum line, therefore	= 0.024"
	0.249"
Let's assume the micrometer range is 2"-3", therefore	= 2"
Total reading	2.249"

Note well: Keep the micrometer, or any other measuring instrument, in a well-protected, clean, dry place. Avoid sudden temperature changes and shock. Never place any parts or tools on the micrometer. (Most precision instruments are provided with a special storage case.)

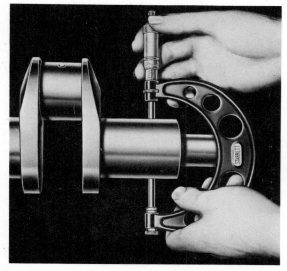

The L. S. Starrett Co.

Fig. 1:88 Measuring a Crankshaft Journal

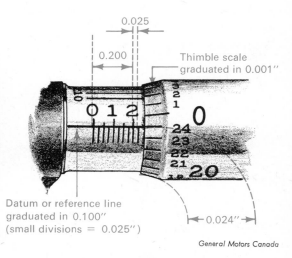

General Motors Canada

Fig. 1:89 Reading a Micrometer. Reading here is 0.200" + 0.025" + 0.24" = 0.249".

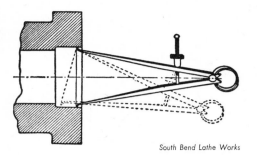

South Bend Lathe Works

Fig. 1:90   Using an Inside Caliper to Measure the Diameter of a Hole

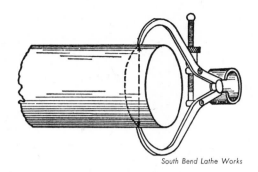

South Bend Lathe Works

Fig. 1:91   Using an Outside Caliper to Measure the Outside Diameter of a Shaft

To avoid distortion in the frame, do not store the instrument with the spindle tip resting on the anvil. Micrometers should be periodically checked for accuracy, and, if necessary, recalibrated by a qualified person.

Calipers

Calipers may be either of the inside type (Fig. 1:90) or of the outside type (Fig. 1:91). They are used in places that are difficult to reach. The dimension obtained with the caliper is then checked on a steel rule or some other measuring device.

Feeler Gauges

These gauges are marked in thousandths of an inch and their purpose is to measure the space between two closely fitting parts. There are two basic types of feeler gauges, the strip type

(Fig. 1:92) and the wire type (Fig. 1:93). Both are made of specially hardened steel to maintain their accuracy. The wire type is used to measure the electrode gap on spark plugs.

The most common types of strip feeler gauges and some of their applications are listed below.

The Feeler Gauge Set

The standard feeler gauge set (Fig. 1:92) usually combines sizes from 0.001" to 0.040". These gauges are used for tune-up work and valve adjustments. Narrow feeler gauges are available for special applications such as the adjustment of electrical contact points.

Snap-on Tools of Canada, Ltd.

Fig. 1:93   Wire Gauge with Gapping Tool

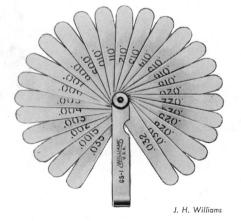

J. H. Williams

Fig. 1:92   Feeler Gauge Set

Snap-on Tools of Canada, Ltd.

Fig. 1:94   Step-cut Gauge Set

General Motors

Fig. 1:95   Checking Piston Clearance with Long Feeler Gauge and Tension Gauge

Go and No-Go Feeler Gauges or Step-cut Gauges

Such gauges are cut as shown (Fig. 1:94) and may be used where specifications allow for a ±0.001″ tolerance. For example, 0.005″ ±0.001″ means that 0.004″ to 0.006″ is acceptable.

Extra-long feeler gauges can be made from rolls of feeler stock. They are ideal where the clearance to be measured is inaccessible, e.g., for checking the fit of a piston in a cylinder bore (Fig. 1:95).

The L. S. Starrett Co.

Fig. 1:96   Screw Pitch Gauge

Note: Feeler gauges that are dented or show other signs of wear must be either replaced or shortened.

The Screw Pitch Gauge (Thread Gauge)

The screw pitch gauge (Fig. 1:96) has toothed blades which, if held against a thread, can determine its specifications.

Dial Indicators

Dial indicators are calibrated in thousandths of an inch. They are used to measure gear and shaft run-out, end- or side-play, gear-lash, valve-guide clearance, and cylinder taper, or to generally check parts for inaccuracies, wear, or movement. Two typical applications are shown in Figs. 1:97 and 1:98.

Note: All measuring devices listed above are available in metric sizes.

There are many other tools used in the automotive trade. Most of them are, however, designed for special purposes. Some of these tools, such as the compression gauge and electrical meters, are discussed in the chapte relevant to their use.

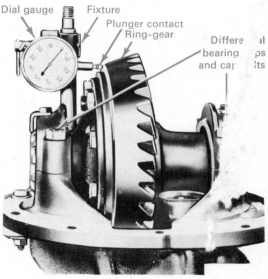

Ford Motor Company

Fig. 1:97   Checking Differential Ring Gear Run-out with a Dial Gauge (To check backlash, place dial contact on a ring gear tooth

General Motors

Fig. 1:98 Measuring Cylinder Bore with a Dial Gauge

RECOMMENDED ASSIGNMENTS

1. Identify the tools in Fig. 1:100 by number, and give at least one typical use for each.
2. List five of the most common abuses of hand tools.
3. The pull applied to a 2'-long hinge handle is 30 pounds. What is the applied torque?
4. How is the swing angle of a single hexagon wrench and that of a double hexagon wrench determined?
5. What type of wrench should be used for hydraulic fittings? Why?
6. Why do many mechanics prefer single hexagon sockets, even though their swing angle is 60°?
7. Why should an ordinary deep socket never be used on a spark plug?
8. What two important rules apply in the choice of a proper socket handle?
9. State briefly four rules for the proper use of screwdrivers.

10. Explain the difference, in both shape and purpose, between the starting punch and the pin punch.
11. Which two safety rules apply to the use of all punches and chisels?
12. Why do most mechanics prefer high-speed hacksaw blades that have 24 teeth per inch?
13. Identify the micrometer settings illustrated here.

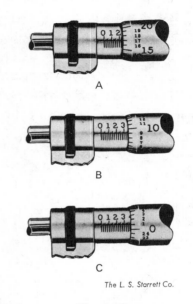

Fig. 1:99

The L. S. Starrett Co.

14. Why has the micrometer 40 threads per inch on the spindle?
15. Why do most modern micrometers include a ratchet stop?
16. What precautions should be taken when handling precision instruments such as micrometers, calipers, and dial gauges?
17. Name six common applications of dial gauges.
18. Change each of the following dimensions into both centimetres (cm) and millimetres (mm): 1", 0.1", 0.01", 0.001", ½", and ¼".

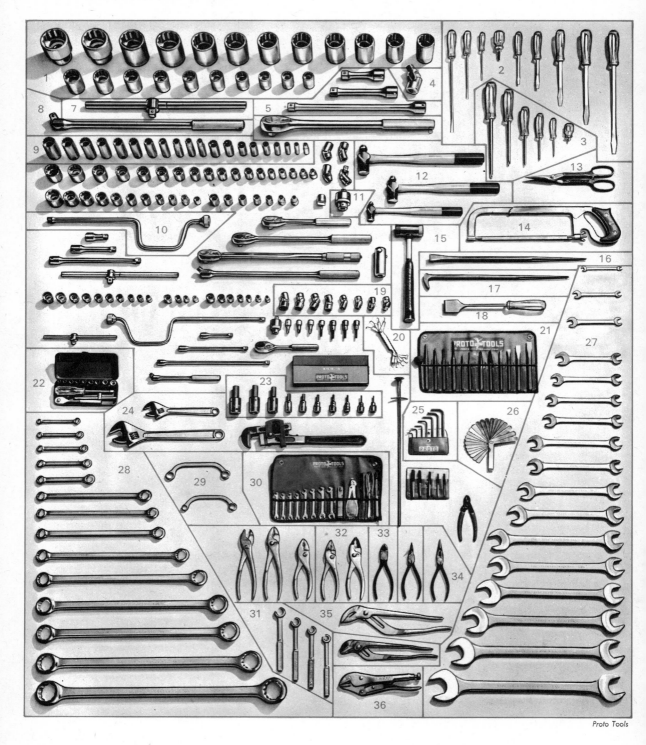

Proto Tools

Fig. 1:100   A Typical Set of Automotive Hand Tools

2

Automotive Fasteners

Study Guide

Every year material and equipment worth millions of dollars is wasted through sheer ignorance of the principles discussed in this chapter (not to mention lost business and injury due to accidents). While it might be too difficult to memorize all details, you should note, very carefully, some of the basic rules and principles governing such matters as torque limits and torque patterns, different thread designs, and the shape and purpose of the hardware involved.

Screws

The most common screw in the automotive field is the *Hexagon Cap Screw* (Fig. 2:1). ("Hexagon" means "six-sided".) Like all screws, it is fastened directly into the material, i.e., a nut is not required. However, screws may have many other head designs. The most common ones are shown in Fig. 2:2. *Phillips Screws* are also available in flat, round, oval, and fillister head designs.

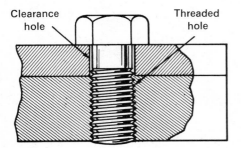

Fig. 2:1   Hexagon Cap Screw

The *Belleville Screw* (Fig. 2:3) has a cup-shaped flange, whose spring action prevents the screw from coming out. This type of screw is widely used on chassis parts, and places where temperature changes and vibration may cause an ordinary screw to lose tension.

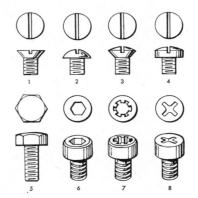

Fig. 2:2   Typical Machine Screws: (1) Flat Head, Counter-sunk; (2) Round Head; (3) Oval Head; (4) Fillister; (5) Hexagonal; (6) Internal Hex (Allen); (7) Fluted; (8) Phillips.

Spae-Naur Products Limited

Fig. 2:3   Belleville Screw

27

Self-tapping Screws, which cut their own thread (Fig. 2:4), and *Sheet Metal Screws* (Fig. 2:5), which are used to fasten panels, are two other popular types of screw.

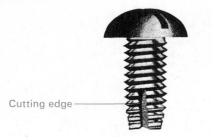

Spae-Naur Products Limited

Fig. 2:4   Self-tapping Screw

Spae-Naur Products Limited

Fig. 2:5   Typical Sheet Metal Screws

The *Hexagon Bolt* (Fig. 2:6) is identical to the hexagon cap screw, except that a nut is used to hold the assembled parts together. The distinction between the two is not always made. For instance, mechanics and manuals often refer to cylinder head bolts, while these are, in fact, screws.

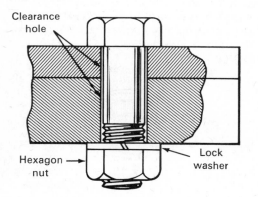

Fig. 2:6   Hexagon Bolt

Set Screws

Set screws (Fig. 2:7), whether of the Allen-head, hex-head, square-head, or slotted type, have a pointed tip to lock or "set" pulleys, gears, handles, and knobs in position on a shaft. The set screw is always at right angles to the shaft. Especially long set screws, which are usually spring-loaded to maintain their adjustment, are employed as linkage stop screws where frequent resetting is required (e.g., throttle or idle stop screws).

Spae-Naur Products Limited

Fig. 2:7   Set Screw

Studs and U-Bolts

Studs (Fig. 2:8) have no heads and are threaded at both ends. In many cases they feature a coarse thread at one end for turning into brittle materials such as cast metals or plastics, and a fine thread at the other end to accommodate steel nuts. U-bolts (Fig. 2:9), which are essentially U-shaped studs, are used to clamp around such parts as exhaust pipes and axle housings.

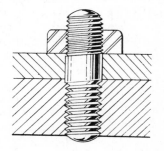

Fig. 2:8   Stud

Nuts

Nuts (Fig. 2:10) are produced in various shapes and designs. Like most other fasteners, they may be made of steel, stainless steel, brass, or

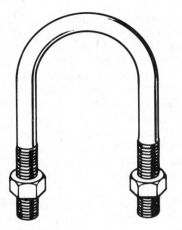

Fig. 2:9   U-Bolt

even plastic. They can be plated with chromium, nickel, zinc, cadmium, lead, and other metals. Some nuts are self-locking; others have a lock washer attached to them.

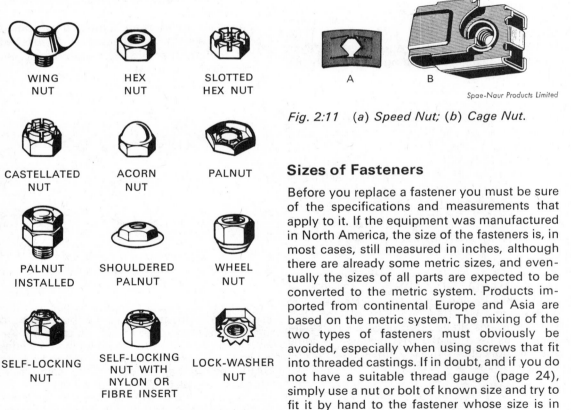

WING
NUT

HEX
NUT

SLOTTED
HEX NUT

CASTELLATED
NUT

ACORN
NUT

PALNUT

PALNUT
INSTALLED

SHOULDERED
PALNUT

WHEEL
NUT

SELF-LOCKING
NUT

SELF-LOCKING
NUT WITH
NYLON OR
FIBRE INSERT

LOCK-WASHER
NUT

Fig. 2:10   Common Shapes and Designs of Nuts

The *Palnut*, which prevents an ordinary nut from shaking loose, should be brought up to finger tightness against the nut to be locked, and then tightened further by approximately one more flat. Note that each nut illustrated in Fig. 2:10 is positioned so that the underside would face the part to be mounted. Threading the nut on the other way could have serious consequences. If, for example, the cone-shaped part of a wheel nut doesn't reach into the stud hole of the rim, the wheel will eventually come off! It should also be noted that many self-locking nuts do not lock reliably if used more than once.

Speed Nuts (Fig. 2:11a) are for light work and where low cost and space are of primary concern (e.g., automotive trim pieces).

Cage Nuts (Fig. 2:11b) are used in inaccessible areas where the nut cannot be reached (e.g., radiator mounts).

A   B

Spae-Naur Products Limited

Fig. 2:11   (a) Speed Nut; (b) Cage Nut.

Sizes of Fasteners

Before you replace a fastener you must be sure of the specifications and measurements that apply to it. If the equipment was manufactured in North America, the size of the fasteners is, in most cases, still measured in inches, although there are already some metric sizes, and eventually the sizes of all parts are expected to be converted to the metric system. Products imported from continental Europe and Asia are based on the metric system. The mixing of the two types of fasteners must obviously be avoided, especially when using screws that fit into threaded castings. If in doubt, and if you do not have a suitable thread gauge (page 24), simply use a nut or bolt of known size and try to fit it by hand to the fastener whose size is in question. In rare cases you may find two threads of the same size that do not match

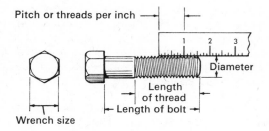

Fig. 2:12   Screw Dimensions

because one has a standard right-hand thread and the other has a left-hand thread. For example, the wheel nuts and studs on the left-hand side of certain models are designed in this way to prevent them from being shaken loose during sudden braking.

The dimensions of a fastener are determined by the method shown in Fig. 2:12. The most common head or wrench sizes can easily be calculated by adding ³⁄₁₆″ to the size of the stem or shank of the fastener. For example, a hexagon bolt with a stem size of ³⁄₈″ requires a wrench size of ⁹⁄₁₆″ (³⁄₈″ + ³⁄₁₆″ = ⁹⁄₁₆″). This formula can be used in reverse to find the stem size of the fastener, providing the wrench size is known.[4]

The two basic types of thread used on domestic vehicles are the UNF (Unified Fine) and the UNC (Unified Coarse) series.[5] Among other things the type of thread is determined by the "pitch", i.e., the number of threads (or turns) per inch. The UNF series, which has more threads per inch than the UNC series, is stronger, and because of its higher friction

factor, is less likely to shake loose. On the other hand, the wider, more deeply cut UNC thread takes a better hold in plastics and in the coarse grain structures of cast metals. It is also more quickly assembled and less likely to seize because of corrosion or high temperatures. The thread sizes of screws, bolts, and studs equal the outer thread diameter as shown in Fig. 2:12. Standard sizes increase in steps of one-sixteenth of an inch, e.g., ¼″, ⁵⁄₁₆″, ³⁄₈″, ⁷⁄₁₆″, etc. Shank sizes smaller than these are expressed in whole numbers, e.g., 12, 10, 8, 6 (size 12 being larger than 10).

If you wished to obtain a UNF hexagon cap screw 2½″ long from the underside of the head to the tip, and with a thread size of ³⁄₈″, you would ask for:

1 hexagon cap screw ³⁄₈″ × 2½″ UNF[6]

Tightening and Loosening Fasteners

You will avoid the worst pitfalls in your work if you observe these simple rules:

1. Standard fasteners are tightened by turning them in a clockwise direction, and loosened by turning them in a counter-clockwise direction (Fig. 2:13).

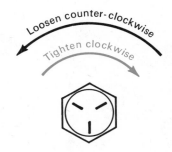

Fig. 2:13   Tightening and Loosening of Standard Right-hand-thread Fasteners

---

[4]Half-inch bolts have wrench sizes of either 1¹⁄₁₆″ or ¾″. It should be noted, however, that if the shank size is more than ½″, the formula cannot be used.

[5]Some manufacturers use the designation NF (National Fine) or SAE Regular (Society of Automotive Engineers) for the UNF series. The designations NC (National Coarse), or USS (United States Standards), or SAE Coarse are sometimes used for the UNC series. For some special applications an extra-fine thread may be used. It is listed as UNEF, or NEF, or SAE Fine.

SAE GRADE 5   SAE GRADE 8

[6]In some cases where the fastener has to withstand heavy loads it may be necessary to specify the grade, i.e., its tensile strength. An SAE grade 5 cap screw, identified by three lines on its head, is, for example, not as strong as an SAE grade 8 cap screw of the same size. Threads are also divided into classes: 1A represents a loose fit; 2A meets most automotive requirements; 3A is for precision equipment. The letters 1B, 2B, and 3B are the equivalents for nuts and other internal threads.

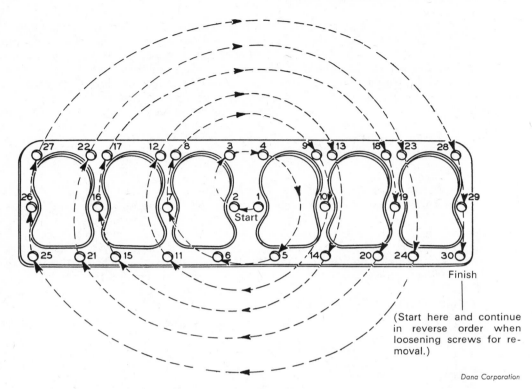

Finish

(Start here and continue in reverse order when loosening screws for removal.)

Dana Corporation

Fig. 2:14   Typical Torque Sequence for Rectangular Parts

2. Non-self-locking fasteners should spin freely until the head touches the part that is being fastened. (A tight thread indicates the wrong size, a dirty or damaged thread, or misaligned parts.)

3. Give all the fasteners on any part several turns before actually tightening any one of them.

4. Refer to the manufacturer's specifications for torque limits and sequence (the degree and order of tightening fasteners).

5. The torque of a fastener is determined by (a) the material of which the part is made; (b) the shape of the part; (c) the intended fit of the part; (d) the size, quality, and condition of the fastener; and (e) the type of gasket material, if a gasket is used.

6. The proper torque sequence for rectangular parts, such as cylinder heads, is illustrated in Fig. 2:14. The proper sequence for circular parts, such as wheels and carburetor and fuel pump covers, is illustrated in Fig. 2:15.

To remove a rectangular part, reverse the

Chrysler Canada Ltd.

Fig. 2:15   Typical Torque Sequence for Bolt Circles

sequence beginning at one of the corners and working towards the centre. In all cases, but especially where cast metal is employed, torque should be increased gradually in two or three steps. Ignoring these precautions will cause misaligned, distorted, or broken parts. For example, if you start to tighten a cylinder head at the corners, the centre will bulge upwards creating excessive stress in this area. The likely result will be a warped head or a leakage of coolant and gases, or possibly both.

Washers

The most common types of washers are shown in Fig. 2:16. The ordinary flat washer, which comes in a variety of sizes and thicknesses, spreads the contact area of the fastener. This is particularly important when one is working with parts made of softer materials (aluminum, plastic, sheet metal, etc.). The *Lock Washer* may be of many different designs but each one has the same purpose: to lock a nut, bolt, or screw so that it cannot back off. *Thrust Washers* are placed between gears, bearings, and other shaft-mounted parts, to absorb thrust loads, to reduce friction, and to maintain the desired clearance (the distance between two parts). Some washers are made of brass, copper, plastic, nylon, fibre, or rubber, in order to serve as seals and electrical insulators or conductors as well as thrust washers.

Rivets

Two kinds of rivets and their application are shown in Fig. 2:17. The *Tubular Rivet* is used to install clutch- and brake-linings. The *Oval Rivet* has a solid stem and is used to assemble heavy frame or suspension parts. When replacing oval rivets, most mechanics drill out the old rivets and put in high-grade bolts and locking devices. These are safer than improperly secured rivets.

Oval   Flat tubular

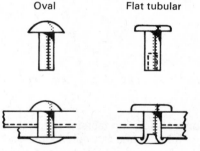

Fig. 2:17   Common Automotive Rivets

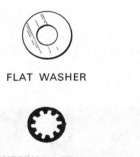

FLAT WASHER

LOCK WASHER

INTERNAL STAR
LOCK WASHER

EXTERNAL STAR
LOCK WASHER

SPELLMAN WASHER

TONGED WASHER

FIBRE WASHER

FINISHING OR
TRIM WASHER

Fig. 2:16   Common Types of Washers

INTERNAL SNAP RINGS

EXTERNAL SNAP RINGS

*Fig. 2:18   Snap Rings (Lock Rings or
Retainer Rings)*

Snap Rings

Snap rings, also known as lock rings or retainer rings (Fig. 2:18), are employed to hold parts such as bearings, gears, piston pins, linkage rods, and washers in position. Snap rings may be of the internal, shaft-mounted type, or of the external, bore-mounted type. A groove must be cut in the part for the ring to fit into, as shown in Fig. 2:19. For the method of installation, see Fig. 1:44.

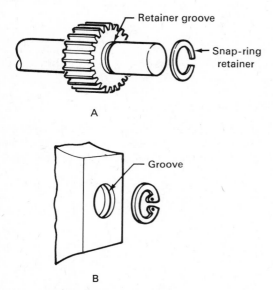

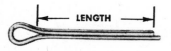

Fig. 2:20   Cotter Pin

Fig. 2:19   Installation of Snap Rings: (a) External Shaft-mounted Ring; (b) Internal Bore-mounted Ring.

Cotter Pins

Cotter pins (Fig. 2:20) are used with castellated or slotted nuts as a safety feature on steering and suspension parts; they are also used to secure linkage rods and clevis pins on brake, transmission, and accelerator linkages. In some cases cotter pins maintain critical torque settings or bearing "preloads" on fasteners such

as the front-wheel-bearing retainer nut. Fig. 2:21 illustrates the proper installation of a cotter pin. Because of the hazards that might be created, never use a cotter pin more than once.

There are other methods of locking fasteners, including folding sheet metal tabs over the fastener's head (Fig. 2:22). In some cases, soft steel wire (mechanic's wire) is used instead of cotter pins. To lock a screw with wire, the screw must be provided with a small hole in its head (Fig. 2:23).

Fig. 2:21   Proper Installation of a Cotter Pin. (1) Head of cotter is inserted firmly in slot. (2) Long end of cotter is bent back to centre of bolt, other end bent down flat. (3) Cotter is tight in nut.

Fig. 2:22   Shim Lock with Folding Tabs

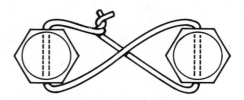

Fig. 2:23   Wire Locking of Fasteners

Keys

To prevent shaft-mounted parts such as timing gears (Fig. 5:24) and pulleys on crankshafts and generators from slipping, keys are installed. The two most common types are the half-moon-shaped "Woodruff" key (Fig. 2:24) and the square key (Fig. 2:25). Another type of key, known as a *Dowel Pin*, is simply an accurately machined steel peg. Dowel pins are

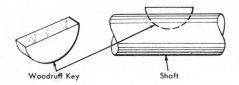

Fig. 2:24   Woodruff Key

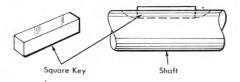

Fig. 2:25   Square Key

Spae-Naur Products Limited

Fig. 2:26   Slotted Tension Pin

semblies, and between the cylinder block and the head (Figs. 5:22 and 5:26).

The Slotted Tension Pin

This pin (Fig. 2:26) is mostly used to hold gears in position where torque requirements are low (e.g., distributor and oil-pump drive gears).

The purpose of the fasteners shown in Fig. 2:27 is self-evident.

pressed into two matching parts that have been provided with corresponding dowel holes. Dowel pins thus ensure a perfectly aligned fit on such parts as some timing gears, transmission housings, and balanced fly-wheel as-

HORSESHOE COTTER
(door handles)

HAIRPIN COTTER
(carburetor linkage)

**CARRIAGE BOLT
OR BUMPER BOLT**
(exhaust brackets and bumpers)

CLEVIS PIN WITH HITCH PIN
(control linkages)

CLEVIS YOKE OR ROD END
(control linkages)

THROTTLE-ROD CLIP
(carburetor linkage)

Spae-Naur Products Limited

Fig. 2:27   Miscellaneous Fasteners

RECOMMENDED ASSIGNMENTS

1. Why do some studs have a fine thread at one end and a coarse thread at the other?
2. Explain why self-locking nuts and wheel nuts, although similar in appearance, are installed in a different manner.
3. Name four types of thread discussed in this chapter, and briefly explain the significance of each.
4. Explain the differences between bolts, studs, and screws.
5. Calculate the proper wrench sizes from the following hexagon bolt sizes: (a) ¼", (b) ⁵⁄₁₆", (c) ⅜", (d) ⁷⁄₁₆", (e) ½".
6. A coarse-threaded hexagon cap screw is 3½" long and ⁷⁄₁₆" in diameter. Express these specifications in the customary formula.
7. Prepare a simple, neat diagram of a hex-agon cap screw. Using labels and dimension lines, illustrate the following: head, stem (or shank), thread, head size, length, diameter, and threads per inch (pitch).
8. Explain briefly the correct way of tightening a palnut.
9. List six important rules that apply to the use of fasteners.
10. Name six likely results if the rules in question 9 are not followed.
11. Prepare a simple diagram to illustrate the proper torque sequence of a cylinder head.
12. Give the names and purposes of three types of washers.
13. Name two types of snap rings, and give the purpose of each.
14. Describe briefly the correct method of installing a cotter pin.
15. Describe the shape and function of a Woodruff key.

3

Gaskets, Sealers, and Seals

In most cases the failure of gaskets and seals is the result of improper installation. Knowledge of their properties will save you from costly and sometimes dangerous mistakes.

Gaskets

The main purpose of a gasket is to prevent the leakage of liquids and gases between two parts. Gaskets must therefore be of a compressible material in which the irregularities of two mating surfaces can embed themselves. Thus, undesirable cavities are filled up, and a leak-proof seal is formed. Some gaskets, especially those made of synthetic rubber, also possess a quality known as resilience or "recovery" (that is, they have the ability to spring back to their original shape once the mounting pressure is removed). Cork, on the other hand, has good compressibility but very little resilience.

In some cases gaskets also serve as shims. By using either a single gasket of suitable thickness or a combination of selected sizes, a desired adjustment or clearance can be obtained.

Gaskets are available in a wide range of materials, shapes, and sizes. The choice of material, which to a certain degree is determined by cost, depends for the most part on the operating conditions involved, as indicated in the chart on pages 38-9.

Although most gaskets may be purchased as separate replacement parts, it is, in many cases, more convenient to purchase an entire set or kit. There are, for example, complete gasket sets available to rebuild engines, cylinder heads, carburetors, transmissions, and differentials. In emergencies it is possible to cut a gasket from a gasket sheet. First, the shape of the part is either traced or imprinted onto the sheet, and the gasket is then cut out with a pair of scissors. In some cases the gasket can be cut on the part itself by light, well-aimed hammer taps along the sharp edges.

The best gasket is only as good as the mechanic who installs it. An over-torqued and split drain-plug gasket can, because of the resulting loss of lubricant, reduce a rebuilt engine to scrap iron in a few seconds. Some carbon deposit left carelessly between the cylinder block and the cylinder head may cause the coolant to leak inside the cylinders. The results can be equally devastating. Leakage is usually the result of one or more of the following conditions: dirt, corrosion, warpage, misalignment, and incorrect torque. Persistent leaks may be due to excessive oil pressure, cylinder "blow-by", improper venting of the engine, of the transmission, or of the differential, plugged return passages, sludge formation, excessive temperatures, high lubricant levels and foaming, or the wrong type of lubricant. In cases where it is possible to install the gasket backwards, you should look for directions such as "Top" or "Front" printed on the gasket. Since temperature changes, pressure, and vibration cause the parts and the gasket to settle, it may be necessary to retorque the screws or bolts to the manufacturer's specifications during the first 300 to 500 miles (500 km to 800 km).

Sealers

Sealers are available in liquid form (applied with a brush), in paste form (applied directly from the tube), and in a semi-solid state (sold in

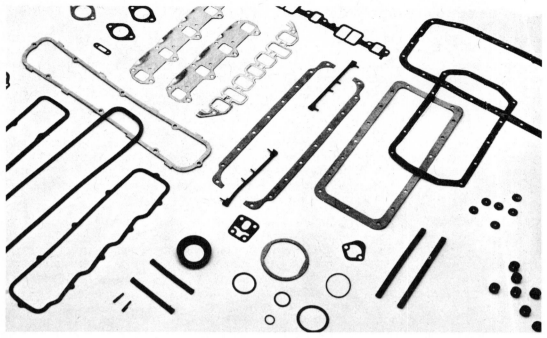

Fel-Pro Incorporated

Fig. 3:1   Typical Automotive Gaskets and Seals

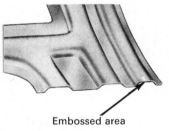

Embossed area

Dana Corporation

Fig. 3:2   Embossed or Beaded Steel Gasket

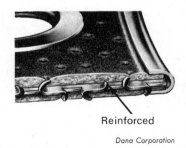

Asbestos filler

Dana Corporation

Fig. 3:3   Copper-Asbestos or Steel-Asbestos Sandwich Gasket

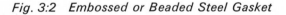

Reinforced

Dana Corporation

Fig. 3:4   Perforated Steel-Asbestos Sandwich Gasket

Gasket Selection Chart

Materials	Properties and Operating Conditions	Typical Applications
Chemically treated paper	Low temperature; high or low pressure; resistant to oil, fuel, water, and antifreeze; flexible, but very limited compressibility; no elasticity or tensile strength	Gear and pump housings, carburetors, transmissions, differentials
Treated fibre, vegetable and asbestos fibre, cork granules, Vellumoid, Felcoid	Low temperature; high or low pressure; resistant to oil, fuel, water, and antifreeze; flexible, soft, good compressibility; moderate tensile strength, with almost no resilience or elasticity	Pump and thermostat housings, carburetors, gaskets for covers of cast materials or heavy steel
Cork and coated cork	Low temperature; low pressure; resistant to oil, fuel, water, and antifreeze; soft, moderate flexibility, and compressibility; little resilience, no tensile strength or elasticity; requires extreme care in storing and handling; tends to shrink and become brittle when left in storage for too long (soaking in warm water or Varsol improves this condition)	Sheet metal covers, oil pans, valve covers, tappet covers, timing-gear covers, differential covers, fuel gauges, etc.
Synthetic rubber and neoprene	Low temperature; low and high pressure; soft, good flexibility and compressibility; good resilience, elasticity, and tensile strength; resists all automotive liquids, including acids; can be reused; advantages outweigh higher cost; easily installed; tough; no storage problems. *Caution:* Oil- and fuel-filter gaskets may leak because of over-torquing! Do not reuse filter gaskets.	Used instead of cork gaskets; also popular as "O" rings, washers, seals, and oil-filter gaskets
Copper	High temperature; good conductor of heat and electrical currents; high mounting- and working-pressures; resists automotive gases and liquids, except acids; slightly soft; can be reused	Gasket washers (fuel system, hydraulic devices, spark plugs, and drain plugs)
Embossed or beaded steel, often aluminum-coated, tin-plated, or stainless steel (Fig. 3:2)	High temperature; good heat transfer; high mounting- and working-pressures; resists automotive gases and liquids, except acids. *Caution:* Handle with extreme care; any dents or wrinkles will cause leakage. Never use embossed steel gaskets twice, regardless of their appearance!	Cylinder head and manifold gaskets

Gasket Selection Chart (Cont'd)

Materials	Properties and Operating Conditions	Typical Applications
Embossed steel, lacquered or resin-coated	As above. Graphite-pigmented resin acts as a heat-activated sealer. Graphite pigments serve as lubricants to allow heat expansion and contraction, especially on manifolds.	As above
Copper-asbestos or steel-asbestos sandwich gaskets (Fig. 3:3)	Same as embossed steel gaskets, but lower heat transfer between parts, and greater thickness. Sandwich gaskets can be used to build up machined surfaces. *Caution:* Handle with extreme care. The straightening of wrinkled gaskets does not restore the damaged asbestos filler inside.	As above
Steel-asbestos, graphite-treated (with steel heat-shield on one side, metal-reinforced asbestos on top side)	As above, and like most gaskets that must resist very high temperatures, they are usually heat-treated by the manufacturer. "Heat-aging", which takes approximately one hour at 750°F, or 400°C, prevents the blistering and peeling of coatings.	As above
Asbestos-steel-asbestos, graphite-treated (a perforated steel sandwiched between two treated asbestos sheets) (Fig. 3:4)	As above	As above
Hard fibre (red, gray, or black)	Resists normal oil- and coolant-temperatures and all liquids; high mounting- and working-pressures; good tensile strength; little compressibility; good insulator	Gasket washers in hydraulic and fuel systems, drain-plug gaskets
Nylon	As above, but slightly more compressible	Ideal as oil pan drain-plug gasket

sticks and applied to pipe threads). They are also available in special dispenser guns. Some sealers can withstand temperatures of up to 600°F (316°C). Most of them are resistant to gasoline, Diesel fuel, grease, oil, antifreeze, and water. Some set quickly; others do not. Some harden, while others remain slightly flexible under heat. Because they withstand constant vibration, contraction, expansion, and pressure changes, and because they do not interfere with the future disassembly of parts, flexible or non-hardening sealer compounds are preferred by most mechanics.

On the other hand, if the proper procedure is followed, the installation of a new gasket usually requires no sealer at all. If conditions, such as pitting, call for a sealer, it should be applied sparingly, for any excess oozing from the gasket may foul up other parts, such as hydraulic valves and passages in an automatic transmission.

Seals

The purpose of seals is to prevent liquids, gases, grease, and dirt from leaving, entering, or by-passing moving parts such as shafts, bearings, valves, hydraulic pistons, and control rods. For example, the seal in the front wheel-hub prevents both the wheel-bearing grease from leaking out and dust and water from leaking in. There are other seals, such as the "O"-ring seal (Fig. 3:5), that are sometimes used as gaskets to seal non-moving parts.

Dana Corporation

Fig. 3:5   Neoprene "O"-Ring Seal

The modern automotive seals employed in engines, transmissions, rear axles, brakes, wheels, steering boxes, and other parts are usually made of synthetic rubber. Leather and felt seals are less common today. A typical seal, sectioned for better viewing, is shown in Fig. 3:6. The two most important dimensions are (a) the OD, or outside diameter, which is determined by the bore of the housing or the

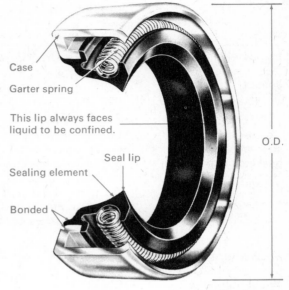

Case
Garter spring
This lip always faces liquid to be confined.
Seal lip
Sealing element
Bonded
O.D.

Dana Corporation

Fig. 3:6   Construction of a Typical Oil Seal

cover into which it is fitted, and (b) the ID, or inside diameter, which is determined by the shaft size. The garter spring not only helps to maintain a uniform pressure of the seal lip against the rotating shaft, but it also compensates for any slight run-out or eccentricity (i.e., wobble) in the shaft. Some seals, such as the crankshaft front main seal, are backed up by oil slingers. By literally slinging the oil away from the shaft, the slinger shields the seal against excessive amounts of lubricant.

The lip of the seal and the garter spring must face the fluid or the area to be sealed. If the seal is installed backwards, the lip will hydroplane, i.e., it will be lifted by the rapid circular flow of the lubricant spinning with the shaft, and by the pressure built up inside the housing by heat, expanding gases, or hydraulic forces. On the other hand, if the seal is installed correctly, these same forces will actually push the lip against the shaft and make a better seal. Even a new seal will leak if there is a misalignment of the shaft or the seal, or if the shaft is rough, worn, pitted, or scratched. It is possible to recondition slightly scored shafts with an abrasive, as long as this doesn't result in any spiral markings, which will pump the lubricant right under the seal. Many seals are ruined due to careless installation. If a proper seal-driver is not available, care should be taken that whatever substitute tool is used, the force applied to drive the seal into position is directed squarely against the whole seal case. The seal lip must be lubricated prior to installation and protected by a suitable sleeve against cuts from splines, key ways, snap-ring grooves, and any other sharp edges or burrs. The excessive use of sealers and the presence of abrasive materials such as sludge, dirt, and rust will lead to premature failure. A leaking seal may also be the result of improper venting, cylinder blow-by, excessively high oil-levels, heat, or shaft run-out. In certain situations where one-piece seals cannot be used, for instance, on some engine rear main bearings, a groove is machined into the material surrounding the shaft (Fig. 3:7). This groove serves as a case into which a short piece of graphite-impregnated wick seal is installed. Wick seals may be made of rope, hemp, or asbestos fibre. Similar seals are also made of synthetic rubber.

Another very common seal, made of synthetic rubber or neoprene, which is available in many sizes, is the "O"-ring seal, mentioned earlier (Fig. 3:5). This type of seal is found in automatic transmissions and other hydraulic devices, and is also placed around tubes and fasteners or fitted into machined grooves to form a high-pressure seal. Some "O"-ring seals, such as the oil-filter gasket, have a square, rather than a round, cross-sectional profile.

The valve-guide seal (Fig. 3:8) may be ring-, washer-, or umbrella-shaped. The basic material is either a special, temperature-resistant synthetic rubber or Teflon. The purpose of the seal is to prevent excessive oil passage between the valve stems and valve guides. If it becomes hard and brittle, it must be replaced. Hydraulic seals, as used in brake cylinders, are basically of two types: the ring-shaped seal and the cup-shaped seal (see Figs. 16:46 and 16:53).

Warning: Hydraulic brake seals deteriorate in ordinary solvents, oils, fuels, and most liquids derived from mineral oils. Since even traces of these liquids adversely affect these seals, you must never use any of them to clean seals or any parts that will come into contact with them.

The size of a hydraulic seal is determined by

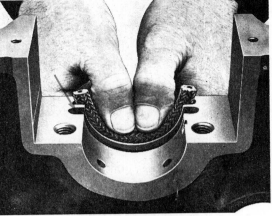

General Motors

Fig. 3:7 Installing the Crankshaft Rear Bearing Oil Seal (Note the second groove for the oil slinger and drainage.)

the size of the bore or cylinder into which it is to be fitted, rather than by the outside diameter of the expanded seal. The surfaces of the cylinder that come into contact with the seal must be free of any roughness or pit marks. The lips of brake seals always face the side from which the hydraulic pressure is applied.

As a rule, all types of seals should be lubricated before installation. On hydraulic brake seals, either a recommended lubricant or the hydraulic fluid normally found in the particular system should be used. Other seals can be coated with motor oil.

Dana Corporation

Fig. 3:8 Valve-guide Seal with Teflon Sleeve

RECOMMENDED ASSIGNMENTS

1. State briefly the purposes of a gasket.
2. Name six types of gaskets and state, in each case, their typical properties and applications.
3. What is the difference between compressibility and resilience?
4. Why is it impossible to salvage a wrinkled sandwich-type gasket?
5. List, in point form, five common causes of gasket leakage.
6. Why are flexible, non-hardening sealers usually preferred to hardening sealers?
7. Explain why excessive applications of sealers should be avoided.
8. What are the two functions of the garter spring?
9. How would you determine whether or not a seal is facing the right way?
10. Give ten causes of premature seal failure.
11. Name three precautions that apply to the installation of a new seal.
12. What is the purpose of the valve-guide seal?
13. How would you determine whether or not a valve-guide seal should be replaced?
14. State three important rules that apply to the installation of cup seals.

TROUBLE-SHOOTING

The following questions are meant to train you to think more deeply about technical problems. They are taken from actual trade experience and relate directly to the topic of this chapter. They are difficult, and to answer them correctly you will probably have to consult someone with experience in the field. The information in brackets following each indicates the minimum number of possible causes.

1. After a new cylinder-head gasket is installed an engine badly overheats. (3)
2. A new "O"-ring-type oil-filter gasket, tightened with a strap wrench, is leaking, and when it is removed there is no sign of any damage. The filter is re-installed by hand and the leak stops. (2)
3. A new gasket leaks as badly as the one it replaced. (several possibilities)
4. The brake-linings are fouled with wheel bearing grease shortly after a new front wheel bearing seal has been installed. (several possibilities)

4

Bearings

Did you know that the average family car, which weighs several thousand pounds, is supported by a bearing surface area smaller than the space occupied by the letters of this sentence? Probably not, but the next time you are handling a front wheel bearing, place the rollers on an ink pad and then stamp a piece of paper with it. The impression left on the paper will show you just how small the area of support really is. Modern engineering, materials, manufacturing processes and especially lubrication have made this miracle possible, but only your skill and know-how can guarantee its functioning.

The purpose of a bearing is to support a rotating part, and to reduce friction and the heat generated by that friction. It is good to keep in mind that mechanical efficiency and the rate of wear are closely related to the last two factors.

Types of Bearings

Bearings can be classified by the direction in which they support their loads:
1. Radial bearings support loads at right angles to the shaft (Fig. 4:1).
2. Thrust bearings support loads parallel to the shaft (Fig. 4:2).
3. Combination bearings combine radial and thrust loads (Fig. 4:3).

There are two common, but distinct, ways of

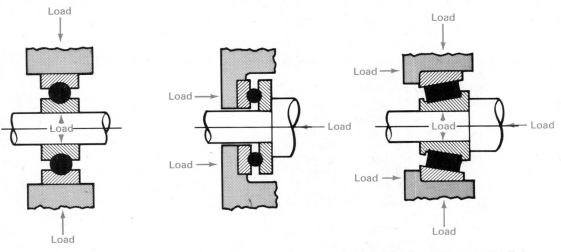

Fig. 4:1   Radial Loads   Fig. 4:2   Thrust Loads   Fig. 4:3   Combination Radial and Thrust Loads

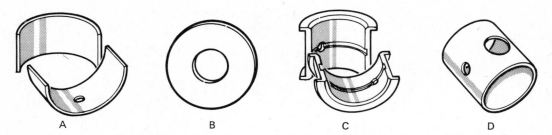

Fig. 4:4   Plain or Friction-type Bearings: (a) Radial (insert type); (b) Thrust; (c) Combination (insert type); (d) Radial (Bushing or Sleeve Bearing).

reducing friction by means of bearings:
1. By using very hard materials, in which case the contacting bearing surfaces are kept small.
2. By using very soft materials, in which case the contacting surfaces of the bearing are relatively large.

As you will see later, each method has both advantages and disadvantages.

There are three general types of automotive bearings:

Plain Bearings or Friction-type Bearings

These bearings, illustrated in Fig. 4:4, derive their names from the fact that they are of "plain" construction and that the contacting bearing surfaces, without the help of any rollers or ball bearings, are subject to sliding friction. To reduce friction the relatively large surface of a plain bearing is usually made of a fairly soft material that has some lubricating qualities of its own. This prevents the bearing from seizing up if there is a momentary lack of lubricant. Also, small abrasive particles, which would otherwise destroy or score the bearing, are able to embed themselves in the material. In addition to embedibility, plain bearings possess conformability; that is, like new shoes they are able to conform to the slight irregularities in the part to which they are fitted. This is the main reason why plain bearings, once used, should never be "switched" but always be refitted in exactly the same position.

Most plain bearings are provided with passage holes or grooves, or both, to allow the lubricant to enter and to surround the moving shaft or part. As a result, some shafts such as the crankshaft and the camshaft, once set in motion, will literally hydroplane over the lubricant.

(See "Hydrodynamic Lubrication", p. 145.)

Plain or sleeve bearings may be made of various types of alloys containing copper, bronze, tin, lead, nickel, and aluminum. In many cases, as shown in Fig. 4:5, several layers of different metals are rolled and fused to a steel or bronze backing.

The plain bearing may be of the split insert type (connecting rod and crankshaft bearings) or it may be a one-piece sleeve (camshaft bearings) (Fig. 4:4). Some sleeve bearings, also called bushings, are made of a porous type of bronze impregnated with a lubricant. The bushings used in starter motors are typical examples. Obviously they must not be exposed to cleaning solvents.

Most insert bearings are designed as radial bearings, but, in a typical bearing set, some (such as one of the engine main bearings) are equipped with thrust flanges, or shoulders, to handle thrust loads as well (Figs. 4:4c, 5:6, and 5:7a). Fig. 4:6 illustrates and explains some important terms such as "spread", "crush", "radial pressure", "locating lug", etc. Without radial pressure, which is a result of spread,

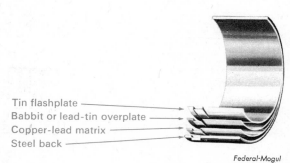

Tin flashplate
Babbit or lead-tin overplate
Copper-lead matrix
Steel back

Federal-Mogul

Fig. 4:5   Overlay Type of Insert Bearing with Load Capacity up to 10,000 psi

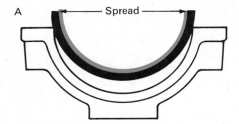

A

"Spread" makes it necessary to snap the insert into the rod or oap and holds the insert in place during assembly of the rod on the crankshaft.

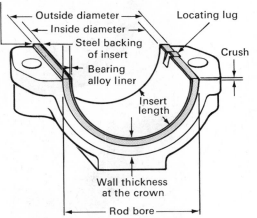

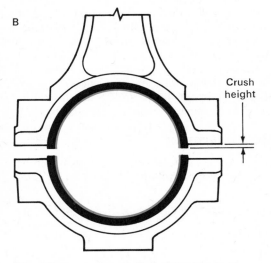

B

"Crush" assures firm seating of the inserts in the rod bore when the bearing cap is tightened. Too much "crush" or too little "crush" will lead to bearing trouble.

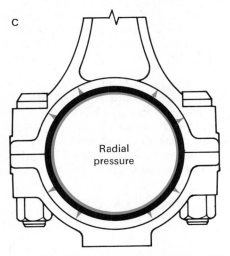

C

Proper "crush" creates a radial pressure which holds the inserts tightly in the rod bore after assembly, assures full contact between inserts and rod.

Sunnen Products Company Limited

Fig. 4:6   Insert Bearing Nomenclature

crush, and proper size, the insert would fail rapidly under the pounding action of the engine. Furthermore, a snug fit ensures that heat can travel freely between the insert bearing and the surrounding material.

Bearing clearance is the amount of free play between the shaft and the insert bearing. If the bearing clearance is too small (i.e., fitted too tightly), the lubricant cannot form an adequately protective film. This causes metal-to-metal contact, scoring, and overheating. In severe cases the shaft seizes, i.e., it locks up in

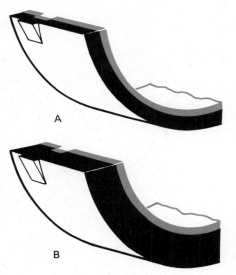

Sunnen Products Company Limited

Fig. 4:7 (a) Precision Insert for a Standard Nominal-Size Crankshaft; (b) Precision Insert for a 0.030" or 0.762 mm Undersize Crankshaft. Note that the difference in insert thickness is made up in the flexible steel backing itself, while the thin alloy lining layer remains constant.

the bearing. On the other hand, if there is too much clearance, the oil simply runs out of the bearing. (See footnote 35, on page 142.) As a result, oil pressure is lost and the bearing, as well as the shaft, is hammered out of shape. The pounding can often be heard, and if ignored, especially at high rpm, the engine will almost tear itself to pieces.

The bearing clearance may be as little as one-thousandth of an inch or even less. Under-size (i.e., thicker) bearings are available (Fig. 4:7) to maintain the correct bearing clearance on slightly worn, undersize, or reconditioned shafts.

To check for a proper fit, a small strip of plastic, known as Plastigage, is placed between the bearing and the shaft (Fig. 4:8a). After torquing the bearing caps (i.e., tightening them to specifications), the flattened Plastigage is measured with a special scale, as shown in Fig. 4:8b. The scale is calibrated in inches on the one side and in millimetres on the other. The widening of the Plastigage under the bearing pressure provides a fast but fairly accurate means of measuring the bearing clearance.

The failure of insert bearings is usually due to dirt, improper installation, misalignment, lack of lubrication, overheating, corrosion, over-loading, poor material, poor finish, high mile-age, or fatigue.

In summary, modern plain bearings are simple, reasonably cheap, reliable, easy to install, compact, light, and available in under-sizes to fit worn or reground shafts.

Ball Bearings

Ball bearings are classified as anti-friction bear-ings because a rolling, rather than a sliding,

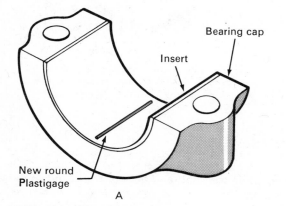

Bearing cap

Insert

New round Plastigage

A

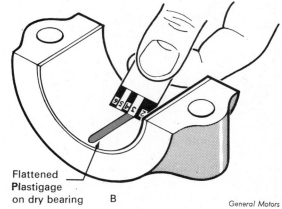

Flattened Plastigage on dry bearing

B

General Motors

Fig. 4:8 Plastigaging an Insert Bearing: (a) Before bearing cap is torqued to specifications; (b) With bearing cap removed again for inspection. Indicated clearance here is 0.003" (0.076 mm) or slightly less.

contact is made between two surfaces. They are made of extremely hard steel alloys and the contacting surfaces of the bearing's members are very small. Their starting friction (i.e., the effort required to set them in motion from a standstill) is therefore very low compared with that of plain bearings.

Automotive ball bearings can be divided into three groups:

1. *Annular Ball Bearings* (Fig. 4:9) are used where mainly radial loads are encountered (generator, water-pump, and transmissions).

2. *Angular Contact Ball Bearings* or *Cup-and-Cone Ball Bearings* (Fig. 4:10) can, for the purpose of cleaning and inspection, be separated into three parts: the inner race, ring, or cone; the bearing cage; and the outer race, ring, or cup. Since they can carry thrust loads in only one direction in addition to radial loads, they are employed in pairs. For example, if they are used as front wheel bearings, care must be taken that their thrust sides oppose each other; otherwise the wheel would simply fall off. When cup-and-cone bearings are installed they must be carefully adjusted to the recommended bearing pressure or preload.

3. *Ball Thrust Bearings* (Fig. 4:11) support loads mainly parallel to the shaft. The clutch release bearing (Fig. 15:2) is a typical example.

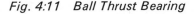
Canadian SKF Company Limited

Fig. 4:10 Angular Contact Ball Bearing or Cup-and-cone Ball Bearing

Canadian SKF Company Limited

Fig. 4:11 Ball Thrust Bearing

Roller Bearings

While roller bearings are not as efficient in reducing friction as ball bearings are, their larger contact surfaces can carry heavier loads, and they tend to last longer.

Roller bearings can be divided into groups corresponding to those for ball bearings:

1. *Straight* or *Cylindrical Roller Bearings* (Fig. 4:12) are used where mainly radial loads are

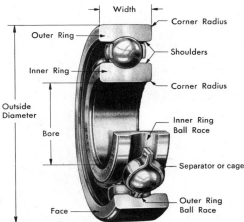

Width
Corner Radius
Outer Ring
Shoulders
Inner Ring
Corner Radius
Outside Diameter
Inner Ring Ball Race
Bore
Separator or cage
Outer Ring Ball Race
Face

Anti-Friction Bearing Manufacturers Assn. Incorporated

Fig. 4:9 Typical Ball Bearing (annular type)

Canadian SKF Company Limited

Fig. 4:12 Straight or Cylindrical Roller Bearing

encountered. In some cases where the roller diameter is very small, the bearing is known as a *needle bearing*. The latter type often has no cage (e.g., universal joint bearings, Fig. 15:26).

2. *Tapered Roller Bearings* (Fig. 4:13) are similar to cup-and-cone ball bearings, in both design and purpose. They are typically combination bearings and are now the most common type of front wheel bearing (Figs. 16:5 and 16:64). They are installed in pairs and are ideally suited for the heavy combination loads encountered in differentials (Fig. 15:31).

3. *Thrust Roller* or *Needle Bearings* support loads mainly parallel to the shaft. Although they are found in some automatic transmissions, they are not commonly used. In most cases plain thrust washers are used instead (Fig. 4:4b).

General Bearing Information

Since all bearings are precision-made, dirt is one of their worst enemies. It is therefore very important that absolute cleanliness be observed whenever bearings are handled. Generally speaking, the most common causes of failure in ball bearings and roller bearings are the same as those listed earlier for insert bearings. There are, however, some special types of failure that are typical of these two kinds of bearings: (a) flaking, or spalling (the hardened surfaces flake off), which is usually the result of metal fatigue; (b) brinelling (roller or needle imprints hammered into the bearing surface), which is due to heavy impact loads or vibration; (c) bent, cracked, or broken cages, rings, and bearing races, caused by corrosion, lack of lubrication, or entry of moisture; (d) pitting, which is due to fatigue, lack of lubrication, tightness, or overloading; (e) spark erosion (minute pitting on generator and electric motor bearings), and (f) overheating (blued bearings) due to lack of lubrication, overloading, or tightness. Any one of these conditions is indicated by abnormal noises, excessive play, or noticeable roughness when the bearing is turned by hand. Always lubricate the bearing with a few drops of oil before testing. Even a brand-new bearing will fail rapidly if it is magnetized. Touching it just once with a magnetized tool will cause it to pick up abrasive steel particles.

Fig. 4:13   Tapered Roller Bearing

Prelubricated bearings (rear axle, generator, and water-pump bearings) are packed with a lubricant during assembly at the factory and then they are sealed (Fig. 4:14). This type of bearing should never be cleaned in solvents as this will ruin the lubricant, and eventually the whole bearing. Due to the drag of the built-in seals and the heavy permanent lubricant, prelubricated bearings do not turn as easily as regular bearings, especially when new. Most other bearings should be lubricated periodically.

To be quite certain of the type and amount of lubricant that should be used, you should always refer to the manufacturer's specifications. This important rule applies equally to procedures of installation and of adjustments.

Never install a bearing without lubricating it, *even if it is connected to a pressurized lubrication circuit.* The adage "An ounce of prevention is worth a pound of cure" was never more true.

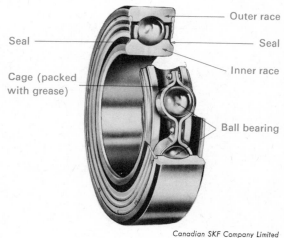

Fig. 4:14   Prelubricated and Sealed Ball Bearing

RECOMMENDED ASSIGNMENTS

1. Define the terms "radial", "thrust", and "combination load".
2. State briefly the main purposes of a bearing.
3. Give three important reasons why plain bearings usually employ soft, rather than hard, bearing surfaces.
4. Why should used bearings never be mixed up?
5. What is an overlay type of plain bearing?
6. Explain the terms "bearing", "spread", and "crush".
7. Comment briefly on the result of incorrect bearing clearance.
8. What is the purpose of Plastigage?
9. Name six advantages of plain bearings.
10. Name three types of ball bearings and give one common automotive application for each.
11. Name three types of roller bearings and give examples of their use.
12. List ten common causes of bearing failure.
13. What precautions should be taken when handling prelubricated bearings?
14. How would you determine whether or not a bearing was adjusted properly?

TROUBLE-SHOOTING

The following cases are typical service problems encountered daily in automotive repair shops. If you are unable to determine the cause or causes of the problem you should discuss it with someone experienced in the field such as a service mechanic. There is at least one cause for each problem.

1. A plain insert bearing is heavily worn right around its inner surface, but much more so towards one edge than the other.
2. The crankshaft of a rebuilt engine seizes up. All main bearings are badly scored.
3. A do-it-yourself motorist finally consults his mechanic after repeated failure of the generator bearings.

5

Engine
Construction

Study Guide

While this chapter involves some basic principles, it is mostly a study of parts—their shapes and functions, and how, when put together, they form a complete piston engine. The actual operating principles of a piston engine are discussed in the following chapters. Wherever possible, our discussion follows the order of engine assembly. If conditions permit, you could actually assemble an old engine step by step as you follow the text. The names of automotive parts are easily remembered if you think of their purpose, action, or shape. For example, a connecting rod is precisely that—a rod that connects, and a rocker arm is an arm that rocks up and down.

General Information

The modern automobile uses an internal combustion engine, which means that the fuel is burned inside the engine's working chamber rather than outside, as is the case with external combustion engines, such as steam engines, Stirling engines, and steam turbines.

Gasoline and Diesel engines convert the chemical energy (potential energy) contained in the fuel into heat energy inside the cylinder. As the hot, expanding gases push against the pistons, this heat is then converted into mechanical energy, which is utilized at the flywheel.

Engine Parts

Cylinder Block and Crankcase

The cylinder block (Fig. 5:5), also known as the engine block or motor block, is in one sense the

foundation of the engine because it determines the basic layout of the engine (straight six, V-8, etc.) and its size (engine displacement). Furthermore, all other major engine parts are attached to it.

Most cylinder blocks are made of a special cast iron, or "alloyed gray iron", which contains small amounts of silicon, manganese, and chromium to increase the hardness and wearing qualities of the cylinder bores. Minute particles of carbon (graphite) embedded in the grain structure of the metal help to reduce friction in the cylinders. Cylinder blocks of cast aluminum are used in some engines, particularly where light weight is a major consideration. They either have cylinder walls specially treated with wear-reducing materials, such as silicone and chrome, or they employ cast iron cylinder sleeves.

The cylinders of liquid-cooled engines are surrounded by cooling jackets (Figs. 5:1-5:4), whereas air-cooled engines are equipped with cooling fins (Fig. 9:6d). Port-like openings on the outside of the cylinder block allow the removal of special sand cores from the cooling jackets after the casting process is completed. Steel plugs, known as frost plugs or core hole plugs, are later pressed into these openings (Fig. 5:5a). (For further information see p. 125.)

The cylinder block is extended downwards to form the crankcase (Fig. 5:5). The crankcase is reinforced by transverse members that support the crankshaft main bearings. To ensure perfect alignment the main bearings and their detachable bearing caps are "line bored" with great accuracy. The main bearing caps are therefore not interchangeable, and if not already numbered, they must be marked before removal to

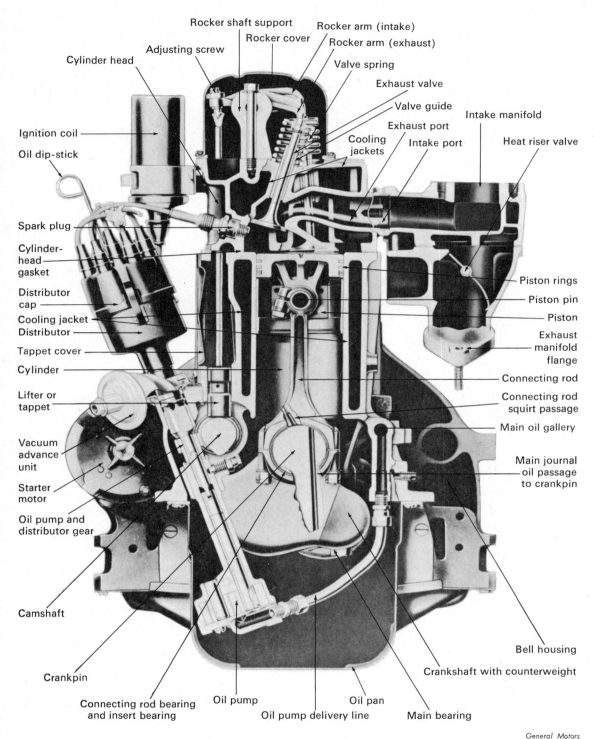

Cylinder head

Rocker shaft support

Adjusting screw

Rocker cover

Rocker arm (intake)

Rocker arm (exhaust)

Valve spring

Exhaust valve

Valve guide

Intake manifold

Ignition coil

Exhaust port

Cooling jackets

Intake port

Heat riser valve

Oil dip-stick

Spark plug

Cylinder-head gasket

Distributor cap

Cooling jacket

Distributor

Tappet cover

Cylinder

Lifter or tappet

Vacuum advance unit

Starter motor

Oil pump and distributor gear

Camshaft

Piston rings

Piston pin

Piston

Exhaust manifold flange

Connecting rod

Connecting rod squirt passage

Main oil gallery

Main journal oil passage to crankpin

Bell housing

Crankpin

Connecting rod bearing and insert bearing

Oil pump

Oil pump delivery line

Oil pan

Main bearing

Crankshaft with counterweight

General Motors

Fig. 5:1   Cross-section of a Six-cylinder Engine

General Motors

Fig. 5:2   Phantom Cross-section of a Six-cylinder Engine

indicate their original positions. Each main bearing is lined with a bearing insert to fit the crankshaft journals. One of the main bearings has thrust flanges to take care of the end-play of the crankshaft (Figs. 5:6 and 5:7a). The rear main bearing is equipped with an oil seal to prevent leakage (Figs. 3:7 and 5:7a).

The Crankshaft

The crankshaft (Fig. 5:7a) receives power from the piston through the connecting rod and converts this reciprocating motion (up and down) and oscillating motion (swinging motion) to rotary motion.

The crankshaft, which may run at speeds of well over 5,000 rpm, is subject to tremendous forces that simultaneously bend and twist it. To produce crankshafts tough enough to with-

stand these forces, special steel alloys and manufacturing methods have been developed. One of the most popular methods is to forge the shaft; that is, a white-hot piece of high-quality steel, such as chrome-nickel steel alloy, is first pounded into the required shape and then machined to size. Oil passages connecting the main journals with the crankpins are drilled into the shaft (Fig. 5:7b). (See also Fig. 5:1.) To reduce wear on the crankpins and main journals they are surface hardened. The whole process results in a rugged yet slightly flexible shaft with an extremely hard and wear-resistant journal finish. The crankshaft is then precision-ground, balanced, demagnetized, and inspected. During the balancing operation, excess material is removed from the counterweights that offset the weight of the crank arms, the crankpins, and the piston and connecting rod

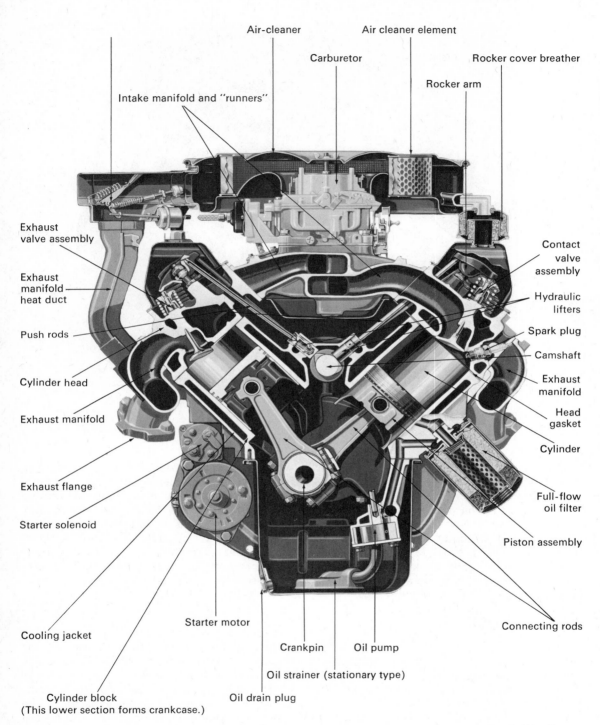

Air-cleaner

Air cleaner element

Carburetor

Rocker cover breather

Rocker arm

Intake manifold and "runners"

Exhaust
valve assembly

Exhaust
manifold
heat duct

Push rods

Cylinder head

Exhaust manifold

Exhaust flange

Starter solenoid

Cooling jacket

Contact
valve
assembly

Hydraulic
lifters

Spark plug

Camshaft

Exhaust
manifold

Head
gasket

Cylinder

Full-flow
oil filter

Piston assembly

Connecting rods

Starter motor

Crankpin

Oil pump

Oil strainer (stationary type)

Oil drain plug

Cylinder block
(This lower section forms crankcase.)

Ford Motor Company

Fig. 5:3   Cross-section of a V-8 Engine

General Motors

Fig. 5:4   Phantom View of a V-8 Engine

assembly. An unbalanced shaft causes heavy engine vibrations, metal fatigue, and finally, breakage. Another very common manufacturing method is to cast the shaft in a sand mould.

Premature crankshaft failures are usually due to improper installation, lack of lubrication, excessive loads, or abrasive materials trapped in the bearings. Worn crankshafts can be reground within specified tolerances and can be fitted with undersize bearings (Fig. 4:7).

The Flywheel

The flywheel (Fig. 5:7a) is fastened to the rear-drive flange of the crankshaft and helps to carry the engine from one power stroke to the next. It also combats torsional crankshaft vibrations, and it supports the starter ring-gear and the clutch cover. The rear face of the flywheel has a smooth finish to provide a frictional surface for the clutch disc. Engines fitted to automatic transmissions are equipped

with a lightweight adapter plate instead (Fig. 5:42a), as the hydraulic coupling or torque converter attached to it is heavy enough to serve as a flywheel. Whichever device is used, it is carefully balanced with the crankshaft; if removed, it must be re-installed in exactly the same position. On many engines, special dowel pins or an irregular screw pattern act as a safeguard against improper installation.

The Piston

The piston (Fig. 5:8) transmits the firing pressures in the cylinder to the crankshaft via the connecting rod. By moving up and down, the piston permits the volume of the cylinder to vary, which allows gases to enter, to be compressed, to expand, or to be exhausted. The piston also guides the upper end of the connecting rod in the cylinder and supports the piston rings.

The trend to high-rpm engines as a means of

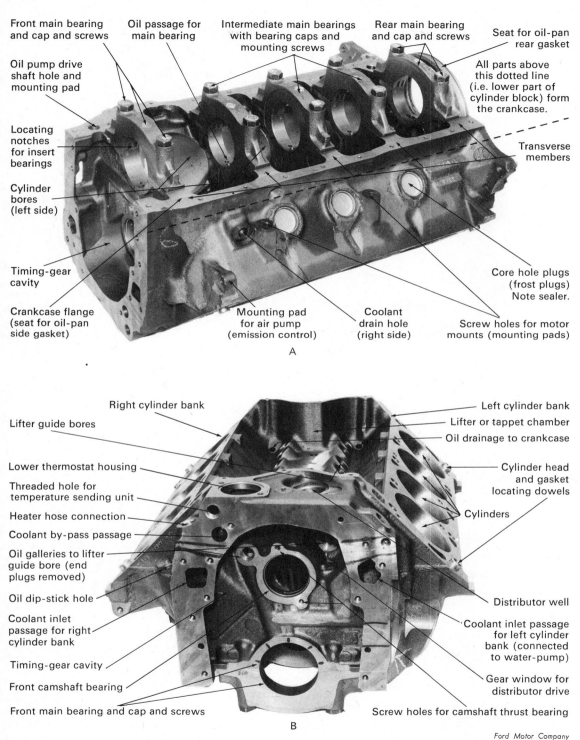

Front main bearing and cap and screws

Oil passage for main bearing

Intermediate main bearings with bearing caps and mounting screws

Rear main bearing and cap and screws

Seat for oil-pan rear gasket

Oil pump drive shaft hole and mounting pad

All parts above this dotted line (i.e. lower part of cylinder block) form the crankcase.

Locating notches for insert bearings

Transverse members

Cylinder bores (left side)

Timing-gear cavity

Core hole plugs (frost plugs) Note sealer.

Crankcase flange (seat for oil-pan side gasket)

Mounting pad for air pump (emission control)

Coolant drain hole (right side)

Screw holes for motor mounts (mounting pads)

A

Right cylinder bank

Left cylinder bank

Lifter guide bores

Lifter or tappet chamber

Oil drainage to crankcase

Lower thermostat housing

Cylinder head and gasket locating dowels

Threaded hole for temperature sending unit

Heater hose connection

Coolant by-pass passage

Cylinders

Oil galleries to lifter guide bore (end plugs removed)

Oil dip-stick hole

Distributor well

Coolant inlet passage for right cylinder bank

Coolant inlet passage for left cylinder bank (connected to water-pump)

Timing-gear cavity

Front camshaft bearing

Gear window for distributor drive

Front main bearing and cap and screws

Screw holes for camshaft thrust bearing

B

Ford Motor Company

Fig. 5:5 Cylinder Block of a V-8 Engine: (a) Top view; (b) Bottom view.

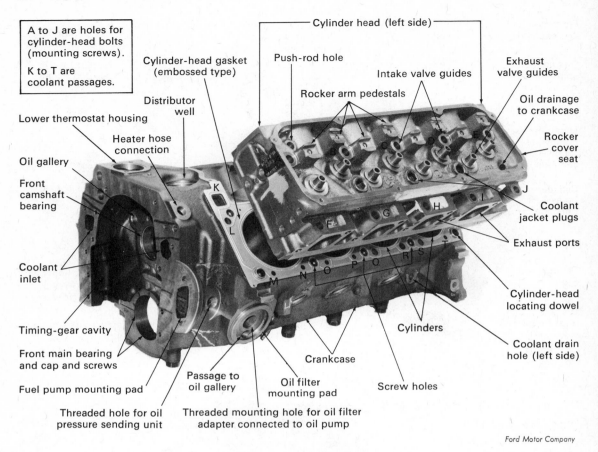

A to J are holes for cylinder-head bolts (mounting screws).

K to T are coolant passages.

Cylinder head (left side)

Cylinder-head gasket (embossed type)

Push-rod hole

Intake valve guides

Exhaust valve guides

Rocker arm pedestals

Distributor well

Oil drainage to crankcase

Lower thermostat housing

Heater hose connection

Rocker cover seat

Oil gallery

Front camshaft bearing

Coolant jacket plugs

Coolant inlet

Exhaust ports

Cylinder-head locating dowel

Timing-gear cavity

Cylinders

Front main bearing and cap and screws

Coolant drain hole (left side)

Fuel pump mounting pad

Passage to oil gallery

Oil filter mounting pad

Screw holes

Crankcase

Threaded hole for oil pressure sending unit

Threaded mounting hole for oil filter adapter connected to oil pump

Ford Motor Company

Fig. 5:5   (c) End View of Cylinder Block of a V-8 Engine.

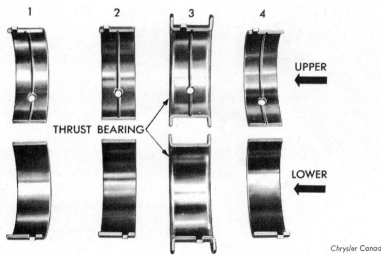

THRUST BEARING

UPPER

LOWER

Fig. 5:6   Set of Main Bearing Inserts

Chrysler Canada Ltd.

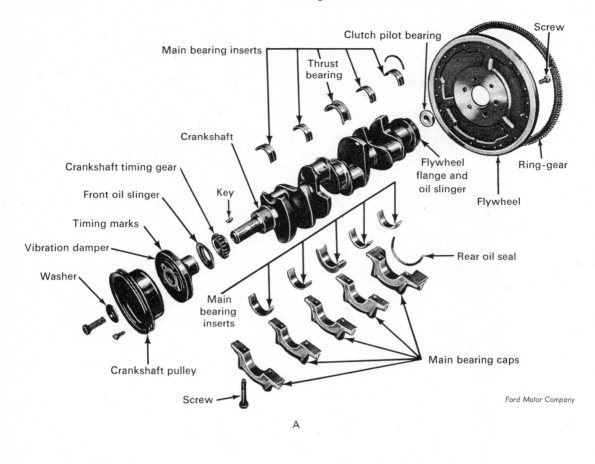

Main bearing inserts

Clutch pilot bearing

Thrust bearing

Screw

Crankshaft

Crankshaft timing gear

Front oil slinger

Key

Timing marks

Vibration damper

Washer

Main bearing inserts

Crankshaft pulley

Screw

Flywheel flange and oil slinger

Ring-gear

Flywheel

Rear oil seal

Main bearing caps

Ford Motor Company

A

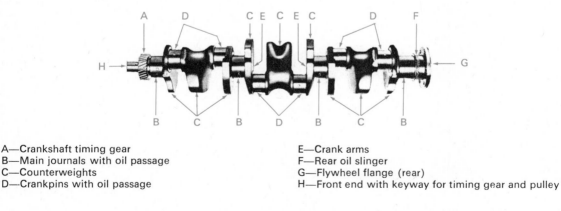

A—Crankshaft timing gear
B—Main journals with oil passage
C—Counterweights
D—Crankpins with oil passage

E—Crank arms
F—Rear oil slinger
G—Flywheel flange (rear)
H—Front end with keyway for timing gear and pulley

B

General Motors

Fig. 5:7   (a) Crankshaft and Related Parts; (b) Details of Crankshaft.

increasing power output led to the development of the aluminum alloy piston. A comparable cast iron piston, which weighs roughly twice as much, causes very high inertia loads. In practical terms, this means that the piston resists the sudden change in velocity near the end of each stroke. The heavier the piston, the more power is wasted to overcome its inertia. The forces may increase to a point where they tear a piston to pieces.[7] Aluminum alloy pistons are now used in all current engines. Various methods had to be applied to overcome three basic problems: (a) aluminum expands one and a half times as fast as cast iron; (b) it melts at roughly 1,200°F (649°C); and (c) if untreated, it doesn't wear as well as cast iron.

The narrow space between the piston skirt and the cylinder wall is called the piston clearance. This space is necessary to provide room for a protective oil film and to reduce friction. On the other hand, if there is too much clearance the piston will be noisy, wear will increase rapidly, the piston rings will not seal properly, and the transfer of heat into the cooling jackets is interfered with. To maintain the specified clearance (which may be as little as 0.0002″, or 0.0051 mm) under all operating temperatures, the following methods are used, either singly or in combination:

1. Cam grinding, i.e., the piston skirt is oval-shaped so that expansion can be relieved towards the purposely undersized skirt area close to the two piston pin bosses (Fig. 5:10).
2. Tapering the cold piston skirt, i.e., the skirt diameter is slightly smaller in the hot upper skirt area than in the cooler lower one. Under normal operating temperatures the

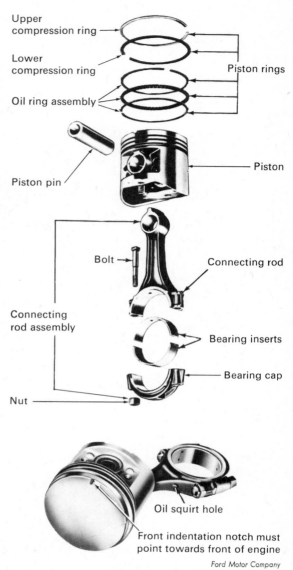

Fig. 5:8 Typical Piston and Connecting Rod Assembly

[7]Some interesting facts: At 4,000 rpm a piston reverses its direction 133 times per second. Firing loads plus kinetic loads may exceed five tons. Depending on engine speed and length of stroke, the piston is sometimes accelerated to over 60 mph (96 km/h) within less than 2″ (5.08 cm). Piston temperatures can reach 600°F (316°C). Aluminum pistons are usually cast, but forged pistons, which are used in some high-performance engines, are stronger and conduct heat more readily. Even in high gear the total distance travelled by all pistons in an eight-cylinder engine is roughly double the mileage covered by the vehicle.

skirt loses most of its taper and a more uniform skirt clearance is obtained.
3. Horizontal oil drain slots are cut into the lower ring groove (Fig. 5:9). This diverts the heat flow from the piston crown into the boss area and away from the skirt. It also allows the oil to return from the oil-scraper ring and at the same time cool the piston from the inside.
4. Shortening the skirt below the piston pin

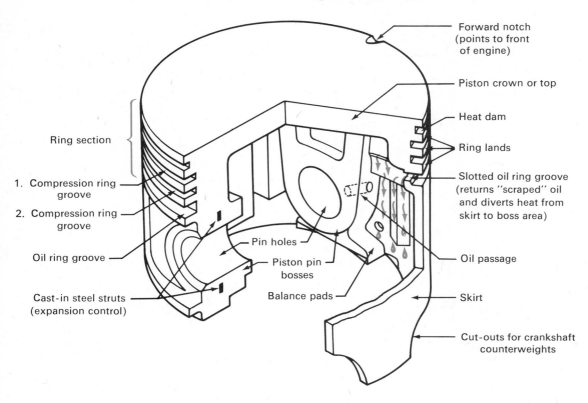

Fig. 5:9   Parts of an Aluminum Alloy Piston (sectional view)

boss area to permit the skirt to expand sideways without changing the piston clearance. This type of skirt, which is known as the "slipper skirt" (Fig. 5:11), also reduces weight and provides more room for the crankshaft counterweights in very compact engine designs.

5. Separating the crown and ring section from the skirt, except for narrow, steel-reinforced struts in the boss areas (Fig. 5:9). The steel struts deflect expansion from the skirt to the boss area. The slots between the crown and the skirt divert the heat as in (3) above.

6. Casting an expansion control ring or band into the piston between the ring section and the skirt. These steel bands deflect expansion from the skirts to the boss areas, which are farther removed from the cylinder wall.

7. The skirt is completely eliminated around the boss area. The latter is moved in from the cylinder wall, sometimes by more than ½" (1.27 cm). This type of piston is very light

yet strong (Fig. 5:12).

8. Horizontal, vertical, slanted, or "T"-expansion slots are cut into the minor thrust side of the piston skirt. This weakens the piston, however, and the method is now rarely used.

To allow for expansion in the piston crown, the entire ring section is undercut by approximately 0.020" to 0.035" (0.508 to 0.889 mm).

Sometimes a small groove, called a heat dam, is cut into the upper ring section between the edge of the crown and the first ring groove (Fig. 5:9). The oil carbon that builds up in the heat dam insulates the upper, and most vulnerable, piston ring against the extremely high firing-temperatures.

The head of the piston (the crown) can be flat, concave, convex, domed, or wedge-shaped, depending on the compression ratio and the combustion chamber design. In high-compression engines the piston head is often provided with valve reliefs, which are indenta-

SIDE VIEW

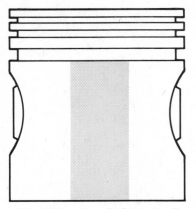

(shaded area in cylinder contact)

SIDE VIEW

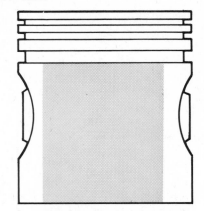

(shaded area in cylinder contact)

BOTTOM VIEW

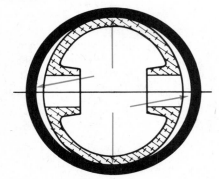

Diagram of a cam-ground piston in a cold engine—"full-cam" position. Note that the piston has cylinder-wall contact in the direction of thrust and has clearance along the axis of the pin bosses.

BOTTOM VIEW

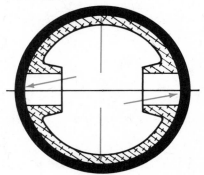

Diagram of a cam-ground piston at engine-operating temperature—"expanded cam" position. The piston has expanded till it is now practically round in the cylinder. Note that the pin bosses are now farther apart than when the piston was cold.

Sunnen Products Company Limited

Fig. 5:10 The Cam-ground Piston

tions to provide sufficient clearance for the overhead valves (Fig. 5:26).

To improve the wear characteristics of the piston skirt, its surface may be hardened by anodizing (i.e., by changing the surface layer electrically to aluminum oxide) or it may be coated with a scuff-reducing metal, such as tin. The skirt can also be knurled (grooved patterns rolled into the thrust sides of the skirt), as in Fig. 5:18. This holds a stronger and cooler oil film, traps abrasive particles, and permits the hot surface-layer to expand. This process is also applied to increase the size of slightly worn pistons. Yet another method is to provide the new skirt with "controlled roughness", i.e., while over-all dimensions are maintained, small threadlike valleys are machined into the skirt to make it more scuff-resistant. Aluminum alloy pistons fitted to aluminum cylinders are often plated with iron or chrome for the same reason.

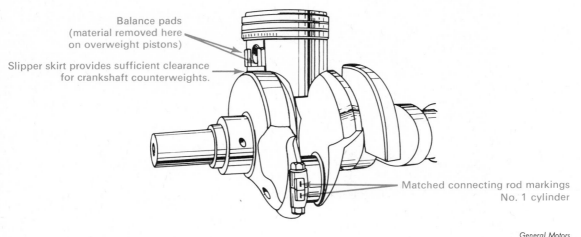

Balance pads
(material removed here
on overweight pistons)

Slipper skirt provides sufficient clearance
for crankshaft counterweights.

Matched connecting rod markings
No. 1 cylinder

General Motors

Fig. 5:11   The Slipper Skirt Piston

General Piston Information

1. Some of the most common causes of piston failure are: misalignment, improper fit, worn cylinders, dirt, lack of lubrication, coolant leakage, oil and fuel deposits, abnormal loads, excessively high engine rpm or temperatures, cheap fuels, wrong types of motor oil, incorrect spark plugs, low coolant levels, and improper carburetor and ignition settings.
2. Pistons should be handled with the greatest possible care. A dropped piston is a damaged piston, whether you can see the damage or not.
3. Pistons are available in oversizes.
4. Used pistons, like any moving part, must never be switched. For installation, always refer to service manuals and use the proper tools. Most pistons bear markings, such as a notch in the piston crown or an "F" in the boss area, to indicate the forward position (Figs. 5:8 and 5:9).[8]
5. All pistons must weigh the same (see balance pads in Fig. 5:11).

[8]On V-8 engines *FL* means "forward left", and *FR* means "forward right". Reversing a piston may cause it to collapse, especially if it is equipped with expansion slots or a piston pin offset towards the major thrust side (see Fig. 7:4).

6. Full throttle and high engine rpm should be avoided until normal operating temperatures are reached.

Piston Rings

The main purpose of the piston rings (Figs. 5:1 and 5:8) is to help the piston to seal the combustion chamber and the cylinder against the crankcase. They also control the thickness of the oil film on the cylinder walls. Furthermore, they transfer the heat from the piston to the cylinder walls and thus to the cooling jackets. Most engine designs use two compression rings and one oil-control ring.

Compression Rings

These are located in the top grooves of the piston (Figs. 5:8 and 5:9). Their primary function is to prevent the passage of gases past the piston, but they also assist in controlling the oil film. When the piston moves downwards, all three rings "peel off" some of the oil thrown against the cylinder walls. While the oil-control ring removes most of the oil, the second and the upper compression rings "shave" the oil film to approximately five ten-millionths of an inch. This very fine oil film is crucial in lubricating and sealing the rings as the piston returns on its upward stroke.

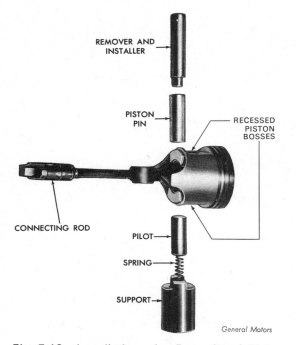

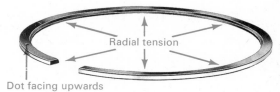

Fig. 5:13 Compression Ring with Molybdenum-filled Groove

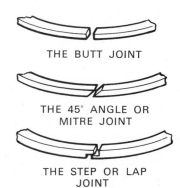

Fig. 5:12 Installation of a Press-fitted Piston Pin (Interference Fit)

THE BUTT JOINT

THE 45° ANGLE OR MITRE JOINT

THE STEP OR LAP JOINT

Fig. 5:14 Types of Piston Ring Joints

Compression rings are usually made of a special cast iron alloy, and are heat-treated and rolled to give them radial tension, i.e., outward tension towards the cylinder wall (Fig. 5:13). Like all piston rings, they are slit to form the ring gap. By far the most common type of ring gap is the straight cut or butt joint. The step joint, also known as the lap joint, and the 45° angle or mitre joint, are rarely found on standard engines (Fig. 5:14). The ring gap closes to a space approximately 0.01″ to 0.03″ (0.254 mm to 0.762 mm) when installed, depending on the cylinder size (Fig. 5:15). The purposes of the gap are (a) to allow installation; (b) to permit heat expansion; (c) to give the ring radial tension so that full contact with the cylinder is maintained at all times; and (d) to compensate for cylinder wear.

There are a great variety of ring profiles. The most common types are shown in Fig. 5:16, and two of these, the tapered ring design and the stepped ring design, require comment.

The *Tapered Ring* (Fig. 5:16b) is similar to hydraulic seals not only in appearance but also in action; that is, it can control the oil flow effectively only if that flow is directed against

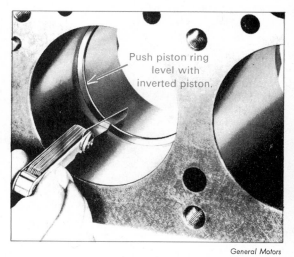

Fig. 5:15 Checking Ring End Clearance or Ring Gap (On used engines this must be done near the bottom of the cylinder at the point of minimum taper.)

A. This is a "plain" or fully rectangular cross-section ring. May be chrome-plated or Ferrox-coated.

B. This ring has a tapered face so that the lower outer corner will have positive contact with the cylinder. May be chrome-plated or Ferrox-coated.

C. The upper inner corner of this ring has a counterbore causing the ring to twist, resulting in a positive lower outer-edge face-contact with the cylinder. May be chrome-plated or Ferrox-coated.

D. This compression ring is both counterbored and tapered to produce a more positive contact at the lower outer edge. It may be phosphate-coated.

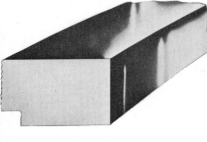

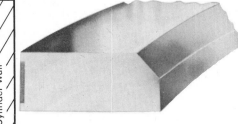

E. This ring has a stopped scraper groove machined in the outer lower corner to cause the ring to twist, resulting in lower outer-edge face-contact.

F. This bevelled or chamfered ring with a molybdenum-filled groove in its face is used in certain applications to prevent scuffing.

Dana Corporation

Fig. 5:16 The Most Common Compression Ring Designs

its raised edge. Therefore, the major advantage of the tapered ring is that it wipes excess oil off the cylinder wall on the down stroke, while it hydroplanes over the oil film on the upward stroke. Rectangular or *plain ring* profiles on the other hand (Fig. 5:16a) tend to leave a thicker oil film behind, which causes higher oil consumption and exhaust emission.

Stepped Rings have a groove cut into either their upper, inner edge (Figs. 5:16c, 5:16d, and 5:16f) or their lower, outer edge (Fig. 5:16e). When a stepped ring is compressed during installation and its gap closes to the specified end-clearance, the lower, outer edge is twisted towards the cylinder wall. The resulting tension is caused by the ring's irregular configuration. Thus, this type of ring normally acts exactly like the tapered ring. During the power stroke, however, and only then, the extremely high firing-pressures momentarily untwist the piston ring so that its full face presses flatly against the cylinder wall. Stepped rings therefore meet four important requirements: (a) they stop blow-by during the power stroke; (b) the twisting action jams the ring against the ring lands (Fig. 5:9) to stop unwanted oil flow through the ring grooves behind the rings and into the combustion chamber; (c) oil film control on the cylinder walls is excellent; and (d) the constant flexing prevents sticky rings (due to carbon deposits). Obviously, if a stepped ring is accidentally turned upside down, it will cause serious problems.

The Oil-control Ring or Oil-scraper Ring

The oil-control ring (Fig. 5:17) controls the oil film in the cylinders. It may be a slotted, cast iron ring, employed either singly or in combination with steel expanders and side rails, or it

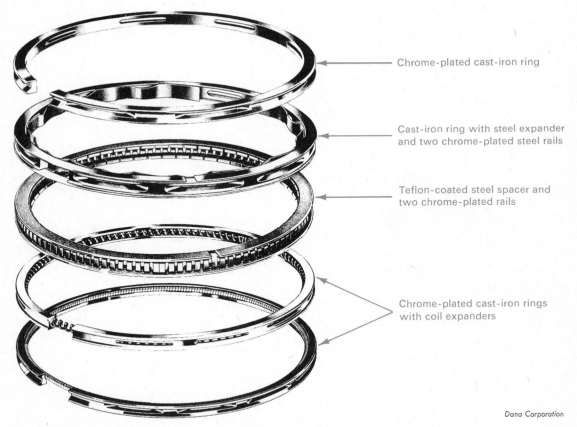

Chrome-plated cast-iron ring

Cast-iron ring with steel expander and two chrome-plated steel rails

Teflon-coated steel spacer and two chrome-plated rails

Chrome-plated cast-iron rings with coil expanders

Dana Corporation

Fig. 5:17 Common Types of Oil-control Rings

may be the widely used sectional type, which is made up of several separate, very flexible steel sections. Each type of ring has channels and openings that serve as oil-return passages into the crankcase. (See also Fig. 5:8.)

General Piston Ring Information

Modern, compact, high rpm engines with high compression, wide cylinder bores, and short strokes require not only shorter pistons but flat rings as well. Compared with older, wider styles, narrow ring faces seal better, are lighter, and are more scuff-resistant. Their drawback is greater wear. To overcome this problem, manufacturers coat the ring faces with hard, wear-resistant materials such as chrome (Fig. 5:16a), molybdenum (Figs. 5:13 and 5:16f), and iron oxide (Fig. 5:16c). In addition, the ring face is sometimes provided with a rippled, threadlike finish that helps to hold the oil (Figs. 5:16a, b, c, d, and e). Thanks to these improvements, the newer, flatter ring designs (Fig. 5:13) actually last longer than the wider types used some years ago, despite the fact that they are more highly stressed.

Fig. 5:18   Checking Minimum Ring-to-groove Side-Clearance with Feeler Gauge

The handling and installation of piston rings require great care and special tools. To prevent their installation upside down, piston rings often bear signs indicating which side faces up (Figs. 5:13 and 5:16). Piston rings are also available in oversizes. You should always refer to manufacturers' instructions when installing piston rings, especially with regard to minimum and maximum ring-gap clearance (Fig. 5:15), ring-to-groove side-clearance (Fig. 5:18), and ring-groove depth.

Generally the causes of ring failure are the same as those listed for piston failure. Rings are particularly sensitive to rich fuel-mixtures because liquid gasoline washes the oil film off the cylinder walls. This in turn leads to carbon deposits, sticky rings, excessive wear, and ring scuffing. Since the oil film is essential for a good ring seal, this condition, known as "gasoline wash", also causes a considerable drop in compression pressure. This is one of several reasons why a flooded engine is hard to start.

The Piston Pin

The piston pin (Fig. 5:8), sometimes called a wrist pin because of its wrist-like action, provides a flexible connection between the piston and the connecting rod. As the piston pin must withstand very heavy loads, sometimes in excess of five tons, it is made of extremely tough chrome-nickel steel alloys. To ensure a perfect, durable fit, the pin is case-hardened (surface-hardened) and lapped (polished) to a mirror finish. The hollow structure results in light weight but great strength, thus reducing inertia loads and power losses.

There are two basic types of piston pin fits: the semi-floating fit and the full-floating fit.
1. The semi-floating fit locks the pin in the upper end of the connecting rod either by a clamping screw (Fig. 5:1 and 5:19a), which is a special locking pin, or by an interference (press) fit (Figs. 5:12 and 5:19b). The piston pin is therefore only free to move in the pin holes of the piston. The pin may also be locked in the piston with a set screw and be free to move in the connecting rod bushing, although this is a less common type of pin fit.
2. The full-floating fit permits pin movement both in the pin holes in the piston and in the

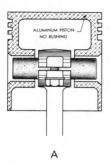

A

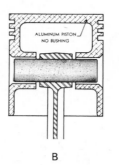

B

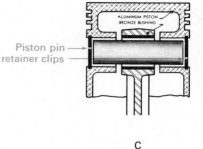

C

Piston pin oscillating in piston, clamped in connecting rod (semi-floating)

Piston pin oscillating in piston, press-fitted into connecting rod (semi-floating)

Piston pin free to move in piston and connecting rod (full-floating)

Sunnen Products Company Limited

Fig. 5:19 Types of Piston Pin Fits

connecting rod bushing. Snap rings in the pin holes prevent the full-floating pin from interfering with the cylinder walls (Fig. 5:19c).

The Connecting Rod

The "con-rod" (Fig. 5:8) connects the piston pin, and thus the piston, to the crankpin of the crankshaft. Its reciprocating or oscillating motion (like the swing of a pendulum) allows the up-and-down motion of the piston to be transformed into the rotary motion of the crankshaft. Modern high-rpm engines require the connecting rod to be exceptionally strong, yet as light as possible to reduce inertia loads and centrifugal forces. For this reason connecting rods are usually steel alloy forgings with a rigid "I"-beam cross-section. They are shot-peened (pellet-blasted) to resist fatigue and distortion. While most "con-rods" have oil spit-holes to lubricate the cylinder walls (Fig. 5:1), those fitted to full-floating piston pins may have a central oil passage joining the lower bearing and the upper bronze bushing. The bearing caps and connecting rods come in matched sets, and their bearing caps must never be switched or reversed. The caps and "con-rods" are usually punch-numbered to indicate their proper installation and cylinder positions (Fig. 5:11). The two parts bolted together, with the bearing inserts held firmly in position, clasp the crankpin of the crankshaft in a hinge-like manner. The bearings, which have a clearance of approximately 0.0002" to 0.003" (0.0051 mm to

0.0762 mm), are pressure-lubricated from the crankshaft oil passages (Fig. 5:1). The connecting rod bolts are of special, high-tensile steel and are locked so that engine vibration cannot loosen them. Connecting rod bearings are available in undersizes (i.e., thicker) to fit slightly worn or reconditioned crankshafts (Fig. 4:7). To avoid serious engine vibrations, all pistons and connecting rods must be of exactly the same weight.

Causes of failure follow closely those outlined earlier for pistons and piston rings. Typical problems arise from connecting rod distortion, misalignment, incorrect bearing clearance, loss of oil pressure, and improper installation. These defects are critical, as they will invariably lead to serious failure of related parts such as crankpins, pistons, and cylinders. In severe cases the entire engine is destroyed.

The Oil-pan Windage Baffle

The oil-pan windage baffle, consisting of a sheet metal tray, is usually mounted to the main bearing caps of some engines (Fig. 11:6). It reduces power-consuming drag caused by the "egg-beater" action of the crankshaft and the connecting rods. The baffle helps to control oil consumption, foaming, and emission.

If we were to assemble an engine in roughly the sequence followed thus far in this chapter, we should continue with the oil pump and the oil intake. Since these parts are discussed in Chapter 11: Lubricants and Lubrication, let us

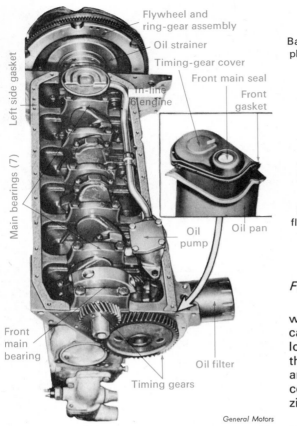

Fig. 5:20 *Bottom View of Cylinder Block Assembly Ready for Installation of Oil Pan*

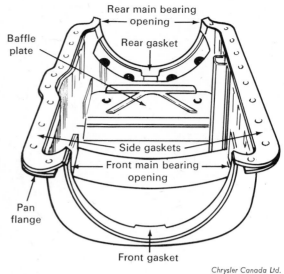

Fig. 5:21 *The Oil Pan*

assume them to be in position for now. The oil pan would then follow.

The Oil Pan

The oil pan (Fig. 5:21) is fitted by means of screws to the lower part of the crankcase (Fig. 5:20), where it is exposed to the air flow. It stores the motor oil that circulates through the engine and cools it as it returns from the hot engine parts. A gasket between the crankcase and the oil-pan flange (mounting edge) ensures an oil-tight seal.

The Camshaft

The camshaft (Fig. 5:22) operates the engine's valve mechanism and, in most cases, the distributor, the oil pump, and the fuel pump as

well (Figs. 5:1 and 5:2). It is either forged or cast. To withstand extremely high pressure-loadings (around 100,000 lb. per square inch) the cams are surface- or induction-hardened and precision-ground. The cams may also be coated with wear-reducing materials, such as zinc phosphate.

The camshaft changes rotary motion into the reciprocating motion of the valve lifters, or tappets, which follow the hump-shaped cams (Figs. 5:1 and 5:35). With the exception of "boxer" engines (Fig. 9:6d), there is one cam on the camshaft for each valve. The design and the relative position of the cam on the camshaft govern the time, the rate, the duration, the lift (height), and the sequence of valve opening. The cam face is often slightly tapered, that is, one edge is roughly 0.0006" to 0.001" (0.0152 mm to 0.0254 mm) higher than the other (Fig. 5:23). In this case, the valve lifters, or tappets, must have convex (spherically ground) bottoms and they are usually slightly offset in relation to the cam face. This design provides better cam-to-tappet contact, improved lubrication, more even wear, and less friction as the taper induces some tappet spin. Since camshafts with a taper use lifters with flat bottoms, care must be taken to identify the style used when installing new parts.

Unless an electric fuel pump is used, the camshaft is equipped with an eccentric to

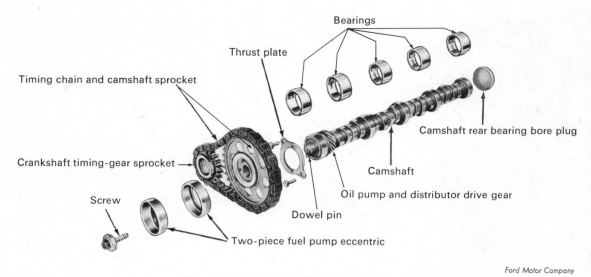

Timing chain and camshaft sprocket

Thrust plate

Bearings

Crankshaft timing-gear sprocket

Camshaft rear bearing bore plug

Screw

Camshaft

Oil pump and distributor drive gear

Dowel pin

Two-piece fuel pump eccentric

Ford Motor Company

Fig. 5:22   Camshaft and Related Parts

operate the rocker arm of the fuel pump. The eccentric as well as the drive gear for the distributor and the oil pump are usually part of the camshaft and may be located anywhere between the cams. On some units they are attached to the timing gear (Fig. 5:22). A special thrust plate (Fig. 5:22) fastened to the cylinder block holds the shaft in position and maintains the end-play at approximately 0.001″ to 0.005″ (0.0254 mm to 0.1270 mm). Too much play affects the valve- and ignition-timing.

The camshaft is driven by the crankshaft timing gear. Only the two most common types are described here.

1. The *Chain Drive* (Fig. 5:24a) employs a crankshaft sprocket and a camshaft sprocket, joined by a timing chain. To reduce noise and chain slack, the timing chain is often kept under tension by mechanical or hydraulic chain tensioners. With the chain drive, both shafts turn in the same direction.

2. The *Direct Drive* uses two helical timing gears (Fig. 5:24b). The crankshaft timing gear is usually made of sintered steel and most camshaft timing gears are made of a different material, such as pressed fibre, nylon, or aluminum in order to reduce gear noise. If the backlash between the two gears increases

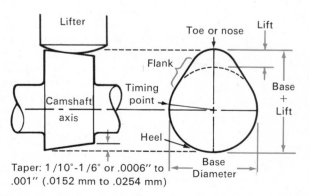

Lifter

Toe or nose

Lift

Flank

Timing point

Base + Lift

Camshaft axis

Heel

Base Diameter

Taper: 1/10°-1/6° or .0006″ to .001″ (.0152 mm to .0254 mm)

Fig. 5:23   Camshaft Taper to Provide Tappet Spin, More Even Wear, and Improved Lubrication (Note: Curved lifter bottom and cam taper are greatly exaggerated in this illustration.)

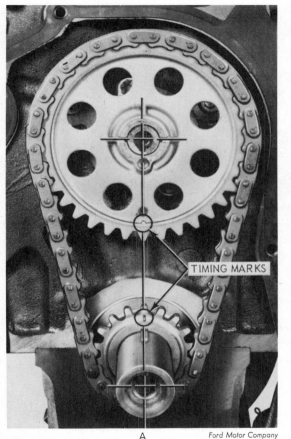

TIMING MARKS

A   *Ford Motor Company*

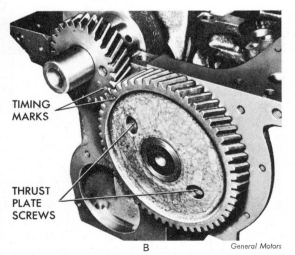

TIMING MARKS

THRUST PLATE SCREWS

B   *General Motors*

Fig. 5:24 (a) Timing Gears or Sprockets (Chain Drive); (b) Helical Timing Gears (Direct Drive).

beyond specified limits owing to wear, either one or both timing gears must be replaced. With the direct drive, the two shafts turn in opposite directions.

The crankshaft must make two revolutions per cycle while the camshaft makes only one. This 2:1 ratio requires that the camshaft sprocket, or gear, have twice as many teeth as the crankshaft gear. The reasons for this are explained in Chapter 6.

Because the relative positions of the two timing gears are critical to the proper timing of the opening and closing of the valves, the gears (and sometimes also the chain) are provided with some type of valve timing mark as shown in Fig. 5:24. Since both gears are keyed to their respective shafts, it is very easy to install them in their correct positions. Improperly timed gears lead to a loss in performance, rough engine idle, or even to collisions between the valves and the pistons.

To prevent oil leakage through the main front seal in the timing-gear cover, the crankshaft timing gear is usually shielded by an oil slinger (Fig. 5:7a). The timing-gear cover is fitted with a gasket, which is placed either directly against the cylinder block or against an intermediate steel plate, known as the front end-plate (Fig. 5:20).

The Crankshaft Pulley

The crankshaft pulley (Fig. 5:7a) is keyed to the front end of the crankshaft, which protrudes through the front-main-seal opening of the timing-gear cover. The crankshaft pulley may be of a single- or multiple-belt design, depending on whether or not the engine is equipped with belt-driven accessories (power steering, air conditioning, certain emission-control devices, etc.) in addition to the standard water pump and generator. The hub of the pulley extends inward into the timing-gear cover and forms the mating seat for the front main seal (Fig. 5:2).

The Vibration Damper or Harmonic Balancer

The vibration damper (Figs. 5:2, 5:7a, and 5:25) is usually part of the crankshaft pulley. Its purpose is to reduce crankshaft vibrations. Basically the damper consists of two steel discs or

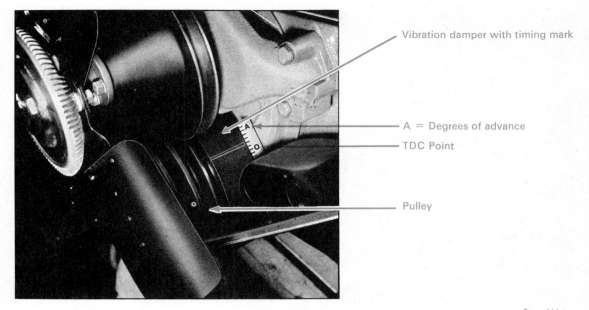

Vibration damper with timing mark

A = Degrees of advance

TDC Point

Pulley

General Motors

Fig. 5:25 Ignition Timing Marks on Vibration Damper and Timing Gear Cover (Note: When zero line is at pointer, No. 1 piston is at TDC, also called UDC or Upper Dead Centre. Compare with Fig. 5:26.)

rings with a friction lining sandwiched between them. Since only one of the discs is rigidly keyed to the crankshaft, the friction lining allows the second disc to shift by a few degrees in either direction. This action tends to cushion the sharp torsional jerks typical of an intermittently firing piston engine. If unchecked, these vibrations may actually snap the crankshaft, especially on the longer six-cylinder designs. The shorter shafts of the more compact V-8 and four-cylinder engines often do not have a vibration damper.

Either the pulley or the damper is, in most cases, provided with timing marks. If the crankshaft of the engine we have discussed is turned over until the piston in No. 1 cylinder reaches its uppermost position (Fig. 5:26), this timing mark would align itself with a stationary timing mark on the timing-gear cover (Fig. 5:25). As you will see later, the timing marks, also known as the TDC marks (Top Dead Centre) or the UDC marks (Upper Dead Centre), are very important for adjusting ignition-timing and, in some cases, valve clearance. Without timing marks the piston's exact position would be

difficult to determine accurately after the cylinder head is installed.

Together, the components so far discussed form the cylinder block assembly.

The Cylinder Head

The cylinder head (Fig. 5:27) is a machined casting that is fitted with the head gasket to the smoothly finished top of the cylinder block (Fig. 5:26). The design of the head varies greatly with the type of engine. Conventional designs contain the combustion chambers, the intake and exhaust ports, the push rod openings, the valves, the thermostat housing, and the cooling jackets. The cooling jackets in the cylinder head are connected to those in the cylinder block by means of several carefully aligned passages (Fig. 5:26). The cylinder head also supports the valve mechanism and the spark plugs, which reach into the combustion chambers. The shape of the combustion chambers, the valve and port arrangement, and the position of the spark plugs are very significant factors in controlling combustion, and hence

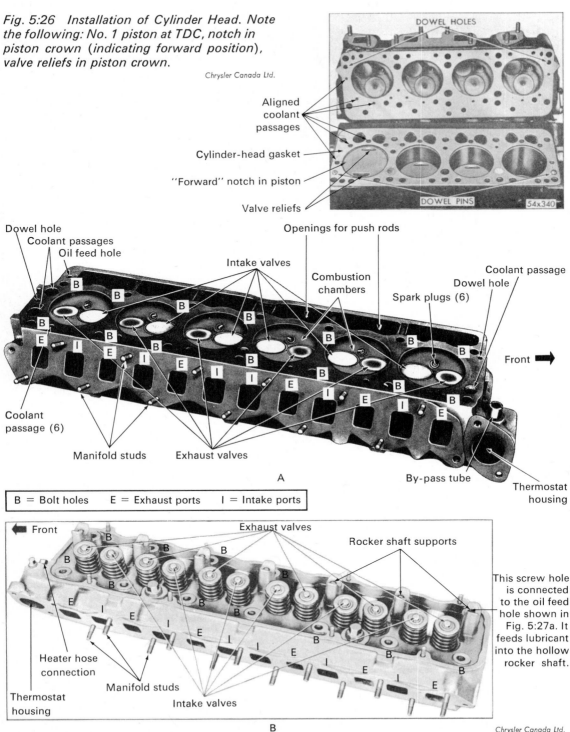

Fig. 5:26 Installation of Cylinder Head. Note the following: No. 1 piston at TDC, notch in piston crown (indicating forward position), valve reliefs in piston crown.

Chrysler Canada Ltd.

DOWEL HOLES

Aligned coolant passages

Cylinder-head gasket

"Forward" notch in piston

Valve reliefs

DOWEL PINS

54x340

Dowel hole
Coolant passages
Oil feed hole

Openings for push rods

Intake valves

Combustion chambers

Coolant passage

Dowel hole

Spark plugs (6)

Front

Coolant passage (6)

Manifold studs   Exhaust valves

By-pass tube

Thermostat housing

A

B = Bolt holes   E = Exhaust ports   I = Intake ports

Front

Exhaust valves

Rocker shaft supports

This screw hole is connected to the oil feed hole shown in Fig. 5:27a. It feeds lubricant into the hollow rocker shaft.

Heater hose connection

Manifold studs

Thermostat housing

Intake valves

B

Chrysler Canada Ltd.

Fig. 5:27 Cylinder Head of a Six-cylinder Engine: (a) Bottom view; (b) Top view.

engine efficiency and exhaust emission.

Like the cylinder block, the cylinder head may be of either cast iron or cast aluminum. The valve guides are, in most cases, separate parts pressed into openings arranged so that they are concentric with the valve seats (Fig. 5:1). The valve guides act as slipper bearings to allow the valves to move freely up and down. They also prevent the passage of gases between the valve ports and the chamber formed by the valve cover. The replacement of worn valve guides requires special tools.

Additional valve-guide seals control the amount of oil that is allowed to enter the valve guides for adequate lubrication. Worn seals are a common cause of high oil-consumption.

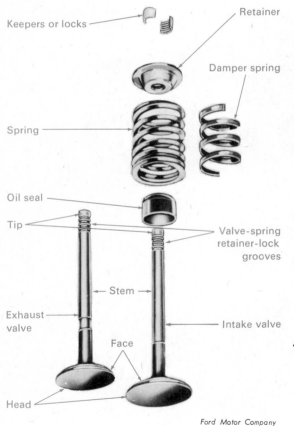

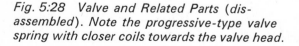
Ford Motor Company

Fig. 5:28 Valve and Related Parts (disassembled). Note the progressive-type valve spring with closer coils towards the valve head.

The Valve Seats

The valve seats (Fig. 5:30) are ring-shaped inserts that reinforce the highly stressed port openings in the combustion chamber. Where no inserts are used, the seats are part of the head (Figs. 5:31 and 5:32). To obtain the necessary toughness, the seat area may be induction-hardened (electrically). Valve guides and insert seats are both made of heat- and wear-resistant alloys. Special skills and facilities are required to install them correctly.

The Valves

The valves (Fig. 5:28) control the gas flow of the engine. There are normally two valves per cylinder. The intake valve is the larger one because it admits the fresh, cool mixture that is under atmospheric pressure, and the more that can get in, the better. The smaller exhaust valve allows the burnt gases to be expelled. These gases are still under such high pressure that the size of the exhaust valve is less important; in fact, a large valve would be unable to cope with the tremendous temperatures —1,100°F to 1,200°F (593°C to 649°C). Under full operating-loads the exhaust valves actually turn red-hot. The heat is kept within safe limits by one or more of the following methods:

1. Heat transfer between the valve stem and valve guide and between the valve face and valve seat into the cooling jackets (Fig. 5:35).
2. Special high-temperature-resistant alloys such as silicon-chromium steel may be used.
3. The valve face or seat may be reinforced with a layer of stellite, a non-ferrous alloy of cobalt, chromium, and tungsten. The hardness of stellite is not materially affected up to 1,500°F (816°C) and actually improves at red heat (Fig. 5:32).
4. Sodium-filled valves may be used. The sodium melts at 208°F (98°C) and, when liquid, helps to transfer heat from the valve head to the cooler area of the stem and valve guide. As a result sodium-filled valves run at temperatures approximately 200F° (93°C) cooler than ordinary valves.

While valves are usually one-piece steel forgings, they can be divided into the following parts for reference purposes (Figs. 5:28 and 5:29):

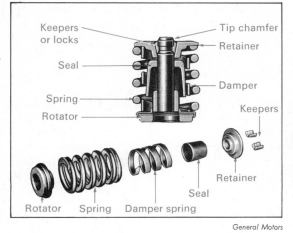

Keepers
or locks

Seal

Spring

Rotator

Tip chamfer

Retainer

Damper

Keepers

Retainer

Seal

Rotator   Spring   Damper spring

General Motors

Fig. 5:29   Valve Spring Assembly (Note: Rotators and dampers are used only on some engines.)

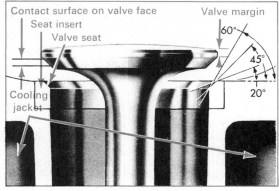

Contact surface on valve face   Valve margin
Seat insert
Valve seat
60°
45°
20°
Cooling jacket

Chrysler Canada Ltd.

Fig. 5:30   Valve Seat Reconditioning Angles

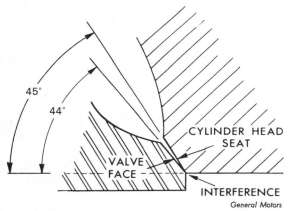

45°
44°
CYLINDER HEAD SEAT
VALVE FACE
INTERFERENCE

General Motors

Fig. 5:31   Interference Fit

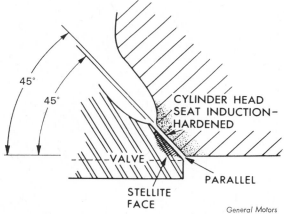

45°
45°
CYLINDER HEAD SEAT INDUCTION-HARDENED
VALVE
STELLITE FACE
PARALLEL

General Motors

Fig. 5:32   Parallel Fit (used on hardened insert seats)

1. *Valve stem tip*—specially hardened and ground to provide smooth contact for the rocker arm.
2. *Tip chamfer*—the tip edge is bevel-ground to avoid "mushrooming", to permit the wiping-action of the rocker arm, and to allow easy insertion of a feeler gauge (Fig. 5:33).
3. *Valve-spring retainer-lock grooves*—interlock with the retainer locks.
4. *Valve stem*—fitted to the valve guide with approximately 0.0005" to 0.003" (0.0127 mm to 0.0762 mm) clearance, and often chrome-plated to reduce wear.

5. *Valve head*—covers the port opening in the combustion chamber.
6. *Valve face*—seals against the valve seat; precision-ground to specified angle (also see Fig. 5:30 for detail).
7. *Valve margin*—leaves sufficient margin for regrinding (Fig. 5:30); the valve overheats if it is ground too thin.

Proper valve seating and heat transfer is crucial if a durable, gas-tight seal is to be made. Best results are obtained with a valve-to-seat contact in the middle of the valve face (Fig.

5:30).[9] The valve seat is usually ground at three different angles, for example 20°-45°-60° (Fig. 5:30). This ensures proper valve contact and discourages the build-up of carbon deposits and gas turbulence. If the valve seat is left too wide, the contact pressure is too low to prevent leakage; if the seat is too narrow, both the seat and the face will overheat and burn out. The actual mating of the valve face and the seat requires great precision. Two methods are commonly used:

1. Both face and seat are ground to the same specified angle, for example, 45°. A grinding or lapping compound is then used between the face and the seat to ensure that they are perfectly mated (Fig. 5:32).

2. The valve is ground at an angle that deviates from the seat by 1° or slightly less. For example, if a seat is ground to a 45° angle, then the valve would be ground to an angle of approximately 44° (Fig. 5:31). If some blueing ink were painted on the valve face, it would leave a very narrow circle imprinted on the valve seat. When the engine is first started up after a valve grind, the narrow contact area causes such high seating pressures that proper seat width is obtained automatically by the pounding action of the valve. The difference between the face angle and the seat angle is known as the interference angle. *Warning:* The interference method does not work with hard stellite valves and induction-hardened seats (Fig. 5:32).

The most common valve failures are due to high mileage, erosion, corrosion, deposits, sticking, burned valve seats and faces, improper fuels, improper carburetor and ignition settings, excessive temperatures, very heavy engine loads and high rpm, lack of lubrication, leakage of coolant, abnormal valve spin, metal fatigue, bent valves, worn valve guides, worn, stretched, or eroded valve stems (called "necking"), worn seats, incorrect spring tension, and,

particularly, improper installation and adjustments.

The Valve Spring

The valve spring (Fig. 5:29) closes the valve after its maximum lift has been reached and keeps it firmly shut until the valve is opened again. Valve springs are highly stressed parts and are made of special heat-set chromium-vanadium or chromium-silicon steels. They may be coated, as corrosion or even a mere surface scratch will eventually cause them to break. When this happens, the valves often collide with the piston, which leads to serious damage. Weakened valve springs usually result in a loss in performance, especially at high rpm. Some engines use two valve springs of different diameters around each valve stem. The smaller inner spring is called a damper spring.

The valve spring is held in position by the valve-spring retainer washer and locks or keepers (Fig. 5:29). The latter are usually of the split, conical type, which increase their holding pressure against the lock grooves of the valve stem as tension increases. The retainer washers are of various designs; some designs are styled to induce a slow valve spin. These valve rotators turn approximately 2° during each opening and closing cycle. This ensures a more even wear, and it helps to wipe off deposits between the valve face and the valve seat. Owing to the better sealing and longer valve life provided, valve rotators also cut down on exhaust emission. Some valve rotators are placed below the valve spring (Fig. 5:29).

Many valve springs are of the progressive type, i.e., one end of the valve spring is more tightly coiled than the other (Fig. 5:28). During the initial stages of valve lift, the more loosely wound coils compress more readily than the tightly wound ones. The latter compress in turn as the valve approaches the fully opened position. This prevents the valves from floating or from continuing their lift towards the approaching piston at high rpm. The tightly coiled end of the spring must rest against the cylinder head, unless the spring is of the conical type. Power-consuming inertia loads are thus reduced, since the heavier part of the spring is allowed to rest, leaving the more widely spaced and lighter coil windings to move with the reciprocating retainer washer at the top.

---

[9]Typical seat widths are 3/64" to 1/16" (1.19 mm to 1.59 mm) for inlet seats and 1/16" to 3/32" (1.59 mm to 2.38 mm) for exhaust seats. The exhaust seat is wider to improve heat transfer. The intake seat, which is cooled by a fresh mixture anyway, is narrower because the spring pressure is distributed over a larger seat area and therefore leakage is more of a problem.

Warning: Never tamper with valve-spring tension. Spacer washers between the spring and the cylinder head should be used only to compensate for the removal of material on the valve seats and valve faces. The penalty for ignoring this warning will be snapped valves, bent push rods, or something even more serious.

The Cylinder-head Gasket

The cylinder-head gasket (Figs. 5:26 and 5:42b) seals the cylinder head and the cylinder block against leakages of gases, coolant, and motor oil. When tightening the cylinder head, it is mandatory to use a torque wrench and to follow strictly the procedures specified (Fig. 2:14). And never loosen a cylinder head on a hot engine! Disregarding these two rules will cause distorted and cracked cylinder heads and cylinder blocks, and coolant leakage. The damage is often beyond repair. (For causes of gasket failure see page 36.)

The Valve Lifters, Tappets, or Cam Followers

The valve lifters follow the contour of the cams, and thereby cause the valves to be lifted off their seats. They are held in position by the lifter or tappet guides in the cylinder block directly above the camshaft (Figs. 5:1, 5:2, 5:3, and 5:34). The valve lifters can be of the hydraulic type or of the mechanical type. Those of the latter type, although often hollow inside, are also known as the solid lifters (Fig. 5:35). While mechanical-lifter-equipped engines require occasional adjustments at the rocker arm to maintain the specified valve clearance (Fig. 5:33), hydraulic valve lifters (Fig. 5:36), once properly set, are self-adjusting. They normally operate with zero valve clearance.

As can be seen from Fig. 5:37b, the one-way check valve traps the non-compressible oil between the lifter body and the plunger in such a manner that the entire lifter assembly acts as a solid member. If, on the other hand, wear on the lifters, push rods, or rocker arms, or metal contraction (due to temperature changes) in any other member of the valve train causes the play between the cam heel and the lifter to increase, the plunger is simply raised in the lifter body (Fig. 5:37a). This is partly accomplished by the plunger spring in the high-

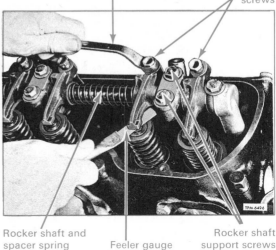

If available, use hinge handle with single hexagon socket instead of box wrench.

Adjusting screws

Rocker shaft and spacer spring   Feeler gauge   Rocker shaft support screws

General Motors

Fig. 5:33   Adjusting Valve Clearance

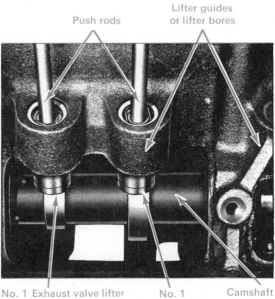

Push rods   Lifter guides or lifter bores

No. 1 Exhaust valve lifter (down position)   No. 1 Intake valve lifter (down position)   Camshaft

General Motors

Fig. 5:34   Relationship of Lifters and Cams When Cylinder No. 1 Is in Firing Position (Cam heels are facing lifter bottoms.)

pressure chamber, and partly by the admission of more oil through the check valve. The oil is supplied from the oil gallery and the feeder passages in the lifter guide bores. When the cam lobe (the toe of the cam) once again raises the lifter, the sudden increase in pressure causes the check valve, which is assisted by a small spring, to snap back onto its seat (Fig. 5:37b). At this point, both the lifter body and the plunger rise as if they were one solid part. If, however, the expansion of any parts (or wear on the valve faces and valve seats) demands that the lifter contract, the plunger will very slowly, and after several camshaft revolutions, displace some of the oil trapped in the high-pressure chamber of the lifter body. The displaced oil does not escape through the one-way check valve but rather through "leak-by" between the closely fitted plunger and the lifter body (Fig. 5:37b). Excessive plunger clearance, however, will lead to partial or complete collapse of the hydraulic lifter. This condition, as well as sticky valve lifters, results in rough engine-idle or excessive noise. The main reasons for sticky valve lifters are contaminated oil, oil sludge (see page 133), and certain sticky deposits (commonly called "varnish"). Hydraulic valve lifters are matched assemblies, i.e., whether used or new, their component parts are not interchangeable. When replacing mechanical lifters with hydraulic lifters (or vice versa), the camshaft must be replaced too, since each type of lifter requires a different cam design.

Push Rods

The push rods (Figs. 5:35 and 5:36) transmit the upward push of the lifters to the rocker arms. The push rods are frequently of a tubular design, which reduces energy-consuming inertia loads and valve-floating at higher rpm. Tubular push rods may also serve as oil passages from the hydraulic lifters to the rocker arms (Fig. 11:8). A bent push rod, which causes improper valve-timing and insufficient lift, is usually easily spotted because of excessive spin.

The Rocker Arms

The rocker arms (Figs. 5:35 and 5:36) convert the upward push of the push rods into the downward movement of the valves. If the

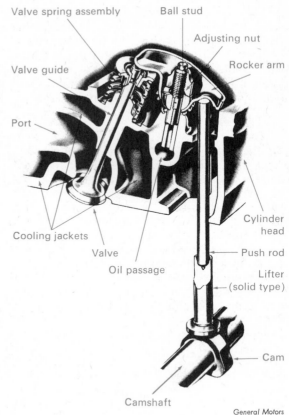

General Motors

Fig. 5:35   Socket or Ball-pivot-type Rocker Arm

position of their fulcrum (pivot) is offset towards the push rod, they also increase the amount and rate of valve lift. Rocker arms may be of stamped steel, forged or cast steel, or pressure die-cast aluminum for light weight. The two most common rocker arm designs are the shaft-mounted type and the socket, or ball-pivot, type. The shaft-mounted type (Figs. 5:33 and 5:36) is suspended from a hollow rocker shaft provided with small lubrication holes for each of the rocker arm bushings. The end of the rocker arm that contacts the valve tip has a slightly curved contour. This reduces friction, allows for the wiping-action of the rocker arm, and facilitates the insertion of a feeler gauge during valve adjustments. The other end is fitted with a special adjusting screw whose spherical tip rests in the cup-shaped upper end of the push rod (Fig. 5:1).

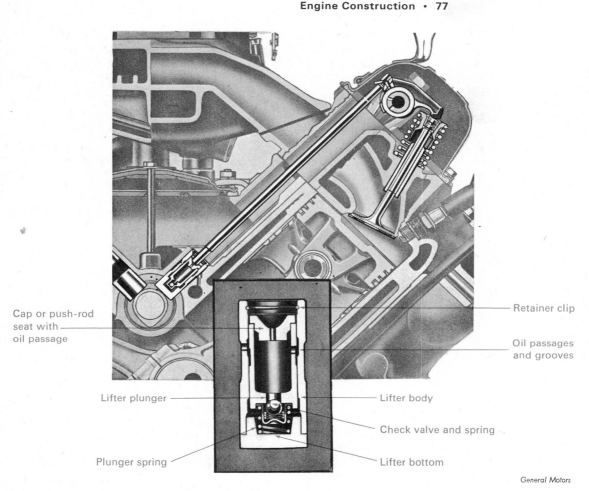

Cap or push-rod seat with oil passage

Retainer clip

Oil passages and grooves

Lifter plunger

Lifter body

Check valve and spring

Plunger spring

Lifter bottom

General Motors

Fig. 5:36   Typical Valve Train with Hydraulic Valve Lifters

The adjusting screw is used to set the specified valve clearance or lash, i.e., the free play that must be maintained between the rocker arm and the valve tip when the cam heel faces the bottom of the lifter (valve fully closed) (Figs. 5:33 and 5:34).[10] Valve clearance makes allowance for heat expansion on engines equipped with mechanical lifters. The adjusting screw is either self-locking or secured by a locking nut.

[10]This is one case where the TDC marks outlined on page 70 are needed. They make it possible to determine the correct piston and valve position for the No. 1 cylinder. However, the adjustment is usually repeated while the engine is at slow idle and under normal operating temperature.

Some engines equipped with hydraulic lifters have non-adjustable rocker arms. (After a valve grind a shorter push rod may have to be installed.) Coil springs or thrust bushings placed between the rocker arms prevent them from shifting sideways (Fig. 5:33).

The socket-type rocker arm is supported individually by stud pedestals, as shown in Fig. 5:35. A self-locking nut maintains the desired height of the entire rocker arm and thus the specified valve clearance.

General Valve Information

1. Used valve lifters, push rods, rocker arms, and valves should be installed in their original positions.

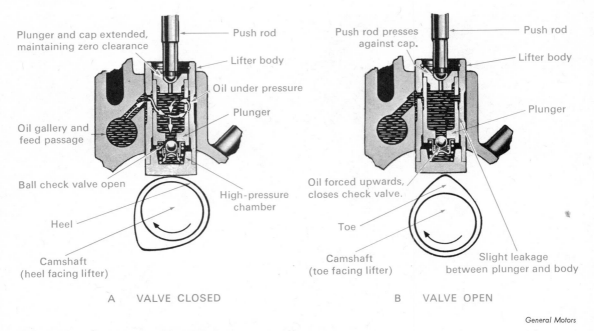

Fig. 5:37   Operation of Hydraulic Valve Lifter Mechanism

2. Never replace any parts unless you have discovered the root cause of the problem.
3. Too little valve clearance causes burnt valves, wrong valve-timing, excessive valve lift, rough engine-idle, and loss of performance. Too much valve clearance causes increased wear and noise, insufficient valve lift, wrong valve-timing, and a loss in performance.

The Valve Cover or Rocker Cover

The valve cover (Fig. 5:42b) is fitted with a gasket to the raised upper edge of the cylinder head and forms an oil-tight enclosure for the valve mechanism. It may be equipped with an oil filler cap and a special venting device (Fig. 5:3). (For information on PCV systems see Fig. 14:2.) The cover is either a sheet metal stamping or an aluminum casting to assist cooling.

The Lifter Cover or Tappet Cover

This covers the entire lifter chamber, or tappet chamber, and is fitted with a gasket against the cylinder block (Fig. 5:42a). On some V-8 engines the intake manifold is shaped in such a way that no separate cover is needed (Fig. 5:3).

The Intake Manifold

The intake manifold (Figs. 5:3, 5:40, and 5:42b) carries the air-fuel mixture from the carburetor mounted on it to the engine intake ports in the cylinder head. On V-8 engines the intake manifold is placed between the heads. The branching of intake ports permits one manifold port to serve two cylinders (Fig. 5:42b). While branched ports reduce cost, they are less effective in terms of "breathing" efficiency. A gasket between the intake manifold and the cylinder head prevents "false air" from being drawn into the manifold. On some V-8 designs the vacuum in the manifold may also cause oil from the lifter chambers to enter the ports. The result is rough engine-idle, poor performance, fouled spark plugs, carbon deposits in the engine, and increased exhaust emission. In many cases separate passages connected to the cooling system and the exhaust (exhaust "cross-over" passages) ensure that the manifold temperature is kept at a level that provides

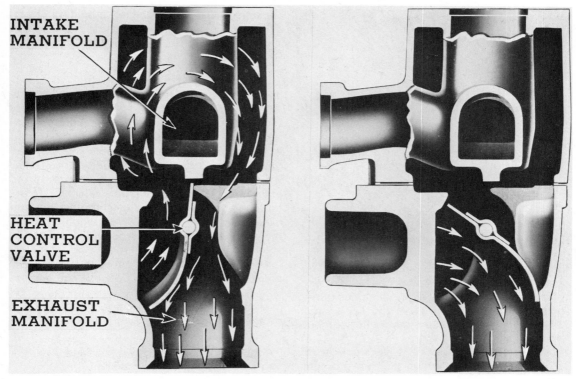

INTAKE
MANIFOLD

HEAT
CONTROL
VALVE

EXHAUST
MANIFOLD

General Motors

Fig. 5:38 Sectional View of Manifold Heat-control Valve: (a) Engine cold; (b) Engine at normal operating temperature.

good engine performance and low emission.

The shape and dimensions of the intake manifold ports, or "runners", are carefully designed to improve "breathing" and to give an equal mixture distribution to all cylinders.

The Exhaust Manifold

The exhaust manifold (Figs. 5:3 and 5:42b) carries the burnt gases from the engine's exhaust ports to the front exhaust pipe. The exhaust manifold may be bolted to the cylinder head on the same side as the intake manifold, or it may be attached separately on the opposite side as it is on V-8 engines. Manifolds are relatively fragile castings that must be handled with care if distortion, breakage, and leakage are to be avoided. Exhaust manifold gaskets are designed to withstand very high flame-temperatures. (See Fig. 5:42b and also Chapter 3.)

The Manifold Heat-control Valve or Heat Riser Valve

The heat-control valve (Figs. 5:38 and 5:39) is located in the exhaust manifold and assists the evaporation of gasoline particles during engine warm-up. When the engine is cold, the valve redirects hot exhaust gases into a heater jacket situated directly below the carburetor. This area is often called the "hot spot". Any condensed particles of fuel clinging to the cold walls of the intake manifold are changed by this heat into the more combustible gaseous state. As a result, cold-start performance, fuel mileage, and emission control are improved. When the engine reaches normal operating temperature, the thermostatic bimetal spring loses its tension. This permits the counterweight, attached to one end of the valve shaft, to open the heat-control valve, and thus

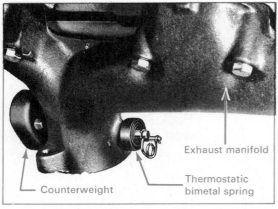

Fig. 5:39 *Manifold Heat-control Valve*

the exhaust gases can no longer reach the "hot spot" (Fig. 5:38b). The shaft of the heat-control valve is offset so that high gas velocities during forced acceleration will push the valve open. This ensures unrestricted exhaust flow regardless of engine temperature.

A manifold heat-control valve stuck in the cold position will result in serious problems (increased back pressure, overheating, burnt exhaust valves, poor performance, etc.).

The Exhaust System

The front exhaust pipe, the muffler, the resonator[11] (if used), and the tailpipe make up the exhaust system (Fig. 5:41). These units carry the burnt gases from the front exhaust pipe to the rear of the vehicle. The exhaust system also reduces engine noise and cools the expelled gases. Most important, it prevents the fumes, which contain deadly carbon monoxide, from entering the interior of the vehicle. Unfortunately, too many motorists forget that the exhaust system offers full protection only if there is no leakage and when the automobile is in motion.

The front exhaust pipe is bolted to the exhaust manifold flange. Because of engine vibration the connection is often made by means of a flexible gasket joint. The other parts of the exhaust system are suspended from

[11]A resonator is essentially a secondary muffler connected to the exhaust system.

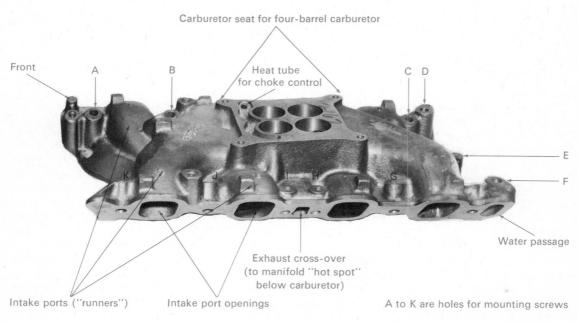

Fig. 5:40 *Intake Manifold for a V-8 Engine with a Four-barrel Carburetor*

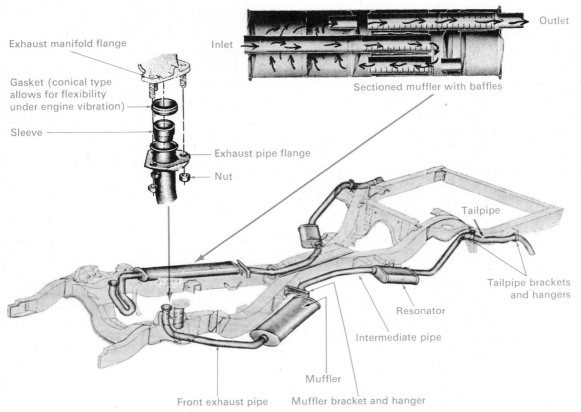

Exhaust manifold flange

Inlet

Outlet

Gasket (conical type allows for flexibility under engine vibration)

Sleeve

Exhaust pipe flange

Nut

Sectioned muffler with baffles

Tailpipe

Tailpipe brackets and hangers

Resonator

Intermediate pipe

Muffler

Front exhaust pipe

Muffler bracket and hanger

General Motors

Fig. 5:41 Typical Dual-exhaust System for a V-8 Engine (Improves breathing efficiency by reducing back-pressure.)

flexible hanger-type brackets in order to insulate the interior against undesirable noise, vibration, and heat. The muffler reroutes the burnt gases through separate chambers and perforated baffle tubes to "muffle" the exhaust noise.

Some vehicles use dual exhaust systems (Fig. 5:41); others have a single system. Single systems can be employed on V-8 engines with two exhaust manifolds if the divided gas flow is joined by means of a cross-over pipe or a suitable "Y" connection (Figs. 16:1 and 16:18).

Further information on exhaust systems is given in Chapter 14: The Emission-Control System.

The Motor Mounts

These are rubber-insulated brackets that support the engine and reduce the transmission of engine vibrations and road shock. The most common method of installation is to attach one of these mounts to each side of the cylinder block. In addition, there is either one mount on each side of the bell housing, or a single one is placed under the transmission. The latter type is called a transmission mount.

The basic cause of motor-mount failure, which may lead to loss of vehicle control, is, in most cases, an oil leak. Since oil and rubber are incompatible, the leak must be stopped before a new mount is installed.

RECOMMENDED ASSIGNMENTS

1. Explain the difference between an internal combustion engine and an external combustion engine.
2. What is the purpose of numbering main bearing caps and connecting-rod bearing caps?
3. What are the functions of the crankshaft?
4. What are the purposes of the flywheel?
5. Prepare a sketch of a piston, and label all parts.
6. Explain five methods designed to maintain the proper piston clearance on aluminum alloy pistons, regardless of whether they are hot or cold.
7. Name three methods employed to make aluminum pistons more wear-resistant.
8. List the most common causes of piston failure.
9. Explain the purposes of compression rings.
10. Explain the purpose of the oil-control ring.
11. Name four functions of the ring gap.
12. What type of piston rings would probably be installed in a slightly worn cylinder?
13. What are the advantages of stepped piston rings, such as the scraper and the counter-bored type?
14. Name three important checks to be carried out when installing new piston rings.
15. What problems are caused by "gasoline wash"?
16. Comment on the two basic types of piston pin fits.
17. Illustrate one system of marking timing gears for correct installation.
18. State the four functions of the crankshaft pulley-and-damper assembly.
19. Why do inlet valves have large heads and narrow seats while exhaust valves have small heads and wide seats?
20. Illustrate a typical valve face-to-seat contact showing all three seat angles and the interference angle.
21. Why is the valve stem tip chamfered?
22. List fifteen common causes of valve failure.
23. Explain the purpose of the progressive type of valve spring with brief reference to its proper installation.
24. Under what circumstances would the check valve of a hydraulic valve lifter be open (cam position, contraction or expansion of parts, etc.)?
25. How could you determine whether or not an engine has hydraulic lifters without actually seeing the lifters themselves?
26. What conditions are indicated by excessive push-rod spin?
27. Give three reasons why the end of the rocker arm that contacts the valve tip should be curved.
28. Comment on the effects of improper valve adjustment (too much valve clearance and too little).
29. What is the purpose of the intake manifold?
30. Explain the function of the manifold heat-control valve with reference to hot and cold positions.
31. Give four reasons why the proper installation of parts in the exhaust system is very important in terms of comfort and safety.
32. Prepare a cross-sectional diagram of a single-cylinder engine. Label all parts.
33. Solve the "Mechanic's Puzzle" in Figs. 5:42a and b by identifying all the parts.

TROUBLE-SHOOTING

All the information you need is contained in this chapter. While some problems may be caused by any of several possible conditions, there is usually only one that is considered typical.

1. A crankshaft occasionally produces a thumping noise. Prying the crankshaft back and forth along its axis when the engine is not running makes a similar noise.
2. A piston and a cylinder are badly damaged. There are deep score marks in the cylinder wall facing one of the piston pin bosses.
3. A piston is replaced. The new piston also fails. Very close inspection shows that both the piston and the connecting rod bearing are worn very unevenly.
4. A compression test indicates valve failure. The valves are removed and show very little wear; however, the valve stems are partly discoloured and are covered with deposits.
5. After a cylinder head has been re-installed, the engine has very little power. There is more exhaust emission than usual. When the oil dip-stick is checked, the oil level appears to have risen.

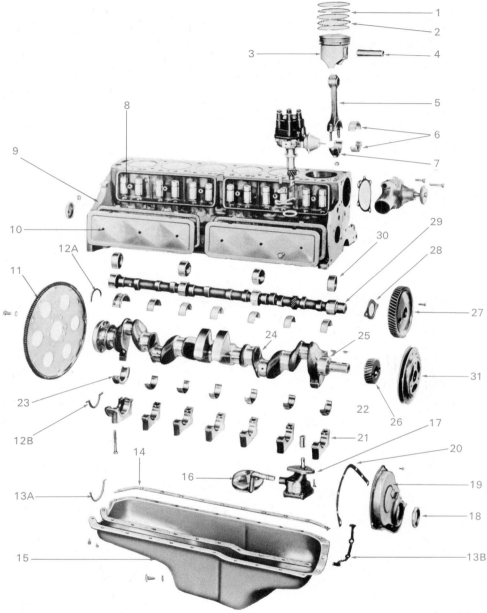

General Motors

Fig. 5:42 (a) Cylinder Block and Associated Parts of a Six-cylinder Engine (For assembled unit see page 67.)

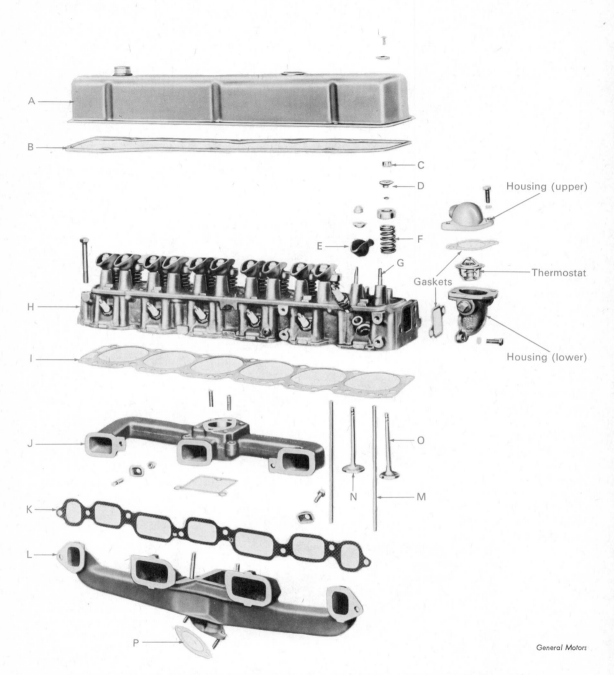

A

B

C

D

Housing (upper)

E

F

Thermostat

G

Gaskets

H

Housing (lower)

I

J

O

N M

K

L

P

General Motors

Fig. 5:42 (b) Cylinder Head and Associated Parts of a Six-cylinder Engine (For assembled unit see page 71.)

6

The
Four-Stroke Cycle

The previous chapter dealt with engine parts and how they relate to each other. In this chapter the emphasis is mainly on operating principles.

Most of today's automotive engines are four-stroke-cycle internal combustion engines; i.e., they burn fuel internally, and their operation is based on four movements that are always repeated in the same order.

The type of cannon you see in old forts and historical movies is essentially a four-stroke-cycle internal combustion engine.[12] Its cycle of operation must follow four repetitive steps or strokes:

1. Intake of the charge (gunpowder as the source of energy).
2. Compressing the charge (to increase firing efficiency).
3. Firing the charge (triggered by a fuse, the hot, expanding gases force the cannon ball out of the barrel).
4. Exhausting or removing the fumes and ashes (preparation for the next intake of a new charge to repeat the cycle).

In the following paragraphs you will notice how closely the gasoline engine follows the cycle just described. However, to harness the power of the four-stroke cycle, engineers had to "borrow" some of the steam engine's parts, such as the piston, the connecting rod, the crankshaft, and the flywheel. The cannon barrel was replaced by the cylinder and its fuse by an electrical wire and a spark plug.

1. The Intake Stroke

During the intake stroke (Fig. 6:1) the crankshaft is turned one half-turn. This causes the piston to move downwards through one whole stroke from Top Dead Centre (TDC) to Bottom Dead Centre (BDC). The downward movement of the piston thereby produces a partial vacuum inside the cylinder; i.e., the pressure decreases in relation to the atmospheric pressure outside the engine.[13] Since the intake valve is already open, the air-fuel mixture prepared outside the cylinder is pushed in. The mixture is preheated as it passes through the ports and into the cylinders. This is one reason why the cooling system must regulate the engine operating

---

[12]The idea of a gunpowder engine was actually proposed by the Dutch scientist Christian Huyghens in 1680. The Frenchman Beau de Rochas is credited with first describing the theoretical principle of the four-stroke cycle in 1862. In 1876, the German engineer Dr. Nikolaus August Otto built an engine based on this principle, also known as the Otto cycle. His colleague, Gottlieb Daimler, placed an improved version of this engine in a modified horse carriage in 1886.

[13]The vast layer of gases in the atmosphere above us exerts a pressure of roughly 14.7 psi (pounds per square inch), at sea level. This gas layer is approximately 78 per cent nitrogen, 21 per cent oxygen, and 1 per cent other gases. Even though we live at the bottom of this "ocean of gases", we don't feel the pressure because our bodies have adjusted to it by exerting as much pressure from the inside out. If high altitudes are reached in an unpressurized plane, the reduced atmospheric pressure will, however, cause blood vessels and body cells to burst.

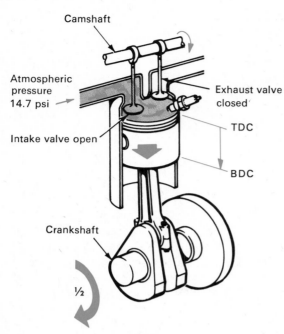

Fig. 6:1   The Intake Stroke

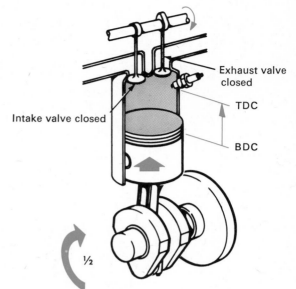

Fig. 6:2   The Compression Stroke

temperature somewhere between 180°F and 240°F (between 82°C and 116°C).

2. The Compression Stroke

During the compression stroke (Fig. 6:2) a further half-revolution of the crankshaft causes the piston to move upwards from BDC to TDC. Since both valves are closed, the mixture is now compressed into the small cavity remaining above the piston. This cavity is called the combustion or firing chamber. The compression pressure may reach anywhere between 120 psi and 180 psi. The friction between the compressed gas molecules causes a further temperature rise of several hundred degrees. This prepares the gas for firing.[14]

---

[14]When you inflate a bicycle tire, the pump cylinder heats up for the same reason. This principle is very important, since the burning of fuel proceeds much more rapidly if it is preheated before it is ignited. Also, without compression, too much heat would be lost through the cylinder walls and the cooling jackets. Good compression is therefore the single most important factor in maintaining engine efficiency, i.e., high performance and fuel mileage, as well as low emission.

3. The Power Stroke or Firing Stroke

The piston now approaches TDC, and both valves remain closed. At this point a carefully timed spark from the spark plug ignites the first "layer" of compressed gas, which in turn ignites the next "layer", and this one, the next, and so on. This results in a rapid but controlled chain reaction until all "layers" of the entire "charge" are ignited. The very high temperatures, which momentarily may approach 5,000°F (2800°C), cause the confined gases, including the relatively inert (chemically inactive) nitrogen, to expand at an extremely fast rate. The resulting high pressure pushes the piston downwards (Fig. 6:3).[15] Thus the *chemical energy* of the fuel is first converted to the *heat energy* of combustion, which in turn is converted to *mechanical energy* at

---

[15]The firing pressure is therefore not the result of a violent, uncontrolled explosion as it is in the case of the cannon. The flame-travel through the combustion chamber takes roughly $1/_{350}$ of a second, and pressure can reach 700 psi or more, i.e., roughly 3½ to 4 times the compression pressure. Normal firing loads of five tons acting on the piston are not uncommon.

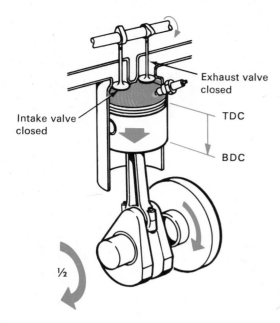

Exhaust valve
closed

Intake valve
closed

TDC

BDC

Fig. 6:3   The Power Stroke (*The flywheel
stores kinetic energy.*)

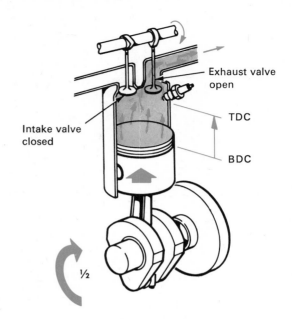

Exhaust valve
open

Intake valve
closed

TDC

BDC

Fig. 6:5   The Exhaust Stroke

the piston. The connecting rod transmits the firing pressure acting against the piston to the crankshaft. In this manner, the reciprocating motion of the piston, like the up-and-down motion of a leg resting on a bicycle pedal (Fig. 6:4), is changed to the rotary motion of the crankshaft. During the power stroke the crankshaft completes a further half-revolution, as it does with any other stroke.

4. The Exhaust Stroke

Most of the useful firing pressure is already spent before the piston reaches BDC. The exhaust valve is now opened and the burned gases escape at high velocity. Once again the piston moves upwards from BDC to TDC, pushing out the remaining gases (Fig. 6:5). This adds another half-revolution of the crankshaft. The cylinder is thus prepared to receive a new charge, and in quick succession the engine

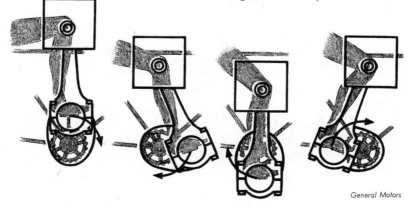

General Motors

Fig. 6:4   *The Change of Reciprocating Motion to Rotary Motion*

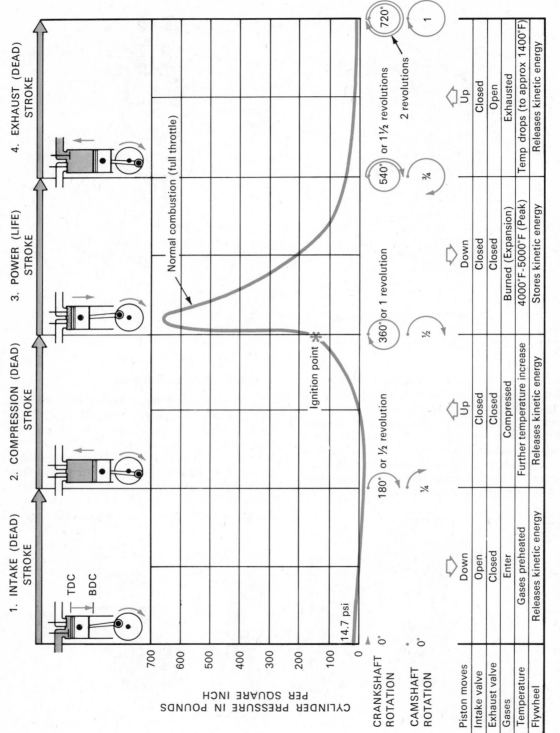

Fig. 6:6 Four-stroke Cycle Pressure or Indicator Diagram and Summary Chart

repeats the four-stroke cycle over and over, always in the same order: intake—compression—power—exhaust.

Since the crankshaft makes half a revolution during each stroke, the four strokes of one complete cycle equal two revolutions of the crankshaft. Because each valve opens only once during the four-stroke cycle, the camshaft, as shown in Figs. 6:1, 6:2, 6:3, and 6:5, makes only one revolution. Therefore, the ratio of crankshaft to camshaft speed (revolutions) is 2:1.

Obviously a single-cyclinder engine will run rather unevenly at lower rpm. The problem is that the power stroke is the only "life stroke"; it is followed by three "dead strokes", namely, the exhaust stroke, the intake stroke, and the compression stroke. This is the main reason why a flywheel is needed. While most of the mechanical energy released by the power stroke is available to do useful work, some of the energy is stored in the flywheel. During the "dead strokes" this energy, called *kinetic energy* (the energy of moving masses), is released to carry the engine from one power stroke to the next without any appreciable change in engine speed. It is like a cyclist taking a brief rest. Even though he may cease pedalling momentarily, the momentum of the wheels, the bicycle frame, and even his body will carry him on for a while.

The chart (Fig. 6:6) summarizes the most important points discussed in this chapter.

RECOMMENDED ASSIGNMENTS

1. Explain the term "four-stroke-cycle internal combustion engine".
2. What causes the air-fuel mixture to enter the cylinder during the intake stroke?
3. State the advantages to be gained by compressing the air-fuel mixture before igniting it.
4. Why would it be incorrect to speak of an "explosion" when referring to the normal ignition of the compressed gas?
5. What are the three forms of energy converted during the power stroke?
6. What is the major function of the crankshaft?
7. Name the four strokes of the four-stroke cycle in the proper order, and give the valve positions for each.
8. How many times do the crankshaft and camshaft rotate during one complete four-stroke cycle? Explain your answer.
9. What is the crankshaft-to-camshaft ratio?
10. What is the main purpose of the flywheel?
11. Identify each stroke in the four diagrams in Fig. 6:7.

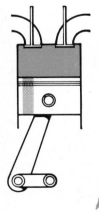 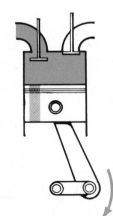 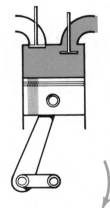 

Fig. 6:7

7

Engine Terms

Study Guide

Wherever possible you should try to relate the following material to the chapters on the four-stroke-cycle engine, and engine construction. The terms listed are not haphazard bits of information but are carefully arranged to show their meaningful connection. Several of the following terms have already been introduced in previous chapters but they are presented here with fuller explanations. The definitions will put you in a better position to understand service manuals, road tests, and motor magazines, and to discuss related topics intelligently.

TDC—Top Dead Centre, the highest point of piston travel.

UDC—Upper Dead Centre, the same as TDC.

BDC—Bottom Dead Centre, the lowest point of piston travel.

BTDC or *BUDC*—Before Top Dead Centre or Before Upper Dead Centre.

Stroke—the distance the piston travels between BDC and TDC, or vice versa, the equivalent of half a crankshaft revolution. The stroke is determined by the crank radius of the crankshaft, i.e., the length of the crank arm or "throw" measured between the centre lines of the crankpin and the crankshaft main journals. Hence the length of the stroke = 2 × the crank radius.

rpm—revolutions per minute. Unless otherwise stated, the term applies to the speed at which the crankshaft is revolving.

Bore-Stroke Ratio—the ratio of the bore to the stroke; e.g., a 3.5:4.0 bore-stroke ratio means the bore is 3.5" and the stroke is 4.0".

Short-stroke Engine—an engine where the bore roughly equals the stroke, or is even larger than the stroke, e.g., 4.25:3.75.

Cubic Inch Displacement (*CID*) or *Engine Displacement*—the volume displaced in the cylinder as the piston moves from BDC to TDC, multiplied by the number of cylinders. The formula used to calculate the engine displacement is

$$\frac{\text{Bore}^2 \times \text{Stroke} \times \pi \times \text{no. of cylinders}}{4}$$

where π is 3.1416 (a constant). The CID of a V-8 engine with a bore-stroke ratio of 4.00:3.75 would therefore be:

$$\frac{4^2 \times 3.75 \times 3.1416 \times 8 \text{ cu. in.}}{4}$$

or

$$\frac{16 \times 11.781 \times 8 \text{ cu. in.}}{4}$$

$$= 32 \times 11.781 \text{ cu. in.}$$

$$= 376.992 \text{ cu. in.}$$

or roughly 377 cubic inches.

cc—cubic centimetre(s). This measurement (also appears as ccm or cm³) can be used with the preceding formula to calculate engine displacement in the metric system. This displacement may also be expressed in litres, where one litre equals 1000 cubic centimetres or 61.025 cubic inches.

Compression Ratio—the degree to which the piston compresses the mixture in the cylinder and the combustion chamber. The compression ratio is calculated by the following formula:

$$CR = \frac{\text{volume above piston at BDC}}{\text{volume above piston at TDC}}$$

This is the same as

$$CR = \frac{\text{displacement volume and clearance volume}}{\text{clearance volume}}$$

(see Fig. 7:1).

Example: Let the total volume in one cylinder and its combustion chamber be 50 cubic inches while the piston is at BDC. Assume that these 50 cubic inches are now compressed by the piston into a space, called the clearance volume, that measures only 5 cubic inches with the piston at TDC. Therefore the compression ratio would be 50/5 or 10:1.

Compression Pressure—the pressure in the cylinder at the end of the compression stroke (piston at TDC). The pressure is measured by a compression gauge calibrated in psi (Fig. 7:2). At full throttle and medium rpm, maximum firing pressure during the power stroke is roughly four times as high as the compression pressure. Since any loss of compression drastically affects engine performance, the compression test is part of every tune-up. (Also

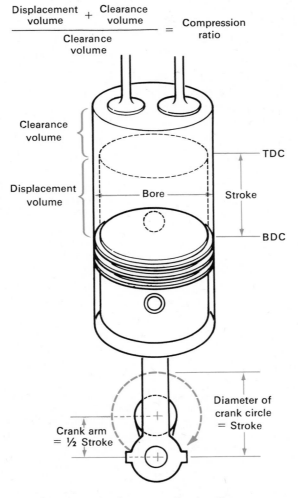

$$\frac{\text{Displacement volume} + \text{Clearance volume}}{\text{Clearance volume}} = \text{Compression ratio}$$

Clearance volume

Displacement volume

Bore

Stroke

TDC

BDC

Diameter of crank circle = Stroke

Crank arm = ½ Stroke

Fig. 7:1   Common Engine Terms

General Motors

Fig. 7:2 Checking Compression with a Compression Gauge. Note carefully: (1) The engine must be at normal operating temperature. (2) The throttle should be fully open. (3) The battery must be fully charged. Warning: Always return the throttle to the closed position after the test is completed!

refer to footnote 14 on page 86.)

Mechanical Efficiency—the ratio of power output to power input. On a piston engine it is the power available at the flywheel, compared to the power developed in the cylinders. Losses in power are due to friction, inertia, heat losses, the power expended in pumping the gases through the ports and cylinders, and the loads imposed by the accessories attached to the engine.

Thermal Efficiency—the ratio between the heat energy converted to mechanical energy inside the engine and the heat energy contained in the fuel. This assumes that the fuel is completely burned. Thermal efficiency, which varies greatly

with engine design, is generally 20 per cent to 30 per cent for gasoline engines. Fig. 7:3 shows the energy distribution in an average gasoline engine.

Volumetric Efficiency—the ratio between the air volume in the cylinder at atmospheric pressure, while the engine is standing still and the piston is at BDC, and the actual volume of air-fuel mixture that is able to enter the cylinder during the intake stroke when the engine is running. Volumetric efficiency varies with engine design and rpm.

Torque—the turning or twisting force produced when a force is applied against a pivoted lever or a similar device (such as a gear tooth). Torque is commonly measured in lb.-ft. (pound-feet) or kg·m (kilogram metres) in the metric system. In a piston engine the force is produced by the firing pressure acting against the pistons, and is transmitted to the crank arms by the connecting rods. Since torque is the product of force × leverage (pounds × feet), the greater the firing pressure and the longer the crank arm, the more torque is developed. Fig. 7:4 will help you to understand the principle of torque. If the 1' radius of the flywheel represents the lever, and the pull of the attached cable, which causes 300 lb. to move upwards, represents the force, the torque of the engine must be 300 lb.-ft. We shall assume in all of our calculations that the radius or lever is one foot long. It would make no difference if the radius was assumed to be 2' long and the weight was reduced to 150 pounds, for 2' × 150 pounds = 300 lb.-ft. Conversely, if the radius were only ½', then the weight could be increased to 600 pounds, for ½' × 600 pounds = 300 lb.-ft.

Maximum Torque—the maximum torque that a given engine can produce with the throttle wide open. On most production engines, maximum torque is reached somewhere between 2,000 and 4,000 rpm. In Fig. 7:5 the graph of a particular 360-cubic-inch engine shows that approximately 356 lb.-ft. of torque are produced at 2,500 rpm. If the load is increased at this point, i.e., beyond the maximum torque stated, the engine simply stalls. However, if the load is decreased, engine speed will immediately increase and then level off at a higher rpm. It is very important to realize that, while the rpm has increased, torque has in fact decreased. The

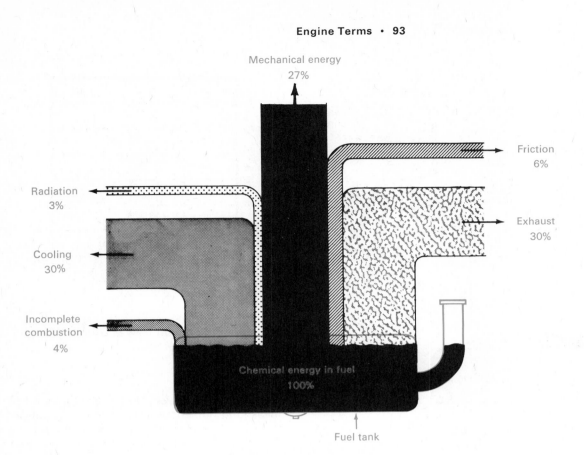

Mechanical energy
27%

Friction
6%

Radiation
3%

Exhaust
30%

Cooling
30%

Incomplete
combustion
4%

Chemical energy in fuel
100%

Fuel tank

Fig. 7:3   Energy Distribution in a Conventional Gasoline Engine

only way that both torque and rpm can rise is by modifying the engine itself. In that case we say that the power or performance is increased.

Horsepower or *hp*—a measure of performance or power, i.e., the rate of doing work or work per unit of time. The term was introduced by James Watt, the great Scottish inventor who redesigned Newcomen's steam engine. Fig. 7:6 illustrates the meaning of 1 hp in a very simple way. If the weight is 550 pounds and the horse takes one step one foot long every second, thus raising the weight an equal distance, the horse produces one horsepower. Hence 1 hp equals 550 ft.-lb. (foot-pounds) per second or 33,000 ft.-lb. per minute. In the metric system 1 hp equals 75 kilogram metres per second (which is 542.4 ft.-lb. per second).

Brake Horsepower or *bhp*—identical to hp. The term refers to the prony brake, a device once used to measure hp. The device consisted of a brake band, which, placed around a drum, made it possible to vary the load imposed on an engine. Because the prony brake tended to overheat, it was replaced by hydraulic or electrical dynamometers.

Fig. 7:4 will make it easy for you to understand and calculate bhp. Assume the engine runs at a steady 4,300 rpm.

(a) Work done
= distance weight raised × force
Work done in one revolution
= circumference of flywheel × force
= 2π × radius × force
= 2π × torque (because torque = radius × force)
Hence work done in one minute
= rpm × 2π × torque

(b) Therefore bhp = $\dfrac{\text{rpm} \times 2\pi \times \text{torque}}{33,000}$

(because 1 bhp equals 33,000 ft.-lb. per minute)

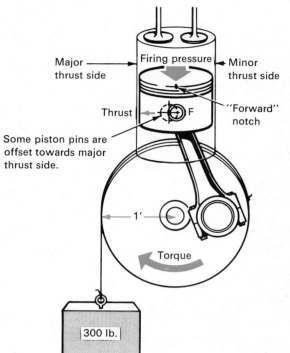

Major thrust side

Firing pressure

Minor thrust side

Thrust

F

"Forward" notch

Some piston pins are offset towards major thrust side.

1'

Torque

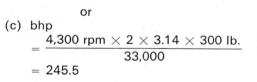

300 lb.

Fig. 7:4   Three Hundred Pound-feet of Engine Torque (Note: The notch in the piston crown and the "F" in the boss area indicate "Front".)

or

(c) bhp

$$= \frac{4,300 \text{ rpm} \times 2 \times 3.14 \times 300 \text{ lb.}}{33,000}$$

$= 245.5$

The power of this particular engine is therefore 245.5 bhp (Fig. 7:5).

For future calculations you could use formula (b) above and simply substitute the rpm and torque specifications for any given engine. This formula applies regardless of what the source of power is or where the power is taken. However, owing to frictional losses, bhp will obviously be less if the dynamometer is applied to the rear wheels rather than to the flywheel.[16]

---

[16]The loss is roughly 7-10 per cent for vehicles equipped with standard transmissions. On automatics approximately 10-15 per cent is lost, causing additional fuel consumption of anywhere between 4 and 10 miles per gallon.

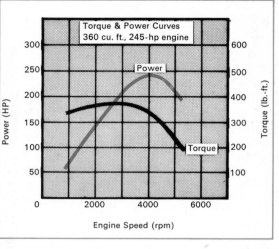

Road & Track

Fig. 7:5   Torque and Power Output of a Modern Piston Engine

SAE Net Horsepower—a controlled method of measuring horsepower according to specifications laid down by the Society of Automotive Engineers. The method specifies, among other things, that permanent accessories necessary for normal operation, such as the water pump, fan, generator, muffler, air-cleaner, radiator, and emission-control system, remain connected during the test,[17] and that the fuel and all engine adjustments be standard. The SAE net horsepower is roughly 30 per cent lower than the gross horsepower. The latter is measured with the engine running under ideally controlled conditions and without any accessories attached.

Reciprocating Engine—an engine whose working parts continuously move back and forth, that is, accelerate in one direction, stop, and then accelerate in the opposite direction. Reciprocating motion wastes more energy than rotary motion. It also imposes high inertia loads on the reciprocating parts, such as pistons, piston pins, rings, connecting rods, lifters, push rods, rocker arms, valves, and valve springs.

---

[17]This excludes accessories such as air conditioners and power steering pumps, which are not considered standard equipment.

Rotary Engine—an engine whose working parts rotate rather than reciprocate (see pages 111–14).

Major Thrust Side—the side of the piston that carries the greatest loads (Fig. 7:4). All conventional automotive engines turn in a clockwise direction at the crankshaft pulley. This means that the lower end of the connecting rod swings to the right when the firing pressure pushes the piston downwards. In other words, the connecting rod assumes a position similar to that of a ladder leaning against a wall. This causes the firing pressure to push the upper part of the connecting rod, and thus the piston, against the left side of the cylinder wall. Since the push has nothing to do with gravitational forces, i.e., the weight of the piston, the major thrust side is always on that side towards which the upper end of the connecting rod is pointing during the firing stroke. The rule therefore applies to all engines, regardless of whether the cylinders are upright, slanted, or horizontal. Proper identification of the major thrust side is very important when installing pistons. A piston with an offset pin hole (Fig. 7:4) to combat thrust loads, or one equipped with expansion slots, will likely collapse if reversed.

Minor Thrust Side—the side opposite to the major thrust side. The thrust loads are reversed during the upward strokes (compression and exhaust) as the lower end of the connecting rod swings to the left. These loads are, however, much less than those encountered during the power stroke, hence the term minor thrust side.

No. 1 Cylinder—the cylinder closest to the front of the engine (pulley and timing-gear side). On V-8 engines it may be on either the left or the right side (refer to the manufacturer's specifications).

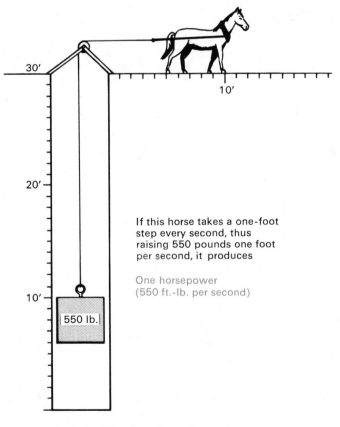

Fig. 7:6 The Meaning of One Horsepower

Firing Order—the order in which the cylinders of an engine fire (page 99).

ICE—internal combustion engine (page 50).

ECE—external combustion engine. Examples: steam engines, steam turbines, and the Stirling engine. In these engines combustion takes place externally, i.e., outside the cylinder or power chamber. The heat generated raises the temperature of the "working fluid"; i.e., water is changed to high-pressure steam, or air is expanded.

Further information on the following terms is given in Chapter 9:

L-Head or *Flat-Head Engine*—side-valve engine with valves located in the cylinder block.

OHV Engine—overhead-valve or I-head engine.

Hemi-Head—cylinder head with combustion chambers in the shape of a hemisphere.

Cross-flow Head—cylinder head with intake and exhaust ports on opposite sides, usually of hemi-head design.

SOC or *SOHC*—single overhead camshaft.

DOC or *DOHC*—dual, or double, overhead camshafts.

Diesel Engine—an engine operating on the Diesel principle, i.e., direct fuel injection and self-ignition by very high compression of air.

Two-stroke-cycle Engine—an engine that completes its cycle in two strokes.

LPG or *LNG Engine*—an engine running on liquefied petroleum or natural gas (page 108).

RECOMMENDED ASSIGNMENTS

1. The distance between the centres of the crankshaft main journals and the crankpins is 2". What is the stroke of the engine?
2. What is the major disadvantage of the reciprocating type of engine?
3. Define the term "short-stroke engine."
4. Calculate the cubic displacement of a V-8 engine with a 4.0:3.5 bore-stroke ratio.
5. What is the cubic displacement of a 4-litre engine expressed in cubic inches?
6. What is the compression ratio of an engine whose cylinders have a displacement volume of 45 cubic inches and a clearance volume of 5 cubic inches?
7. Define the following terms: mechanical efficiency, thermal efficiency, volumetric efficiency.
8. Calculate the bhp for an engine producing 460 lb.-ft. of torque at 4,500 rpm.
9. Where are the major thrust sides on the left and on the right cylinder bank of a V-8 engine?

SUGGESTED FURTHER READING

Study the specifications of service manuals and sales brochures, and read test reports published in motor magazines.

8

Valve-Timing and Firing Orders

In Chapter 6 you learned how a four-stroke-cycle engine works. This chapter explains how the engine can be made to run more efficiently and smoothly.

Valve-Timing

How fast you can run very much depends on your ability to breathe properly. The same applies to internal combustion engines. The point is that,as engine speed increases, there is less and less time to fill the cylinder with the air-fuel mixture. As a result, volumetric efficiency decreases (see p. 92). Nor is there sufficient time to remove the exhaust fumes during the exhaust stroke. This causes the fresh mixture going in to be diluted with the exhaust gases remaining in the cylinder. In other words, the engine can neither "inhale" nor "exhale" properly, and its breathing efficiency is impaired. One solution would be to charge the engine, i.e., to force the mixture into the engine by means of some type of air pump, known as a compressor or a blower. While this is sometimes done on high-performance engines, it is a fairly expensive and complex method (Fig. 9:5). Fortunately, there are several cheaper ways of improving breathing efficiency. One is to streamline and enlarge the ports. The widening of the cylinder bores on modern engine designs was done partly to allow the installation of larger valves and ports, especially on the intake side. Even on production engines the intake valve may be 2" or more in diameter and have a lift of roughly ½".

The major problem is, however, lack of time. For example, at 6,000 rpm there is only ¹/₂₀₀ of a second for each stroke. To gain time and to make use of the momentum or inertia of the moving gases, the valves are simply opened sooner and closed later than was customary on older designs with much lower engine speeds.

Intake-Valve Timing

The time, the rate, the duration, and the degree of valve opening is governed by the shape of the cams on the camshaft (Fig. 8:1). To gain

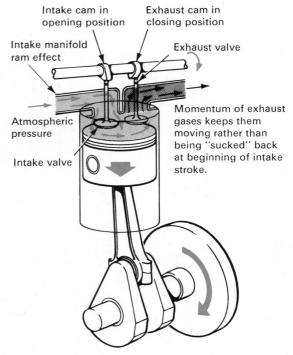

Fig. 8:1 Valve Overlap Between the Exhaust Stroke and the Intake Stroke (Intake valve is opening while exhaust valve is still closing.)

time for the admission of the fresh mixture and to ensure quiet valve action and minimum wear, it is necessary for the valves to open and close smoothly yet rapidly. It also means that they must open as soon as possible and stay open for as long as conditions will permit.

The intake valve opens before TDC, i.e., at the end of the exhaust stroke, while the piston is still moving upwards and the exhaust gases are continuing to shoot out of the open exhaust port. This is possible because the departing gases create a draft effect, and because the new mixture has sufficient momentum to force its way inside the cylinder. It should be realized that the mixture never stops moving completely (Fig. 8:1). Even at moderate engine speeds, the continuous stream of air and fuel particles speeding through the intake port literally piles up against the closed valve, ready to rush into the cylinder when the valve opens once again. This principle, which is often referred to as the "ram effect", can be encouraged by the proper shaping of the ports. The particles act some-

what like people rushing through the hall of a theatre. When the entrance door (the intake valve) momentarily closes, their ranks close up or compress, and when the usher suddenly opens the door, they "fall" into the theatre. Together, the valves work like two doors in a smoke-filled room; the fresh air enters through one, while the smoke moves out through the other. As the piston moves downwards during the intake stroke, cylinder pressure decreases and atmospheric pressure pushes the mixture through the intake manifold into the cylinder. The gas flow speeds up and the momentum of the high-velocity gases is such that the inward gas movement continues during the initial stages of the compression stroke, and well beyond the BDC point. The intake valve is closed when the pressure between the intake manifold and the cylinder is roughly equal. The exact point of closing depends on the engine design, particularly the bore-stroke ratio, the size and shape of the intake ports, and the normal rpm range of the engine.

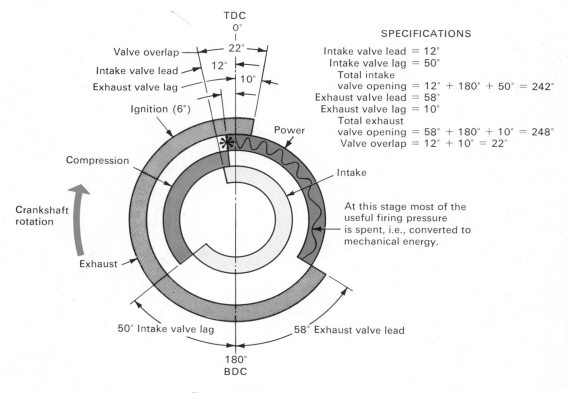

Fig. 8:2   Valve-Timing Diagram

Exhaust-Valve Timing

Exhaust-valve timing goes hand in hand with intake-valve timing. If the exhaust pressure in the cylinder is too great at the end of the exhaust stroke, the new mixture obviously cannot enter. And when it does, the fresh mixture is diluted with burnt gases that didn't have sufficient time to leave. The result is a considerable drop in engine performance. To improve the situation, the exhaust valve is opened near the end of the power stroke when pressure is already low. While this causes some waste of unused energy, the over-all effects of proper valve-timing are more than enough to make up for these losses. The exhaust valve closes after TDC at the beginning of the intake stroke (Fig. 8:1). This enables the spent gases to keep moving out of the exhaust port as the piston starts on its way down. The exhaust valve is closed before the exhaust gases can be drawn back into the combustion chamber.

It is apparent, therefore, that the whole concept of valve-timing depends on the rapid motion of gases. In other words, the system works efficiently only at higher rpm. At very low engine speeds the exhaust would actually begin to back up through the carburetor. "Hot valve-timing" is one reason why idle speeds and shift points[18] had to be raised considerably on modern engines. If the timing marks on the timing gears are incorrectly aligned or the timing chain is worn and stretched, the engine will not run properly.

Valve-Timing Terms

Valve-timing is expressed in degrees of crankshaft rotation, as shown in the valve-timing diagram (Fig. 8:2).

Valve Lead is the number of degrees a valve opens before TDC or BDC.

Valve Lag is the number of degrees a valve closes after BDC or TDC.

Valve Overlap is the total number of degrees the intake and exhaust valves of a given cylinder are open at the same time.

Total Valve Opening is the total number of degrees that a given valve stays open. Total Valve

---

[18]The engine rpm at which the transmission is shifted into another gear.

Opening = Valve Lead + 180° (the equivalent of one stroke) + Valve Lag. On some high-performance engines, total valve opening may be 300° or more. This represents a gain of 120° in valve opening over an engine without any valve lead or lag.

Firing Orders of Multi-cylinder Engines

The flexibility and smoothness of modern automobile engines cannot be obtained from one or two cylinders. While some well-designed four-cylinder engines may be very smooth, generally speaking, more cylinders mean less vibration. The absence or presence of these vibrations depends, among other things, on "mechanical balance" and "power balance". Mechanical balance has nothing to do with the static, or dynamic, balance of the rotating parts mentioned in Chapter 5. It is achieved when the reciprocating parts, particularly those of the piston and connecting rod assemblies, are so arranged that they counterbalance each other. On a four-cylinder engine, for example, the two pairs of pistons always move in opposite directions (Fig. 8:3a). However, for geometric reasons the pistons approaching TDC move faster than the pistons approaching BDC. This means that perfect mechanical balance cannot be obtained from a four-cylinder engine because the upward "kick" of the one pair of pistons is greater than the downward "kick" of the other pair. Thus a four-cylinder engine literally "shakes its head", especially at lower rpm. The condition is compounded by the sideward thrust of the counterweights in mid-stroke position. The spacing of the crankpins on six- and eight-cylinder engines permits these forces to be fairly well-balanced.

Power Balance

Power balance is governed by the firing order of the cylinders and the ability of each cylinder to produce equal power. By selecting a suitable firing order, e.g., 1-5-3-6-2-4 (Fig. 8:3b) the power pulses are distributed evenly, instead of all occurring first at one end of the crankshaft and then at the other. If, in fact, this were not done, an out-of-balance condition would arise, resulting in heavy vibrations and torsional crankshaft stresses. Power balance can be upset if one or more cylinders do not develop full

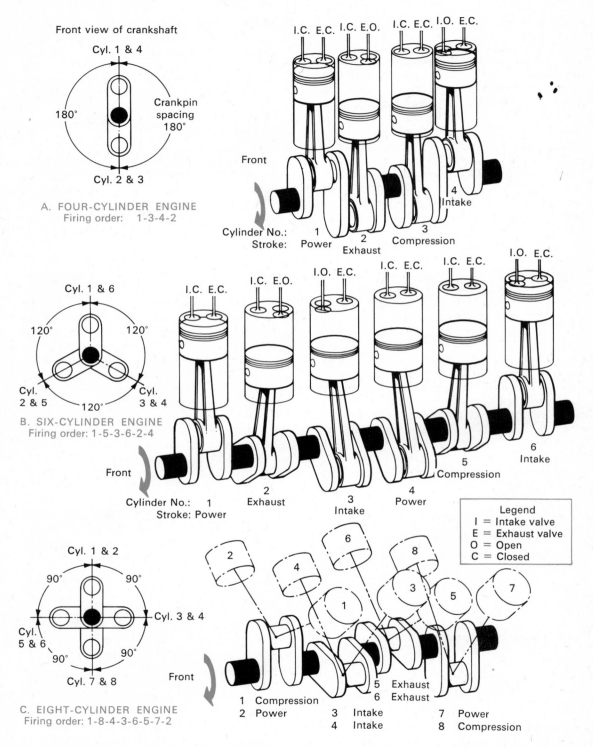

Front view of crankshaft

Cyl. 1 & 4

180°

Crankpin spacing 180°

Cyl. 2 & 3

A. FOUR-CYLINDER ENGINE
Firing order: 1-3-4-2

I.C. E.C.   I.C. E.O.   I.C. E.C.   I.O. E.C.

Front

Cylinder No.:   1   2   3   4
Stroke: Power   Exhaust   Compression   Intake

Cyl. 1 & 6

120°   120°

Cyl. 2 & 5   Cyl. 3 & 4
          120°

B. SIX-CYLINDER ENGINE
Firing order: 1-5-3-6-2-4

I.C. E.C.   I.C. E.O.   I.O. E.C.   I.C. E.C.   I.C. E.C.   I.O. E.C.

Front

Cylinder No.:   1   2   3   4   5   6
Stroke: Power   Exhaust   Intake   Power   Compression   Intake

Legend
I = Intake valve
E = Exhaust valve
O = Open
C = Closed

Cyl. 1 & 2

90°   90°

Cyl. 5 & 6   Cyl. 3 & 4

90°   90°

Cyl. 7 & 8

Front

C. EIGHT-CYLINDER ENGINE
Firing order: 1-8-4-3-6-5-7-2

1 Compression   5 Exhaust
2 Power   6 Exhaust
3 Intake   7 Power
4 Intake   8 Compression

Fig. 8:3 Crankshaft Configurations of Engines. Note valve positions, piston movement, strokes, and firing order.

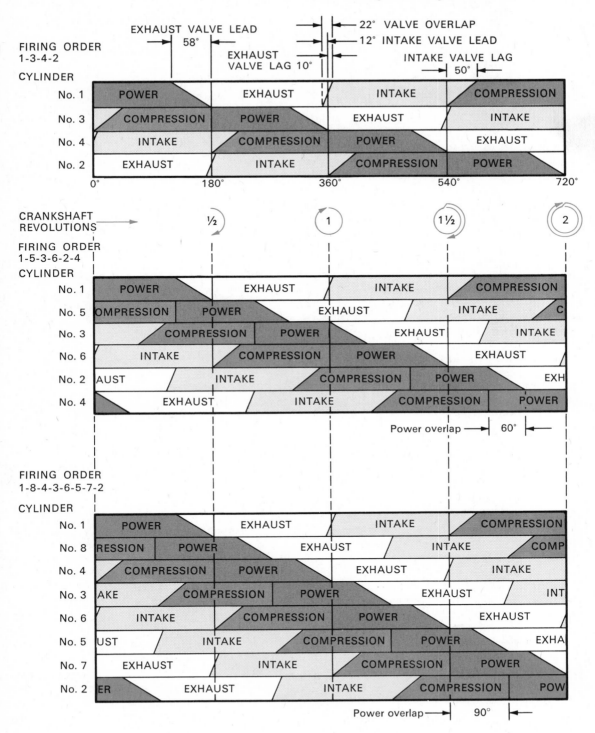

Fig. 8:4 Typical Stroke Charts of Engines: (top) Four-cylinder; (centre) Six-cylinder; (bottom) V-8.

power owing to such conditions as low compression or fouled spark plugs.

Power Overlap

Power overlap is obtained when the firing of one cylinder overlaps that of another. It occurs on automotive engines with six or more cylinders. Fig. 8:3a shows the typical 180° crankpin configuration of a four-cylinder engine. Note that crankpins No. 1 and No. 4 are at the beginning of the power and the intake strokes, respectively; i.e., they are both in TDC position, while No. 2 and No. 3 are both in BDC position at the beginning of the exhaust and the compression strokes. The top section of Fig. 8:4 is a stroke chart for two crankshaft revolutions of a four-cylinder engine. A stroke chart simply represents two crankshaft revolutions of a complete four-stroke cycle in a straight line. It is like placing the uncoiled starter rope of a lawnmower straight on a table. The chart shows very clearly that four cylinders give a continuous flow of power; i.e., there is one·power stroke for each half-turn of the crankshaft. But there is no power overlap. Another very important fact should be noted, namely, that it requires only two turns of the crankshaft for all cylinders to fire once. Since this applies to all four-stroke-cycle engines, regardless of the number of cylinders employed, it is now quite apparent that flexibility and smoothness are improved by increasing the number of cylinders. For example, an eight-cylinder engine fires eight times during two revolutions. The firing order of 1-3-4-2, illustrated in Fig. 8:3a, is the most common for straight four-cylinder engines. Another firing order that is sometimes used is 1-2-4-3. On a six-cylinder crankshaft the crankpin angle is 120°, i.e., the crankpins are set apart by 120°. It can be seen from Fig. 8:3b that as soon as crankpin "A", now in firing position, has been driven through 120°, crankpin "B" will receive the next power pulse. However, since crankpin "A" still has to go 60° to complete its firing stroke, there are in fact two cylinders firing together for a period of 60°. Hence the power overlap is 60° (Fig. 8:4).[19]

With very few exceptions the firing order of six-cylinder engines is as shown in the second stroke chart of Fig. 8:4, namely 1-5-3-6-2-4. The crankshaft of a V-8 engine has four crankpins spaced at 90°, and each serves two connecting rods (Fig. 8:3c). Power overlap is 180° − 90° = 90°. As the firing order of a V-8 engine varies with both the design and the method of numbering the cylinders, it is best to refer to the manufacturer's specifications. In many cases the firing order is inscribed on the intake manifold or on some other engine part.

V-6 crankshafts are very similar to V-8 shafts, except that they have three crankpins spaced at 120°. V-6 engines have irregular firing patterns, and this is often the cause of slight vibrations at lower engine speeds.

RECOMMENDED ASSIGNMENTS

1. What factors are determined by the shape of the cam lobe?
2. Define the following terms: (a) valve lead, (b) valve lag, (c) valve overlap.
3. What are the purposes of valve lead and valve lag?
4. Explain why the exhaust gases normally do not escape through the intake port despite valve overlap.
5. Draw a valve-timing diagram with the following specifications: intake valve lead 8°, intake valve lag, 50°, exhaust valve lead 58°, and exhaust valve lag 11°.
6. Calculate from the specifications given in question 5 (a) the valve overlap, and (b) the total valve opening for each valve.
7. What is the difference between mechanical balance and power balance?
8. Give two reasons why a six-cylinder engine usually produces less vibration than a four-cylinder engine.
9. How many crankshaft revolutions would it require for all cylinders to fire once in a twelve-cylinder engine?
10. How many degrees apart are the crankpins on (a) a four-cylinder crankshaft, (b) a six-cylinder crankshaft, and (c) an eight-cylinder crankshaft?
11. (a) What is power overlap? (b) How much power overlap is there in a four-, six-, and eight-cylinder engine?
12. How does exhaust valve lead affect power overlap?
13. Define the difference between an ICE and and ECE, and give examples of each.

---

[19]If the effects of exhaust valve lead are included, the latter would have to be subtracted.

9

Engine Types and Designs

The material in this chapter is largely a survey of power plants with brief comments on their main features.

There are at present three basic types of mass-produced automotive engines: the gasoline-piston engine, the Diesel engine, and the Wankel engine. The gas turbine has, outside its traditional applications in aviation and other areas, been used commercially only in trucks and buses. Among other reasons, high cost and a relatively high output of nitrogen oxides have, so far, prevented wider acceptance of it. While Diesel engines are used in some cars, especially of European origin, they are also, because of high cost and a fairly low power-to-weight ratio, mostly confined to heavy-duty equipment.

Cars powered by steam and electricity are still in the experimental stage, and their future appears uncertain at present. Compared with ordinary steam engines, the type of unit needed for modern cars with their high output, light weight, and compact size would be very expensive and complicated. Also, the condensers that are required to recycle the used steam are still too heavy and bulky to be practical. Low efficiency, high fuel consumption and maintenance cost, and safety risks are other problems associated with the steam engine. The electric motor would offer great advantages if it were possible to store the necessary energy in some device comparable in size, weight, and energy content to automotive fuel tanks. A lead-acid battery weighs approximately one hundred times as much as the quantity of gasoline required to produce an equivalent amount of energy! So far no suitable substitute battery has

been developed. The claim that electrical cars are "clean" overlooks the fact that the necessary generating plants for recharging the batteries are contributory sources of pollution (sulphur oxides, heat pollution of waterways, radioactive waste materials, etc.). Our discussion will therefore be confined to those internal combustion engines currently being mass-produced.

The Two-stroke-cycle Engine

Although there are very few mass-produced automobiles with two-stroke-cycle engines, the principle involved is of very great interest. This type of engine is widely used for lawn mowers, motorcycles, outboards, snowmobiles, snowblowers, model engines, chain saws, auxiliary generators, and in other situations where small motors are required. Also, many Diesel engines work on the two-stroke-cycle principle, and you should become familiar with it.

There are two common types of two-stroke-cycle engines: those with two ports and those with three ports.

The Two-port Type

Referring to Fig. 9:2a, you can see that, as the piston moves upwards, the volume of the tighly sealed crankcase cavity increases. The pressure in the crankcase therefore decreases, causing the atmospheric pressure to lift the reed valve off its seat. The air-fuel mixture prepared in the carburetor is then able to enter through the crankcase intake. The reed valve is usually a thin, razor-blade-like flutter valve

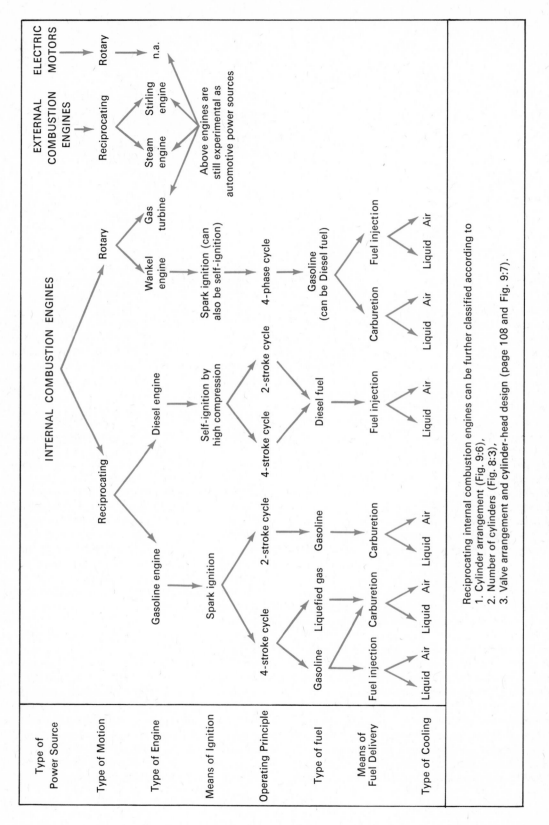

Reciprocating internal combustion engines can be further classified according to
  1. Cylinder arrangement (Fig. 9:6),
  2. Number of cylinders (Fig. 8:3),
  3. Valve arrangement and cylinder-head design (page 108 and Fig. 9:7).

Fig. 9:1 Types of Automotive Power Plants

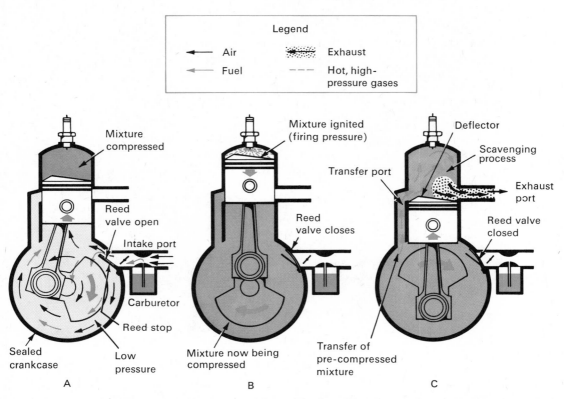

Fig. 9:2 *Operating Principles of a Two-stroke-cycle Gasoline Engine (two-port type)*

made of very flexible spring steel. If it were heavier, it wouldn't be sensitive enough to react to sudden pressure changes. To prevent it from opening too far, it is provided with a back stop. The reed valve remains open until the crankcase pressure equals the intake manifold pressure. This occurs at the beginning of the downward stroke, which follows. Very often a pair of reed valves is used for each cylinder.

Meanwhile a fresh mixture, admitted during the previous cycle, is compressed in the upper cylinder as the piston approaches TDC. The spark from the spark plug now ignites the compressed mixture (Fig. 9:2b) and the hot, expanding gases drive the piston back towards BDC. Just before reaching this point (Fig. 9:2c), and after most of the heat energy has been converted to mechanical energy, two things happen in the following sequence; (1) the exhaust port is uncovered by the piston crown and the burnt gases escape; and (2) the transfer port connected to the crankcase, which is slightly lower

than the exhaust port, now opens to admit a fresh mixture into the cylinder. The transferred mixture is under considerable pressure as it was trapped and pre-compressed in the crankcase during the downward stroke of the piston. When the piston returns to the position shown in Fig. 9:2a, the transfer and exhaust ports are closed once again, and the two-stroke cycle repeats itself.

You will notice that the crankshaft has made only one revolution to complete one two-stroke cycle, compared with the two revolutions made by the crankshaft in a four-stroke-cycle engine. Since the opening and closing of the reed valve is determined solely by pressure conditions inside and outside the crankcase, and not by a camshaft, it follows that the reed valve times itself; i.e., it closes later at high rpm than it does at low rpm. Higher gas velocities may retard its closing to a point well beyond TDC. Another style of two-port design uses a crankshaft-mounted rotary valve that covers and uncovers the crankcase intake

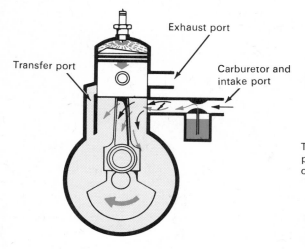

Fig. 9:3 *The Three-port Two-stroke-cycle Engine*

at carefully timed intervals.

The Three-port Type

The three-port type, shown in Fig. 9:3, operates exactly like the two-port type, except it has an intake port located at the lower end of the cylinder wall. Since the opening and closing of the intake is controlled by the piston skirt sliding up and down in the cylinder, the position of the port opening is carefully chosen to give the best results during a given rpm range.

Both types of engine require some arrangement to reduce the loss of the mixture through the exhaust port and the mixing of the fresh and the burnt gases. The controlled process of gas exchange with the piston at or near BDC, where the ingoing and outgoing gases assist each other without undue mixing, is called *scavenging* (Fig. 9:2c). In fact, the scavenging process could be compared to the period of valve overlap in the four-stroke-cycle engine where two ports are kept open at the same time (see pages 97-9). To improve scavenging, some pistons are equipped with a deflector as shown in Fig. 9:2. The deflector diverts the incoming mixture upwards into the combustion chamber where it must curve around to push the remaining burnt gases out through the exhaust port. On other two-stroke-cycle engines with more or less flat piston tops, the gas flow from

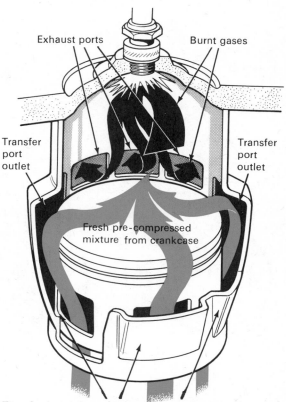

Transfer port inlets connected to crankcase and controlled by "windows" cut into piston skirt
Evinrude Motors

Fig. 9:4 *The Schnuerle System ("Loop-charging" improves scavenging.)*

the crankcase to the cylinder is channelled through several transfer ports so arranged as to introduce a controlled swirl (Fig. 9:4). This widely used method, known as the Schnuerle system, improves scavenging; i.e., it removes the burnt gases more completely and mixture losses through the exhaust ports are reduced.

To improve volumetric efficiency (i.e., the ability to "pump" the mixture) and to increase pre-compression, the sealed crankcase of conventional two-stroke-cycle engines is kept as small as possible to eliminate any unnecessary cavities.

In the ring grooves are small locating or "knock" pins that are indexed with the intended ring-gap position to prevent the piston rings from turning and getting their ends caught in the port openings. Since there is no need for an

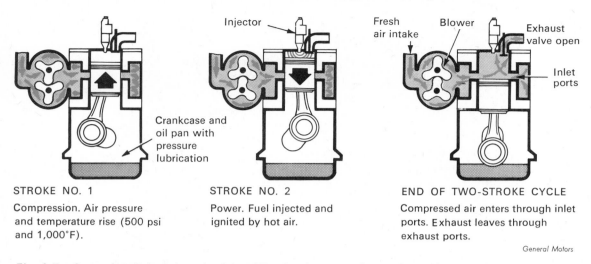

STROKE NO. 1

Compression. Air pressure and temperature rise (500 psi and 1,000°F).

STROKE NO. 2

Power. Fuel injected and ignited by hot air.

END OF TWO-STROKE CYCLE

Compressed air enters through inlet ports. Exhaust leaves through exhaust ports.

General Motors

Fig. 9:5   Operating Principles of a Diesel Engine (two-stroke-cycle type)

oil-scraper ring, there are usually only two compression rings.

The advantages of the two-stroke-cycle engine are obvious: the engine fires twice as often as the four-stroke-cycle engine, and therefore its flexibility is almost as great, as that of an engine with double the number of cylinders. It is also very simple, compact, light, and cheaper to produce and to repair. Because it has no reciprocating valve mechanism, the two-stroke-cycle engine is capable of relatively high rpm. The cylinder head and cylinder block can be cast in one piece, and because of its uncluttered design, the two-stroke-cycle engine is very easily air-cooled, although this does raise the noise level. It can also be water-cooled. Maintenance is fairly simple.

The disadvantages may be less obvious. There is usually no pressure lubrication, and the oil must either be mixed with the gasoline[20] or be supplied directly to the engine by a metering pump. Exhaust emission is high, particularly of unburned hydrocarbons (oil and gasoline). The engine is very sensitive to mixture adjustments, and the wrong mixture can cause fouled spark plugs, rough engine-idle, or even "four-stroke cycling" (i.e., the engine skips one power stroke, with the result that there is only one

power stroke for every two crankshaft revolutions). The exhaust system may clog up with carbon deposits, and proper lubrication requires close attention. The theoretical claim that the power-per-engine displacement is doubled is not possible with ordinary designs, partly due to scavenging and transfer problems. Nor do the two systems described work very well with large-bore engines. Some Diesel engines that work on the two-stroke cycle are therefore equipped with regular exhaust valves in the cylinder head and several intake ports in the cylinder. This arrangement also permits the use of a pressurized lubrication system with a conventional oil pan because the air is forced into the cylinder by a "blower" and not by means of crankcase precompression (see below).

The Diesel Engine

This engine (Fig. 9:5), so named after its inventor, Dr. Rudolf Diesel, compresses air to such a high degree that the air temperature rises to approximately 1,000°F (540°C) as the piston approaches TDC. At this point, fuel is injected directly into the cylinder by a high-pressure injector. When the fine fuel spray hits the hot, compressed air, ignition takes place. Injection actually continues during the initial stages of firing. The remainder of the process closely follows that of the gasoline engines

---

[20]The fuel-oil mixture is usually between 25:1 and 20:1; i.e., there is between 4 per cent and 5 per cent motor oil in the gasoline.

already described. Diesel engines operate on either the four-stroke-cycle or the two-stroke-cycle principle. The compression ratio of Diesel engines is approximately 17:1 and the compression pressure is roughly 500 psi (35 kg/cm^2). This is the main reason why the Diesel's thermal efficiency is approximately 7 per cent to 10 per cent higher than that of the gasoline engine. Fuel consumption is therefore 30 per cent to 35 per cent less. A further important advantage is that Diesel engines always take in a full charge of fresh air and therefore the fuel is more completely *oxidized*, or burned. This also explains why the engine's exhaust, despite its more objectionable odour, contains practically no carbon monoxide. It should be emphasized at this point that a well-designed, properly adjusted Diesel engine doesn't produce any more smoke than a gasoline engine.[21] The engine speed of a "Diesel" depends solely on the amount of fuel injected and the load imposed on the engine. The amount of fuel injected is controlled by the throttle position and a special governor.

The LPG (Liquefied Petroleum Gas) and LNG (Liquefied Natural Gas) engines are practically identical with the gasoline engine, except that the means of mixing the air and the fuel are different. The gas is stored in special pressurized steel tanks. Liquefied propane is also used as an automotive fuel.

The survey chart Fig. 9:1 shows that piston engines can be either liquid-cooled or air-cooled. The number and arrangement of cylinders in automotive engines is partly covered in Chapter 8. The most common arrangements are illustrated in Fig. 9:6.

Valve Gear and Cylinder Head Design

Hardly any other aspect of the engine has so much effect on engine efficiency, power output, and exhaust emission as the valve gear and the cylinder head arrangement. As a result there are a great variety of designs. The following is a brief description of the most important ones. All four types are illustrated in Fig. 9:7.

[21]One of the first two engines to pass the stringent 1975-6 emission control laws was a passenger car Diesel engine!

The L-Head, Flat-Head, or Side-Valve Engine

Advantages: simplicity; compactness; no reciprocating push rods or rocker arms; low manufacturing cost; easily serviced.

Disadvantages: low volumetric efficiency; suitable only for lower compression ratios; low performance; large combustion chamber surfaces; fairly high emission of pollutants.

The OHV (Overhead-Valve) or I-Head Engine

Advantages: allows the ports and the combustion chamber to be shaped for improved volumetric efficiency, high compression, clean combustion, and large valves. This means good performance and less emission. The most efficient design is the "hemi-head" which has hemispherical combustion chambers, angled valves, and streamlined cross-flow porting; i.e., the mixture and the exhaust enter and leave at opposite sides from one another. The spark plug can be positioned centrally between the valves to reduce flame travel and detonation.

Disadvantages: complex, expensive design; many reciprocating parts; less compact.

SOHC (Single Overhead Camshaft) and DOHC (Double or Dual Overhead Camshaft)

Advantages: In addition to the advantages offered by the overhead valve and the hemi-head design, the overhead camshaft engines have fewer reciprocating parts and therefore allow higher rpm and sometimes substantial increases in performance. Valve control is more precise; there is little heat expansion in the valve train; and therefore less valve clearance is needed than on push-rod activated valves.

Disadvantages: complex gearing, unless a toothed fibre belt is used; high, costly cylinder head. The DOHC layout is very expensive.

Short-stroke Engines

Whether or not an engine is a short-stroke engine depends on the bore-stroke ratio. If the ratio is, say, 3:4 (i.e., the stroke is longer than

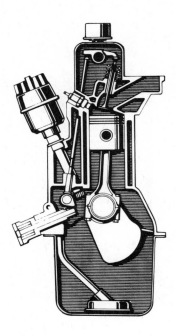

A. IN-LINE OR "STRAIGHT" ENGINE

B. SLANTED OR "SLANT" ENGINE

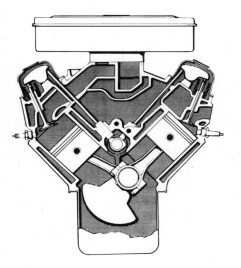

C. V-ENGINE (usually of 90°)

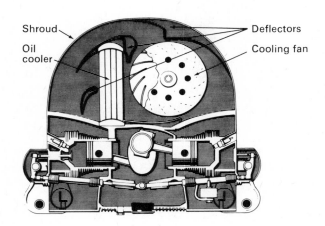

D. HORIZONTALLY OPPOSED ENGINE (AIR-COOLED)
(also called "flat", "pancake", or "boxer" engine)

Fig. 9:6   Common Cylinder Arrangements of Automotive Engines

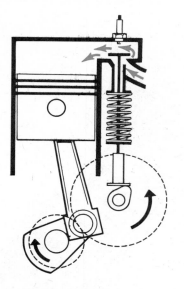

THE L-HEAD ENGINE

(also known as Flat-Head or Side Valve Engine.
The second valve is behind the one shown.)

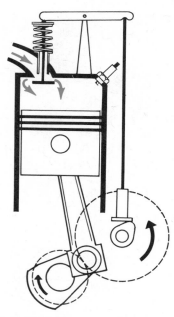

THE OVERHEAD VALVE ENGINE

(also called I-Head Engine. The second
valve is behind the one shown.)

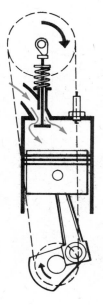

SINGLE OVERHEAD CAMSHAFT ENGINE

(The second valve is behind the one shown.)

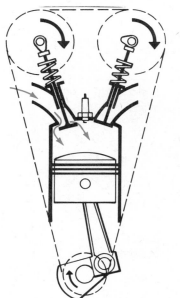

THE DOUBLE (OR DUAL) OVERHEAD CAMSHAFT ENGINE WITH HEMI- OR CROSS-FLOW CYLINDER HEAD.

(Note the dome-shaped high compression piston and the
centre position of the spark plug.)

Fig. 9:7 *Four Common Valve Arrangements and Cylinder Head Designs (Diagrams are greatly simplified.)*

the bore), it is considered a long-stroke engine. If the stroke is roughly equal to, or shorter than, the bore, it is said to be a short-stroke engine. Consider, for example, three different single-cylinder engines all with the same displacement of roughly 50.3 cubic inches. Their respective bore-stroke ratios are 3.58:5, 4:4, and 4.28:3.5. Obviously the first engine would be a long-stroke engine and the other two would be short-stroke engines. The last engine, however, has a stroke that is even shorter than the bore. Such an engine is often referred to as an "oversquare" engine.

There are several reasons why the trend has been away from long-stroke engines. One way of getting more power out of an engine is to increase rpm. To prevent excessive piston speeds, the length of the stroke has to be reduced. Obviously a piston with a stroke of 4" will move more slowly than one with a stroke of 5" at the same rpm. Short-stroke engines are also more compact in design, and their smaller, lighter crankshafts provide better acceleration

and higher rpm. In addition, wider bores permit the use of larger valves and valve ports. This increases volumetric efficiency. However, there are limits to this trend. One reason is that a "square" bore-stroke ratio, such as 4:4, gives the greatest cylinder volume with the smallest surface area (cylinder wall, piston top, and combustion chamber). If the square ratio is changed very much, either one way or the other, heat losses are greater and larger surfaces increase exhaust emission due to fuel condensation and "flame quenching".

The Wankel Engine

Named after its inventor, Dr. Felix Wankel, this engine (Fig. 9:8) uses a triangular rotor revolving inside a housing which, in a sense, serves as both cylinder and crankcase. The rotor divides the housing into three variable cavities, or sliding chambers, in such a way that they either increase or decrease their volumes as the rotor turns around (Fig. 9:9).

Audi-N.S.U.

Fig. 9:8   Two-rotor Wankel Engine (sectional view). Cubic displacement: 1000 cubic centimetres or 61 cubic inches. Horsepower: 120 SAE. Note torque converter at rear of engine and front wheel drive with inboard disc brakes.

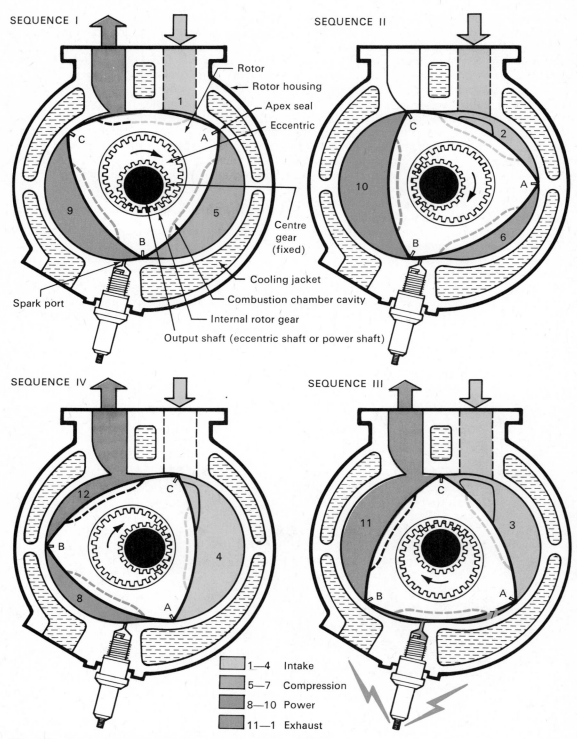

SEQUENCE I

SEQUENCE II

Rotor
Rotor housing
Apex seal
Eccentric
Centre gear (fixed)
Cooling jacket
Combustion chamber cavity
Internal rotor gear
Output shaft (eccentric shaft or power shaft)
Spark port

SEQUENCE IV

SEQUENCE III

	1—4	Intake
	5—7	Compression
	8—10	Power
	11—1	Exhaust

Fig. 9:9 Operating Principle of a Wankel Rotary Engine

The rotor itself, indicated by dotted lines, has a small combustion chamber cavity in each of its slightly arched sides.

Sequences I, II, III, and IV of Fig. 9:9 represent a continuous motion study of the Wankel engine and its operating cycle. (In the following description be careful not to confuse the terms "sequence", "stage", and "phase"!)

The Intake Phase

The upper chamber in stage 1, sequence I, is at its minimum volume, and any further movement of the rotor will cause it to increase. This is the beginning of the intake or induction phase. The chamber volume continues to increase through stages 2 and 3 and reaches its maximum in stage 4 (end of induction phase).

The Compression Phase

Let us assume the rotor continues and is once again in the position shown in sequence I. It can be seen that the fresh mixture that entered during the induction phase is now compressed at stage 5, and more so at stage 6, until at stage 7 it reaches its minimum volume and maximum pressure (end of compression phase).

The Expansion, or Power, Phase

At stage 7, sequence III, an electrical spark ignites the fully compressed mixture, with the result that the gases expand and push against the arched side BA of the rotor through stages 8, 9, and 10. This causes the rotor to force the eccentric,[22] which is part of the shaft, to turn in a clockwise direction. If the spark were improperly timed, the rotor might easily reverse itself in sequence III. If timed correctly, however, the momentum of the rotating parts carries the rotor to sequence IV. In sequence IV the distance from apex B to the centre line of the engine is greater than the distance from it to apex A, and as a result, the engine will always turn in the intended direction. At stage 10 apex

---

[22]An eccentric is an off-centred disc. You can easily demonstrate its movement by pushing a pencil part way through a coffee-cup lid slightly off centre. If you now hold the pencil and rotate it and the lid, you can observe the movement of an eccentric.

C has reached the exhaust port, and this ends the power phase.

The Exhaust Phase

In stages 11 and 12 the burned gases, with most of their heat energy and pressure converted to mechanical energy, are now exhausted as apex C of the rotor uncovers the exhaust port. In stages 12 to 1 apex seal B sweeps the wall of the rotor housing to remove any remaining combustion residues. This is the end of one Wankel cycle and the beginning of the next one.

How far did the eccentric shaft turn during this cycle? Note that the eccentric is in the upper position in sequence I. In sequence III the eccentric is in its down position, and in sequence I it again returns to its original position; i.e., the eccentric shaft (also called the power shaft or output shaft) has made one revolution. If you fix your eyes on one of the apexes or tips of the rotor, and follow its movement for the same period, you will discover that the rotor ABC has made only one third of a turn. This means that if the rotor makes one whole revolution, as it did during the complete four-phase cycle described above, the output shaft makes *three* revolutions. The shaft-to-rotor ratio is therefore 3:1. You must remember, however, that in our description of the Wankel cycle, we have followed only one of the combustion chambers on its way around. We overlooked the fact that there are three chambers working simultaneously and firing one after the other. This means that there are three firings or power phases for each rotor revolution. Since one rotor revolution equals three output shaft revolutions, there is one power pulse for every shaft revolution!

We have avoided a discussion of the gears so far because they have little to do with the Wankel principle itself. Their sole purpose is to give the rotor mechanism more stability or orientation in the housing. The internal rotor gear turns with the rotor, while the centre gear is fixed. The latter is rigidly attached to one of the side housings, and its centre opening forms one of the main bearings for the output shaft.

The main advantages of the Wankel engine over the piston engine are that it has no reciprocating parts. Hence there is less vibration; its size and weight is roughly half; there is an uninterrupted power flow even with only one rotor; the engine fires twice as often per rotor as the cylinders of a standard engine; and there are fewer parts, especially moving parts. A further important advantage is the fact that power can be increased by simply adding more rotors to the basic design. Some parts of a two-, three-, or four-rotor Wankel engine are therefore interchangeable. The emission of nitrogen oxides is quite low because combustion temperatures are less than in most standard piston engines. Wankel engines can be either water- or air-cooled, or they can even operate on the Diesel principle.

One disadvantage of the engine is that if one rotor fails to fire, it causes the equivalent power loss of two cylinders. This is one reason why some Wankel engines employ two spark plugs for each rotor. (Two spark plugs also improve combustion.) Since the rotors tend to throw oil and mixture particles against the spark plugs, the electrodes of the plugs are shielded against the combustion chambers by means of small spark ports. The emission of unburned hydrocarbons and carbon monoxide is at present somewhat higher than on conventional piston engines. Since most engines now require so-called "after burners" or "thermal reactors" to meet the latest emission standards, this disadvantage is of little concern. A more serious criticism of present Wankel engines is the claim that they consume more fuel per horsepower.

RECOMMENDED ASSIGNMENTS

1. Describe what happens in the crankcase and the cylinder of a two-port two-stroke-cycle engine as the piston moves (a) from BDC to TDC, and (b) from TDC to BDC.

2. Prepare labelled diagrams to show the difference between a two-port and a three-port two-stroke-cycle engine.
3. Explain two common methods employed to improve scavenging.
4. What controls the opening and closing of the reed valve?
5. Why should the crankcase on standard two-stroke-cycle engines not have any unnecessary cavities?
6. What is the purpose of the "knock" pins in the piston-ring grooves?
7. Discuss the relative advantages and disadvantages of the two-stroke-cycle engine.
8. Explain the main differences between a Diesel engine and a gasoline engine.
9. How is engine speed regulated on a Diesel engine?
10. (a) By means of simple sketches, illustrate three common cylinder head designs using different valve arrangements.
(b) List briefly the advantages and disadvantages of each system.
11. Define the term "short-stroke engine" and explain its advantages.
12. Name, in proper order, the four working phases of a Wankel cycle.
13. How far does the rotor of a Wankel engine turn during one complete four-phase cycle?
14. What is the ratio between the rotor and the eccentric shaft (output shaft) in a Wankel engine?
15. (a) Explain two methods employed to prevent spark-plug fouling on Wankel engines.
(b) Give two reasons why electrode fouling can be a serious problem with Wankel engines.

10

The
Cooling System

The simplicity of the cooling system combined with the fact that we cannot see how the coolant does its work causes many people to overlook its importance, and as a result, it is frequently neglected. However, it often proves to be the root cause of many seemingly unrelated problems. Its proper functioning, or its failure, affects every single part of the engine, from the carburetor and the spark plug down to the oil in the oil pan.

The internal combustion engine is, as the name implies, a heat engine. Within the limits outlined below, high operating temperatures tend to raise thermal efficiency; as a result, both fuel economy and engine performance are increased. However, materials such as aluminum, steel, oil, and fuel, and the expansion clearances needed for such parts as pistons and valves require that normal operating temperatures be regulated somewhere between 180°F and 250°F, or 82°C to 121°C. A further important consideration is emission control. Low temperatures cause an increase of unburned hydrocarbons, carbon monoxide, and soot, whereas very high temperatures encourage the formation of nitrogen oxides. In summary, the purpose of the cooling system is to maintain the engine at the most efficient operating temperature and thereby ensure the best results in performance, fuel mileage, engine life, and emission.

There are two basic types of cooling systems used with today's engines—direct-air cooling and liquid cooling.

Direct-air Cooling

This cooling system (Fig. 9:6d), used in some automobile engines and lawn mowers, employs forced-air circulation, which requires the use of a fan. In the case of other types of engines, such as those in motorcycles, no fan is needed, and the circulation of air depends upon the forward movement of the vehicle. Since there is no liquid involved, the engine heat is transferred directly from the cooling fins to the air, where it is dissipated. The cooling fins, which are part of the engine, increase the surface area for better heat transfer between the hot metal and the cool air. Systems with forced circulation usually employ shrouds and deflectors to direct the air in a circular flow around, and between, the cylinders and the cylinder heads. In some cases, a thermostatic temperature control is included to increase or decrease the airflow as the need arises.

Although this type of cooling system eliminates the problems of coolant leakage and antifreeze protection, it has its drawbacks. It is noisier (there are no noise-insulating cooling jackets); it requires a fairly complex design; the shrouding makes accessibility for servicing more difficult; temperature rises sharply (although only momentarily) as the engine is shut off; and it often requires an additional heating system in colder climates. Mainly because of its light weight, air cooling has been used on some economy cars, high-performance cars, and aircraft.

Liquid Cooling

This is by far the most common type of cooling system used with automotive engines (Fig. 10:1). The coolant circulates through the cooling jackets surrounding the hot cylinders and the combustion chambers, and, after absorbing the excess heat, carries it to the radiator. Here

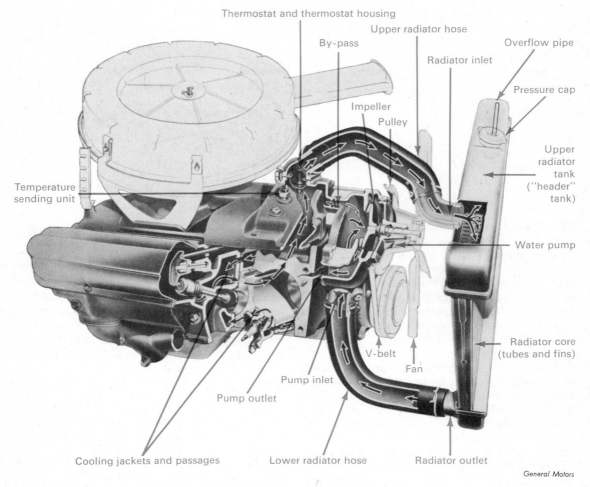

Fig. 10:1 *Liquid Cooling* (*forced circulation of a slanted four-cylinder engine*)

the heat is transferred to the radiator core where it is dissipated by the air that passes through the core. In this sense, even liquid-cooled engines are air-cooled. The coolant simply acts as a medium to carry heat from one area to another where it is more easily disposed of. The cooling jackets also throw off a certain amount of heat that is dissipated by the airflow passing over the outside of the engine.

The Cooling Jackets

The cooling jackets (Fig. 10:1) surround the cylinders, valve ports, valve seats, valve guides, combustion chambers, and spark-plug holes. Since the exhaust-valve seats tend to heat up

more than any other part in the cylinder head, special ports or nozzles convey low-temperature coolant from the water pump to these "hot spots". The high-speed circulation that is used in modern engines allows the use of very narrow cooling jackets. This reduces wear and exhaust emission by shortening warm-up periods, and has resulted in lighter and more compact engines.

Thermostats

Thermostats (Fig. 10:2) are automatic devices that hold the operating temperature of the engine within a specified range. A typical thermostat may be set to open at 185°F (85°C)

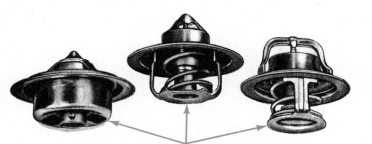

Heat sensor with wax pellet must face hot coolant side.

THREE WAX-PELLET-TYPE THERMOSTATS

Chrysler Canada Ltd.

BELLOWS-TYPE THERMOSTAT

General Motors

Fig. 10:2   Common Types of Thermostats

and to be fully open at 210°F (99°C). The two most common types of thermostats are the bellows type, which is filled with ether or some other volatile liquid, and the solid state, or wax pellet, type. The extent to which the thermostat opens determines the coolant temperature in the engine by regulating the coolant flow between the cooling jackets and the radiator. To ensure that hot liquid reaches the thermostat during the warm-up period, small seepage holes or gaps allow a trickle flow even in the closed position. This also prevents an air lock when the cooling system is filled.

The more widely used solid state type of thermostat is controlled by a linkage rod embedded in a wax-filled copper socket, which is sealed with a rubber sleeve or diaphragm. As the temperature rises, the wax expands and gradually begins to squeeze the sleeve and pin out of the socket, thus opening the valve attached to the other end. As the temperature drops, a calibrated return spring partly or fully closes the valve. The temperature at which the thermostat valve begins to open is stamped on the unit. The temperature at which the fully opened position is reached lies about 25F°, or 14C°, higher than this. While some manufacturers have installed the bellows-type thermostat in pressurized cooling systems, solid state thermostats are less affected by pressure changes.

The opening and closing of suspect thermostats can be tested with a thermometer and a suitable container filled with a regular antifreeze solution. Thermostats that have failed usually remain in the open position. If a thermostat has to be replaced, the safest practice is to buy the same type of unit that was used originally. *Note:* The heat sensor (wax pellet or bellows) is installed facing the hot coolant side. Reversal will cause severe overheating and serious damage! Unless otherwise specified, the same thermostat should be used in summer and winter.

By-pass Recirculation

By-pass recirculation (Fig. 10:3 and 10:1) allows the coolant during engine warm-up to circulate through the cooling jackets without entering the radiator. This system, which is used on all automotive engines, prevents the premature opening of the thermostat, and is designed to equalize the coolant temperature and the metal expansion in the cylinder and combustion chamber region. Without the by-pass, cylinder distortion may be so severe that the pistons will seize up. Some cooling systems include separate passages connected to the intake manifold to regulate the temperature of the fuel-air mixture passing through the ports.

The Water Pump

The water pump (Fig. 10:4) maintains the circulation of the coolant. All modern engines use the permanently sealed type of impeller pump with prelubricated bearings. The pump is usually mounted to the front of the engine between the cylinder block and the radiator, and it is driven by a V-type belt powered by the crankshaft pulley. The coolant enters the inlet pipe of the pump, which is connected to the radiator outlet. The coolant is caught by the

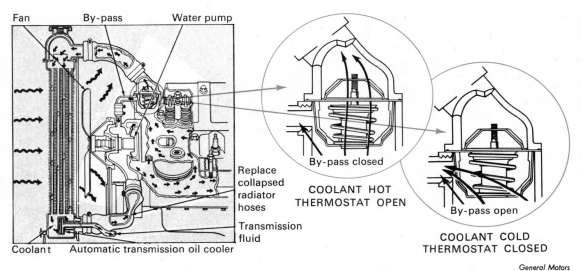

Fan   By-pass   Water pump

By-pass closed

COOLANT HOT
THERMOSTAT OPEN

By-pass open

COOLANT COLD
THERMOSTAT CLOSED

Replace
collapsed
radiator
hoses

Transmission
fluid

Coolant   Automatic transmission oil cooler

General Motors

Fig. 10:3   Operation of a Thermostat with By-pass Circuit

rotating blades of the impeller at the centre of the pump and thrown outwards by centrifugal force. The blades impel the coolant around the pump housing until the outlet, which leads to the cooling jackets, is reached. The rate of flow and the pressure of a given pump depends mostly on the rpm.[23] When the engine stops, the water pump ceases to operate, and the temperature in the cylinder block rises momentarily as the hot metal of the engine continues to transfer heat to the coolant. Fortunately, circulation does not come to a complete standstill because the hot coolant, which in its expanded condition is lighter than the cooler liquid entering from the radiator, rises to the upper outlet by itself. This principle, known as *convection*, was once used in automotive cooling systems that were not equipped with water pumps. These thermo-syphon systems, as they are called, are, however, inadequate for today's engines and are no longer used.

The Cooling Fan

The cooling fan (Figs. 10:4 and 10:5) is usually attached, with the pump pulley, to the front

[23]At 4,000 rpm the rate of flow of an average pump is approximately 60 gallons (273 litres) per minute; i.e., the entire coolant volume is recirculated at least 10 times every minute. To do it, the water pump may absorb as much as 8 hp!

part of the water pump shaft. The fan creates a low-pressure area that draws the air through the radiator, cooling the liquid in the radiator core. The heat is discharged past the engine and down under the floor pan. This helps to cool the outside of the engine block and, especially, the exhaust manifold. Cooling fans may range from simple, less efficient two-blade steel stampings, to carefully balanced five-to-seven-blade designs with variable pitch or speed.

The *Variable Pitch* or *Flex-blade Fan* (Fig. 10:5b) is either made of a tough plastic or has flexible steel blades riveted to the fan hub. On both types the pitch, or angle, of the blades is reduced at higher rpm, owing to centrifugal forces and an increase in air pressure. This, in turn, cuts energy-consuming drag and noise. To lessen noise further, the blades are usually spaced unevenly on the hub.

The *Fluid Fan Drive* or *Torque-control Drive* has a silicone-fluid-filled coupling that connects the fan to the pulley. As rpm and drag increase, the coupling permits the fan to slip at a controlled rate. This coupling also reduces engine loads and noise.

The *Thermostatically Controlled Fan Drive* (Figs. 10:5c and 10:6) employs either a magnetic coupling (less common) or the fluid drive described above, in conjunction with a thermostat. The thermostat responds to the temperature of the coolant or, more commonly, to that of the radiator discharge air coming through

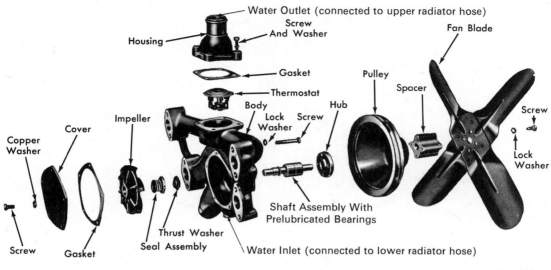

Fig. 10:4 *Water Pump and Fan (disassembled)*

A. STANDARD CROSS FAN

B. FLEX-BLADE FAN

C. THERMO CLUTCH FAN

Fig. 10:5 *Three Common Types of Cooling Fan*

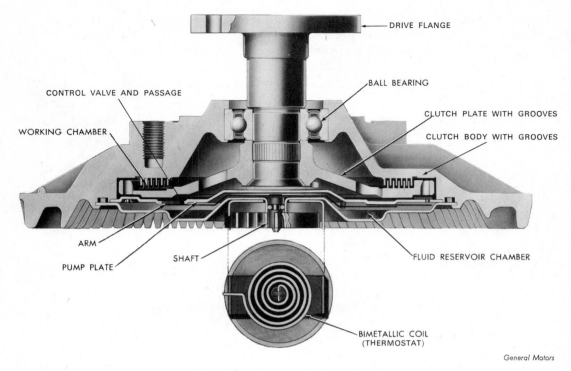

DRIVE FLANGE

BALL BEARING

CONTROL VALVE AND PASSAGE

CLUTCH PLATE WITH GROOVES

WORKING CHAMBER

CLUTCH BODY WITH GROOVES

ARM

SHAFT

FLUID RESERVOIR CHAMBER

PUMP PLATE

BIMETALLIC COIL
(THERMOSTAT)

General Motors

Fig. 10:6 Automatic Fan Clutch

the radiator core. When the temperature of the discharge air is sufficiently low, the fan clutch simply disengages or "free-wheels". On the other hand, if the discharge temperature rises to, say, 160°F or 71°C and beyond in response to increased engine loads, the fan clutch is either partly or fully re-engaged and the fan speed starts to increase. The shifting is governed by a bimetallic coil (the thermostat) in the centre of the automatic clutch (Fig. 10:6). The thermostatic coil in turn controls the flow of the silicone fluid between the reservoir of the hydraulic clutch and its working chamber by means of a special valve. If the fluid from the reservoir is admitted to the working chamber, it fills the grooves of the clutch plate and the clutch body. The shearing action between the two members causes the clutch to engage. If the fluid, however, flows again in the opposite direction, the fan slows down or even begins to "windmill".[24] At very high rpm the coupling

also allows the fan to slip at a controlled rate.

Note: While two fluid-drive couplings may appear to be identical, the viscosity of the fluids inside could, in fact, differ depending on the engine size, the drive ratios, and whether or not an air conditioner is used.

The Fan Belt

The fan belt (Figs. 10:7 and 10:1) is also known as the *V-belt* because its cross-section is

---

[24]A certain manufacturer determined that during normal highway operation the fan needs to

run only 40 out of every 1,000 miles (i.e., 64 out of every 1600 km), as ram air created by the movement of the vehicle is quite sufficient to cool the radiator. A standard fan will therefore unnecessarily consume roughly 8 hp and one gallon (4.55 litres) of gasoline every 300 miles (480 km). Thermostatically controlled fans also reduce engine warm-up and choking time. They are usually standard equipment with air-conditioned vehicles, which do not need the extra output of their oversized fans during the cooler seasons. In the latter case, fuel savings of well over 10 per cent have been reported.

shaped like the letter "V". This enables the belt to wedge itself into the pulley groove, which results in better traction. The fan belt usually drives the fan, the water pump, and the generator. The generator is suspended from an adjustable bracket to permit the setting of proper belt tension. To adjust belt tension to the manufacturer's specifications, a proper tension meter should be used (Fig. 10:7). Because pulley distances and belt loads vary from one engine to another, the old rule of thumb that belt deflection under approximately 20 lb. of thumb pressure should equal belt width is inaccurate. Correct belt tension is very important. A loose setting results in slippage, overheating, belt wear, and belt squeal, especially under sudden acceleration and heavy generator loads. If the belt is too tight, it causes excessive wear of the belt and the water pump bearings. As fan belts are made of fabric-reinforced rubber, they stretch when they are new. Therefore, when a new belt is installed, either the tension must be set slightly above that of used belt specifications, or the belt should be retightened after a running time of roughly one hour. Lubricants must never be applied to noisy belts since this causes slippage and deterioration of the rubber.

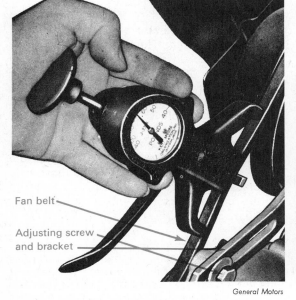

Fan belt

Adjusting screw and bracket

General Motors

Fig. 10:7 Checking Fan Belt Tension with a Tension Meter

The Radiator

The radiator (Figs. 10:1 and 10:16) cools the hot coolant that is pumped into it from the cooling jackets. The liquid enters the upper radiator tank, or "header" tank, through the upper radiator hose, passes through small tubes or passageways, and then enters the outlet tank (lower tank). The outlet tank is connected to the low-pressure side of the water pump by means of the lower radiator hose. To increase the surface area of the radiator core, and thus its cooling capacity, the tubes along which the coolant travels from the header tank to the outlet tank, pass through very thin sheets of copper, called cooling fins.

There are two basic types of radiator cores, the cellular type and the tubular type (Figs. 10:8 and 10:9). Of the two, the cellular type is more efficient, but it is also more expensive and is generally confined to heater cores.

The coolant flow through the radiator core may be either vertical or horizontal. Radiators with a horizontal flow have their header and outlet tanks mounted on each side of the radiator core and are called cross-flow radiators. This design allows lower hood lines on the automobile, which in turn improve visibility, streamlining, and styling. The radiator is often equipped with a fan shroud. Both the radiator and the shroud are mounted in a single frame called the radiator yoke or cradle. The shroud

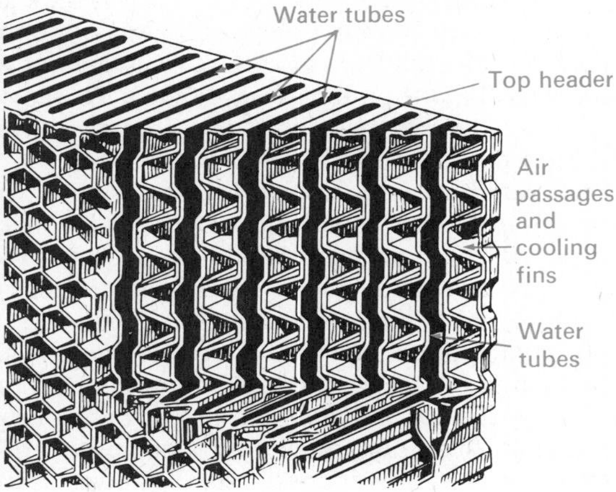

Water tubes

Top header

Air passages and cooling fins

Water tubes

Ford Motor Company

Fig. 10:8 Cellular-type Radiator Core

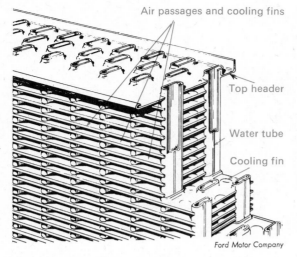

Air passages and cooling fins

Top header

Water tube

Cooling fin

Ford Motor Company

Fig. 10:9   Tubular-type Radiator Core

ensures that air is moved through the entire core area, preventing hot air under the hood from recirculating behind the radiator. For the same reason, the upper part of the radiator is usually sealed against the hood by a long piece of rubber stripping along the top edge of the yoke frame. This also forces the ram air, entering through the grille at higher driving speeds, to travel directly through the radiator core. On vehicles equipped with automatic transmissions, one of the radiator tanks usually includes a coiled tube and suitable connectors to permit the cooling of the transmission fluid (see Fig. 10:16, items 10 and 18). The cooling system is filled through the filler neck, which is either a part of the upper radiator tank or a part of a separate expansion tank (Fig. 10:16). To allow for sufficient expansion, the coolant level should never be higher than that specified by the manufacturer, usually at least one inch below the lower inner edge of the filler neck (Fig. 10:11). The filler neck has an overflow pipe and a hose to provide an escape for excess coolant and vapour pressure.

Most radiators are made of copper and brass. Both metals are good heat conductors, are easily soldered, and are more or less corrosion-resistant. Aluminum, which is much lighter and even better as a heat conductor, has been used on several models. (Processing costs and repairs, however, pose certain problems.) Radiators are painted black to give off heat more

readily. Vehicles equipped with air conditioning usually require oversized radiators to absorb the extra heat generated by the increased engine loads, and a condenser, which is mounted in front of the radiator.

You will appreciate the role of the radiator more fully if you consider that at normal highway speeds it gives off approximately 129,000 BTU[25] per hour, which is about the amount of heat needed by a foundry to melt down an entire cylinder block! (Fig. 7:3 shows how the heat energy released in the cylinder is distributed.)

The Radiator Pressure Cap

For reasons of safety the filler neck of the radiator is provided with stepped cam notches. When the radiator pressure cap (Fig. 10:10) is turned to the first notch, vapour pressure is relieved, and when it is turned further, the cap can be removed (provided the engine is well below operating temperatures!)

The pressure relief valve in the radiator cap has three functions:

1. It releases excess coolant and vapour pressure if the system is overfilled or overheated, thus preventing ruptured radiator- and heater-cores and hoses.

2. It makes possible higher and more efficient operating temperatures than could be attained without it. The boiling point of water at sea level, where the atmospheric pressure is 14.7 psi (about 100 kilopascals), is 212°F or 100°C. For every added pound per square inch of pressure, the boiling point is raised by approximately 3F°, or 1.7C°. Therefore, if water, without the addition of antifreeze, were used as a coolant, and if the pressure cap were labelled with a blow-off pressure of 15 psi, or 103 kPa, above atmospheric pressure, the boiling point of the water in the cooling system would be raised by 15 × 3F°, or 45F°, to 257°F (125°C).

---

[25]One BTU, or British Thermal Unit, can raise the temperature of 1 lb. of water by 1 Fahrenheit degree. One gallon (4.55 litres) of gasoline contains roughly 129,000 BTU. The average house furnace is rated at a maximum of 80,000 BTU.

Fig. 10:10 "Earless" Radiator Pressure Cap for Coolant Reserve System

Besides permitting higher operating temperatures, the pressure cap prevents coolant loss when a hot engine is stopped suddenly. In this case the coolant temperature rises momentarily because of the continuing heat transfer into the cooling jackets. Without the pressure cap most of the liquid in the cooling system would be vaporized. Not only would this vapour escape from the radiator, but since it is an extremely poor coolant, it would seriously damage the engine by cracking the cylinder head and

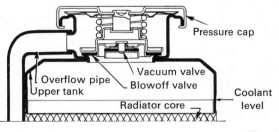

Fig. 10:11 Radiator Pressure Cap Installed

distorting engine parts. For this reason and for reasons of your own safety, *never* remove the pressure cap on a hot engine. Wait until the radiator can be touched by hand.

3. It prevents excessive cavitation and coolant surge. The coolant inside the pump housing cannot keep up with the rapid rotation of the impeller, and vacuum bubbles are therefore formed by cavitation on the trailing sides of the impeller blades. These bubbles are undesirable because they can reduce the efficiency of the pump by more than 50 per cent during acceleration and at high rpm. They also encourage coolant surge under sudden deceleration; that is, momentarily there may be more water entering the radiator than leaving it. With a pressurized system these problems are much less likely to occur.

The vacuum valve opens when the pressure inside the radiator drops to approximately 1.5 psi, or 10.335 kPa, below atmospheric pressure. This prevents the collapse of radiator hoses and pump seals as the engine cools off.

When replacing a pressure cap, you must be sure that the new cap matches the old one, not only in pressure setting but in design (locking cams, depth, etc.) as well.

The Coolant Recovery System or Coolant Reserve System

The coolant recovery system (Fig. 10:12) employs a non-pressurized, vented coolant reservoir or reserve tank connected to the pressurized radiator by means of a connecting tube. The pressure relief valve in the radiator cap releases the expanding coolant into the reservoir when the cooling system heats up. When the liquid cools down and contracts, the vacuum valve permits the coolant to return to the radiator. The reservoir is usually made of transparent plastic so that the coolant level can be checked at a glance. The main advantage of sealed systems is that the reservoir cap on a hot engine can be safely removed without any loss in vapour pressure; thus, damage and injury caused by coolant loss and boiling is prevented. Furthermore, the harmful formation of sludge and corrosion is reduced since no fresh air is allowed to enter the cooling system. To discourage the unauthorized removal of the radi-

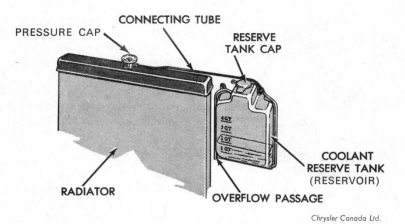

Fig. 10:12 Coolant Recovery System (Coolant Reserve System)

ator pressure cap on sealed systems, it is purposely made round and smooth; that is, it does not have the "ears" found on conventional pressure caps (Figs. 10:1 and 10:10).

Radiator Hoses

Radiator hoses are made of a fabric-reinforced synthetic rubber that is not affected by approved coolants. They provide a flexible connection between the radiator and the engine. The use of so-called universal flex-hoses instead of properly shaped, genuine replacement hoses should be avoided. Owing to engine vibrations and torque reaction in the motor mounts, these hoses put too much stress on the radiator tanks. This eventually leads to cracks and leaks.

Some hoses are reinforced with removable wire coils to prevent kinks and flow restrictions.

Caution: To avoid scalding yourself, never squeeze a hot pressurized hose. Do not use oil when installing a tight hose. If necessary, use water, antifreeze, or brake fluid. Non-adjustable, wire-type hose clamps (Fig. 10:1) should not be reused.

Temperature Gauges and Warning Lights

These allow the operator to adjust his manner of driving to the temperature conditions of the engine. He should avoid heavy engine loads until the normal operating temperature has been reached or, if the engine overheats, he must stop the engine before serious damage is done.

There are two basic kinds of temperature gauges: the capillary type and the electrical type. They are generally non-serviceable replacement items.

The capillary-type gauge employs a small liquid-filled cartridge, or "immersion bulb",

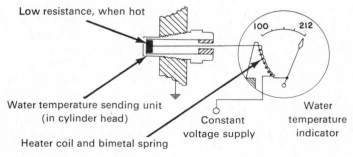

Fig. 10:13 Electrical Temperature-gauge Circuit

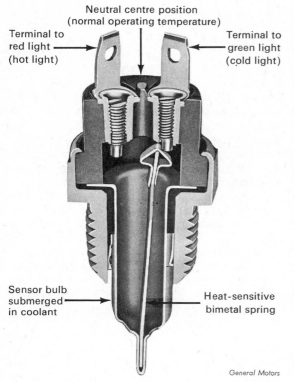

Neutral centre position
(normal operating temperature)

Terminal to
red light
(hot light)

Terminal to
green light
(cold light)

Sensor bulb
submerged
in coolant

Heat-sensitive
bimetal spring

General Motors

Fig. 10:14 Cross-section of a Temperature Sending Unit for Warning Lights (Do not disturb factory-set adjusting screws unless a master gauge is available.)

that is screwed into the hottest part of the cooling jacket, usually in the cylinder head or the thermostat housing. The immersion bulb, commonly known as the *sending unit*, is connected to the *dash unit* (also called the *receiver*, or *indicating*, *unit*) by means of a flexible, but non-elastic, capillary tube. When the liquid in the sending unit is heated by the coolant, it expands and the pressure increases. The dash unit contains a coiled Bourdon tube, which, like a rolled-up garden hose, straightens in response to the increase in pressure. The Bourdon tube is linked to the indicator arm of the dash unit, and thereby indicates the temperature on the calibrated dial face of the gauge.

There are several types of electrical temperature gauges, but all work on principles similar to the ones described below.

The sending unit contains an electrical device which, as the temperature rises, increases the current flow in the circuit connected to it (Fig. 10:13). Therefore, as the coolant heats up, the current flow to the dash unit increases as well. This causes a tiny heater coil wound around a bimetal spring to heat up. The bimetal spring, which is inside the dash unit, consists of two fused layers of dissimilar metals. As each of these metals expands at a different rate, the spring deflects when it is heated. In other words, the higher the coolant temperature is, the more current flows, which determines the degree of heat deflection of the bimetal spring and the indicator arm attached to it.[26] Other dash units use a pair of electromagnetic balance coils, such as those used in fuel gauges (Fig. 13:3). By regulating the magnetic force of one coil over the other, the varying flow of current received from the sending unit causes the indicator arm to register the coolant temperature. Since electrical temperature gauges are sensitive to voltage fluctuations, separate low-voltage regulators are often employed.

Instead of calibrated temperature gauges, simple warning lights may be used. The cold light, usually green, will stay on until the temperature is above 110°F (43°C). The hot warning light, in most cases red, will light up somewhere above 240°F (116°C). Both lights are controlled by a single sending unit that connects either one or the other light to ground, i.e., negative. In the centre position (normal operating temperature) both lights are out (Fig. 10:14).

Unfortunately, none of the systems described can detect any local hot spots in the cooling system. An overheated valve or piston may remain undetected until the damage has already been done.

Frost Plugs, Heater Connections, and Drain Taps

The frost plugs are round steel stampings pressed into port-like openings in the sides of the cylinder block (Figs. 10:16 and 5:5b). Once removed, they must be replaced. Their fit is so controlled that, in the event of a freeze-up, the expanding ice will push them out, rather than crack the cylinder block. Unfortunately,

[26]With some electrical gauges the current flow is highest at low temperatures, and lowest at high temperatures.

this system of frost plugs often fails to prevent serious damage. The plugs are removed during major engine overhauls because they are often corroded and they allow the removal of deposits in the cooling jackets. The openings are also convenient for the installation of electric block heaters needed in colder climates.

The "hot" connection for the heater core is usually located in the cylinder head or the thermostat housing. The cold return connection feeds into the low-pressure area of the water pump (Fig. 10:16, items 12H and 17).

There are usually two or three taps or plugs to drain the coolant. One is at the lowest point in the radiator and one is on the outside of the cylinder block (Fig. 10:16, items 1RT and 1ET). On V-8 engines there is one at each cylinder bank.

Antifreeze Solutions

You will have noticed that the term "water cooling" has been avoided throughout this chapter. The reason for this is that modern engines require a solution of antifreeze and water all the year round. Antifreeze solutions not only prevent freeze-ups in cold weather; they also have a higher boiling point than water (Fig. 10:15). If only pure water or alcohol solutions are used, the boiling point may be reached before the temperature warning light comes on. In addition, good brands of antifreeze contain special soluble oils to provide lubrication for the water pump seals. These oils do not have any harmful effects on the radiator hoses. Other agents are added to discourage deposit formation, corrosion, and foaming. Methyl and ethyl alcohols are rarely used now as antifreeze, except as windshield washer solvents. These antifreeze compounds evaporate easily, they have a low boiling point, they are highly flammable, and they react with aluminum parts. The most common antifreeze solution, adequate for summer and winter, is roughly half ethylene glycol and half water. Undiluted ethylene glycol antifreeze is non-flammable and odourless, has little effect on paint, and boils at 330°F (165.5°C). But it turns to sludge at 9°F (−13°C). A solution of 68 per cent antifreeze and 32 per cent water, which has a freezing point of −92°F (−69°C), offers maximum protection against freeze-ups. However, such a high concentration is not recommended, as it impairs efficient cooling. A 50/50 antifreeze solution has a freezing point of roughly −34°F (−37°C) and a boiling point of 228°F (109°C)[27]. Because glycol-base antifreeze does not evaporate under normal temperatures, it is also called "permanent antifreeze". Manufacturers recommend, however, that it be changed every one or two years. The use of widely advertised coolant additives, such as rust and foam inhibitors, pump lubricants, and sealers, is not recommended because they may react with similar agents contained in adequate amounts in any good antifreeze.

A special hydrometer is used to test the strength of the antifreeze solution, i.e., its ability to protect the system against freezing. The hydrometer must be calibrated for the particular type of antifreeze in question. Some of these instruments can measure the solution while it is hot or cold; others may be used only when the coolant is at a specified temperature.

Caution: The mixing of certain types of antifreeze may produce a jelly-like sludge and cause overheating. This is particularly a danger with imported automobiles, whose cooling systems may be filled with different solutions from those available here. Antifreeze leakage inside the engine caused by defective head gaskets or cracks in the cooling jackets will lead to serious engine failure. Ethylene glycol is incompatible with motor oil, and it forms a sticky, varnish-like deposit when it mixes with oil. Piston and bearing failures are the most common results.

General Cooling System Information

One of the most common causes of overheating is deposits in the cooling system. For example, a 1/16" (0.16 cm) layer of lime and rust affects heat transfer in the same way that an increase of over four inches (10.16 cm) in the thickness of the cylinder wall would. Deposits in the radiator seriously impair its efficiency by plugging the core passages. Usually the deposits can be dislodged by a mild reverse flushing, i.e., flushing in the opposite direction to normal pump flow. To reverse-flush the radiator, the

[27]With a 15 psi, or 103.35 kPa, pressure cap, the boiling point of this solution would be 273°F, or 134°C.

Ethylene Glycol Base

FREEZE PROTECTION TABLE

Total Cooling System Capacity in Quarts	Quarts of concentrated Antifreeze required for protection to temperatures (°F) shown.									
	2	3	4	5	6	7	8	9	10	11
8	10	– 8	–34							
9	14	0	–21	–50						
10	16	4	–12	–34	–62					
11	18	– 8	– 6	–23	–47					
12	19	10	0	–15	–34	–57				
13	21	13	3	– 9	–25	–45				
14		15	6	– 5	–18	–34	–54			
15		16	8	0	–12	–26	–43			
16		17	10	2	– 8	–19	–34	–52		
17		18	12	5	– 4	–14	–27	–42		
18		19	14	7	0	–10	–21	–34	–50	
19		20	15	9	2	– 7	–16	–28	–42	
20			16	10	4	– 3	–12	–22	–34	–48
21			17	12	6	0	– 9	–17	–28	–41
22			18	13	8	2	– 6	–14	–23	–34
23			19	14	9	4	– 3	–10	–19	–29
24			19	15	10	5	0	– 8	–15	–24
25			20	16	12	7	1	– 5	–12	–20
26			21	17	13	8	3	– 3	– 9	–16

For cooling system larger than shown use double the quantity required for system one half as large.

BOIL PROTECTION TABLE *†

Total Cooling System Capacity in Quarts	Quarts of concentrated Antifreeze required for protection to temperatures (°F) shown.									
	2	3	4	5	6	7	8	9	10	11
8	218	221	228							
9	216	220	224	229						
10	219	219	222	228	232					
11	215	218	221	224	229					
12	215	218	220	223	228	231				
13	215	216	219	222	225	228				
14		216	218	221	223	228	230			
15		216	218	220	222	225	228			
16		216	218	219	221	224	228	230		
17		215	217	218	221	223	225	228		
18		215	216	218	220	222	224	228	229	
19		215	216	218	219	221	223	225	228	
20			216	218	219	220	222	224	228	229
21			216	217	218	220	222	223	225	228
22			215	216	218	219	221	223	224	228
23			215	216	218	219	220	222	224	225
24			215	216	218	218	220	221	223	225
25			215	216	217	218	219	221	222	224
26			215	216	216	218	219	220	222	223

* Boiling points at sea level. Temperature decreases 2 F° for each 1,000 feet of altitude.

† Boiling points increase 3 F° for each psi of pressure exerted by pressure cap.

Gulf Canada

Fig. 10:15 Antifreeze Tables

thermostat is removed and a garden hose is inserted into the thermostat housing. With the radiator drain tap open, the water is left running for several minutes. Detergents and pressure flushing should be applied only in severe cases. Frequent topping-up or refilling adds to deposit formation and corrosion. Because the coolant becomes diluted, adequate summer and winter protection may also be lost. When a cooling system on a cold engine is being refilled, it may take twenty minutes to remove all the air trapped by the thermostat. The filling must be completed while the engine is running, but before the engine temperature rises too high. The whole cooling system can be pressurized by means of a special hand pump attached to the filler neck. This will reveal any loose connections or leaking gaskets, pump seals, hoses, or radiators (Fig. 10:16). The same device can be used to check the pressure relief valve in the pressure cap. On very hot days, and especially in slow, stop-and-go traffic, an automatic transmission should be placed into neutral when the vehicle is at a standstill. This helps cooling for several reasons. Without any load, the torque converter in the transmission generates considerably less heat. As a result, temperatures in both the transmission oil cooler and the radiator are lowered. At the same time, engine-idle is raised, and thus more air is moved by the cooling fan. If the radiator boils over, *do not remove the pressure cap!* First turn the heater on, and then stop the engine and wait. The radiator must never be filled or "topped up" when the engine is hot. "Cold showering" can cause serious distortion or even cracks in the engine. This warning does not apply to coolant reserve tanks.

Damaged or loose fins, and insects, leaves, or paper entering the radiator core are very often overlooked. All of these restrict the airflow and the normal transfer of heat. The use of radiator blinds is undesirable for the same reason. Thermostatically controlled shutters, such as those used on heavy-duty equipment, regulate the entire airflow only when needed, whereas pieces of cardboard do not. Overheating under heavy loads or snapped fan blades are possible results. Since the airflow is restricted only in one area, the blades are subjected to uneven loads and vibrations that may eventually lead to metal fatigue.

Replacement parts, such as gaskets, thermostats, pulleys, fans, and pumps, must match the originals, especially in size and type. For example, a small pulley combined with an oversized impeller can cause sufficient pressure to "blow" a heater core.

The proper functioning of the cooling system is closely connected with general engine performance, fuel economy, heater output, and oil consumption. Because parts are fitted with clearances calculated for normal operating temperatures, temperature regulation also relates directly to engine noise and the rate of wear. Abnormal coolant temperatures cause excessive fuel and water condensation, sludge formation, corrosion, backfiring, pre-ignition, detonation, increased exhaust emission, and "dieseling", i.e., the engine continues to run with the ignition turned off.

One of the most popular misconceptions is that it is good for the engine if the full operating temperature is reached before the car is put into motion. In fact, this method is bound to upset everything at once. The balance of normal heat distribution (heat converted to mechanical energy as opposed to heat absorbed and rejected by the cooling system), proper lubrication, carburetion, ignition, emission control, and fuel conservation are all interfered with by this bad practice. The best warm-up procedure is to reach specified operating temperature under low-to-medium working loads.

Was the comment in the first paragraph of this chapter an overstatement? A survey conducted by the Imperial Oil Company in collaboration with CAT (Canadian Automotive Trade Magazine) revealed that 144 cars out of 200 required some type of cooling system service. In many cases it was only a matter of topping up the coolant, replacing dirty coolant, adding antifreeze, or removing insects from the radiator core. However, 58 per cent needed new radiator caps, over one-third required either belt adjustment or replacement, 12 per cent had defective radiators, and 6 per cent needed new radiator or heater hoses. An earlier survey showed that 33 per cent had to be replaced.

RECOMMENDED ASSIGNMENTS

1. Prepare a labelled schematic diagram of a complete cooling system. Use arrowheads to indicate the direction of the coolant flow. The coolant should be shown in colour.
2. Why do modern cooling systems operate between 180°F and 250°F (82°C and 121°C)?
3. What is the purpose of the thermostat?
4. Explain the operation of the thermostat.
5. Why do most cooling systems have by-pass recirculation?
6. How is by-pass recirculation accomplished?
7. Why does the coolant not completely stop circulating when a hot engine is turned off?
8. Describe the operation of a water pump. Illustrate your answer.
9. Name three common fan designs and explain their main features.
10. Discuss the problems caused by improper tension of the fan belt.
11. What are the purposes of the fan shroud and the yoke seal?
12. What is the proper coolant level and why must it be maintained?
13. Explain the difference between the following two terms: (a) pressurized cooling system, and (b) forced circulation.
14. State the four functions of the radiator pressure cap.
15. What is the purpose of the cam notches on the radiator filler neck?
16. Give three reasons why the pressure cap must never be removed while the engine is hot.
17. In what respects is the sealed cooling system an important improvement?
18. List four types of temperature gauges and explain their key features.
19. What is the technical name of the special steel plugs pressed into the side of the cylinder block? What is their purpose?
20. What would be the boiling point of a cooling system with a 14-psi pressure cap and a 50/50 antifreeze solution?

21. Explain the term "permanent antifreeze".
22. Why do better brands of permanent antifreeze contain certain additives?
23. What methods are used to determine (a) the strength of an antifreeze solution, and (b) coolant leakage?
24. List the likely consequences of ethylene glycol leaking into the cylinders and the oil pan.
25. Name two common causes of an internal antifreeze leakage.
26. Name eight common causes that will lead to the failure of the cooling system.
27. How does the proper functioning of the cooling system or its failure affect general engine performance?

TROUBLE-SHOOTING

(There is at least one solution to each problem.)
1. A driver complains that his temperature gauge never reaches normal operating temperature. A master gauge, installed temporarily, rules out any defects in the gauge or the sending unit.
2. Excessive bubbling can be observed when looking down the filler neck. The condition gets worse when the transmission is in "drive" and power is applied with the brakes on.
3. The red warning light stays on regardless of the temperature.
4. A radiator is refilled and pressure-tested by a mechanic. There are no leaks or other abnormal conditions. The owner is puzzled because he replaced the antifreeze himself just half an hour earlier but lost almost all of it because of boiling.
5. A motorist removes the thermostat completely. To his surprise both performance and fuel mileage drop. Why?
6. On a cold winter's day, the radiator boils over through the pressure cap and the overflow, yet the lower portion of the tank feels cold to the touch.
7. Name the likely causes or problems identified by numbered "trouble spots" in Fig. 10:16.

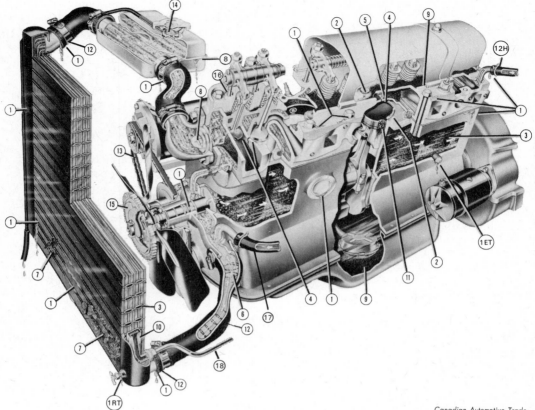

Canadian Automotive Trade

Fig. 10:16 "Lots of Trouble". How good are you at identifying each problem ?

11

Lubricants and Lubrication

While there are some terms and abbreviations that should be committed to memory, the emphasis in this chapter is on a few basic principles and circuits.

The Purpose of Lubrication

Without lubrication the automobile and most moving machinery would be unthinkable. By the same token, the lack of lubrication is probably the most common cause of excessive wear and of the premature failure of parts.

The main purpose of lubrication is to reduce friction. As you know, friction is the resistance to motion between two bodies that are in contact with each other. A piston moving against the cylinder wall or the crankshaft revolving in the main bearings are typical cases where friction comes into play. If lubrication did not reduce friction to acceptable levels, too much energy would be wasted in overcoming it. Furthermore, the constant rubbing action would cause very rapid wear and considerable heat. Obviously this condition exists not only in the engine but also throughout the vehicle, wherever there are moving parts.

Motor Oils

The motor oil must do all of the following: lubricate and cool the engine, seal the piston rings, keep the engine clean (Fig. 11:1), protect against corrosion and cushion impact loads, and transmit hydraulic pressure.

In order to lubricate sliding parts such as pistons, rings, and valve lifters, the motor oil must be able to maintain a thin, slippery oil film under high pressure. This type of lubrication is known as boundary lubrication.[28] To fulfil this role effectively the oil must have lubricity (oiliness) and adhesion, i.e., a natural affinity for metals that causes it to cling tenaciously to their surfaces. Adhesion must be maintained under high temperature and high pressure, and shaft rotation and the scraping action of piston rings must not be allowed to displace the oil film. If severe damage (such as ring scuffing and scored bearings) is to be avoided during cold starts, the lubricant must stay put when the vehicle is not in use. Furthermore, the oil film forms a protective layer against corrosion due to condensation and the formation of acidic combustion by-products. The oil must also possess cohesion, or film strength. Cohesion means that the tiny molecules of the lubricant cling to one another, so that even the high surface-pressures encountered between the teeth of gears or inside a bearing cannot penetrate the protective boundary layer.[29]

Viscosity

Viscosity is the ability of a liquid to resist flow. It is closely related to cohesion. An oil of high viscosity, or "weight", will normally resist

---

[28]"Boundary", or thin film, lubrication measures a few ten-millionths of an inch in thickness. "Thick" film lubrication, such as that found in insert bearings, is usually around 0.0001" to 0.001" (0.0025 mm to 0.025 mm).

[29]You can verify this by coating the striking surface of a hammer with a good lubricant. Even a forceful hammer blow will not displace the boundary layer.

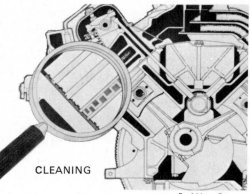

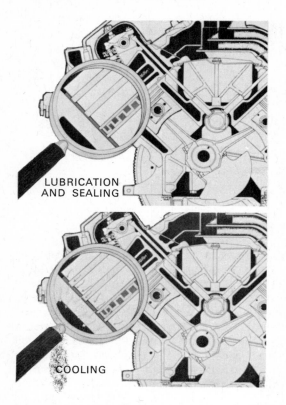

Ford Motor Company

Fig. 11:1   The Purposes of Motor Oil

shearing and rupture more effectively than a lubricant of low viscosity. This property is particularly important where a thick oil film must be maintained on rotating parts and where impact loads are high. Adhesion and viscosity help to prevent undesirable cavitation (page 123) and foaming. Adhesion and viscosity are also needed to seal the piston rings and thus stop undesirable blow-by. Obviously, a very viscous and therefore thicker oil cannot seep between tightly fitted parts. Its rate of flow through the oil passages is also reduced. On the other hand, if the viscosity is too low, the oil film will be too thin to give adequate protection, and, when the engine is stationary, will not stay put on the cylinder walls or anywhere else. Either extreme leads to excessive wear, oil consumption, emission, and deposit formation.

Viscosity is measured in a viscometer, or viscosimeter, a funnel-like arrangement with a calibrated orifice (opening) and a flask (Fig. 11:2). The time that it takes for a given amount of oil to pass through the orifice at 210°F (99°C) determines the viscosity rating assigned to the oil sample. A motor oil with a viscosity rating of

SAE 10 is less viscous than one labelled SAE 20. Standard motor oils may have any one of the following SAE viscosity ratings: 5, 10, 20, 30, 40, or 50. Viscosities of 10, 20, and 30 are the most widely used. The viscosities of winter oils, such as 5 W, 10 W, or 20 W, are determined at 0°F rather than at 210°F. The viscosity selected depends, among other factors, on operating temperatures, engine loads, climatic conditions, and engine design. For example, an air-cooled engine or one with greater bearing clearances may require a more viscous oil.

The Viscosity Index (V.I.)

You probably know that motor oil runs more freely when it is hot. However, two brands of oil with the same SAE viscosity at 210°F (99°C) may behave very differently at −30°F or 310°F (−34°C or 154°C). As engines are designed with a more or less constant viscosity in mind, the better oil would be the one whose viscosity is the least affected by any changes in temperature. If the oil is very thick at low temperatures, too much power is needed to overcome friction and the lubricant is unable to penetrate between closely fitted parts. In fact, in cold weather, the starter motor may be unable to produce adequate cranking speeds. On the other hand, if the viscosity drops sharply at very high temperatures, the oil film will be too thin to provide adequate protection, and the engine will start to burn oil.

The viscosity index, therefore, rates a motor oil on its ability to resist changes in viscosity due to variations in temperature. The V.I.

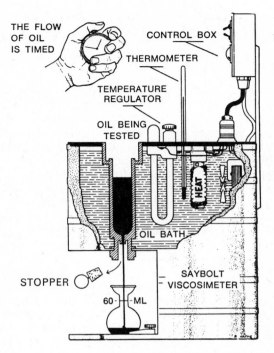

THE FLOW
OF OIL
IS TIMED

CONTROL BOX

THERMOMETER

TEMPERATURE
REGULATOR

OIL BEING
TESTED

HEAT

OIL BATH

STOPPER

SAYBOLT
VISCOSIMETER

60 — ML

Fig. 11:2   Saybolt Viscometer or Viscosimeter

originally ranged from 0 to 100. The value of 0 was assigned to naphthene oils made from California crude because, in the unrefined state, their viscosity changes drastically with temperature. The very stable, paraffin-type oils from Pennsylvania were assigned the number

Viscosity

100. However, improvements in refining and the use of special additives can raise the V.I. value far above 100. This is not to say that V.I. grades above 100 do not change their viscosity at all. Even the very best oils change their viscosity to some extent.

Multi-grade Motor Oils

While the V.I. number itself is not usually indicated on regular cans of oil, multi-grade labels such as 10W-30 or 20W-50 are an indication of a high V.I. rating. For example, a 10W-30 motor oil signifies that at 0°F (−18°C) it behaves like an SAE 10 winter oil and at 210°F (99°C) it behaves like a regular SAE 30 oil. A winter oil has a specially low "pour point", whereas a regular SAE 30 either becomes too thick for the oil pump to handle or ceases entirely to flow at temperatures below 0°F. Because of its high V.I. rating, a multi-grade oil can be used all year round, and this simplifies the problem of keeping many different grades in stock.[30] It should be noted that even the best multi-grade oils change their V.I. if contaminated by condensation and sludge formation.

Additives

Additives are chemical compounds that improve a lubricant's natural qualities and "tailor" it to meet specific demands. While these additives are extremely effective, they may amount to less than half a drop per gallon or one average oil filling.

Detergents are added not to clean a dirty engine but to keep a clean engine clean; i.e., they prevent the build-up of deposits, especially carbon. Some so-called "drastic detergent oils" may plug the oil filter if the engine is very dirty or if a non-detergent oil was used previously. Detergent oils are sometimes referred to as heavy-duty oils.

Dispersants disperse those contaminating substances that are too small to be removed by even the most efficient oil filter. Most of the contaminants, such as carbon, water, acids, and lead salts, enter the crankcase through blow-by. These abrasive and corrosive ma-

[30]Some top-line motor oils have such a high viscosity index that they are rated as SAE 5W-10W-20W-30W or simply 5W-30.

terials join together to form black, jelly-like deposits, known as sludge. Dispersants not only reduce sludge formation by holding these minute particles in suspension, but they allow them to be removed during regular oil changes. Detergent-dispersant additives were first introduced in the automotive field with the use of hydraulic valve lifters, which are extremely sensitive to any kind of oil impurity or deposit.

Note: Because of their high detergent content, it is the nature of HD, or *Heavy Duty*, oils to turn gray within a few hours of engine operation.

Oxidation Inhibitors are additives that reduce the rate of those chemical reactions in which oxygen combines with oil to form larger and more viscous molecules, or even corrosive acids and sludge.

Corrosion Inhibitors are added to protect metal parts against the corrosive effects of water and acids.

Foam Inhibitors do not prevent foam, which results from the whipping action of moving parts, but they cause it to settle more quickly. Foaming is undesirable because it encourages the breakdown of oil films, and in severe cases the lubricant will simply be lost. It also interferes with the hydraulic action of the oil pump and with the valve lifters, which would fail to adjust and become very noisy as a consequence.

V.I. Improvers and *Pour Point Depressants* help reduce the thinning of the oil when it is hot and undue thickening when it is cold. The pour point is the temperature below which the oil ceases to flow because the wax in the oil solidifies. Pour point depressants are widely used in winter oils.

Anti-Wear and Pressure Additives improve pressure resistance and lubricity.

Caution: Never mix different brands of oil, since certain additives are incompatible. If a switch of brands is made, both the oil and the oil filter must be changed.

Oil Changes

Because additives are eventually depleted, a point may be reached where they no longer prevent deposit and sludge formation. Unfortunately, there is no definite rule that states when an oil change must be made. This largely depends on operating conditions, climate, type of fuel, the quality of the motor oil, the condition of the engine, driver habits, dust conditions, condensation, etc. Condensation can make the oil so stiff that starting is impossible on very cold days. Furthermore, a vehicle driven mostly at highway speeds and over long distances does not require oil changes as frequently as, for example, a city taxi operating under low-speed, stop-and-go conditions. A particularly important factor is operating temperature. While low temperatures encourage condensation, high temperatures cause an increase in the rate of oil oxidation. The rate of oxidation, like most chemical reactions, roughly doubles for every 18F°, or 10C°. Under ideal conditions and with crankcase temperatures of around 230°F, or 110°C, oil change intervals of up to 4,000 miles (6400 km) or four months may be maintained. However, an air conditioner or trailer can each raise this temperature by as much as 15F° (8.3C°) and the motor oil may have to be changed every 1,500 miles (2400 km) instead, especially in warmer climates. To complicate matters even more, the addition of certain emission-control devices has, in some cases, raised oil temperatures up to 300°F (149°C).

Source of Motor Oils

Modern motor oils are mineral oils which, like gasoline and Diesel fuel, are obtained by fractional distillation from petroleum, or crude oil. They are further refined to obtain additional desired properties. Vegetable oil (castor oil) is sometimes used in certain small racing engines and model engines because of its very good lubricity and high-temperature performance.

Special oils, such as lock oil, penetrating oil, and oils for two-stroke-cycle engine lubrication, are formulated to meet special requirements.

Witco Chemical Canada

Foam Inhibitors

API Service Classifications

The API service classifications were originally laid down by the *American Petroleum Institute* to divide different types of oils into groups according to specific operating conditions. In 1969 and the years following, the API, the *Society of Automotive Engineers* (SAE), and the *American Society for Testing Materials* (ASTM) collaborated in a revision of these classifications. Since service manuals may use either the old or the revised system, the reference chart below lists the new classifications and their approximate equivalents in the old system. The service designation is usually stamped on the can of oil with the SAE viscosity rating.

Classification of Motor Oils

New SAE and API Performance Classifications	Original API Classification	Summarized Service and Oil Descriptions according to API and ASTM
SA	ML (Motor Light)	Light operating conditions; no additives except perhaps pour point and/or foam depressants.
SB	MM (Motor Medium)	Medium operating conditions; contains some corrosion and anti-scuff properties.
SC	MS (Motor Severe) 1964 specifications	Satisfies 1964-67 warranty requirements; improved anti-sludge and anti-corrosion performance.
SD	MS 1968 specifications	Satisfies 1968 warranty requirements; superior to SC oils.
CA	DG (Diesel General)	Mild to moderate Diesel engine operation using high-quality, low-sulphur fuels, and without blower or turbo-charger; occasionally used in gasoline engines under mild operating conditions; protection against high-temperature deposits and corrosion.
CB	DM (Diesel Medium)	Mild to moderate Diesel engine operation using lower-quality, higher-sulphur-content fuel, and without blower or turbo-charger; occasionally used in gasoline engines under mild operating conditions; protection against high-temperature deposits and corrosion.
CC	DM (Diesel Medium)	Moderate to severe Diesel engine operation with light supercharging; used in certain heavy-duty gasoline engines; protection against high- and low-temperature deposits and corrosion.
CD	DS (Diesel Severe)	Supercharged Diesel engines operating on low- or high-quality fuels, high engine speed, and high output requiring highly effective wear and deposit control.

Automatic Transmission Fluid

Automatic transmission fluid (ATF) is a highly refined oil that serves as a hydraulic liquid, and also as a transmission coolant and lubricant. For smooth performance and proper shifting regardless of temperature conditions, as well as trouble-free operation, the automatic transmission fluid must have a very high viscosity index (around 130) and contain additives to prevent sludge, varnish, oxidation, foaming, cavitation, wear, and scoring. It must also have low volatility to prevent fluid losses, and it should keep the seals soft and pliable, possess low-temperature fluidity, and have a high flash point.[31] A change from 60°F to 240°F (16°C to 116°C) causes a volume increase of approximately 8 per cent; as a result the average transmission level will vary by roughly 1" (2.54 cm). To facilitate the detection of leaks, a strong red dye is added to the fluid. Automatic transmission fluid is also used as a hydraulic fluid in most power steerings.

ATF with Dexron, a special additive (formerly type A, suffix A), is required by the majority of automatic transmissions. It must not be replaced or mixed with ATF, type F. The latter fluid contains frictional additives for "quick grip" band and clutch action designed into some types of automatics.

Note: The ATF level is usually checked with the transmission lever in "Park" and while the engine is running. On some models it must be done in the "Neutral" position and while the engine is running. Always make sure that the ATF type used meets the manufacturer's specifications.

Gear Lubricants

Gear lubricants must be able to withstand the extreme pressures and the wiping action between the teeth of the gears without separating.[32] They must also be able to prevent "channelling" at low temperatures. This occurs when the rotating gears cut a channel into the oil so that the displaced lubricant cannot flow between the meshing gear teeth. Foaming may lead to a rupture of the oil film and thus cause direct metal-to-metal contact, excessive wear, or even "stripped gears".

Gear lubricants may vary from high-viscosity motor oils to various types of so-called EP (extreme pressure) gear lubricants. Standard viscosities are SAE 75, 80, 90, 140, and 250. Multiple SAE grades of 80-90, 90-140, and 80-90-140 are also available. SAE 90 is usually used above 10°F (−12°C), SAE 80 below 10°F. The gear lubricants SAE 75, 80, and 90 are the most common, and their viscosities are roughly equivalent to motor oils SAE 10W, SAE 20, and SAE 50 respectively. The so-called multi-purpose gear lubricants can be used in some standard transmissions, rear axles, and steering boxes.

By definition, an EP gear lubricant is any lubricant that has a greater load-carrying-capacity than a refined, straight mineral oil.

As it did for the service classifications of motor oils, the API published in 1969 specific service designations for lubricants used in manually shifted transmissions and axle drives. The gear lubricant classifications bear the designations API-GL-1, 2, 3, 4, 5, and 6. The first type is a straight mineral oil without any special anti-wear or EP additives, although it may contain oxidation and foaming inhibitors and pour point depressants. It is not satisfactory for most modern transmissions. The gear lubricants API-GL-2 to 6 are compounded with increasing amounts of anti-wear and EP additives. Beginning with API-GL-4 the lubricants are suitable for the higher pressures, speeds, and torque loads encountered in modern hypoid differentials. Accordingly, these special EP lubricants are often called hypoid oils. Each of the six types is available in the various viscosities listed earlier. Incorrect viscosity can cause serious damage, noisy operation, gear chatter, and leakage. It may also interfere with the proper shifting and synchronization of transmission gears.

Note: Discolouration or darkening of the gears due to EP lubricants is normal. Certain

---

[31]The flash point is the temperature at which the surface vapours of the oil ignite. The flash point of good motor oils is somewhere around 400°F, or 204°C. The burning point, i.e., the temperature at which the oil burns continuously, is usually above 500°F, or 260°C. The temperature is kept below these points, even in the cylinder, by adequate cooling.

[32]Pressure loadings of certain hypoid gears

(Fig. 15:10g) may be as high as 400,000 psi (2 756 000 kPa).

additives react with the metal to form a very thin protective layer against corrosion and wear. However, these agents can be harmful to non-ferrous worm gears, which are used on some imported cars. Limited slip differentials also require special lubricants with "friction modifiers" to prevent clutch plate chatter during turns. In all cases manufacturers' specifications are to be followed. Overfilling will cause foaming, abnormal pressures, and excessively high temperatures, as well as loss of lubricant. The mixing of brands should be prevented. Some EP lubricants have a fairly strong odour and they are usually black-brown in appearance.

Lubricating Greases

When it is necessary to hold a lubricant in certain areas without it running off, or where parts are inaccessible, grease is used. Grease is actually a lubricating oil to which certain highly adhesive thickening agents have been added. The thickening agents are called soaps and, depending on the operating requirements, they may consist of aluminum, barium, calcium (lime), lithium, or sodium compounds. These metallic soaps are oil-soluble rather than water-soluble, and they have a higher affinity for metals than do liquid lubricants.

Not only must a good-quality grease be a good lubricant; it must also have very high

Witco Chemical Canada

Gear Lubricants

adhesion, must not leak or drip, and must be resistant to impact loads, centrifugal throw-off, water, and oxidation. It must often withstand high temperatures and protect against corrosion; under very low temperatures it should not become stiff if channelling is to be avoided. It is also very important for the grease to have high mechanical stability; i.e., the constant kneading action of moving parts must not affect its quality. In addition, grease often helps to seal parts against the entry of dust, water, and even antifreeze.

NLGI grade numbers ranging from 0 to 6 were introduced by the *National Lubricating Grease Institute* to describe grease consistency (thickness). Automotive greases are usually in the grade 1 to grade 3 range (soft to medium consistency). Although the grades are in no way a measure of quality, it is obvious that a very soft, low-grade grease is more likely to leak than a harder grease. On the other hand, a stiffer, high-grade grease increases friction and undesirable channelling where rapid motion is involved, especially at low temperatures. A very peculiar but important quality of grease is its ability to form a thin film, which, like ice, changes to a liquid when placed under high pressure. Because this change, known as directional fluidity, occurs only in the direction of the motion, the grease does not cause leakage or centrifugal spin-off under normal operating conditions. This characteristic is particularly important in front wheel bearings. It is obvious that a particular type of lubricating grease designed for a specific application will possess certain qualities that will make it less ideal for other applications.

Chassis Grease is a relatively soft grease that can be applied through a grease fitting (Fig. 11:4) by means of a grease gun. It also has the ability to penetrate between tightly fitted parts. Because of the exposed position of many chassis components, chassis grease must resist the entry of water and dust. Special grades are available for extreme weather conditions.

ELI (Extended Lubrication Interval) Chassis Grease is a lubricant of very high quality used in specially sealed joints or bearings that require less frequent service. Excessive lubricating pressures will damage the seals and defeat the intended objectives.

EP Greases must be able to withstand extreme pressure and impact loads. They often

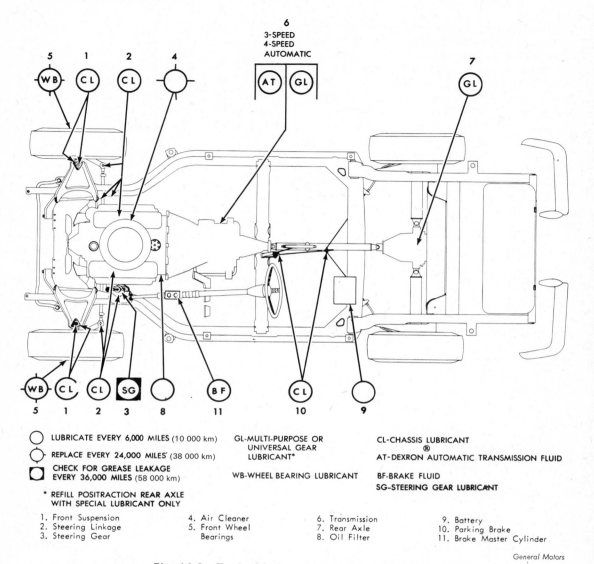

Fig. 11:3   *Typical Lubrication and Service Chart*

◯	LUBRICATE EVERY 6,000 MILES (10 000 km)
◗	REPLACE EVERY 24,000 MILES (38 000 km)
◻	CHECK FOR GREASE LEAKAGE EVERY 36,000 MILES (58 000 km)

* REFILL POSITRACTION REAR AXLE WITH SPECIAL LUBRICANT ONLY

GL-MULTI-PURPOSE OR UNIVERSAL GEAR LUBRICANT*

WB-WHEEL BEARING LUBRICANT

CL-CHASSIS LUBRICANT
AT-DEXRON® AUTOMATIC TRANSMISSION FLUID

BF-BRAKE FLUID
SG-STEERING GEAR LUBRICANT

1. Front Suspension
2. Steering Linkage
3. Steering Gear
4. Air Cleaner
5. Front Wheel Bearings
6. Transmission
7. Rear Axle
8. Oil Filter
9. Battery
10. Parking Brake
11. Brake Master Cylinder

General Motors

contain solid lubricants, such as graphite and molybdenum disulphide, which give some protection even if the grease itself should be displaced. (Molybdenum disulphide grease is often referred to as a "moly" grease.) These greases are used for ball joints, leaf springs, shaft splines, brake cables, universal joints, and the "fifth wheel" on tractor trailers. Some manufacturers specify EP grease for regular chassis lubrication.

Wheel Bearing Grease is a relatively thick and

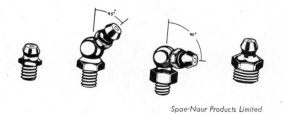

Spae-Naur Products Limited

Fig. 11:4   *The Most Common Types of Grease Fittings*

extremely adhesive type of grease. While most greases are fibrous in nature, certain wheel bearing greases are often visibly so when pulled apart. Some car manufacturers prohibit the use of so-called "long fibre" greases. Sodium, barium, or lithium soap greases are particularly popular because their high adhesion to metal prevents dry friction, leakage, and rusting. These greases also have a high dropping point, i.e., the temperature at which a grease liquefies. To cope with the increased wheel bearing temperatures of vehicles equipped with disc brakes, specially formulated lubricants such as aluminum complex soaps, with dropping temperatures of around 500°F, or 260°C, are used. Not only is a grease that is subjected to temperatures close to its dropping point likely to spin off under centrifugal forces, but it will oxidize as well. An oxidized grease tends to harden; it has a dry or dark appearance, and it may have a foul smell. Oxidation also causes the grease to decompose, lose its lubricity, and form certain corrosive acids. This is one reason why front wheel bearings should be thoroughly cleaned and relubricated every 25,000 miles (40 000 km) or thereabouts. It also prevents damage due to trapped abrasive particles and water.

Multi-purpose Grease is, under normal operating conditions, suitable as a general chassis lubricant and as a lubricant for some front wheel bearings.

Steering Gear Lubricants

Steering gear lubricants may range from a multi-purpose gear lubricant to an automatic transmission fluid for power steerings. Some manufacturers recommend special semi-liquid gear lubricants, while others recommend EP gear oils. As usual, manufacturers' specifications must be followed closely.

Special lubricants are available for speedometer cables, window regulators, door locks, brake cables, distributor cams, lubricating cups, mechanical fuel pumps, certain water pumps, limited slip differentials, rubber parts, and so on. Parts subjected to high temperatures, such as spark-plug threads (especially in aluminum heads) and heat riser valves, can be lubricated with suitable graphite compounds that do not turn into hard carbon deposits.

Lubrication

Fig. 11:3 shows a typical lubrication chart. The recommended lubrication intervals vary with different makes of automobiles and different operating conditions. In many cases the use of special seals and lubricants has greatly extended the intervals of chassis lubrication. With permanently sealed joints no servicing is required at all. Remember that the adhesive or "sticky" nature of oils and greases makes cleanliness all the more important. A dirty funnel, container, grease fitting, filler plug, or grease gun can cause excessive wear, and even failure of parts. Modern power assists, such as power steering, and the use of very effective noise insulation also tend to act as a "cover-up" for tight and dry parts. If the vehicle is not serviced regularly, these conditions will likely go undetected until serious damage has been done.

The Engine-lubrication System

Engines are lubricated in various ways. Oil may be mixed with the fuel, as it is on two-stroke cycle engines; it may be splashed onto parts; or it may be pressure-fed to the parts through small passages. Although modern automotive engines are all pressure-lubricated (Figs. 11:5 and 11:8), a number of parts are still lubricated

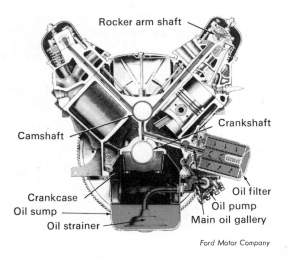

Ford Motor Company

Fig. 11:5 Pressure Lubrication of a V-8 Engine (cross-sectional view)

by splash, gravity flow, and oil mist.[33] The importance of the lubricant as a coolant should once again be pointed out in this connection.

The Oil Pan

The oil pan (Fig. 11:6. See also Fig. 5:21) provides a storage place for the motor oil. It also acts as a catch basin for the hot oil dripping back from the engine parts. To improve heat dissipation, it is made of either stamped sheet metal or ribbed cast aluminum. Built-in baffles and a deep sump stabilize the oil during acceleration, hill climbing, and sharp turns. The oil pan and crankcase are vented to improve cooling, remove vapours, and relieve blow-by pressure from the cylinders. (For more detail see Fig. 14:2.) The oil can be removed through a drain plug situated at the lowest point of the oil sump (Fig. 11:7). Sludge deposits and sediments should be flushed out while the oil is still hot and flowing freely. All standard engines have the wet-sump system described above, but some high-performance engines employ a dry-sump system. In the latter system the oil returning from the engine is pumped through an oil cooler into a separate oil reservoir and is then recirculated.

The Oil Intake and Strainer

As shown in Fig. 11:8, the oil enters the oil pump through the oil intake and strainer. The strainer is a fine wire-mesh screen that prevents the entry of large particles. There are two types of oil intakes: the floating type (Fig. 11:9) and the stationary type (Fig. 11:10). The floating type has the advantage of being able to adjust itself to the oil level, which prevents sludge and sediments from plugging or passing through the strainer.

The Oil Pump

The oil pump is either inside (Fig. 11:8) or outside the crankcase (Fig. 11:5) and draws the

---

[33]Some older engines had dippers attached to the connecting-rod bearing-caps. Part of the oil scooped up by the dippers was channelled to the crank journals and the remainder would splash against the other parts inside the engine. A similar system may be found in some lawn mower engines.

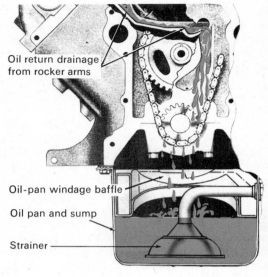

Oil return drainage from rocker arms

Oil-pan windage baffle

Oil pan and sump

Strainer

Ford Motor Company

Fig. 11:6   The Oil Pan—a Storage Tank, Catch Basin, and Cooling Place for the Motor Oil

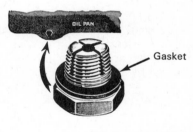

Gasket

Spae-Naur Products Limited

Fig. 11:7   Oversized Self-tapping Drain Plug to Repair Stripped Threads

lubricant through the oil intake. It maintains oil circulation throughout the engine lubrication system. The two most common types of oil pumps are the rotor type (Fig. 11:9) and the gear type (Fig. 11:10). While some oil pumps are driven by the crankshaft, most are geared to the camshaft.[34]

---

[34]At higher engine speeds the oil pump may recirculate the entire oil content almost four hundred times in one hour.

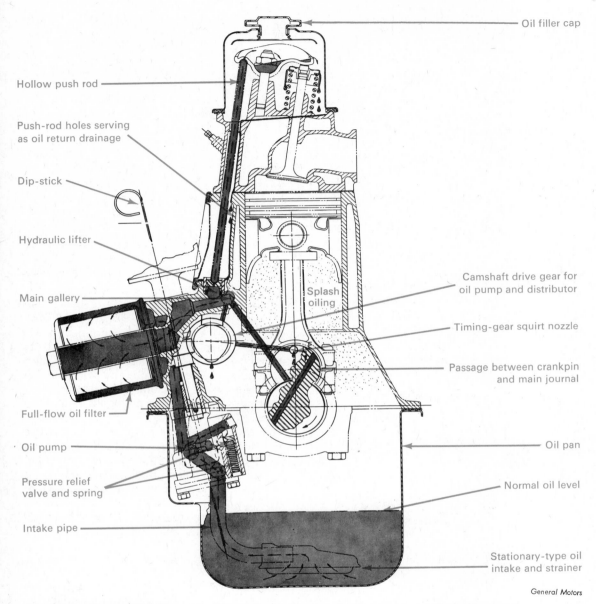

Oil filler cap

Hollow push rod

Push-rod holes serving
as oil return drainage

Dip-stick

Hydraulic lifter

Main gallery

Splash
oiling

Camshaft drive gear for
oil pump and distributor

Timing-gear squirt nozzle

Passage between crankpin
and main journal

Full-flow oil filter

Oil pump

Oil pan

Pressure relief
valve and spring

Normal oil level

Intake pipe

Stationary-type oil
intake and strainer

General Motors

Fig. 11:8 Typical Oil Flow in a Six-cylinder Engine. Note pressure relief valve in oil pump, main gallery above camshaft, and hollow push rod.

The Pressure Relief Valve

The pressure relief valve (Figs. 11:8, 11:9, and 11:10) ensures that the oil pressure does not exceed a predetermined level (40 to 70 psi, 275 to 482 kPa). If excess oil pressure were not relieved, it would, among other things, cause abnormal pump loads, oil consumption, and emission. It could also interfere with the operation of the hydraulic valve lifters. Oil pumps are designed to produce sufficient pressure and output under the worst conditions, such as low engine rpm and heavy loads. Further allowances must be made for hot, low-viscosity

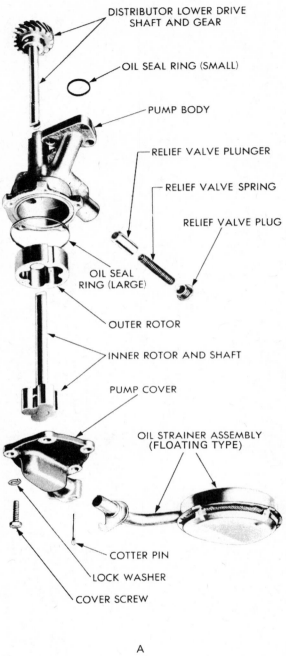

DISTRIBUTOR LOWER DRIVE
SHAFT AND GEAR

OIL SEAL RING (SMALL)

PUMP BODY

RELIEF VALVE PLUNGER

RELIEF VALVE SPRING

RELIEF VALVE PLUG

OIL SEAL
RING (LARGE)

OUTER ROTOR

INNER ROTOR AND SHAFT

PUMP COVER

OIL STRAINER ASSEMBLY
(FLOATING TYPE)

COTTER PIN

LOCK WASHER

COVER SCREW

A

Chrysler Canada Ltd.

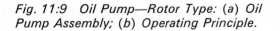

Fig. 11:9 Oil Pump—Rotor Type: (a) Oil Pump Assembly; (b) Operating Principle.

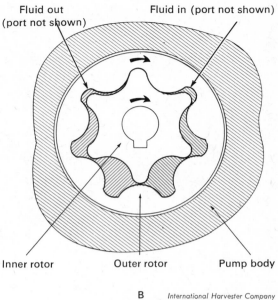

Fluid out
(port not shown)

Fluid in (port not shown)

Inner rotor   Outer rotor   Pump body

B   *International Harvester Company*

motor oil and for the normal wear of bearings.[35] Obviously, then, a new engine running at its maximum rpm would produce extremely high oil pressure if there were no provision made to relieve the excess pressure. This is particularly true if the engine oil is still cold and more viscous.

The oil pressure relief valve is basically a spring-loaded check valve calibrated in such a way that, when maximum pressure is reached, some of the oil is bled off, either into the pump inlet or into the oil pan. The pressure relief valve may be in the oil pump itself, between the pump and the oil filter, or even between the oil filter and the main oil gallery.

The Oil Filter

Oil filters (Figs. 11:5 and 11:8) prolong the life of the engine by removing trapped dust, deposits, carbon particles, and metallic pieces, all of which may get into the oil, causing scored bearings, excessive wear, and sticking hydraulic valve lifters.

There are two types of oil filters: the full-flow

[35]An increase of crankshaft bearing clearance from 0.0015″ to only 0.003″ (0.038 mm to 0.076 mm) due to wear causes the oil flow to increase by five times!

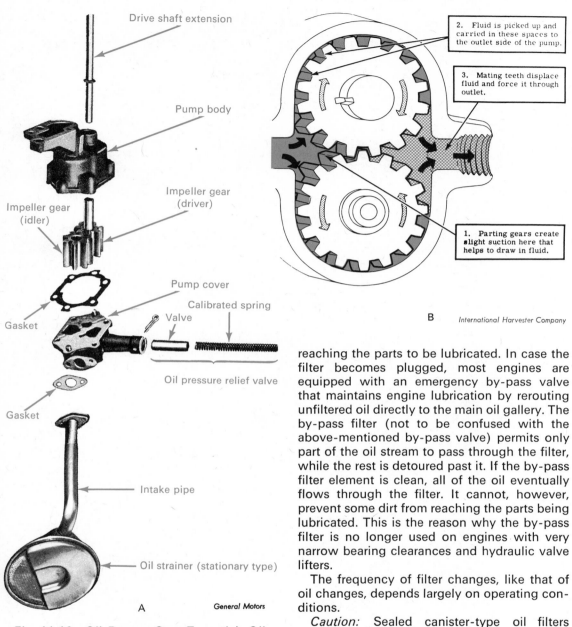

2. Fluid is picked up and carried in these spaces to the outlet side of the pump.

3. Mating teeth displace fluid and force it through outlet.

1. Parting gears create slight suction here that helps to draw in fluid.

B   *International Harvester Company*

Drive shaft extension

Pump body

Impeller gear (driver)

Impeller gear (idler)

Gasket

Pump cover

Calibrated spring

Valve

Gasket

Oil pressure relief valve

Intake pipe

Oil strainer (stationary type)

A   *General Motors*

Fig. 11:10 Oil Pump—Gear Type: (a) Oil Pump Assembly; (b) Operating Principle.

type and the by-pass type. The full-flow filter is used on most modern engines.

The names of these two filters explain how they work. "Full-flow" indicates that all the engine oil must flow through the filter before reaching the parts to be lubricated. In case the filter becomes plugged, most engines are equipped with an emergency by-pass valve that maintains engine lubrication by rerouting unfiltered oil directly to the main oil gallery. The by-pass filter (not to be confused with the above-mentioned by-pass valve) permits only part of the oil stream to pass through the filter, while the rest is detoured past it. If the by-pass filter element is clean, all of the oil eventually flows through the filter. It cannot, however, prevent some dirt from reaching the parts being lubricated. This is the reason why the by-pass filter is no longer used on engines with very narrow bearing clearances and hydraulic valve lifters.

The frequency of filter changes, like that of oil changes, depends largely on operating conditions.

Caution: Sealed canister-type oil filters should be tightened by hand; overtorquing causes leakage! Always lubricate the filter gasket before installation to prevent it from wrinkling. And remember that a new filter takes ½ to 1 quart of extra motor oil after it is installed. Where possible, the new filter should be filled with clean motor oil before installation, especially after an engine overhaul!

The Main Oil Gallery

The main oil gallery is connected to the pressure side of the oil pump, or to the outlet of the oil filter if one is used (Figs. 11:8 and 11:5). It could be considered the "main artery" of the engine lubrication system as it feeds various passages and secondary galleries leading to the bearings and other pressure-lubricated parts. The ends of the main gallery are sealed with removable plugs so that sludge can be removed during engine overhauls (Fig. 5:5C).

Pressure- and Splash-lubricated Parts

In most engine designs the main gallery is connected directly to the crankshaft main bearings. The oil flows from the "mains" to the connecting-rod bearings via small passageways that join the crankshaft main journals and the crankpins (Fig. 11:8). The lower end of the connecting rod is usually provided with a squirt hole that directs a jet of oil towards the cylinder walls (Fig. 11:11). On some V-8 engines the jets are directed into opposite cylinders.[36] Where a full-floating piston pin is employed, a long, narrow "rifle bore" may connect the lower and upper ends of the connecting rod. The pin holes in the piston are usually lubricated by oil passages in the piston bosses (Fig. 5:9). The oil throw-off from all of these parts lubricates the cylinder walls, the pistons, the oil pump drive gear, the camshaft eccentric, and other parts. The importance of oil to the proper sealing of the piston rings should be repeated here. The camshaft bearings receive oil either directly from an oil gallery or by branch passages from the main bearings (Figs. 11:5 and 11:8). The tappet guides and rocker arms are pressure-fed in similar fashion. In some cases, especially where hydraulic valve lifters are used, oil may reach the rocker arms via hollow push rods (tubular type, Fig. 11:8). The timing gears may be lubricated by a small squirt nozzle located between them or by drainage oil from other areas (Figs. 11:8 and 11:6). Engines equipped with hydraulic timing-chain tensioners use oil pressure to remove chain slack.

The remaining parts, such as the valve guides, the valve springs, the insides of the pistons, the

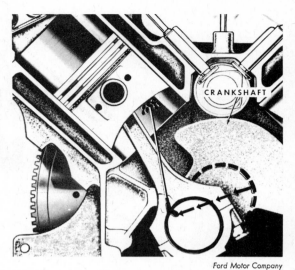

Ford Motor Company

Fig. 11:11   Connecting-rod Squirt Hole for Cylinder and Piston Lubrication

piston bosses, and any other exposed surfaces inside the engine, are supplied by oil drainage, splash, and mist (Fig. 11:8). In some areas the lubricant is used solely as a cooling and cleansing agent. Suitable drainage holes in the cylinder head, the lifter chamber, the timing-gear cavity, and the rear main bearing allow the hot oil to return to the oil pan for recirculation (Fig. 11:6). On "in-line" engines the push rod holes usually serve as the oil return (Fig.

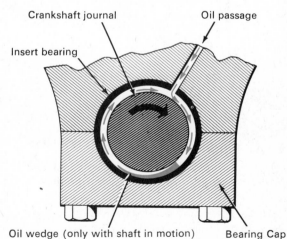

Crankshaft journal   Oil passage

Insert bearing

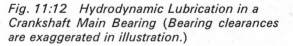

Oil wedge (only with shaft in motion)   Bearing Cap

Fig. 11:12   Hydrodynamic Lubrication in a Crankshaft Main Bearing (Bearing clearances are exaggerated in illustration.)

---

[36]The squirt holes may or may not face the major thrust side. Be sure to follow the manufacturer's instructions.

11:8). If the drainage holes become plugged, the likely result is oil leakage and consumption, as well as increased exhaust emission, indicated by blue or white smoke.

Hydrodynamic Lubrication

When an engine is shut off and the oil pump stops, the crankshaft and camshaft rest in their respective bearings. Only a very thin film of oil prevents metal-to-metal contact. With a good motor oil this "boundary layer" will stay put for days. When the engine is restarted and the oil pressure builds up, the shafts are raised from the boundary layer and "thick-film" lubrication measuring 0.0001" (0.0025 mm) or more is established. As the shafts rotate, adhesion causes the oil nearest the shaft to rotate with it, while the oil layer attached to the bearing shell remains more or less stationary. The result is that an oil wedge is formed, which causes the shafts to skim or "hydroplane" over the oil like a water ski. Thus the ability of the lubricant to re-

duce friction and to carry heavy loads is greatly increased. This important principle is known as hydrodynamic lubrication (Fig. 11:12).

Bearing Eccentricity

Modern connecting-rod insert bearings are usually of a slightly eccentric design; i.e., the insert is thinner close to the parting line (Fig. 11:13). The reason for this is that the large bearing bore of the connecting rod is momentarily elongated (i.e., stretched slightly out of roundness) by the tremendous inertia forces when the piston approaches TDC. Since some new bearing designs may leave as little as 0.0001", or 0.0025 mm, for oil clearance, even the slightest distortion would cause scoring at the parting line, or the bearing might even seize. The extra-thick oil pockets at the parting line provided by the eccentric design prevent this. The additional clearance is otherwise of little consequence since the major firing loads are not absorbed in this area.

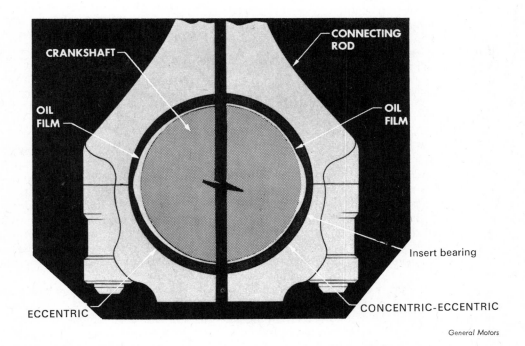

General Motors

Fig. 11:13   Two Types of Bearing Inserts to Provide Additional Side Clearance: (left side) Eccentric Design; (right side) Concentric-eccentric Design.

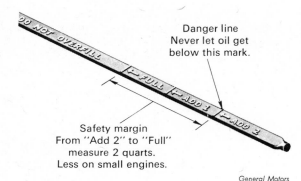

Danger line
Never let oil get
below this mark.

Safety margin
From "Add 2" to "Full"
measure 2 quarts.
Less on small engines.

General Motors

Fig. 11:14   Typical Dip-stick Markings

The Dip-stick

The dip-stick (Fig. 11:14) is provided with at least two markings: the "add" line and the "full" line. The level must always be checked with the engine stopped. Since new oil filters will take up as much as one quart of oil, it is necessary, after a filter change, to run the engine at medium rpm for roughly one minute before the final dip-stick check is made. This procedure will also determine whether there are any leaks in the filter. A replacement dip-stick must match the original one exactly.

Oil Pressure Gauges and Warning Lights

The mechanical oil pressure gauge is almost identical with the mechanical temperature gauge already described on pages 124-5. Their open-ended capillary tube is connected directly to the main oil gallery.

An electrical oil pressure gauge is similar to an electrical temperature gauge (Fig. 10:13) except that the sending unit contains a device which, as pressure changes, varies the current flow through the dash gauge to which it is connected. Thus, the dash gauge electrically registers the oil pressure in the engine.

Instead of a pressure gauge, most cars are equipped with a coloured, low-pressure warning light. The light is connected to a sending unit that contains a diaphragm, a calibrated spring, and a set of breaker points. When the oil pressure reaches a predetermined value, the switch is opened by the diaphragm, and the warning light goes out. Some of these switches are set to open at only 3 psi, or 21 kPa.

Needless to say, the warning light is much less effective than a pressure gauge in monitoring engine conditions. For example, if the light should come on while the engine is operating at medium to high rpm, serious damage may have already occurred.

RECOMMENDED ASSIGNMENTS

1. List seven important functions of motor oil.
2. Define the terms "adhesion" and "cohesion".
3. Explain the difference between "high viscosity" and "high-viscosity index".
4. What is the difference between an SAE 30 and an SAE 10W-30 motor oil?
5. Explain the purpose of the following additives: detergents, dispersants, inhibitors, V.I. improvers, and pour point depressants.
6. Why is a low flash point undesirable?
7. Name the factors that determine the frequency of oil changes.
8. What SAE service designation would you recommend for an ambulance driven in both high-speed and stop-and-go traffic?
9. List the three important points to be observed when checking the ATF level.
10. (a) What causes channelling? (b) What are its effects? (c) How can it be prevented?
11. Explain the term "hypoid oil".
12. What are the characteristics of a good-quality grease?
13. Describe six different types of grease and their typical applications.
14. Give two reasons why a grease should not operate close to its dropping point.
15. Why is cleanliness of extreme importance when dealing with lubricants?
16. Explain the major purposes of the following: (a) the oil pan, (b) the oil intake and strainer (two types), (c) the oil pump, (d) the pressure relief valve, (e) the oil filter (two types), and (f) the main oil gallery.
17. What is the purpose of crankcase ventilation?
18. Prepare a schematic diagram of a complete engine lubrication system. Label all the parts and show the direction of the oil flow by arrows. Use colour to indicate the lubricant.

19. List under two separate headings the engine parts lubricated by oil pressure and by splash or mist.
20. What is hydrodynamic lubrication?
21. What is the difference between thick-film lubrication and boundary film lubrication?
22. Explain the purpose of bearing eccentricity.
23. Describe the proper method of checking the oil level after changing the motor oil and filter.
24. (a) Explain three methods of monitoring oil pressure at the instrument panel. (b) Why is one of these methods not too reliable?

TROUBLE-SHOOTING

There are at least two solutions to each problem.
1. A relatively new engine is hard to turn over in cold weather, even though the starter and the battery are in good condition.
2. A motorist has the motor oil changed by a reputable garage. When he checks the oil level on the same day after a long drive, he is surprised that the oil looks as dark as the old oil.
3. The front wheel bearings of a vehicle are repacked with the recommended grease and the seal is replaced. The customer returns the same day with leaking front wheel hubs.
4. A motorist lubricates the distributor cam. Half an hour later the engine begins to misfire, and finally it stops altogether.
5. The oil pressure warning light flickers in fast turns.
6. The indicator arm of the oil pressure gauge goes clearly beyond the normal pressure range.
7. A motorist is surprised that the oil level in the engine actually increased during the last 1,000 miles.

SOME SUGGESTED ADDITIONAL READING

Fuels and Lubricants, Second Edition, Imperial Oil Ltd., 111 St. Clair Avenue West, Toronto M5W 1K3.

"Pride of Performance" . . . , Pennsylvania Grade Crude Oil Association, Oil City, Pennsylvania.

12

The
Electrical System

One of the great appeals of automotive mechanics is that it combines many different interesting fields. The electrical system is a typical example. A working understanding of the basic principles involved is essential for any well-trained mechanic. In the majority of cases where a motorist seeks his service, the mechanic must apply some of these principles, whether it be in the matter of a routine tune-up, a safety check, or a service call, or in the actual repair of some electrical circuit or device.

Magnetism

Magnetism is a peculiar force of attraction first observed centuries ago in connection with a certain iron ore known as magnetite. The ability of the mineral to serve as a compass led to the name "leading stone" or "lodestone". While magnetism can penetrate any material known, only iron, cobalt, nickel, or alloys of these materials are normally attracted by magnetism.

The magnetic forces are strongest at the ends or "poles" of a magnet. The end seeking the geographic north pole, which, magnetically speaking, is really a south pole, is labelled the *N-pole*; similarly, the end seeking the geographic south pole is labelled the *S-pole*. The molecular theory of magnetism holds that each of the vast number of molecules that make up a magnet is itself a tiny magnet, and each has a north pole and a south pole. While the poles are arranged in a haphazard way in the unmagnetized state, they align themselves in an organized way when exposed to a magnetic field. As shown in Fig. 12:1, the arrangement of north and south poles is very similar to a group of flashlight batteries with their negative and positive poles connected in series. In both cases there is a cumulative effect. The polarity of the magnetic field can be determined with an ordinary field compass. While the magnetic field of force itself is invisible, the lines in Fig. 12:2 illustrate its pattern. The law of magnetic poles states that unlike magnetic poles attract each other, while like poles repel each other.

There are three basic types of magnets. *Natural magnets* are naturally occurring magnetic minerals which have little practical use. While they are in a sense also *permanent magnets*, this term is usually applied to much stronger man-made magnets of iron alloys containing silicon, nickel, cobalt, and aluminum. Once magnetized (usually electrically), permanent magnets stay magnetized unless they are demagnetized by high temperatures, hammering, or opposing magnetic forces. Permanent magnets are used in speedometer heads, some oil drain plugs (to collect abrasive metal shavings), magneto-type ignition systems, pick-up tools, and electrical meters. *Electromagnets* (Fig. 12:23) require an electric coil and current for magnetization. The core material is often made of soft iron to allow both quick magnetization and fast demagnetization when the current travelling through the coil is turned on and off.

What Is Electricity?

No one knows the complete answer to this question. However, we can safely say that it is a form of energy. In its normal state, the atom, which is the basic "building stone" of all matter, is electrically neutral. The positively charged *protons* in its core, or *nucleus*, balance an equal number of negatively charged *elec-*

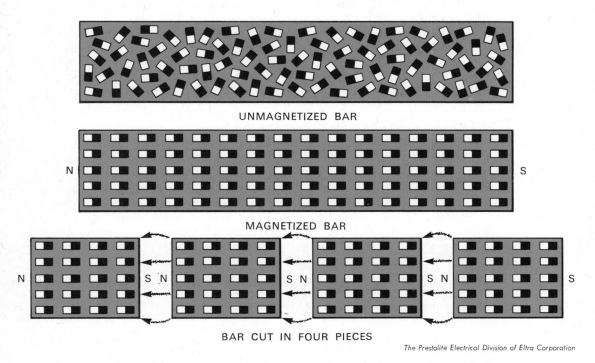

UNMAGNETIZED BAR

MAGNETIZED BAR

BAR CUT IN FOUR PIECES

The Prestolite Electrical Division of Eltra Corporation

Fig. 12:1   An Experiment Demonstrating the Molecular Theory of Magnetism. Note the attraction of unlike magnetic poles.

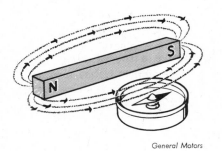

General Motors

Fig. 12:2   Pattern of Magnetic Field of Force

trons surrounding it (Fig. 12:3). If one electron is removed, however, it causes an imbalance, and the system is no longer neutral, for there would be one positive proton without its negative "partner". This gives the whole atom a positive charge. Such an atom is called a *positive ion*. Conversely, if an electron is added to a previously neutral atom, a negative charge is obtained, resulting in a *negative ion*. Scientists believe that the force of attraction that

exists between the positive protons and the negative electrons is the source of electrical energy. However, for any useful energy to be obtained, the number of electrons has to be astronomical. It also follows that a negatively charged object has a surplus of electrons, and a positively charged object has a deficit of electrons.

Static Electricity

Static electricity consists of an electrical charge that remains on an object and does not flow. Common examples of static electricity are the electrical charges you pick up when you comb your hair or walk over carpets. A commercial application of this principle is the electric capacitor, or condenser (page 178). Static electricity can be described in terms of an object having either a surplus or a deficit of electrons.

Electrical Current

Electrical current is the most common form of electricity. It involves the flow of electrons

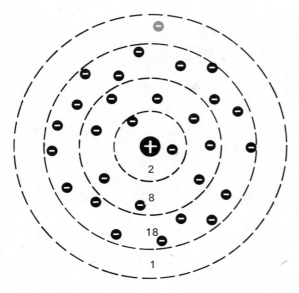

Positively charged nucleus contains 29 positive protons and other neutral particles (neutrons)

Fig. 12:3 Representation of an Electrically Neutral Copper Atom. The indicated number of electrons surrounding the positive nucleus may be anywhere within the dotted regions or "boundary surfaces". Contrary to common belief, the electrons hover, rather than orbit, around the nucleus.

through a conductor (Fig. 12:4). While an electrical current cannot be seen, sparks and electrical light are visible signs that electrons have, in fact, been set in motion.

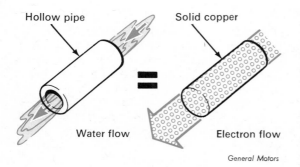

Hollow pipe   Solid copper

Water flow   Electron flow

General Motors

Fig. 12:4 Comparison of Water Flow in a Pipe and Electron Flow in an Electrical Conductor

Direct Current

Direct current, or simply D.C., means that the current flows in one direction only. The electron theory, as applied in this text, holds that the electrical current flows from negative to positive.

Alternating Current

Alternating current, or simply A.C., is a current that "alternates", or changes its direction; that is, the electrons are constantly pushed back and forth in the electrical circuit. The A.C. delivered to your home alternates its polarity or swings back and forth, sixty times a second; hence the term *60 cycles per second*.

Electrical Terms and Units

The number of electrons moving through a given circuit is so vast that it is impractical to express a charge or a current in numbers of electrons. A more convenient means had to be devised for the purpose of exact measurements. While many experts reject the idea of comparing current flow to the flow of water, we have used this comparison for the purpose of illustration and to explain the electrical units given below (Fig. 12:4). However, you will see later that important differences do exist.

Amperage measures the amount of current, i.e., the number of electrons flowing through an electric circuit in a given time. Amperage is roughly equivalent to the amount of liquid moving through a pipe. The *ampere* is an arbitrarily chosen amount of current.

Voltage or *Electromotive Force (EMF)* or *Potential* is electrical "pressure", i.e., the moving force of electrons. Voltage is similar to pressure in a water-pipe. One *volt* is the EMF required to produce a current of one ampere through a conductor with a resistance of one ohm (see following definition).

Resistance is measured in *ohms* and could be compared to the internal friction of a pipe restricting the flow of a liquid. A resistance of 1Ω (one ohm) will permit a current flow of one ampere in an electrical circuit if the applied voltage is one volt.

Capacitance is the ability of certain devices such as *capacitors* (also known as *condensers*) to store an electric charge. The *microfarad*

(μF) is the most common unit used to measure capacitance.

Wattage is a measure of electrical power, i.e., the rate at which electrical work is being done. For example, 746 watts = 1 horsepower. Wattage equals volts $\times$ amperes. A headlight connected to a 12-volt battery drawing 4 amperes would be rated at 48 watts because $12 \times 4 = 48$.

Ohm's Law

While our understanding of electrical current is very limited, the rules that govern its behaviour are well established. For the electrician and automotive mechanic Ohm's Law is the most important of these rules.

It states that in an electric circuit the amperage (amount of current) varies directly as the voltage (electrical pressure) and inversely as the resistance. (Ohm's law can also be stated as "Voltage is equal to amperage times resistance.") This is really what one would reasonably expect. For example, the amount of water flowing in a pipe varies directly with the pressure. On the other hand, any restrictions in the pipe reduce that flow. Applied to an electric current, it simply means that the higher the voltage and the lower the resistance, the more current will flow. Ohm's Law is usually expressed by the following formula:

$$\text{Amperage} = \frac{\text{Voltage}}{\text{Resistance}}$$

$$I = \frac{V}{R}$$

or

$$V = I \times R$$

or

$$R = \frac{V}{I}$$

The advantage of these formulas is that, if only two values are known, the third can be easily calculated. If, for example, the voltage is 12 and the amperage is 2, the resistance must be 6 ohms, because $R = \dfrac{12 \text{ volts}}{2 \text{ amperes}}$.

Conductors

Electrical conductors are materials that permit the flow of an electrical current. The conductivity of an electrical conductor depends primarily on the type of material, the size and length of the conductor, and its temperature. Some common electrical conductors are silver, copper, aluminum, zinc, brass, platinum, iron, steel, nickel, tungsten, and lead. Liquids that conduct an electric current, such as the sulphuric acid solution employed in automotive storage batteries, are called *electrolytes*. Copper is used in automotive wiring because it is one of the best conductors known. The reason for this lies in the arrangement of its twenty-nine electrons (Fig. 12:3). Apparently twenty-eight of these electrons shield the nucleus of the copper atom in such a way as to prevent the last and twenty-ninth electron from joining them. It is this single electron that makes copper an ideal conductor, since the flow of current appears to be nothing more than the movement of these "free" electrons being "pushed" from one atom to the next.

Insulators

Insulators, also called *dielectrics* and *nonconductors*, are materials that resist the flow of electrical current because their atomic structure does not have any "free" electrons to be "pushed around". The most common automotive insulators are rubber, cotton, fibre, mica, glass, plastics, nylon, fibreglass, bakelite, certain varnishes and lacquers, treated paper and wood, porcelain, and aluminum oxide. All modern spark-plug insulators are made from aluminum oxide, a material that, because of its white appearance, is often mistaken for porcelain. Note that while metals are good conductors, their oxides, commonly referred to as corrosion or rust, are extremely good insulators. Many "mysterious" electrical failures are caused by some oxide formation between wire and terminal connections, for example, the black, white, and even turquoise oxide deposits on some badly serviced car batteries.

Electrical Wires and Terminals

Since the gauge and the length of the wire largely determine the resistance of a conductor, and thereby the amount of current that can be

6-Volt System		12-Volt System		Total Length of Cable in Circuit from Battery to Most Distant Lamp									
Amperes (approx.)	Candle Power	Amperes (approx.)	Candle Power	2.5 Feet	5 Feet	10 Feet	20 Feet	30 Feet	40 Feet	50 Feet	60 Feet	80 Feet	100 Feet
				Gauge	Gauge	Gauge	Gauge	Gauge	Gauge	Gauge	Gauge	Gauge	Gauge
0.5	3	1.0	6	20	20	20	20	20	20	20	20	20	18
0.75	5	1.5	10	20	20	20	20	20	20	20	20	18	18
1.0	8	2	16	20	20	20	20	20	20	18	18	16	16
1.5	12	3	24	20	20	20	20	20	18	18	16	16	14
2.0	15	4	30	20	20	18	20	18	16	16	16	14	12
2.5	20	5	40	20	20	18	18	18	16	14	14	12	12
3.0	25	6	50	20	20	18	18	16	16	14	14	12	12
3.5	30	7	60	20	20	18	18	16	14	14	12	12	10
4.0	35	8	70	20	20	16	16	16	14	12	12	10	10
5.0	40	10	80	20	18	16	16	14	12	12	12	10	10
5.5	45	11	90	20	20	18	16	14	12	12	10	10	8
6.0	50	12	100	20	20	18	16	14	12	12	10	10	8
7.5	60	15	120	20	20	18	14	12	12	10	10	8	8
9.0	70	18	140	20	20	16	14	12	10	10	8	8	8
10	80	20	160	20	18	16	12	12	10	10	8	8	6
11	90	22	180	20	18	16	12	10	10	8	8	8	6
12	100	24	200	20	18	16	12	10	10	8	8	6	6
18		36		20	16	14	10	8	8	8	6	6	4
25		50		18	16	12	10	8	6	6	4	4	2
50		100		14	12	10	6	4	4	2	2	1	0
75		150		14	10	8	4	2	2	1	0	00	000
100		200		12	8	6	4	2	1	0	00	000	0000

General Motors

Fig. 12.5 How to Select the Correct Wire Gauge

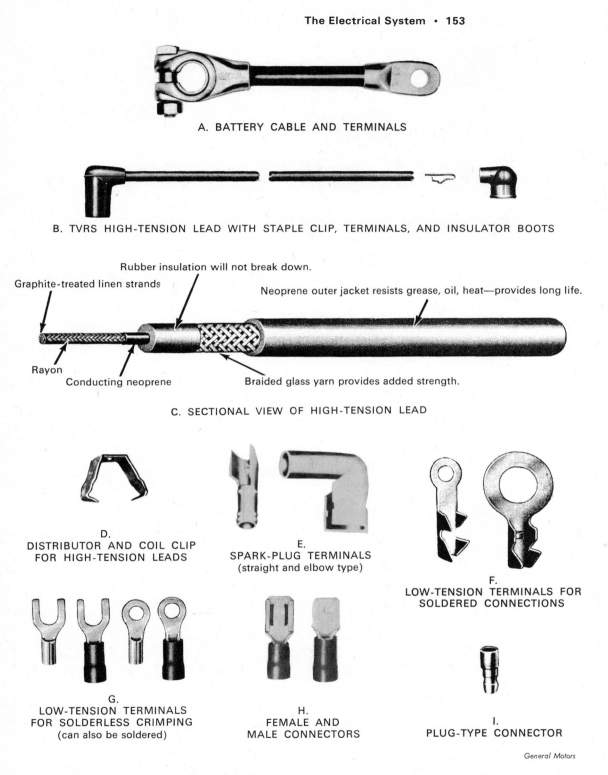

A. BATTERY CABLE AND TERMINALS

B. TVRS HIGH-TENSION LEAD WITH STAPLE CLIP, TERMINALS, AND INSULATOR BOOTS

Rubber insulation will not break down.

Graphite-treated linen strands

Neoprene outer jacket resists grease, oil, heat—provides long life.

Rayon

Conducting neoprene

Braided glass yarn provides added strength.

C. SECTIONAL VIEW OF HIGH-TENSION LEAD

D.
DISTRIBUTOR AND COIL CLIP
FOR HIGH-TENSION LEADS

E.
SPARK-PLUG TERMINALS
(straight and elbow type)

F.
LOW-TENSION TERMINALS FOR
SOLDERED CONNECTIONS

G.
LOW-TENSION TERMINALS
FOR SOLDERLESS CRIMPING
(can also be soldered)

H.
FEMALE AND
MALE CONNECTORS

I.
PLUG-TYPE CONNECTOR

General Motors

Fig. 12:6   *Some Common Automotive Terminals, Connectors, Insulators, and Conductors*

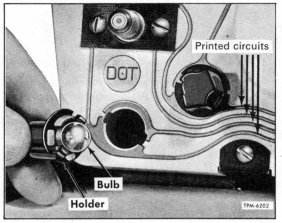

Printed circuits

Bulb

Holder

TPM-6202

General Motors

Fig. 12:7 Rear Side of a Dash Panel with Printed Circuits

recommended will cause overheating, fires, and unsatisfactory performance of the electrical units connected to the conductor. For better flexibility most external automotive conductors are of the stranded type. (Those used inside generators, electric motors, coils, etc., are not.)

A conductor is only as good as its connection. Fig. 12:6 shows some common automotive terminals and connectors. So-called solderless terminals require that a special pair of pliers be used for installation. Electrical wires may also be secured by a terminal screw or by soldering.

In a *printed circuit* (Fig. 12:7) a conductive material "printed" or bonded onto some insulated material (ceramic or plastic) replaces the wiring used in conventional circuits. Printed circuits are used in some instrument panels, electronic devices, and radios.

carried safely, care must be taken when choosing the correct type of wire for a given circuit. (Similar rules apply when selecting the size and the length of water-pipes.) The chart in Fig. 12:5 will help you to determine these factors. The use of wire gauges smaller than those

Fuses, Circuit Breakers, and Fusible Links

Fuses

Fuses (Fig. 12:8) are electrical "safety valves". When there is an excessive flow of current,

Fuse caps
(copper or brass, nickel- or cadmium-plated)

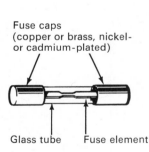

Glass tube   Fuse element

Fig. 12:8 Parts of a Fuse

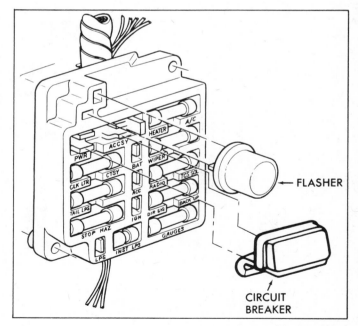

FLASHER

CIRCUIT BREAKER

General Motors

Fig. 12:9 Automotive Fuse Panel

such as that caused by a short or an overload, the fuse simply burns out, or "blows", before any serious damage is done to the devices connected to the circuit. This also prevents fires due to sparks or overheated conductors. Obviously the cause of the problem must be rectified before a new fuse can be installed. It is very important that the replacement fuse have the proper rating. For instance, if a 14A fuse is installed where a 9A fuse is specified, adequate protection is lost. Automotive fuses usually have a 10 per cent overload capacity; they blow in less than one hour under a 35 per cent overload, and in less than 30 seconds with a 50 per cent overload.

Circuit Breakers

Circuit breakers (Fig. 12:9) either reset themselves or they must be reset manually after they have been "tripped" by an overload. In automotive circuit breakers, such as those used in most headlight circuits, a thermostatically controlled set of breaker points opens if the current and thus the temperature, exceeds certain limits. This causes the current flow to stop; the temperature then drops, and the points close again. The cycle continues until either the overload ceases or the current is shut off. Circuit breakers are also employed where the improper operation of such accessories as

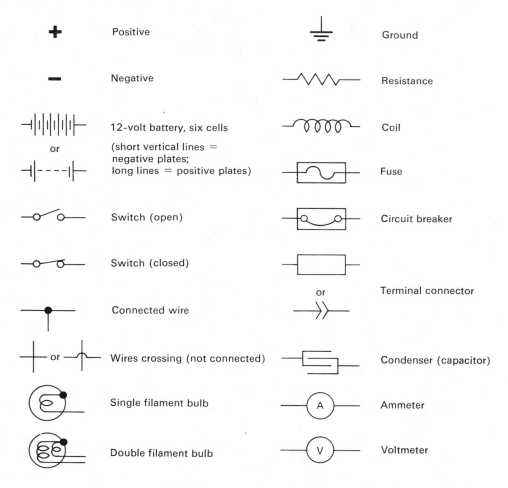

Fig. 12:10 Common Electrical Symbols

cigarette lighters and power windows may cause temporary overloads.

Fusible Links

Fusible links look like ordinary electric wires except that they contain a special conductor that burns out under an overload. Fusible links are often used to protect major wire harnesses or charging circuits. The dense white smoke and the smell of a burned-out fusible link serve as effective warning signals.

Electrical Symbols

Electrical symbols, as shown in Fig. 12:10, greatly simplify the drawing of schematic diagrams. You should be familiar with them.

Electric Circuits

An electric circuit includes the path of an electric current through the source, the switch that controls the circuit, the conductors, and the electrical devices connected to them. In an automobile the source may be either the storage battery or the generator.

Most automotive circuits are negative ground-return circuits. This means that the current travels from the negative side of the battery or the generator directly to *ground*, i.e., to the chassis, the body, the engine, and other parts connected to the battery. From here the current flows through such electrical devices as the starter motor and the lights, and then returns to the positive terminal of the battery or the generator via a switch and an insulated conductor.

Note: Most automotive electrical systems have negative ground. Some imported cars and older domestic models may have positive ground.

A *Series Circuit* exists when two or more electrical units are so connected that the same current flows through all of them without an alternate path. It follows that, if the current is interrupted by any unit connected in series, the current flow will stop in all parts of the circuit. In a circuit such as the one shown in Fig. 12:11 this could be caused by an open switch, a burned-out filament, a loose, broken, or disconnected conductor, or a failure in the source itself. While the current flow (amperage) is the same in all parts of a series circuit, the voltage is divided up among the units connected to it (Figs. 12:11 and 12:81).

A *Parallel Circuit* (Fig. 12:12) exists when two or more electrical units are connected to the source in such a way that more than one path is provided for the flow of the current. The voltage applied to all units connected in a parallel circuit is equal to that of the source. The sum of the currents (amperage) in the branches of the circuit is equal to the current flowing through the source.

A *Shunt Circuit* is also a parallel circuit. The term usually applies to generators, electric motors, regulators, and electrical meters.

A *Series-Parallel Circuit* is a combination of series and parallel circuits.

An *Open Circuit* is a circuit that is broken or incomplete, so that the flow of the current is interrupted. The circuit may be open because of a severed conductor, a blown fuse, or a loose connection, or simply because a switch is left open.

A *Closed Circuit* is a circuit that is complete, permitting the current to flow (Figs. 12:11 and 12:12).

An *"Unintentional" Ground* is a grounded connection caused by a badly insulated wire touching the metal of some part of the frame or a body panel (Fig. 12:13).

A *Short Circuit* occurs when the current follows a route shorter than that of the intended

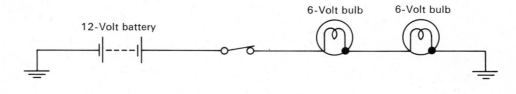

Fig. 12:11   Series Circuit (closed)

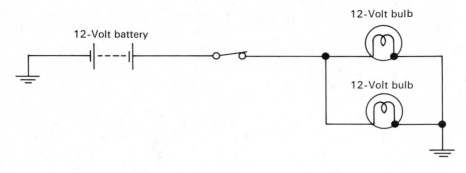

Fig. 12:12   Parallel Circuit (closed)

circuit. For example, in Fig. 12:13 two badly insulated wire loops allow the current to take a shorter path back to the source. In this sense, most grounds are also shorts. If, however, a horn is controlled by a switch connected to its grounded side rather than to its "positive" side, a bare wire touching another grounded part could cause the horn to continue sounding. This is a case of an unintentional ground and not of a short circuit.

A *Dead Short* occurs when the current returns directly to the source without meeting any resistance other than that of some connecting conductor. A poorly insulated, positive battery cable touching the body or the frame could cause such a short. Dead shorts can lead to serious injury, sparks, fires, explosions, and damaged parts. The grounded battery cable should be removed before undertaking electrical repairs.

The Battery

The lead-acid storage battery (Fig. 12:14) is an electrochemical device that converts chemical energy stored in its cells into electrical energy, and electrical energy back into chemical energy, depending on whether the battery is discharged or charged. Its main purpose is to provide a source of current when the engine is not running, for such devices as the starter motor, the ignition system, the lights, the radio, and other electrical accessories. It also helps to balance the charging circuit as electrical load conditions fluctuate.

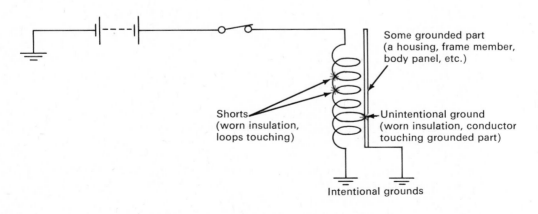

Fig. 12:13   Examples of Shorts and Unintentional Grounds

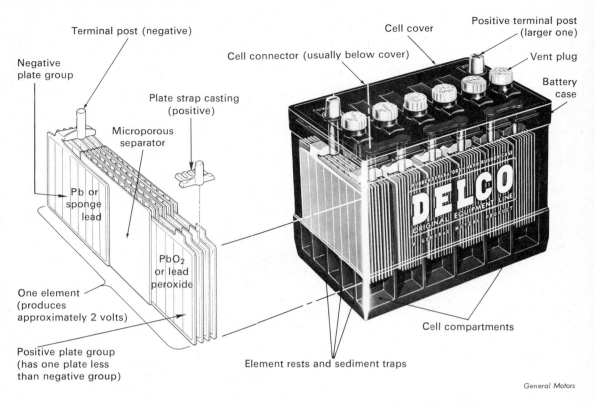

Terminal post (negative)

Negative plate group

Plate strap casting (positive)

Microporous separator

Pb or sponge lead

PbO₂ or lead peroxide

One element (produces approximately 2 volts)

Positive plate group (has one plate less than negative group)

Cell cover

Cell connector (usually below cover)

Positive terminal post (larger one)

Vent plug

Battery case

DELCO
ORIGINAL EQUIPMENT LINE

Cell compartments

Element rests and sediment traps

General Motors

Fig. 12:14 Parts of an Automotive Storage Battery (12 volts)

Battery Construction

The battery case is usually a one-piece, acid-proof moulding of hard rubber or plastic. The case is divided into several cell compartments, each with plate or element rests at the bottom. The element rests also form sediment traps that prevent shorting between the plates due to plate fall-out. Since each cell normally produces slightly over two volts, modern 12-volt car batteries have six cells connected in series. A number of alternating negative and positive plates, separated by insulators, form a battery element. In each element there is one more negative plate than there are positive plates. Immersed in the electrolyte of the battery compartments, the elements make up the individual cells. The positive and negative plates are held together in two separate groups by plate straps. This arrangement increases the amount of active chemical material within a relatively small area, and thus the capacity or output of the battery. The cells in turn are connected to one another in series by cell connectors. The two end posts, called the *battery terminal posts*, protrude through the sealed cell cover. The battery cables are fastened to the tapered terminal posts with special clamp-type connectors. In some cases the cables are connected to screw-type terminals that are mounted on the side of the battery case.

The polarity of the battery posts or terminals is indicated by lettering or by a + and a − symbol. It should also be noted that the positive terminal is 1/16″ (1.6 mm) larger in diameter than the negative terminal.

Each cell has a vent plug that acts as an escape hole for gases and also as a filler plug. The electrolyte level should be 1/4″ to 1/2″ (6 mm to 12 mm) above the separators, or at the point fixed by some type of level indicator. To maintain this level, distilled water or clean water with

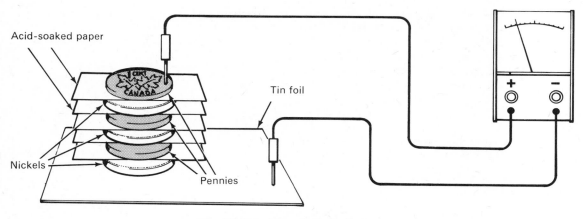

Fig. 12:15   Simple Coin Battery

low mineral content is added when necessary.[37] Some storage batteries are completely sealed, and therefore require no topping up.

The electrolyte is a liquid conductor of current and consists of a solution of water (H_2O) and sulphuric acid (H_2SO_4). If the battery is fully charged, it contains approximately 36 per cent sulphuric acid by weight and about 25 per cent by volume. This corresponds to a specific gravity of 1.270 measured at 80°F, or 27°C; i.e., the electrolyte is 1.270 times heavier than an equal amount of pure water at the same temperature.

Operating Principles of a Storage Battery

Let us consider the simple experiment shown in Fig. 12:15. A strip of shim stock or tin foil is placed on a table. A copper penny and a nickel coin, separated by a piece of thin paper soaked with battery acid, is then placed upon it. (Any acid, even grape juice or saliva, will do.) Thus a single battery cell in its most basic form is created; i.e., it includes one positive plate and one negative plate of dissimilar metals, a porous separator, and some electrolyte. Best results are obtained if several such coin cells, with paper separators between each coin, are stacked in series. If you begin with a copper

penny, you should end with a nickel. When the test leads of a low-reading voltmeter (0 to 1 Volt) are connected to the metal strip and the last coin, the meter will register a flow of current. Close examination will show that:

1. The chemical reaction involved causes a surplus of electrons at the negative terminal, while creating a deficit of electrons at the positive terminal.
2. The reaction requires two dissimilar metals and an electrolyte.
3. The voltage increases with the number of plates connected in series.
4. The more cells connected in series, the higher the voltage is.
5. The more cells connected in parallel, the higher the amperage is.
6. The amperage also increases with the size of the plates and the weight of the active material.
7. If the cell is fully discharged, there would be an equal electron charge at both end terminals.
8. The process stops when the acid is used up and mostly water remains in the separators.
9. If the current flow is reversed by means of a D.C. generator, i.e., by "pumping" the electrons back to the negative terminal, the chemical reaction can also be reversed, thus recharging the battery.

The same general principles apply to the lead-acid storage battery. When the battery is fully charged, the active material of the positive plates is lead peroxide (PbO_2), which is brown in colour (Fig. 12:14). The compound is made porous so that, by allowing the sulphuric acid

---

[37]Approximately 1-2 fluid ounces, i.e., one or two tablespoons of water per month or every 1,000 miles (1600 km). If water consumption is higher, the battery is either overcharged or gets too hot.

(H_2SO_4) of the electrolyte to penetrate very deeply, more of the material participates in the reaction. This is important if the battery is to supply a heavy current over long periods without any appreciable drop in voltage. The negative plate contains gray, spongy lead (Pb). The two active materials are held firmly in place by lead-antimony grids. These grids also serve as conductors, connecting the active material to the cell straps and terminals. The separators are made of some such permeable dielectric (insulator) as cellulose, glass fibre, microporous rubber, or plastic.

When the battery discharges (Fig. 12:16), the sulphuric acid reacts with the originally dissimilar negative and positive plates and gradually turns *both* into lead sulphate. As a result the electrolyte is weakened; i.e., the acid concentration of the solution is diluted and mostly water is left behind. (Since water is lighter than sulphuric acid, a very convenient means is provided of checking whether or not a battery is charged.) Therefore, when the battery is discharged, the specific gravity decreases, and when the battery is charged, the specific gravity increases. In the latter case the direct current produced by the charging circuit flows through the battery and the electrolyte in the opposite direction, thus reversing the reaction. In the process the sulphate (SO_4^{-2}), which reacted with the plates during discharge, is once again released into the electrolyte, and the battery is restored to its charged condition. This means that the positive plates revert to lead peroxide, the negative plates revert to spongy lead, and the electrolyte concentration increases to normal strength.

It is very important that the battery, once activated, remain fully charged. A discharged battery deteriorates more quickly, and the weakened electrolyte will freeze in cold weather, causing cracked plates and battery cases. Furthermore, battery output is very sensitive to temperature changes. For example, a drop from 80°F to 0°F (27°C to −18°C) causes a power loss of roughly 40 per cent, while the required cranking power is more than doubled owing to an increase in oil viscosity. To simplify storage and to reduce safety hazards, such as acid spillage, freeze-ups, and shorts, most batteries are now of the *dry charged* type. The dry charged battery contains plates that have been pre-charged without the use of electrolyte. The

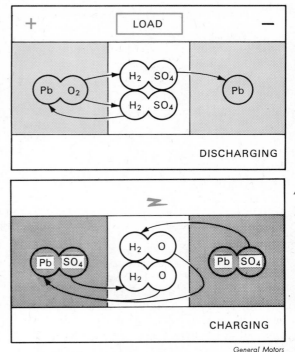

Fig. 12:16 Chemical Changes During Discharging and Charging of a Lead-Acid Storage Battery

General Motors

electrolyte is not added until shortly before the battery is put into service. Electrolyte of proper strength can be obtained in sealed safety containers. It is, however, not possible to restore the battery to a dry charged condition by simply draining the electrolyte. Once activated, the battery must remain connected to a charging circuit or be recharged at least every 30 days. A fully charged battery, especially when kept in a warm place, will discharge slowly on its own if not recharged by the generator. Any dirt, moisture, or acid residues will increase the rate of self-discharge across the battery cover. It is therefore imperative that the battery be kept clean. To remove and neutralize acidic deposits, a solution of water and baking soda or household ammonia can be used. (But never let any of these solutions enter the cells!) Then flush the outside of the battery with clean water.

The Safe Handling of Batteries

Storage batteries should be carried in a battery cart or with properly placed battery straps

(Fig. 1:67). The cells should never be overfilled or tilted. When charging, "boosting", testing, connecting, or disconnecting a battery, recommended procedures must be followed closely. Never expose a battery to sparks or flames. Oxygen and hydrogen generated during charge and discharge form an extremely dangerous explosive gas that may accumulate below the vent plugs for several hours. Wear safety glasses and never rub your eyes after touching a battery. The best first-aid treatment for acid burns is plenty of fresh water.

When disconnecting a negatively grounded battery, remove the ground cable first; and when connecting a negatively grounded battery, attach the ground cable last. This prevents injuries, shorts, fires, and battery explosions. The terminals must never be hammered and they should be free of oxides, acid, and dirt. After the cable terminals are connected to the battery post, they are coated with grease to prevent corrosion. Reversed polarity will instantly cause serious damage to the charging circuit. The same thing may happen if the battery cables are not disconnected during a fast recharge. Connect and disconnect the battery with all accessories and switches in the "off" position to prevent sparks and battery explosions.

Battery Tests and Checks

1. Visual checks will reveal such defects as cracks, leakage, distorted plates, bad connections, improper electrolyte levels, corrosion, and deposits.
2. Electrical tests may involve various voltage and amperage tests. The voltage of the battery must be within specified limits, both with and without battery loads. The loads can be imposed normally by using the starter motor, the lights, and other electrical equipment, or by connecting a variable resistor, which allows the battery to discharge at a controlled rate.
3. The hydrometer test (Fig. 12:17) measures the specific gravity of the electrolyte, which, as we have learned earlier, is a fairly reliable indicator of battery-charge conditions. Since specific gravity is affected by temperature changes, it is important to correct the cell readings if they are obtained at electrolyte temperatures below 80°F or above 80°F

(27°C). For every 10F° below 80°F (every 5½C° below 27°C), 0.004 must be subtracted from the reading, and for every 10F° above 80°F, 0.004 must be added. For example, if a reading of 1.215 is obtained, it would appear, according to the chart in Fig. 12:18, that the battery is three-quarters charged. Let's assume, however, that the electrolyte temperature is 10°F, or 70°F lower than 80°F. It follows that the value to be subtracted would be 7 × 0.004 or 0.028. The corrected reading is therefore 1.215 − 0.028 = 1.187. Now we see that the battery is less than three-quarters charged, hardly enough to start an engine on such a cold day. You will not forget whether you should subtract or add, if you remember this: When the electrolyte is hot it expands, and since an equal volume of the same liquid is now lighter, we must add to compensate for the loss in weight.

Note: An improper electrolyte level, water that is added and not fully mixed with the solution, and spillage will all result in false hydrometer readings.

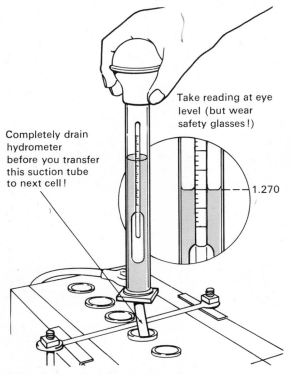

Take reading at eye level (but wear safety glasses!)

Completely drain hydrometer before you transfer this suction tube to next cell!

1.270

Fig. 12:17 The Hydrometer Test

CHEMICAL CHANGES IN BATTERY
DURING DISCHARGE

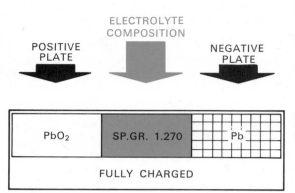

Battery Ratings

The *Voltage* of a new, fully charged battery is determined by the number of cells. Each cell produces slightly over two volts. The 12-volt battery is now used in all standard cars. The main advantages of the 12-volt system over the 6-volt system are that more power is produced; conductors of smaller gauge size can be used; the performance of the ignition system is improved; and, particularly, it increases the starter motor torque needed for large, high-compression engines.

The *Ampere-hour (A·h) Rating* is determined by the amount of current delivered by a battery at 80°F, or 27°C, over a period of 20 hours without the cell voltage falling below 1.75 volts. The A·h rating of a battery depends primarily on the weight of the active material and the size and the number of the plates. A 100 A·h battery can produce 5 amperes for 20 hours.

The *Watt-hour (W·h) Rating* is a performance rating obtained by multiplying the A·h rating by the battery voltage. For example, a 6-volt and a 12-volt battery both advertised at 70 A·h would, at first, appear to be equal. The performance rating reveals the difference: the 12-volt battery is rated at 840 W·h (70 × 12) while the 6-volt battery is rated at only 420 W·h (70 × 6).

Battery Charging

Batteries are normally recharged by the vehicle's own charging circuit. However, if the lights are left turned on while the car is parked for several hours, or if for any other reason the battery becomes discharged, it will be necessary to recharge it by other means. If time permits, slow charging at around 5A is preferable. Fast or "boost" charging at rates of 30A or more doesn't completely penetrate the plates and results in a partly charged battery. Whatever the charging rate, electrolyte temperatures of over 125°F, or 52°C, must be avoided, even if this means interrupting the charging process.

Electromagnetism

Whenever an electric current is flowing, a magnetic field is set up around the conductor. This can be proven by sprinkling iron filings on a piece of paper surrounding the conductor (Fig. 12:19) or by using a compass (Fig. 12:20).

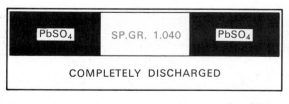

General Motors

Fig. 12:18

Magnetic lines of force lie at right angles to the conductor, and they decrease in strength or "density" as the distance from the wire increases. If the flow of current is increased, the magnetic field of force also increases. Furthermore, if the current flow is reversed, the compass needle will point in the opposite direction, an indication that the polarity of the electromagnetic field has been reversed as well.

Where a compass is unavailable or it is impractical to use one, the so-called *Left-hand Rule* can be used to determine the direction of the lines of force (Fig. 12:20). Grasp the conductor in your left hand with your thumb pointing in the direction of the electron flow. Your fingers will now point in the direction of the lines of force.

It is obvious that the electromagnetic field described above lacks sufficient strength to be of practical use. By coiling the wire, however, a much stronger magnetic field is obtained. Let us study this very important principle in more detail. To simplify matters, let us assume that we could see an individual electron coming and leaving like a dart; one way we would see its point, the other way its tail feathers (Fig. 12:21). Fig. 12:22a and b shows that, if the current travels in opposite directions through two adjacent parallel conductors, their magnetic fields, while opposite in polarity, travel in the same direction between the conductors. The high density of this inner magnetic field causes the conductors to repel each other. If,

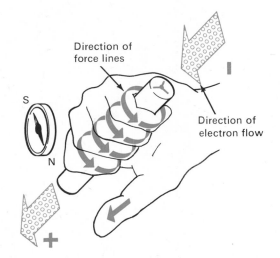

Fig. 12:20 Left-hand Rule for Determining the Direction of Lines of Force Around a Conductor

on the other hand, the current travels in the same direction (Fig. 12:22c), the two magnetic fields combine and the conductors attract one another. In fact, the two conductors could be compared to the separate strands of a larger, two-ply wire that forms one strong continuous magnetic field. In a sense, the magnetic lines of force act like rubber bands and pull the conductors together.

It follows that in a wire coil the magnetic field of each loop of wire no longer acts individually but joins the others to produce a single magnetic field of much greater strength and density. A still stronger electromagnet may be obtained by placing a piece of iron in the centre

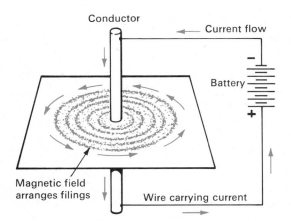

Fig. 12:19 Electromagnetic Field Surrounding an Electrical Conductor

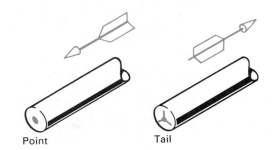

Fig. 12:21 Points and Tails of Arrows Indicating Current Flow in Electrical Conductors

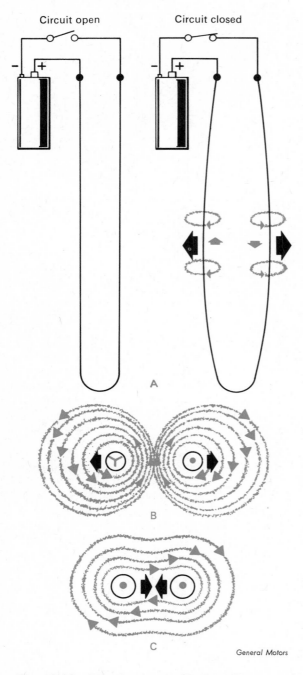

Circuit open   Circuit closed

Fig. 12:22 The electromagnetic fields of force surrounding adjacent conductors repel each other if the flow of current is in opposite *directions. The fields of force of adjacent conductors combine with one another and cause the conductors to be attracted if the flow of current is in the* same *direction.*

General Motors

of the coil (Fig. 12:23). Because magnetism acts more easily through a magnetic material than it does through air, which is said to be less "permeable", the presence of the iron in the centre of the coil greatly strengthens the coil's magnetic field. In fact, it would require a fairly strong force to pull the core out of the coil against the magnetic pull. The magnetic lines of force, as we stated earlier, act like rubber bands. They hold the core in a position that minimizes tension. This important principle is applied in relay switches and solenoids. The latter devices are designed to activate levers in certain types of starter motors (Fig. 12:24).

The strength of the electromagnetic field created by an electric coil is determined by the ampere-turns, i.e., by the product of amperage × the number of turns of wire.

The polarity of a coil is governed by the direction of the current flow, and by whether the coil is wound to the right or to the left. To establish the polarity, either a compass or the left-hand rule (Fig. 12:25) can be used. Care must always be taken not to reverse the intended polarity (in ignition coils, starter and generator windings. battery connections, etc.).

The Generator

The generator produces the current needed by the electrical devices and it keeps the battery charged. The generator is driven by a V-belt connected to the crankshaft and water pump pulleys. There are two types of generators (Fig. 12:26): the older D.C. type and the more modern A.C. generator, usually referred to as an *alternator*.

Just as electricity can produce magnetism, magnetic fields of force can be employed to create an electric current. All that is required is that a conductor connected to an electric circuit be exposed to a magnetic field of varying density. Whether that condition is met by moving the conductor in a magnetic field, or by moving the magnetic field, or by changing the strength of the magnetic field itself, doesn't matter (Fig. 12:27). As you will see, all three methods are employed in various electrical devices. The principle involved is known as *electromagnetic induction*. It should be noted that the magnitude of the current induced depends on the strength of the magnetic field, the number of conductors, and the rate at

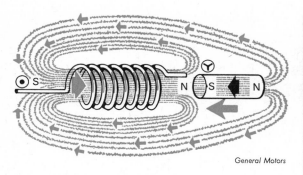

Fig. 12:23 Electromagnetism

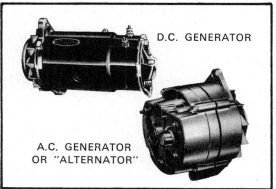

Fig. 12:26 Types of Generators

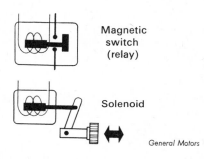

Magnetic
switch
(relay)

Solenoid

General Motors

Fig. 12:24 Two Automotive Applications of
the Electromagnet

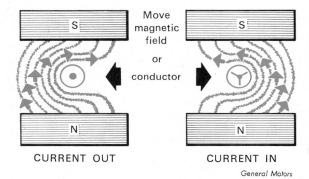

CURRENT OUT   CURRENT IN

General Motors

Fig. 12:27 Electromagnetic Induction

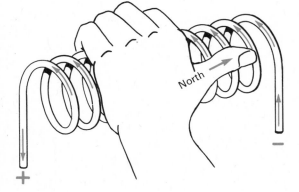

Fig. 12:25 Left-hand Rule for Coils

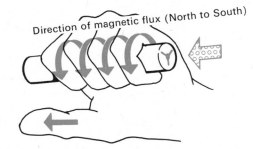

Direction of current flow

Fig. 12:28 Left-hand Rule Applied to
Electromagnetic Induction

which the density or the strength of the magnetic field is being changed.

Figs. 12:27 and 12:28 show that the direction of the induced current flow depends on both the direction of conductor movement and the polarity of the magnetic field. It follows that the current induced in the rotating wire loop shown in Fig. 12:29 is flowing in opposite directions. In the left conductor, which moves upwards in the magnetic field, the flow is in one direction, while in the right conductor, which moves downwards, it is in the other. Since the two conductors are really one continuous wire loop, the current, in effect, makes

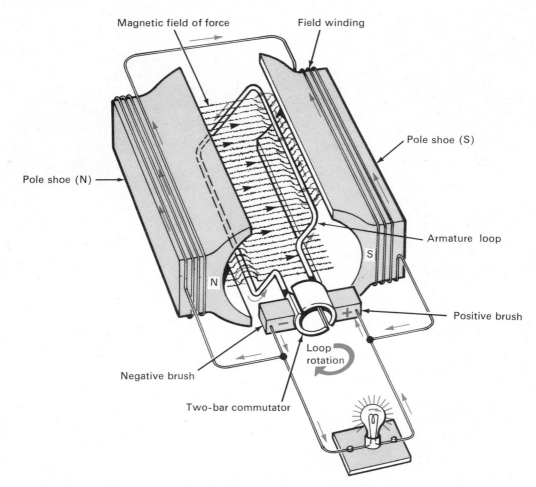

Magnetic field of force

Field winding

Pole shoe (N)

Pole shoe (S)

Armature loop

Positive brush

Negative brush

Loop rotation

Two-bar commutator

Fig. 12:29 Operating Principles of a D.C. Generator

a complete circuit. The current continues on its path through the left commutator bar, the negative brush, the external circuit, and the bulb, and finally re-enters through the positive brush on the right. Note that this would also be the case if the loop were turned by half a rotation. The commutator, which acts as a mechanical rectifier, ensures that the current always flows in the same direction, hence the term *D.C. generator*. A parallel circuit, also called a "shunt" circuit, connected to the brushes forms the field windings that magnetize the two pole shoes. Because the pole shoes are attached to a common steel housing, they are, in fact, the north and south poles of one and the same electromagnet and are often called the *pole pieces*.

The D.C. generator described above would

be very inefficient. By adding more loops, which are wound onto a highly permeable *armature* core, the output can be greatly increased (Fig. 12:30).

The demands placed on modern generators by air conditioners, radios, power windows, additional lights, and other electrical accessories could not be met satisfactorily by merely changing the sizes of pulleys and generators. Another problem with the D.C. generator is that an increase in rpm may cause the armature windings to be thrown out of position by centrifugal forces.

In the A.C. generator, or alternator (Fig. 12:31), the alternating magnetic fields created by the *rotor* winding (the field coil in this case) are moved, while the conductor in which the current is induced (the *stator* winding) is held

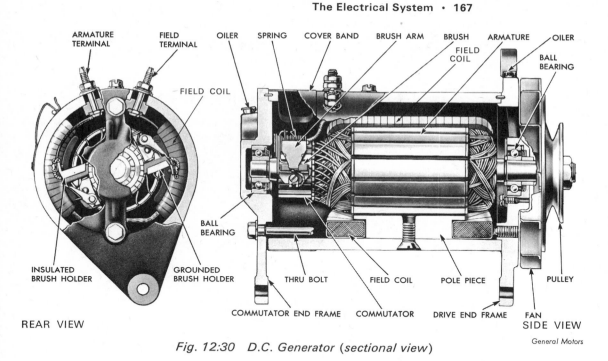

ARMATURE TERMINAL · FIELD TERMINAL · OILER · SPRING · COVER BAND · BRUSH ARM · BRUSH · ARMATURE · OILER

FIELD COIL · FIELD COIL · BALL BEARING

BALL BEARING

INSULATED BRUSH HOLDER · GROUNDED BRUSH HOLDER · THRU BOLT · FIELD COIL · POLE PIECE · PULLEY

COMMUTATOR END FRAME · COMMUTATOR · DRIVE END FRAME · FAN

REAR VIEW · SIDE VIEW

General Motors

Fig. 12:30   D.C. Generator (sectional view)

stationary (Fig. 12:32). The output of alternators is much greater than that of D.C. generators of equivalent size and weight, especially at low speeds, because the stator has more windings than common D.C. armatures (Fig. 12:33) and there are many more poles (Fig. 12:32). Owing to the fairly large circumference of the rotor, the relative speed between the conductor and the magnetic lines of force is also considerably greater. Furthermore, the very compact rotor design also permits higher rpm without affecting its winding. Since the battery and the ignition system can operate only on D.C., the A.C. produced by the alternator is

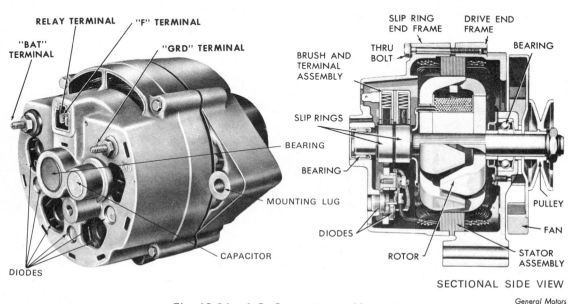

RELAY TERMINAL · "F" TERMINAL · "BAT" TERMINAL · "GRD" TERMINAL

SLIP RING END FRAME · DRIVE END FRAME · THRU BOLT · BEARING

BRUSH AND TERMINAL ASSEMBLY

SLIP RINGS

BEARING · BEARING

MOUNTING LUG · DIODES · PULLEY · FAN

DIODES · CAPACITOR · ROTOR · STATOR ASSEMBLY

SECTIONAL SIDE VIEW

General Motors

Fig. 12:31   A.C. Generator or Alternator

rectified or changed electronically to D.C. by diodes mounted in the "heat sink" of the alternator housing (Fig. 12:31). The operation of the diodes could be compared to the one-way valves in a fuel pump that allow the gasoline to travel in only one direction. Similarly, the diodes are so designed and arranged that the current leaving the main terminal of the alternator travels in one direction only. The

slip rings and brushes are needed to energize the rotor winding with a current of relatively low amperage (Figs. 12:32 and 12:31).

Voltage Regulators

Voltage regulators control the voltage in the electrical system and thus prevent the generator from overcharging the battery. Excessive volt-

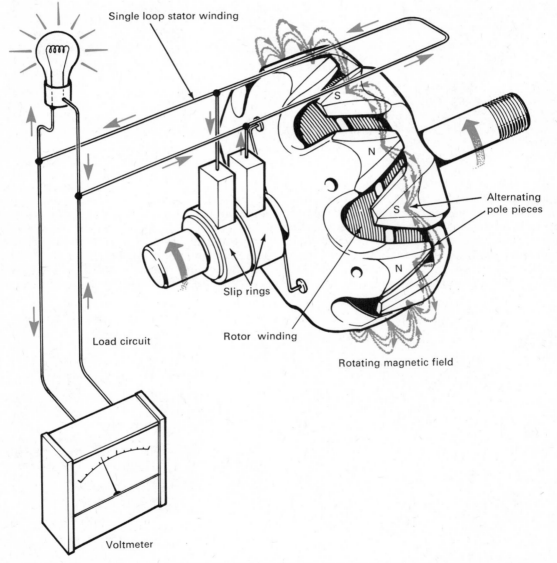

Fig. 12:32 The rotating magnetic field produced by the rotor assembly induces current in the stator winding. Note the use of two slip rings to conduct current from brushes to rotor winding.

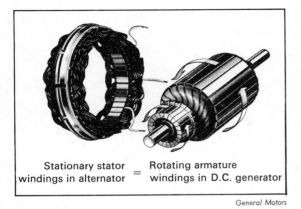

Stationary stator windings in alternator = Rotating armature windings in D.C. generator

General Motors

Fig. 12:33 Two Different Types of Generator Windings Used to Induce an Electric Current

age would also reduce the service life of most electrical components or cause them to burn out. Regulators connected to D.C. generators (Fig. 12:34) include a current regulator and a cutout relay. The current regulator limits the maximum amperage output of the generator, thus protecting the unit against overloads and overheating. The cutout relay opens the charging circuit when the generator voltage drops to a level at which the current would reverse itself. If this were allowed to happen, the battery current would flow into the generator and burn out its windings. No cutout relay is needed with alternators because the principal feature of

diodes is that they permit current flow in only one direction. Since the maximum amperage output of an alternator depends primarily on its basic design, no current regulator is required either.[38] Most A.C. regulators therefore consist only of a voltage regulator (Fig. 12:36). In some cases, the latter is built right into the alternator itself.

The operation of standard voltage regulators (Fig. 12:35) is based on contact points whose opening and closing is controlled by the opposing pulls of small electromagnets and calibrated springs. The position of the contact points regulates the current flowing through the field windings, and thus the output of the generator itself. To accomplish this, the contact points either open or close the circuit to which they are connected, or reroute the current through a resistor. The built-in type of voltage regulator used in some alternators is of the *solid state* type; i.e., it employs a combination of transistors, resistors, and capacitors to control the voltage electronically.

The *ignition light* is actually a charging light that goes out when generator voltage exceeds

---

[38]The A.C. voltage in the stator winding induces an opposite voltage in the same winding. Such a voltage is called a *counter-electromotive force* or, for short, *counter-e.m.f.* At high rpm the counter-e.m.f. is sufficient to limit the maximum output of an alternator.

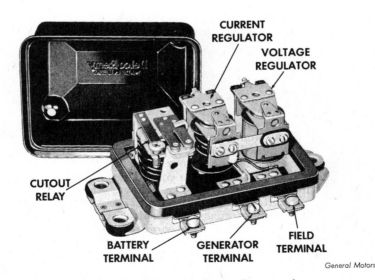

CURRENT REGULATOR

VOLTAGE REGULATOR

CUTOUT RELAY

BATTERY TERMINAL

GENERATOR TERMINAL

FIELD TERMINAL

General Motors

Fig. 12:34 Typical Three-Unit D.C. Regulator with Cover Removed

battery voltage, i.e., when the battery is being charged (Fig. 12:35). Where more precise information is required, a dash-mounted *ammeter* is connected to the charging circuit.

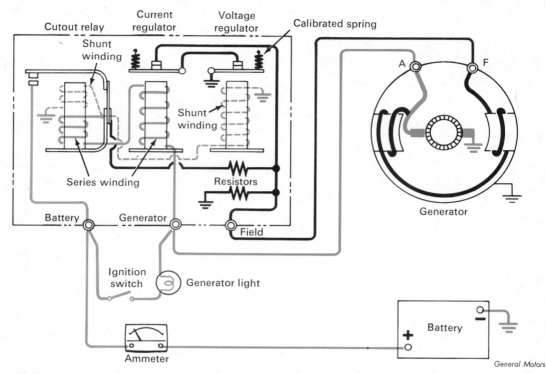

Fig. 12:35 *Standard Three-Unit Regulator. The series windings in the cutout relay and current regulator are shown as a solid coloured line. The shunt windings in the cutout relay and voltage regulator are shown as a broken coloured line. The field circuit and resistors are shown in black.*

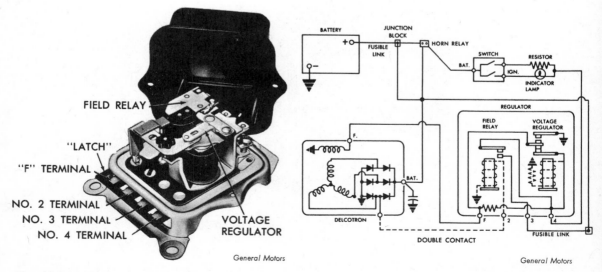

Fig. 12:36 *Typical A.C. Voltage Regulator*

Fig. 12:37 *Detail of an A.C. Charging Circuit*

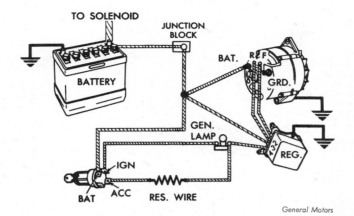

Fig. 12:38   Typical Wiring Diagram of an A.C. Charging Circuit

The Starter Motor

The starter motor, also called the *cranking motor* or simply the *starter* (Figs. 12:39 and 12:40), is located at the rear of the engine. By means of a small pinion gear, which engages the flywheel ring-gear, the starter "cranks" the engine until it operates under its own power. The gearshift lever must always be placed into neutral before the engine is started. On vehicles equipped with an automatic transmission, a "neutral switch" controlled by the shift lever linkage prevents the operator from starting the engine in any position other than "Neutral" or "Park" (Fig. 12:39 and Fig. 16:14).

Basically, a starter motor is a D.C. generator in reverse. In fact, a generator could be turned into an electric motor by connecting it directly to the battery. You will remember that like poles repel each other. It is this force of magnetic repulsion that causes the conductors in the armature of a starter motor to develop the necessary torque (Fig. 12:41). The conductors and their own magnetic fields are subjected to the very dense magnetic lines of force that emanate from the north pole of the field winding and re-enter the south pole through the armature core itself. As a result, the conductors are pushed from an area of high-flux density between the pole shoes to an area of low-flux density adjacent to the pole shoes.

While there are great similarities between D.C. generators and starter motors, very important differences do, in fact, exist:
1. The windings are made of copper ribbon with very low resistance; therefore they conduct much heavier currents.
2. The field windings are connected to the armature in series rather than in parallel, so that the full current travels through the field coils and the armature (Fig. 12:41).

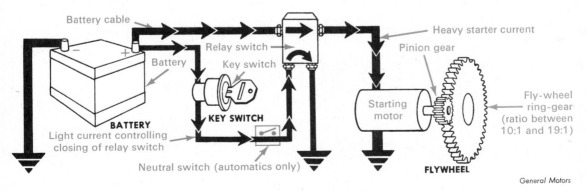

Fig. 12:39   The Cranking Circuit (schematic diagram)

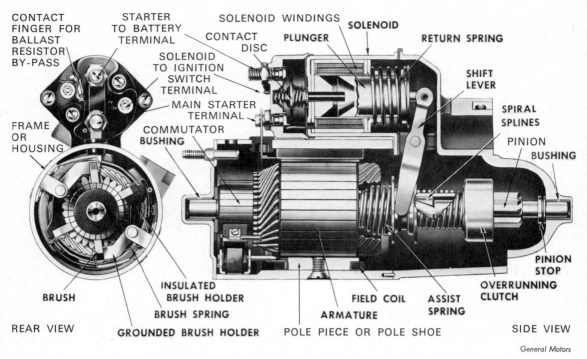

CONTACT FINGER FOR BALLAST RESISTOR BY-PASS

STARTER TO BATTERY TERMINAL

CONTACT DISC

SOLENOID WINDINGS

PLUNGER

SOLENOID

RETURN SPRING

SOLENOID TO IGNITION SWITCH TERMINAL

SHIFT LEVER

MAIN STARTER TERMINAL

SPIRAL SPLINES

FRAME OR HOUSING

COMMUTATOR BUSHING

PINION BUSHING

BRUSH

INSULATED BRUSH HOLDER

BRUSH SPRING

PINION STOP

OVERRUNNING CLUTCH

GROUNDED BRUSH HOLDER

FIELD COIL

ASSIST SPRING

ARMATURE

REAR VIEW

POLE PIECE OR POLE SHOE

SIDE VIEW

General Motors

Fig. 12:40 Solenoid-type Starter Motor (sectional view)

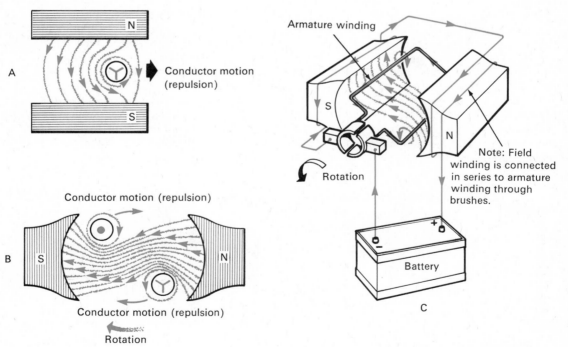

A

N

S

Conductor motion (repulsion)

Armature winding

S

N

Rotation

Note: Field winding is connected in series to armature winding through brushes.

Conductor motion (repulsion)

B

S

N

Conductor motion (repulsion)

Rotation

Battery

C

The Prestolite Electrical Division of Eltra Corporation

Fig. 12:41 Operating Principle of a Starter Motor

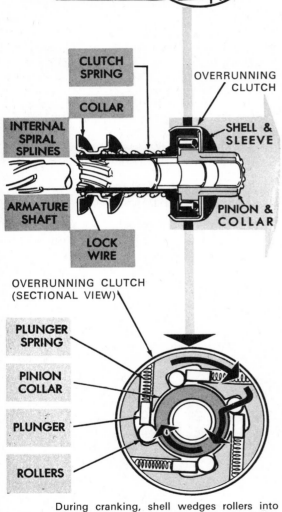

3. There are usually four pole shoes instead of two as in conventional D.C. generators.

All three factors result in extremely high torque. However, starter motors develop so much heat that they can be employed for only a few seconds at a time.

To increase torque even more, the gear ratio between the pinion gear and the flywheel ring-gear is between 10:1 and 19:1 (Fig. 12:39). In some cases the starter motor itself is equipped with an additional reduction gear.

Starter Drives

The *Solenoid-type Starter Drive* (Fig. 12:42) engages the pinion gear by means of a solenoid-activated lever (Figs. 12:24 and 12:40). In the event that the pinion teeth do not line up with the teeth of the ring-gear, the lever compresses the clutch spring (Fig. 12:42), causing the interfering teeth to be pressed together. The armature shaft, which already begins to turn at this point, can now drop the pinion gear into mesh with the stationary ring-gear.

The *Bendix drive* (Fig. 12:43) utilizes the

During cranking, shell wedges rollers into collar of pinion, transmitting torque to pinion. During engine firing, rollers and plungers are "unwedged" in clockwise direction.

General Motors

Fig. 12:42 Operating Principles of a Solenoid Drive

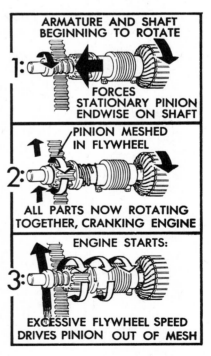

General Motors

Fig. 12:43 Operating Principles of the Bendix Drive

sudden acceleration of the armature shaft to propel the pinion gear into the flywheel ring-gear by means of a *screw shaft*. The inertia of the pinion gear mounted on the screw shaft causes it to accelerate at a slower rate than the armature shaft. (To increase its inertia, the pinion gear is often equipped with a counter-weight.) As a result, the pinion gear, like a nut on a screw, moves along the extended arma-ture shaft into the ring-gear. The purpose of the very heavy coil spring at the end of the armature shaft is to cushion the sudden torque applica-tion of the starter. As soon as the engine fires and the switch is released, the pinion gear is kicked back into its retracted position.

The *Integral Positive-Engagement Drive* (Fig. 12:44) features a movable pole shoe and an actuating lever. When the starter is activated, a heavy current flows through a grounded "pull-in" winding. This causes the movable pole shoe to be drawn into the starter frame, and the actuating lever attached to the pole shoe engages the pinion gear with the ring-gear. The actuating lever also opens the ground contacts of the "pull-in" winding, thereby con-necting the winding in series with the armature. The "pull-in" winding and movable pole shoe thus become a regular pole shoe assembly which, together with the other three field wind-ings and pole shoes, produces the full starter torque. An additional "hold-in" winding en-sures that the movable pole shoe is held in

cranking position. After the engine fires and the ignition switch is released into the run position, the current stops and the actuating lever return spring disengages the pinion gear.

Most starter drives employ some type of over-running clutch whose action is somewhat simi-lar to that of a freewheeling bicycle hub (Figs. 12:42 and 12:44). The clutch protects the armature windings against overspeeding, in case the pinion gear remains engaged beyond the point of engine firing. On the Bendix drive, a set of locking pins unlock under high cen-trifugal forces, i.e., when the engine begins to fire and the flywheel speeds up. This permits the pinion to disengage and return to its resting position on the screw shaft. A ratchet-like *dentil clutch* lets the pinion freewheel, while keeping it still engaged if the engine speed is not yet high enough to deactivate the locking pins. Because this feature prevents disengage-ment if the engine fires only intermittently, the action is called "Follo-Thru".

The Starter Circuit or Cranking Circuit

The starter circuit, or cranking circuit, is shown in Fig. 12:39. Since an ordinary ignition switch cannot handle the very heavy starter currents, which are sometimes well in excess of 100 amperes, the starter motor is controlled by some

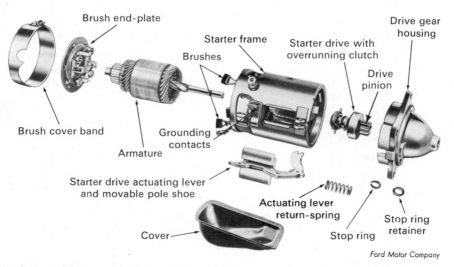

Brush end-plate

Starter frame

Starter drive with overrunning clutch

Drive gear housing

Brushes

Drive pinion

Brush cover band

Grounding contacts

Armature

Starter drive actuating lever and movable pole shoe

Actuating lever return-spring

Stop ring retainer

Cover

Stop ring

Ford Motor Company

Fig. 12:44 Starter Motor with Integral Positive Engagement Drive (disassembled)

type of relay switch. The relay switch connects the starter motor directly to the main battery cable. When the ignition key is turned to the "Start" position, the magnetic pull of the relay winding closes the main circuit. With the solenoid type of starter motor (Fig. 12:40) the two functions of engaging the pinion gear and of closing the main circuit are combined by the solenoid.

The Ignition System

The ignition system produces the spark that ignites the fuel-air mixture. It must also distribute this spark to the cylinders in the proper firing order and at exactly the correct time, if good performance and low emission of pollutants are to be maintained.

The Ignition Coil

The ignition coil (Fig. 12:45) is essentially a step-up transformer that increases the battery voltage to a level sufficient to cause the spark to jump the electrode gap at the spark plug. Spark voltage depends on many factors; it may be less than 6,000 volts at engine idle, and be above 20,000 volts under heavy engine loads or with worn spark plugs. Even with an ignition system in perfect working order, the coil output is largely determined by the varying resistance between the electrodes of the spark plug, i.e., the density of the mixture, the size of the electrode gap, the formation of deposits, etc.

The ignition coil consists of two well-insulated windings and a laminated or layered soft iron core. The windings and the core are placed inside a metal container, which is hermetically sealed by the coil tower to prevent moisture from entering. The tower is made of a moulded insulating material and has three terminals: the negative and positive *primary terminals* and the *secondary high-voltage terminal*. The coil assembly is filled with a transformer oil to improve insulation and to dissipate heat. The primary winding is made up of several hundred turns of fairly heavy insulated copper wire, and the secondary winding consists of many thousand turns of very fine, insulated copper wire. This wire is as thin as a human hair. In a 100:1 ratio coil the primary winding may have 200 turns, and the secondary winding 20,000 turns. Ratios of up to 400:1 are in use. The number of turns in the secondary winding roughly equals the maximum voltage output. In other words, one turn equals approximately one volt.

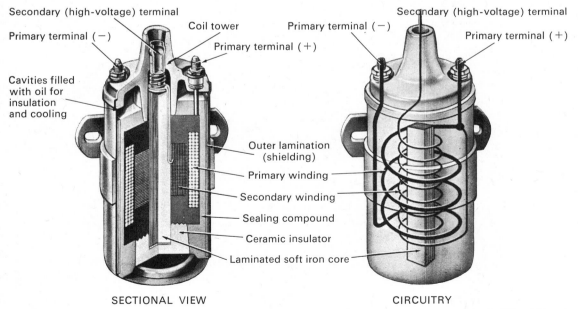

SECTIONAL VIEW   CIRCUITRY

Robert Bosch (Canada) Limited

Fig. 12:45 The Ignition Coil

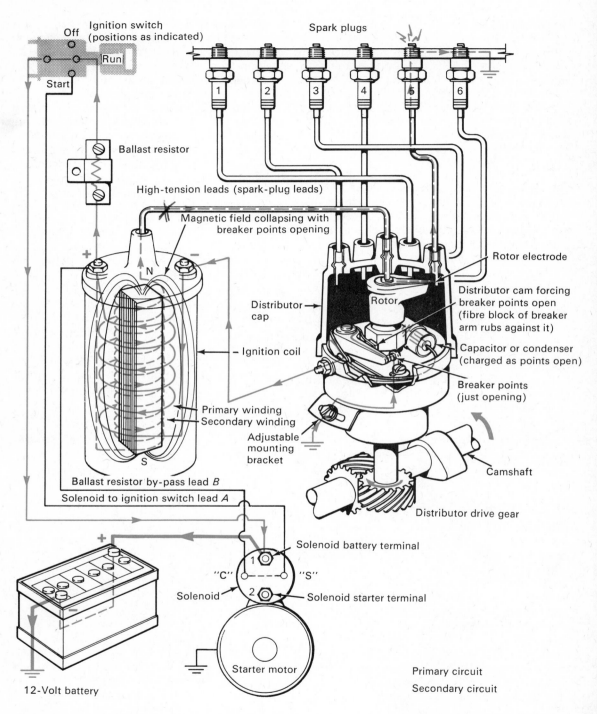

Fig. 12:46 Standard Ignition System for a Six-cylinder Engine (Firing order 1-5-3-6-2-4) (*Note: Current flow in the primary ignition circuit is in the opposite direction to that of the secondary ignition circuit.*)

Operating Principles

When the primary terminals are connected to the source, the primary winding inside the coil sets up a strong electromagnetic field (Fig. 12:46). If the circuit is now suddenly broken, the magnetic field will collapse and cut across the primary and secondary windings, which are joined together inside the coil at one of the primary terminals. *The collapsing magnetic field causes a high-voltage current of opposite polarity to be induced in both windings.* This is not surprising, since we learned earlier (page 164 and Fig. 12:27) that any movement between a magnetic field and a conductor causes electromagnetic induction. It does not really matter whether it is the conductor or the magnetic field that moves. The cycle described above repeats itself each time the primary circuit is closed and then opened. If the primary connections at the coil tower are properly made, the spark will jump the spark-plug gap from the centre electrode to the ground electrode. Reversed polarity would force the spark to move in the opposite direction, a condition that leads to loss of performance or even misfiring. The reason is that it takes about an extra 5,000 volts to make the spark jump the gap from the relatively cool ground electrode to the hotter centre electrode.

Since the collapse of the magnetic field causes induction in both coil windings, the principle involved is often called *mutual induction*. The voltage induced in the primary winding can be as high as 250 volts. Because currents are induced in any conductor that is subjected to a magnetic field, the coil core is not made of a solid piece of iron but of laminated iron strips (Fig. 12:45). This reduces undesirable "stray" or "eddy" currents that increase coil temperatures and lower efficiency. A special type of soft iron is used for the core and the outer lamination because it magnetizes and demagnetizes very rapidly. (The laminated shielding also reduces radio interference.) The more completely the magnetic field expands and the quicker it then collapses, the higher the output of the ignition coil is.

The Ignition Circuits

The ignition circuits, as shown in Fig. 12:46, begin at the positive battery terminal; that is, if we follow the order in which the various components are connected rather than the actual direction of current flow, as indicated by the arrowheads. The primary ignition circuit consists of all those parts that connect the primary coil winding to the battery. The secondary circuit is composed of the secondary coil winding, the high-tension leads, the distributor cap and rotor, and the spark plugs.

The Primary Ignition Circuit

The *Ignition Switch* connects the ignition coil to the source. If the key is in the "Start" position, the solenoid is energized through lead *A*. This closes the starter-solenoid circuit through main terminals 1 and 2. It also impresses the full battery voltage of 12 volts on the primary coil winding through the terminals *S* and *C* and the ballast resistor by-pass *B*. (The contact finger closing circuit *S-C* can be seen in Fig. 12:40.) The by-pass circuit thus ensures that the coil produces sufficient output during cranking. This is all the more important if the momentary voltage drop in the battery circuit, caused by the heavy current draw of the starter, is not to weaken the spark. The brief dimming of the headlights observed when a car is being started is visible evidence of this voltage drop. As soon as the engine fires and the key is in the "Run" position, circuit *A* is opened, the solenoid is de-energized, the starter motor disengages and stops, and the ballast resistor by-pass circuit *B* is opened as well. The current now travels through the "Run" terminal of the ignition switch, the ballast resistor, and the positive primary coil terminal. The ballast resistor (approximately .5 to 1.8Ω) reduces the normal operating voltage applied to the entire primary ignition circuit to roughly 7.5 volts. This prevents excessive coil loads and prolongs the life of the breaker points. Some ignition systems employ a special ballast resistor wire that connects the ignition switch directly to the positive coil terminal. Others use a heat-sensitive resistor wire which, when the engine is started, momentarily feeds a heavier current to the primary coil winding. After the engine fires, the wire heats up, its resistance increases, and the primary current is reduced. Obviously, this eliminates the need for a by-pass circuit. The ballast resistor also acts as a current regulator. At low rpm and relatively long closing

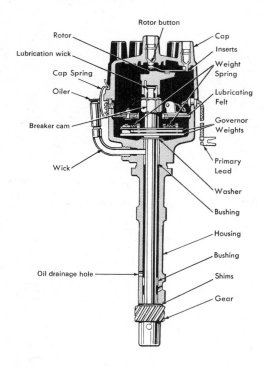

Fig. 12:47   Distributor (sectional side view)

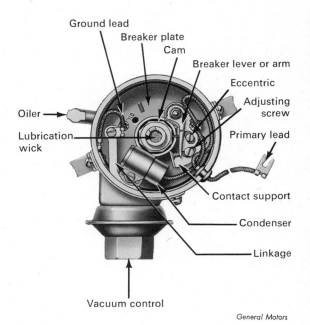

Fig. 12:48   Distributor for Eight-cylinder Engine (top view)

General Motors

times of the breaker points, the resistor heats up and resistance increases. Hence, the current flow is reduced and so is coil temperature and breaker point arcing. Conversely, short closing times at high rpm cause the resistor to cool off, primary current flow increases, and thus a strong spark is maintained.

The *Breaker Points* in the distributor (Figs. 12:46 to 12:48) complete and break the primary circuit and thus control the build-up (expansion) and collapse of the electromagnetic field in the ignition coil. The opening and closing of the breaker points is controlled by the breaker cam, which rubs against the fibre or nylon block of the insulated, movable breaker arm. The latter is kept under tension by a calibrated leaf spring.[39] There is one breaker cam lobe for each cylinder or spark plug. The distributor shaft,

---

[39] A special breaker point lubricant with a high dropping point is applied to the distributor cam to reduce wear on the fibre block and the cam. Breaker point tension is checked with a special tension gauge. Low tension causes high-speed "missing". High tension results in rapid wear.

which is attached to the breaker cam, is usually driven by the engine camshaft and makes one complete revolution for every two revolutions of the crankshaft. The stationary part of the breaker points is grounded to the distributor housing and thus completes the primary circuit when the points are closed. To reduce heat and prolong service life, some breaker points are of the vented design; i.e., the stationary contact point has a vent hole through the centre.

The *Condenser*, or *Capacitor* (Figs. 12:48 and 12:52), performs two very important functions:
1. It speeds up the collapse of the magnetic field in the coil and thereby intensifies the spark.
2. It reduces excessive arcing (sparking) between the breaker points, a condition that causes pitting and burning of the contact surfaces. The metal oxide that is formed as a result may increase primary resistance to a point where coil output is no longer sufficient to ignite the mixture in the cylinders.

Without a condenser, the current induced in the primary coil winding (up to 350 volts) seeks, in the form of a spark, to jump the breaker points when they open and the circuit is broken (Fig. 12:49). This delays the collapse of

Current causes arcing and pitted breaker points.

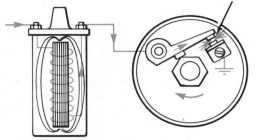

Magnetic field collapses too slowly.

*Fig. 12:49   Primary Circuit without Condenser
(points opening)*

Current charges condenser instead.

No arcing

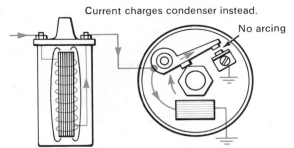

Magnetic field collapses more quickly.

*Fig. 12:50   Primary Circuit with Condenser
(points opening)*

the magnetic field in the coil, thus reducing the high voltage output of the secondary winding. However, with the condenser connected in parallel to the points, this current is diverted into the condenser (Fig. 12:50). In fact, the electrons rush into the condenser so fast that it is momentarily overcharged. The electrons "bounce" back and, with the breaker points now open, they travel back into the primary coil winding (Fig. 12:51). This reverse current causes a very rapid collapse of the magnetic

field and, as a result, the high voltage output is greatly increased. The electron flow oscillates (swings back and forth) between the primary winding and the condenser until all the coil energy is dissipated. (These oscillations can be compared to sound waves or echoes.)

The condenser (Fig. 12:52) consists basically of two very thin, rolled-up sheets of aluminum foil insulated against each other by strips of high-quality insulation. The foils are hermetically sealed in a container, as entry of

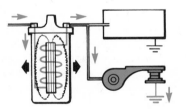

A. Points closed, magnetic field builds up, condenser discharged.

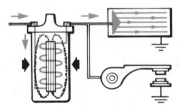

B. Points open, magnetic field collapses, condenser charged.

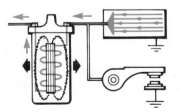

C. Points still open, condenser discharges into primary winding.

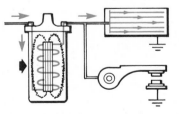

D. Points still open, condenser recharged (first oscillation completed).

General Motors

Fig. 12:51   Operation of a Condenser (Coil and Condenser Oscillations)

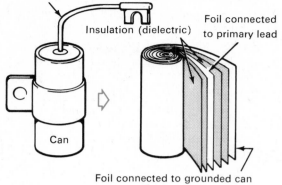

Wire connected to primary lead of breaker points

Foil connected to primary lead

Insulation (dielectric)

Can

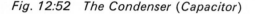

Foil connected to grounded can

General Motors

Fig. 12:52 The Condenser (Capacitor)

any moisture would prevent them from holding a charge.[40]

The Secondary Ignition Circuit

The secondary ignition circuit (Fig. 12:46) produces and distributes, in the proper firing order, the high-voltage current needed at the spark plugs. When the breaker points "break" the primary circuit, and the electromagnetic field in the coil collapses, the induced high-tension current leaves the secondary windings through the centre terminal of the coil tower.[41] The current continues via the high-tension lead of the coil to the centre terminal of the distributor cap. The latter is provided on the inside with a carbon brush, sometimes called the rotor "button", that rides on the distributor

---

[40]The three layers of cloud, air, and earth represent a natural capacitor. During an electric storm, however, the insulation of the air breaks down, resulting in the discharge of lightning.

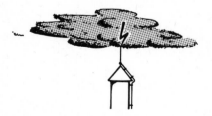

[41]Since the induced current is of opposite polarity, its direction is from the coil towards the grounded spark plugs.

rotor. The distributor rotor is made of a moulded insulator and is equipped with an electrode (conductor tip). The rotor revolves with the distributor cam to which it is attached. The outer distributor cap terminals, which are connected to the spark plugs by means of the high-tension leads, protrude through the inside of the cap. As the rotor tip passes them—and they are passed at precisely the moment the breaker points open and induction takes place —the current momentarily changes into a spark and jumps onto the opposite cap terminal (also called an "insert").[42] The current continues through the high-tension leads to the centre electrode of the spark plug and causes a spark discharge at the electrode gap inside the combustion chamber. Thus, the mixture is ignited. The current returns to the source by way of the spark-plug ground electrode.

Electronic Ignition Systems

One of the most popular electronic ignition systems is shown in Fig. 12:53. The coil still produces the high voltage in the usual manner, except that the current flow in the primary winding is interrupted by a transistor in the control unit.[43] This occurs when the latter receives a signal voltage, i.e., an electrical pulse, from the specially designed distributor. The pick-up coil, the pole piece attached to the permanent magnet, and the reluctor form what could be considered a miniature A.C. generator. In Fig. 12:55a the magnetic lines of force are "reluctant" to cross the air gap between the pole piece and the reluctor because the resistance of the widened gap is too high for the magnetic flux. Note that the pole piece has a small induction coil or "pick-up" coil wound around it (Fig. 12:54). In Fig. 12:55b one of the teeth of the reluctor—and there is one for each cylinder—is very close to the pole piece (about 0.008") and the path for the magnetic lines of

---

[42]To reduce radio interference the gap between the rotor tip and the cap inserts may, in some cases, be as much as 0.060" or 1.5 mm.

[43]A transistor is an electronic device that acts as an electric switch. A weak signal current applied to one of its circuits can turn the transistor "on" or "off". This allows the control of a much heavier current through the main circuit to which the transistor is connected.

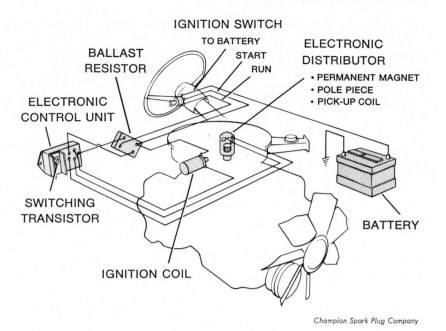

IGNITION SWITCH
TO BATTERY
START
RUN

BALLAST RESISTOR

ELECTRONIC DISTRIBUTOR
• PERMANENT MAGNET
• POLE PIECE
• PICK-UP COIL

ELECTRONIC CONTROL UNIT

SWITCHING TRANSISTOR

BATTERY

IGNITION COIL

Champion Spark Plug Company

Fig. 12:53   Under-hood Arrangement of an Electronic Ignition System for an Eight-cylinder Engine

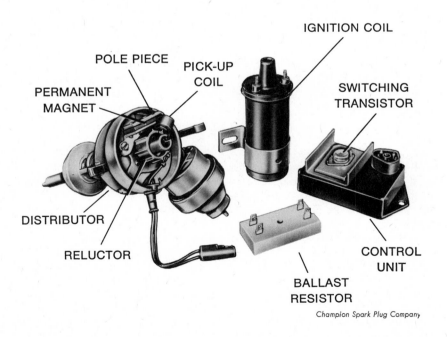

POLE PIECE
PICK-UP COIL
PERMANENT MAGNET

IGNITION COIL
SWITCHING TRANSISTOR

DISTRIBUTOR

RELUCTOR

CONTROL UNIT

BALLAST RESISTOR

Champion Spark Plug Company

Fig. 12:54   Component Parts of an Electronic Ignition System for an Eight-cylinder Engine

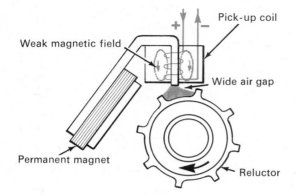

A. Air gap offers resistance or "reluctance" to magnetic field entering reluctor.

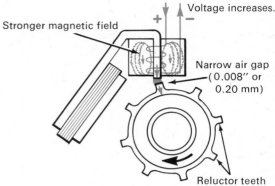

B. Reluctor tooth opposite pole piece. Magnetic lines of force enter reluctor unhindered; magnetic field expands; thus, pick-up coil voltage increases.

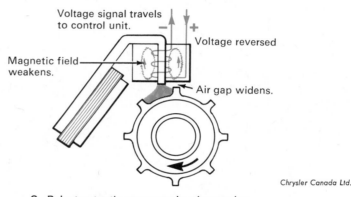

C. Reluctor tooth passes pole piece, reluctance is high, magnetic field collapses inducing voltage signal for control unit (point of ignition).

Chrysler Canada Ltd.

Fig. 12:55

force is strengthened. As a result, the magnetic field expands, thereby inducing a low voltage in the pick-up coil, whose two leads are connected to the control unit. In Fig. 12:55c the same reluctor tooth has passed the pole piece, the air gap increases, and thus the magnetic field collapses. This again induces a voltage in the pick-up coil, which, as indicated, is now of opposite polarity at the terminals. It is this reverse voltage signal that "turns off" the switching transistor in the control unit. Thus, the current flow in the primary coil winding stops abruptly and the coil discharges in the usual manner (Fig. 12:56). In other words, the electronic control unit takes the place of the breaker points in conventional systems since it controls the current flow through the primary winding of the ignition coil. The low-voltage signal from the pick-up coil simply tells the switching transistor when to break the current flow through the primary coil circuit. And it does so at the exact time that ignition is to take place. The same cycle is repeated as long as the reluctor rotates. With the reluctor in the positions shown in Figs. 12:55a and b, the current flows through the control unit, and the primary coil winding once again builds up a strong magnetic field (Fig. 12:57). This period of coil "saturation" is measured in degrees of distributor shaft rotation and is called *dwell*.

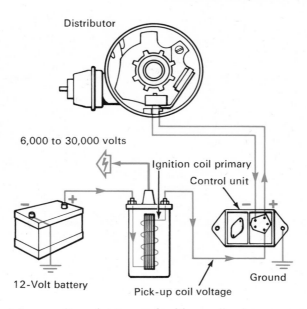

Distributor

6,000 to 30,000 volts

Ignition coil primary

Control unit

12-Volt battery

Pick-up coil voltage

Ground

Chrysler Canada Ltd.

Fig. 12:56   Negative pick-up voltage interrupts ignition coil primary current (point of ignition).

The advantages of an electronic ignition system are obvious. For example, on an eight-cylinder engine equipped with a conventional distributor, the breaker points open and close 12,000 times per minute at 3,000 rpm. Owing to spark erosion and fibre block wear on the breaker points, neither ignition-timing nor dwell settings will remain within exact specifications for more than a few thousand miles at best. On electronic systems, however, no periodic adjustments are needed because the systems operate without breaker points, and the correct amount of dwell is designed into the control unit. This is very important if good performance and low emission are to be maintained over extended mileage intervals. Furthermore, without breaker points, there is no need for a con-denser. On some electronic ignition systems, the ignition coil is built right into the distributor cap. They can be easily recognized, since the centre high-tension terminal in the distributor cap is omitted on these systems.

Magneto-Ignition

Magneto-ignition is employed in some high-performance vehicles, motorcycles, and small engines used in outboards, snowmobiles, lawn mowers, etc. In this system a rotating permanent magnet induces a high-voltage current in a stationary induction coil. The advantages are simplicity, light weight, no need for a battery, and an increase in the intensity of the spark with rpm.

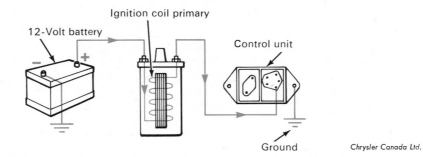

Ignition coil primary

12-Volt battery

Control unit

Ground

Chrysler Canada Ltd.

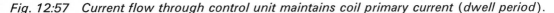

Fig. 12:57   Current flow through control unit maintains coil primary current (dwell period).

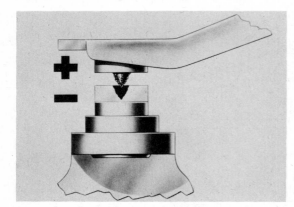
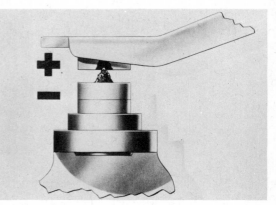

Metal transfer from the negative to the positive point (condenser has insufficient capacitance)

Metal transfer from the positive to the negative point (condenser has too much capacitance)

General Motors

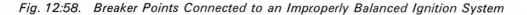

Fig. 12:58.   Breaker Points Connected to an Improperly Balanced Ignition System

The High-tension Leads

The high-tension, or spark-plug, leads (Figs. 12:6b and c) are heavily insulated and contain, in most cases, a graphite-treated fibre core instead of a wire. Special staple clips pushed into the leads connect the fibre core to the terminals. To prevent damage to TVRS (Television-Radio-Suppressor) leads, the conductor must be removed by pulling at the terminal ends. Contrary to common belief, the high resistance does not weaken the spark needed to fire the mixture. It does, however, cut out objectionable refirings that are caused by condenser coil oscillations. It is the radio waves emitted by these refirings that cause interference in television and radio reception.

Since the sequence of the high-tension leads

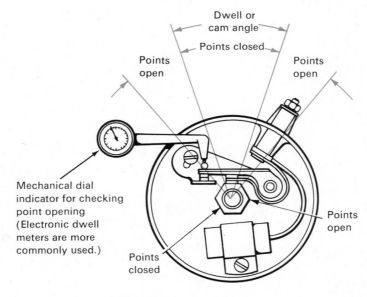

Fig. 12:59   Cam Angle

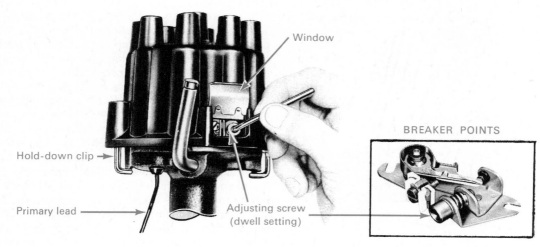

Fig. 12:60   Breaker Points with Dwell-adjusting Screw

in the distributor cap is determined by the firing order of the engine, the position of the leads must never be switched (Fig. 12:46).

Caution: Modern ignition systems are "balanced" systems; i.e., the performance characteristics of the ballast resistor, the coil, the high-tension leads, the rotor, the breaker points, the condenser, the spark plugs, etc., are tuned to one another (Fig. 12:58). Only recommended replacement parts should therefore be used.

The Cam or Dwell Angle

The cam or dwell angle (Fig. 12:59) is the angle during which the breaker points "dwell" in the closed position. The specified cam angle must be maintained to give the coil enough time to build up an adequate magnetic field (coil saturation). Special dwell meters are needed to obtain the proper setting. Some breaker points are equipped with adjusting screws that permit dwell to be set while the engine is running (Fig. 12:60). The screw is first turned inwards (clockwise) until the points stay practically closed and the engine begins to misfire. The screw is then turned outwards (anti-clockwise) as specified (e.g., ½ turn) to obtain the desired dwell setting. On the electronic ignition system, dwell is governed by the control unit and is therefore non-adjustable.

The Breaker Point Gap

The breaker point gap (Fig. 12:61) is the distance between the contact surfaces of the breaker points when the fibre or rubbing block of the movable breaker arm rides one of the crests of the breaker cam. The gap is measured with a narrow feeler gauge. Since a change in

The Prestolite Electrical Division of Eltra Corporation

Fig. 12:61   Adjusting Breaker Point Gap

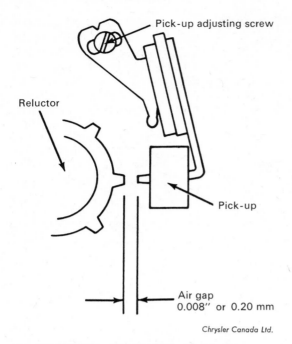

Pick-up adjusting screw

Reluctor

Pick-up

Air gap
0.008″ or 0.20 mm

Chrysler Canada Ltd.

Fig. 12:62 The Reluctor Tooth Air Gap

time is reduced to under 6/1,000 of a second. The result is incomplete combustion, with adverse effects on performance, mileage, and exhaust emission. To gain additional firing time, the spark is introduced at the end of the compression stroke before the piston reaches TDC. Although the advanced spark initiates combustion before TDC, the full firing pressure, involving the entire mixture, develops only after the piston has reached TDC. The desirable degree of ignition advance depends also on many additional factors besides engine speed. For example, the highly compressed, hot, dense mixture obtained under heavy engine loads with wide-open throttle and low rpm will fire much more rapidly than a lighter and cooler mixture at part throttle. Thus, less spark advance is needed in the first case than in the second one.

dwell will also affect the breaker point gap, it is customary to set either one or the other. Because a feeler gauge cannot account for the effects of pitted points, or of play in the distributor shaft, setting dwell is the more accurate method and therefore preferred.

The Reluctor-Tooth Air Gap

The reluctor-tooth air gap (Fig. 12:62) does not require periodic adjustments. If a defective pick-up is replaced, the air gap is reset to specifications with a non-magnetic feeler gauge or a piece of brass shim-stock of equivalent size. Never file the reluctor teeth, as rounded edges will cause erratic low-voltage signals.

Ignition-Timing

Ignition-timing determines at which point the spark is introduced into the combustion chamber. Ignition-timing is expressed in the number of degrees of crankshaft revolution at which firing occurs before or after TDC.

At an idle speed of 500 rpm, less than 6/100 of a second is available to fire the mixture during the power stroke. At 5,000 rpm, the

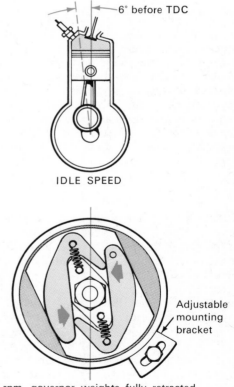

6° before TDC

IDLE SPEED

Adjustable mounting bracket

Low rpm, governor weights fully retracted, no centrifugal advance but 6° basic ignition-timing set at bracket

General Motors

Fig. 12:63 Basic Ignition-Timing

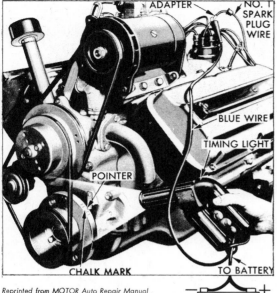

Fig. 12:64 Setting Ignition-Timing with a Timing Light

Some other factors involved are: type of fuel used, atmospheric conditions, compression ratio, combustion chamber design, valve-timing, cylinder temperature, and method of emission control.

Basic Ignition-Timing

Initial, or basic, ignition-timing is the specified number of degrees of spark advance while the engine is at slow idle and the vacuum advance unit is disconnected.[44] Basic timing can be adjusted by loosening the distributor mounting bracket (Figs. 12:46 and 12:65) and rotating the entire distributor housing. If it is moved in the direction of distributor shaft rotation, the spark is retarded; if it is turned in the opposite direction, the spark is advanced. The operation requires a stroboscope, which is an electronic device commonly called a *timing light* (Fig. 12:64). The stroboscope has two light alligator-

[44]Always refer to the manufacturer's specifications, especially on engines equipped with dual-action vacuum advance units (see Fig. 14:6). On some emission-controlled engines, ignition-timing may be set to fire the mixture after, rather than before, TDC.

clip leads, which are connected to the battery terminals, and one more heavily insulated lead, which is connected to the No. 1 spark-plug lead. Each time the No. 1 spark plug fires, the timing light produces a very bright flash. When aimed at the crankshaft pulley, these intermittent flashes make the timing marks easy to see.

Mechanical (Centrifugal) Spark Advance

Mechanical (centrifugal) spark advance is controlled by the engine speed. As the engine rpm increases, centrifugal force pushes the hinged fly-weights of the distributor governor outwards against the tension of calibrated springs (Fig. 12:65). As a result, the distributor cam,

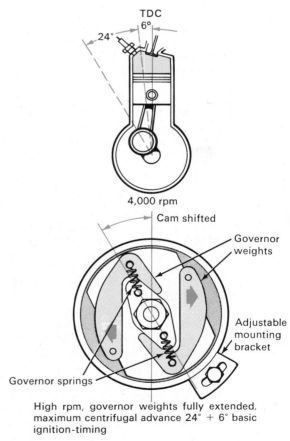

High rpm, governor weights fully extended, maximum centrifugal advance 24° + 6° basic ignition-timing

General Motors

Fig. 12:65 Centrifugal Advance

which is mounted freely on the distributor shaft, advances a few degrees relative to the distributor drive shaft in the direction of its rotation. This advances the time of point opening, and therefore the spark. As rpm decreases, centrifugal force lessens, the springs retract the advance mechanism, and the spark is retarded correspondingly.

Vacuum Spark Advance

Vacuum spark advance is controlled by the intake manifold vacuum; i.e., the spark is advanced or retarded in response to the throttle position and engine loads. (On engines with emission controls, vacuum advance may also depend on the engine temperature.) As shown in Fig. 12:66, the vacuum advance unit, which is connected to the manifold by means of a vacuum line, changes spark-timing by shifting the position of the breaker plate or, in some cases, the entire distributor. Under a high-manifold vacuum the spring-loaded diaphragm inside the vacuum advance unit is drawn into the advanced position. Under a low-manifold vacuum, which exists, for example, at low rpm with wide-open throttle and heavy engine loads, the diaphragm spring pushes the breaker plate into the retarded position. If this were not done, the full mixture entering the cylinders would fire rather violently (if not destructively), since the piston is still going up on the compression stroke.

The amount of centrifugal advance, vacuum advance, and initial timing is a function of engine design and varies with models and makes. It also depends on the octane rating of the fuel used (page 221). The specifications for a typical six-cylinder engine may read as follows: Ignition-timing 6° BTDC; Spark advance 24° at 4,000 rpm, 22° at 15″ of mercury manifold vacuum; Firing order 1-5-3-6-2-4.

Note well: Centrifugal and vacuum advance (not basic timing!) are often specified in degrees of distributor rotation rather than of crankshaft rotation. Since the distributor turns 1° for every 2° of crankshaft rotation, it may be necessary to convert the specifications. In the specifications quoted above, the same amount of advance may be listed as 12° at 2,000 rpm and 11° at 15″ of mercury, *distributor specifications.* Which system is used depends on whether the distributor is tested while the

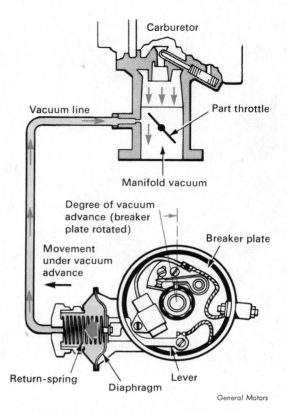

Fig. 12:66   *Vacuum Advance Mechanism*

engine is running, or separately in a special device known as a *synchrograph.*

The Spark Plugs

The spark plug (Fig. 12:67) provides the electrode gap necessary for the high-tension current to produce a spark, and thus ignite the fuel-air mixture in the combustion chamber.

Spark plugs come in different sizes, measured according to the diameter and the length of their thread. Standard spark-plug thread diameters (Fig. 12:68) are usually given in metric rather than in inch sizes (10 mm, 12 mm, 14 mm, or 18 mm), whereas the length of the thread, or reach, is given in fractions of an inch (e.g., 3/8″, 7/16″, 1/2″, 3/4″). The threaded part of the spark plug must not extend into the combustion chamber as it will cause hot spots or mechanical damage. Some spark plugs feature a "projected core-nose"; i.e., their electrodes and insulator tips reach right into the combus-

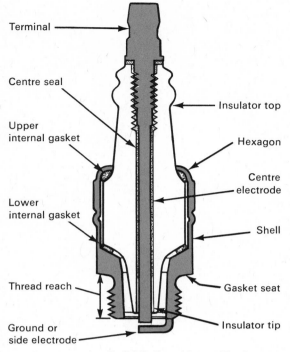

Terminal

Centre seal

Upper internal gasket

Lower internal gasket

Thread reach

Ground or side electrode

Insulator top

Hexagon

Centre electrode

Shell

Gasket seat

Insulator tip

The Prestolite Electrical Division of Eltra Corporation

Fig. 12:67   The Spark Plug (sectional view)

tion chamber. At higher engine speeds the cool incoming mixture "charge cools" the firing tip and the electrodes. This type of plug also reduces fouling at low speeds and idle (Fig. 12:69). Spark plugs with tapered seats require no gaskets.

The insulator, which is made of aluminum oxide, is often ribbed to prevent flash-over between the terminal and the shell, especially when the humidity is high. Obviously, the ribs are only effective if kept perfectly clean. The thread size and reach are usually indicated by letters on the insulator.

Resistor-type Spark Plugs have the same purpose as resistor-type ignition cables. Each spark actually consists of several electrical discharges. Only the first and strongest discharge is needed to ignite the mixture. The added resistance of the resistor-type spark plug limits the unnecessary refirings that cause television and radio interference.

Note: While it has little effect on performance if resistor-type spark plugs are connected to TVRS leads (Fig. 12:6 and page 184), the use

of high-tension leads with wire cores is recommended.

Some spark plugs are equipped with an auxiliary gap, also called a booster gap (Fig. 12:70), which causes a voltage build-up before the spark jumps the main electrode gap. This increases spark intensity, and thus, misfiring due to deposit foulings is reduced. Without the gap, voltage may be drained off across the insulator nose if it is contaminated with residues.

Heat Range of Spark Plugs

Spark plugs also come in different heat ranges suitable for all types of engines and different driving conditions. As shown by the arrows in Fig. 12:71, it takes longer for the heat to travel from the tip of the centre electrode to the coolant on a hot plug than on a cold one. When the proper heat range is chosen, electrode temperatures (700°F-1700°F or 371°C-927°C) are just sufficient to burn off deposits that otherwise cause fouling and misfiring. If, however, electrode temperatures exceed 1700°F, "pre-ignition" will occur, which means that the fuel is ignited before the spark jumps the electrode gap. In some cases, especially where pre-ignition takes place well ahead of TDC, severe damage may result, particularly to the pistons, rings, valves, and engine bearings. In brief, then, an engine operating under relatively *low combustion-chamber temperatures* requires a *hot plug* to keep the plug "face" clean, and one operating under *high combustion-chamber temperatures* requires a *cool plug* to prevent the plug from overheating. A hot plug has a low heat range; i.e., it heats up quickly. A cold plug has a high heat range, for it transfers the heat more readily to the cooling jackets. It can therefore function under more varied operating conditions. On North American-produced spark plugs the higher the number inscribed on the insulator, the hotter the plug is. On most imports the higher the number, the cooler the plug is.

Spark-plug Service is mostly confined to (1) visual inspection, (2) cleaning, (3) filing the centre electrode to remove rounded edges (Fig. 12:72), (4) re-gapping the electrode to specifications, usually 0.032" to 0.035", or 0.80 mm to 0.90 mm (Fig. 12:73), and (5) testing. The inspection of the plug's faces shows whether or not the engine is operating properly and if the heat range chosen is the correct one.

18 mm thread, $^{13}\!/_{16}''$ hexagon, tapered or "conic" seat (no gasket required), $^{1}\!/_{2}''$ reach, projected core-nose

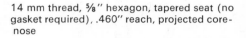

14 mm thread, $^{5}\!/_{8}''$ hexagon, tapered seat (no gasket required), .460″ reach, projected core-nose

14 mm thread, $^{13}\!/_{16}''$ hexagon, gasket required, short reach ($^{3}\!/_{8}''$), projected core-nose

14 mm thread, $^{13}\!/_{16}''$ hexagon, gasket required, long reach ($^{3}\!/_{4}''$), projected core-nose

12 mm thread, $^{11}\!/_{16}''$ hexagon, gasket required, $^{1}\!/_{2}''$ reach, retracted core-nose

10 mm thread, $^{5}\!/_{8}''$ hexagon, gasket required, $^{1}\!/_{2}''$ reach, retracted core-nose

Champion Spark Plug Company

Fig. 12:68   Some Common Spark-Plug Types and Sizes

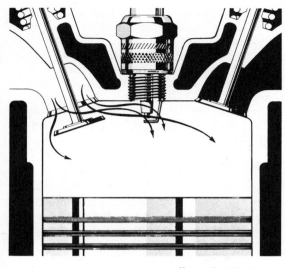

Champion Spark Plug Company

Fig. 12:69   Charge Cooling of Spark Plug with Projected Core-Nose Design

BOOSTER GAP

Champion Spark Plug Company

Fig. 12:70   Auxiliary or Booster Gap

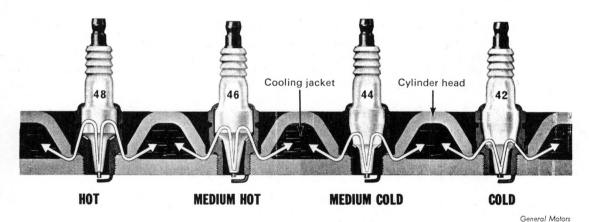

Cooling jacket

Cylinder head

48   46   44   42

HOT   **MEDIUM HOT**   **MEDIUM COLD**   **COLD**

General Motors

Fig. 12:71   Heat Range of Spark Plugs

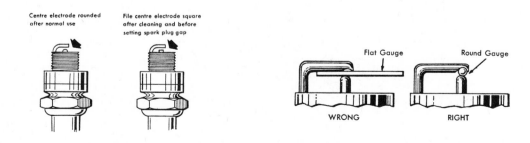

Centre electrode rounded after normal use

File centre electrode square after cleaning and before setting spark plug gap

Flat Gauge   Round Gauge

WRONG   RIGHT

Fig. 12:72   Filing the Centre Electrode   *Fig. 12:73   Regapping the Electrodes*

Some fuel additives, however, may cause residues that are quite deceptive. The insulator tip of a "normal" spark plug should have a grayish or yellowish-to-brown appearance. If the plug is carbon-fouled, the fuel mixture is too rich (sticking choke, flooding carburetor, dirty air-cleaner, etc.), or the plug is too "cold", and the heat range should be changed. Oil-fouled plugs indicate that too much oil is entering the combustion chamber. Often this is a sign that the engine is badly worn. If the plug's "face" shows evidence of overheating (severely eroded electrodes, metal beads on a light-coloured insulator tip, etc.), the plug may be too "hot", the mixture may be too lean, the ignition-timing could be out, or the valves aren't closing properly. Both filing and re-gapping will usually improve engine performance greatly, as this reduces voltage requirements for a good, strong spark. Deposits are removed with a sandblasting device that is also designed for testing spark plugs under simulated compression pressures. Some manufacturers, especially those of two-stroke-cycle engines, do not recommend the sandblasting of spark plugs. Spark plugs fitted to aluminum cylinder heads and Wankel engines should be lubricated with a suitable graphite compound. Ordinary lubricants change to very hard carbon deposits under high temperatures, and this often causes the threads to seize up.

While some spark plugs may last for more than 12,000 miles (19 200 km) under ideal conditions, most manufacturers recommend that they be changed every 6,000 miles (9600 km). This not only ensures maximum performance but it has also become necessary to meet stringent emission-control requirements. Normal wear of the centre electrode is roughly 0.001" per 1,000-2,000 miles, or 0.025 mm per 1600-3200 km.

The Light Circuit

The wiring diagrams in Figs. 12:74 and 12:75 show the connections of all the electrical units already described in this chapter, as well as those of the lights and switches discussed below.

Automotive Bulbs

Automotive bulbs, or "lamps" (Fig. 12:76), come in various standard sizes and shapes. They are usually rated according to voltage, amperage, and candle power (cp). For example, a dash bulb may have 2 cp, a dome light 6 cp, and a park light 4 cp.[45] Two-filament bulbs, such as those combining the park and

---

[45]With small bulbs (not sealed beams), the cp is roughly eight times the amperage draw of the bulb. The metric unit of light intensity is the candela (cd).

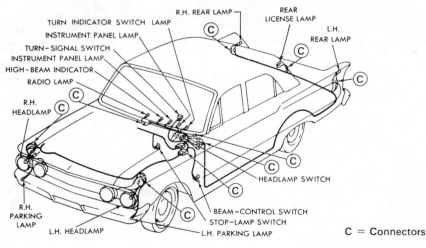

C = Connectors

Ford Motor Company

Fig. 12:74 Typical Light Circuit

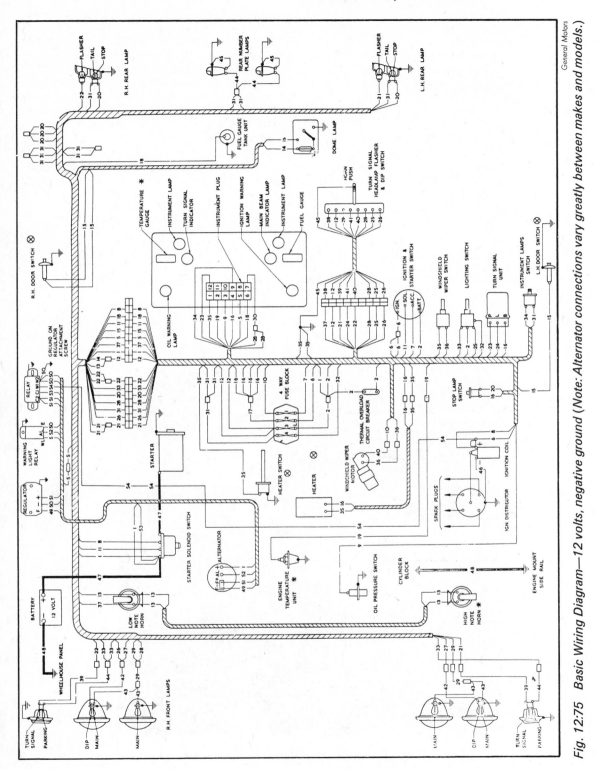

Fig. 12:75 Basic Wiring Diagram—12 volts, negative ground (Note: Alternator connections vary greatly between makes and models.)

General Motors

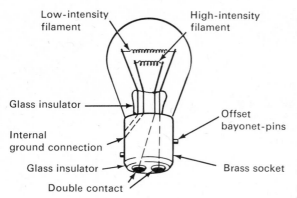

Low-intensity filament

High-intensity filament

Glass insulator

Offset bayonet-pins

Internal ground connection

Glass insulator

Brass socket

Double contact

Fig. 12:76 Two-filament Bulb (Note: Single-filament bulbs have bayonet pins at same level.)

stop lights in one bulb, may be rated as 4/32 cp. The bases of single-filament bulbs have straight lock pins, while those of two-filament bulbs have offset lock pins to prevent improper installation. The pins interlock with corresponding "bayonet" slots in the bulb socket so that a

good connection is maintained even under vibration. The incandescence or light of the bulb is the result of the intense heat generated by the electron flow through the filament (usually a very fine, coiled tungsten wire). To prevent the filament from oxidizing, i.e., burning out, some type of inert gas is substituted for air inside the bulb.

Improper bulb sizes or ratings will, among other things, cause overheating, overloaded circuits, blown fuses, improper flasher speeds, very intense or weak lights, and shortened service life.

Sealed Beam Lamps

Sealed beams (Fig. 12:77) are used in headlights. They are basically oversized bulbs with built-in reflectors. The lens, which is also part of the sealed beam, has a "prismic" finish to reduce glare and to provide a more concentrated, flatter beam of light. Three aiming lugs or pads on the lens assist the adjustment of the headlights. It is, however, quite common to

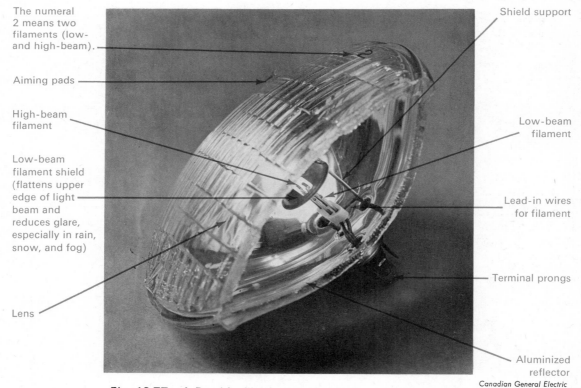

The numeral 2 means two filaments (low- and high-beam).

Shield support

Aiming pads

High-beam filament

Low-beam filament

Low-beam filament shield (flattens upper edge of light beam and reduces glare, especially in rain, snow, and fog)

Lead-in wires for filament

Terminal prongs

Lens

Aluminized reflector

Canadian General Electric

Fig. 12:77 A Double-filament Sealed Beam (sectional view)

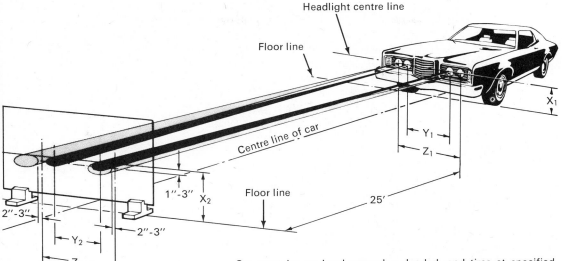

Headlight centre line

Floor line

Centre line of car

Floor line

X_1

Y_1

Z_1

1"-3" X_2

25'

2"-3"

2"-3"

Y_2

Z_2

Car must be on level ground, unloaded, and tires at specified
pressure. Adjust inner lights ⬤ with outer lights ⬭
covered. The outer lights are adjusted on low beam only. Verify
above specifications with current federal and provincial laws.

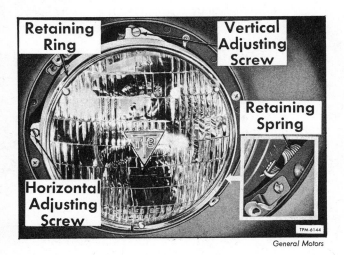

Retaining Ring

Vertical Adjusting Screw

Retaining Spring

Horizontal Adjusting Screw

TPM-6144

General Motors

Fig. 12:78   Headlight Adjustments

adjust the lights by placing the unloaded
vehicle 25 feet in front of a screen or wall provided with aiming lines (Fig. 12:78). The
centres of the bright spots of the high beams
illuminating the screen are set 1 to 3 inches, or
approximately 2.5 cm to 7.5 cm, lower than
height X , which equals the height of line X_1
joining the centres of the headlight lenses. The
low-beam spots are so adjusted that their upper
edges just touch the same horizontal centre
line, while their left edges are 2 to 3 inches, or
approximately 5 cm to 7.5 cm, to the right of

vertical centre lines Z_2, that is, as seen from the
driver seat. This reduces glare for oncoming
drivers, and it improves curbside and shoulder
illumination for better orientation. The less
intense lower beams are also used during fog,
as they cause less reflection. On vehicles
equipped with four headlights, the two outer
units have two filaments (low-beam and high-
beam), and the two inner units have only one
high-beam filament each. A double-filament
sealed beam is equipped with three terminal
prongs (low, high, and ground) and has the

number *2* cast into the upper part of the lens (Fig. 12:77). Sometimes a third, low-intensity filament is added for safety in case the other filaments burn out. A single-filament unit has only two terminal prongs and is identified by the number *1*. It is used for the inner headlights on vehicles equipped with four headlights. At present the *total output* of the high beams may not exceed 75,000 cp (Canada and U.S.A.). This regulation is under review and the cp output will likely be increased. The most common lens sizes are 5¾" and 7".

The *dimmer switch*, which is usually foot-controlled and mounted on the toe board, permits the driver to select either the low beam or the high beam. Since certain light conditions make it difficult to tell which beam is working, the high beam is connected to a coloured pilot light in the dash panel (Fig. 12:7). Some vehicles employ an automatic dimmer switch that is controlled by a photo-electric sensor mounted behind the windshield. The sensor is a light-sensitive device similar to that used on automatic lawn lights, and it is triggered by the light beams of oncoming cars. The *main light switch* usually includes a *rheostat* (variable resistor) to control the brightness of the dash lights. The switch often incorporates fuses, a circuit breaker, and a dome-light switch (Figs. 12:79 and 12:80).

The *stop-light switch* is either of the hydraulic or the mechanical type and is connected to the *turn-signal switch* (Fig. 12:75) in such a manner that if both are engaged at the same time, one stop light is flashing while the other stays on until the brake is released. The *flasher*

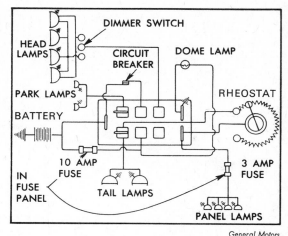

General Motors

Fig. 12:80   The Main Light Switch Circuit

unit itself (Fig. 12:9) is essentially an electric circuit breaker. As such, the device depends on a given amperage draw. Loose connections, a poor ground, a burned-out bulb filament, or the wrong type of bulb will affect its flashing speed and operation.

The Horns

The horns are connected to the *horn relay*, which in turn is activated by a switch in the steering wheel assembly. This switch is not heavy enough for the horns to be connected directly. The sound is generated by a steel diaphragm attached to a vibrating electro-magnet. The pitch is often adjustable.

Electrical Meters

Where an electric device, such as a bulb, fails because of old age, it is simply replaced. However, a blown fuse, a weak spark in the ignition system, insufficient starter torque, or a discharged battery, to name just a few typical examples, are usually signs of more serious problems. Electrical meters provide, in many cases, the only reliable means of determining the source of these problems. While it is not possible here to give detailed instructions for their proper use, much can be learned from the brief descriptions and examples given below. If the readings obtained deviate from those given in the manufacturer's specifications, the unit in question must be repaired or replaced. In many cases Ohm's Law can be applied to calculate voltage, amperage, or resistance (see

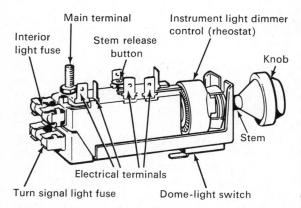

Fig. 12:79   The Main Light Switch (Release button may be on opposite side.)

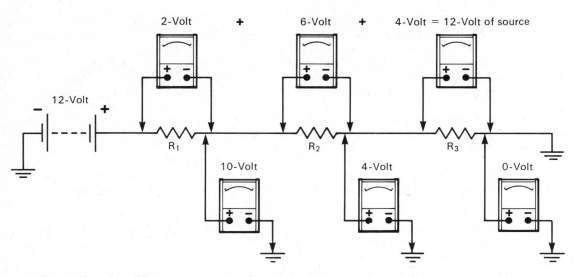

Fig. 12:81   *Checking Voltage Drop and Circuit Resistance with a Voltmeter*

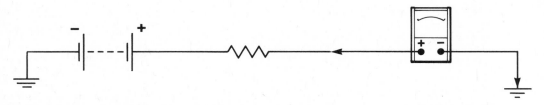

Fig. 12:82   *Checking Current Flow (Amperage Draw) in a Circuit with an Ammeter*

page 151).

The *Voltmeter* is connected in parallel as shown in Fig. 12:81. The example shows that the total of the voltage drops in a series circuit (2V + 6V + 4V) equals the applied voltage (12V). Each voltage drop is the result of the resistance in the circuit section tested.

Caution: Observe the proper polarity when connecting the test leads, and don't exceed the rated voltage of the meter.

The *Ammeter* is usually connected in series as shown in Fig. 12:82 and with the circuit closed. Observe the proper polarity and never exceed the amperage rating of the meter. For example, connecting a 60A ammeter to a starter circuit will burn out the meter instantly. Amperage readings higher than those specified usually indicate a short, while lower readings indicate high resistance, such as that caused by a poor connection (assuming the battery is fully charged).

The *Ohmmeter* is connected in series to the unit to be tested (Fig. 12:83). Ohmmeters

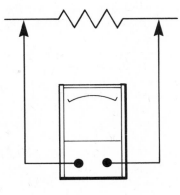

Fig. 12:83   *Checking Resistance with an Ohmmeter (Note:* ‑Ɱ‑ *in above diagrams represents any resistance, e.g., light bulb, electric motor, coil, poor connection, etc.)*

usually have their own source of power. Never hook up an ohmmeter to a circuit under power. Since the resistance of electrical devices varies greatly, a meter of suitable range must be chosen. Before use, always test the ohmmeter by connecting the two test prongs directly to one another. If the reading obtained is not zero, the meter needs calibration, new batteries, or repairs. Turn the meter off when it is not in use. If it is left on, the batteries will discharge, and if they begin to leak, the meter will be damaged.

RECOMMENDED ASSIGNMENTS

1. State the law of magnetic poles.
2. Name the factors that determine (a) the strength of an electromagnetic field and (b) its polarity.
3. What is electricity? Write a brief paragraph explaining what it is.
4. Explain the difference between A.C. and D.C.
5. Define in point form (a) voltage, (b) amperage, (c) resistance, (d) wattage.
6. Define I, V, and R in terms of Ohm's formula.
7. What factors determine the correct choice of electrical wires?
8. Comment on the differences between fuses, circuit breakers, and fusible links.
9. What may be the results if a fuse of incorrect rating is installed?
10. Explain the term "negative ground-return circuit".
11. Illustrate by means of two simple diagrams the difference between a parallel circuit and a series circuit.
12. Define the following terms: (a) open circuit, (b) closed circuit, (c) ground, (d) short circuit, (e) dead short.
13. What are the two major functions of the storage battery?
14. How is the proper electrolyte level of a storage battery determined?
15. Give two reasons why very low temperatures reduce cranking speeds.
16. Give two reasons why a battery must be fully charged even if kept in storage.
17. List ten important safety precautions to be observed when working with storage batteries.
18. In what respect does the electrolyte of a fully charged battery differ from that of a discharged battery?
19. Calculate the correct hydrometer readings for the following electrolyte samples, and indicate in each case the percentage of charge: (a) Specific gravity 1.250 at 120°F; (b) Specific gravity 1.260 at 0°F; (c) Specific gravity 1.270 at 80°F.
20. A 12-volt battery discharges 6A for 20 hours (temperature is 80°F and cell voltage remains at over 1.75V). What is the watt-hour rating of this battery?
21. What is the purpose of the commutator on a D.C. generator?
22. Explain the difference between the field windings of an A.C. generator and a D.C. generator.
23. Why is it necessary to rectify the A.C.?
24. What is the purpose of the voltage regulator?
25. What are the two major differences between the field windings of a generator and a starter motor?
26. Explain the difference between a solenoid-type starter drive and a Bendix-type starter drive.
27. What is the function of the overrunning clutch used in starter drives?
28. Prepare a labelled diagram of the ignition coil, and explain the purpose of the following parts: (a) the primary winding, (b) the secondary winding, (c) the laminated soft-iron core.
29. Why is the coil core laminated, and why is it made of soft iron?
30. Explain briefly the principle of electromagnetic induction.
31. Prepare a labelled schematic diagram of a complete ignition circuit (primary and secondary circuits).
32. State the functions of (a) the breaker points, (b) the condenser, and (c) the rotor.
33. What are the main advantages of an electronic ignition system?
34. Explain the purpose of (a) the reluctor and pick-up assembly, and (b) the electronic control unit.
35. Why is dwell not adjustable on electronic ignition systems?

36. Why should the reluctor never be filed?
37. (a) What is the difference between an ordinary electric wire and a high-tension lead? (b) How should high-tension leads be removed?
38. What does the term "balanced ignition system" mean?
39. Define the terms "cam angle" and "breaker point gap". (Illustrate your answer with a simple sketch.)
40. What is the purpose of (a) centrifugal advance and (b) vacuum advance? How are both types of spark advance controlled?
41. (a) What is the purpose of initial timing? (b) How is it adjusted?
42. What is the purpose of the auxiliary gap in some spark plugs?
43. Explain the function of the projected core-nose design of some spark plugs.
44. For a doctor who makes house calls, would you recommend a spark plug of slightly higher heat range than normal or one of slightly lower heat range? Explain your answer.
45. List in proper order the necessary operations involved in the reconditioning of a spark plug.
46. (a) Name four points to be considered when selecting the correct bulb. (b) List six possible problems caused by neglecting the above points.
47. By means of a simple sketch, show how a voltmeter could be used to check an ignition ballast resistor for an open circuit.
48. The normal draw of a primary coil winding is 4A. (a) How would you connect an ammeter to check the amperage draw? (Illustrate your answer.) (b) What condition would be indicated if the draw was 5A? (c) If the draw was 0A?

TROUBLE-SHOOTING

There is at least one solution to each problem.

1. An engine starts and fires normally with the ignition key in the "start" position; in the "run" position, however, the engine stalls.
2. After a new ignition coil is installed, the engine develops a bad "miss", especially under heavy loads.
3. The owner of an almost new car replaces the spark plugs before going on a long trip. A few hours later the engine develops severe piston failure.
4. A driver has changed a set of spark plugs. When he starts the engine, it backfires, and the carburetor catches fire.
5. The correct stop-light bulb is installed, but the light appears very dim.
6. A customer complains that both the cigarette lighter and the wiper motor work fine when used singly, but when both are operated together, the fuse blows.
7. A friendly neighbour helps a motorist to get his car started by offering a "boost" with his own battery. When the engine finally runs, the charging light stays on.
8. A customer claims that the fan belt squeals as soon as he turns the lights on.
9. A motorist complains that his radio developed serious interference noises after a major tune-up was carried out.
10. A car owner installs a new set of breaker points. Surprisingly, performance drops, and a loud pinging noise is heard under sharp acceleration.

13

The Fuel System

The purpose of the fuel system (Fig. 13:1) is to store the fuel and to deliver the correct air-fuel mixture to the cylinders. It consists of the following basic units:

1. The fuel tank (Fig. 13:2)
2. The fuel gauge circuit (Fig. 13:3)
3. The fuel pump and fuel filter (Fig. 13:11)
4. The carburetor and air-cleaner (Figs. 13:13 and 13:25)
5. The intake manifold (Fig. 13:14)
6. Various emission-control devices (Chapter 14)

The Fuel Tank

The fuel tank (Fig. 13:2) stores the fuel and is usually located at the rear of the vehicle. On rear-, or mid-engined cars, the tank is often in the front. The tank is equipped with a vent to relieve back pressure during refuelling, to prevent a vacuum as the tank empties,[46] and to release vapour pressure due to temperature changes when, for instance, the car is parked

---

[46]If the vent is plugged, the fuel pump vacuum is sufficient to collapse the entire fuel tank.

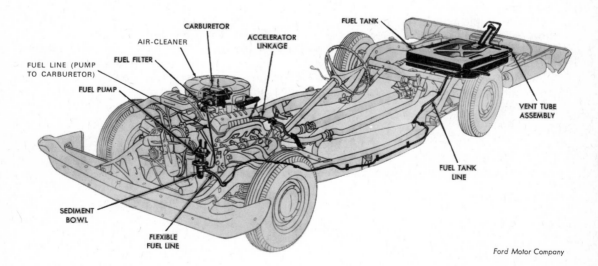

Ford Motor Company

Fig. 13:1   Components of a Basic Fuel System (For emission-control systems, see Chapter 14.)

in the hot sun. The tank may include any of the following devices: a drainage plug, a fuel strainer, and baffles to reduce surge. Some fuel tanks also incorporate an expansion tank that prevents overfilling (Fig. 14:1).

The Fuel Gauge Units

The *sending unit* (Figs. 13:2 and 13:3), mounted inside the tank, consists of a variable resistor, often called a rheostat, which is connected to the *fuel gauge dash unit*. The resistance, and thus the amount of fuel indicated, varies as the float arm that controls the sending unit moves with the fuel level. Fig. 13:3 shows the float just below the half-empty position and the sliding contact of the rheostat almost centred. Under this condition the current, after passing through the left-hand coil of the dash unit, is divided in such a way that approximately one-third of the current flows through the right-hand coil and the remainder flows through the rheostat. The resulting balance of magnetic forces causes the armature and the indicator

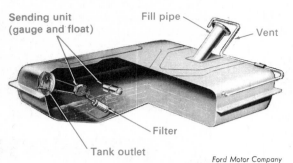
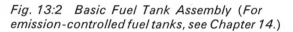

Ford Motor Company

Fig. 13:2 Basic Fuel Tank Assembly (For emission-controlled fuel tanks, see Chapter 14.)

arm attached to it to move into the position shown. When the tank is empty, the float lowers the resistance of the rheostat to almost zero, since the sliding contact arm provides a direct path to ground for the connecting wire. The current now takes the path of least resistance, i.e., through the left-hand coil only. The magnetic pull of this coil causes the armature and the pointer to move to the *E* (empty)

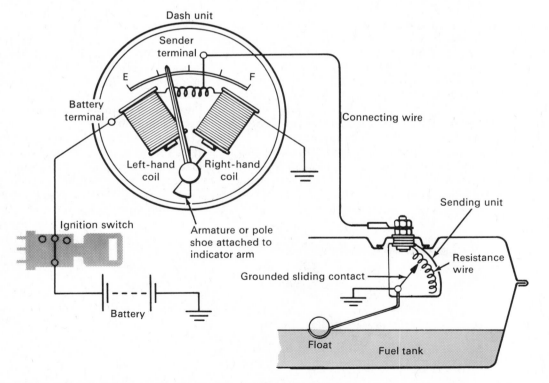

Fig. 13:3 Circuit Diagram of a Fuel Gauge (Note: The sliding contact and resistance wire form a variable resistor, often called a rheostat.)

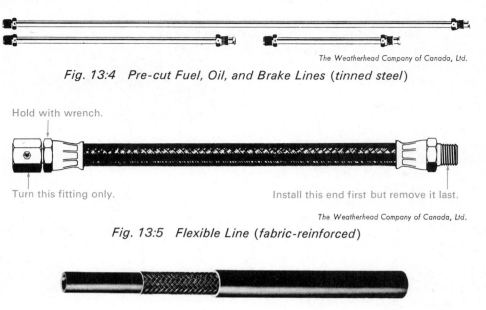

The Weatherhead Company of Canada, Ltd.

Fig. 13:4   Pre-cut Fuel, Oil, and Brake Lines (tinned steel)

Hold with wrench.

Turn this fitting only.

Install this end first but remove it last.

The Weatherhead Company of Canada, Ltd.

Fig. 13:5   Flexible Line (fabric-reinforced)

The Weatherhead Company of Canada, Ltd.

Fig. 13:6   Low-pressure Fuel Hose (fabric-reinforced; no fittings needed) (exposed view)

position. If the tank is refilled, the float rises to its upper limit and so does the resistance of the rheostat. The current, after passing through the left-hand coil, is thus divided equally between the rheostat and the right-hand coil. The latter now has sufficient magnetic strength to move the pointer to the *F* (full) position. On many fuel gauges the circuit is arranged in the opposite way; i.e., the resistance of the rheostat is highest when the tank is empty and lowest when it is full. Others employ an electrically heated bimetal spring of the type used in certain temperature gauges. In this case the fuel gauge, the temperature gauge, and the oil pressure

gauge are usually all of the bimetal type. (For principles of operation see page 125 and Fig. 10:13.) Because the accuracy of these gauges depends on a supply of uniform voltage, they are all connected to a common low-voltage regulator set at approximately 5 volts. As a further refinement, a low-fuel-level warning light is sometimes added.

Caution: The repair of fuel tanks and sending units should be left to experts. Report leaking tanks immediately. Broken exhaust pipes, shorts, sparks, static electricity, hammering, welding, or drilling can cause an explosion. Never refuel with the engine running or near an open flame!

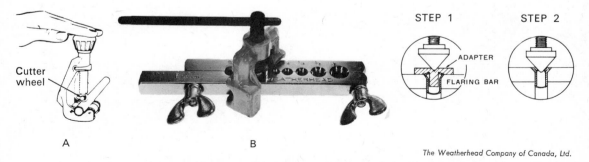

Cutter wheel

STEP 1

ADAPTER

FLARING BAR

STEP 2

A   B

The Weatherhead Company of Canada, Ltd.

Fig. 13:7   Tube Cutter and Flaring Tool (45°)

The Fuel Lines

The fuel lines (Figs. 13:1, 13:4, 13:5, and 13:6) carry the fuel from the tank to the fuel pump and from there to the carburetor. The most common materials are tinned steel, fabric-reinforced synthetic rubber, and neoprene. The last two materials are used where vibration or movement is encountered, for example, between the chassis and the fuel pump.

The size of fuel line tubing is determined by its outside diameter, whereas fuel line hoses are usually specified according to their inside diameters. It is quite common for the mechanic to make up his own fuel lines from suitable stock. The operation requires a special *tube cutter* and a *flaring tool* (Fig. 13:7). The funnel-shaped "flare" at each end of the tube acts as a leakproof seal between the two fittings to which the line is connected. Automotive flares must be double flares; i.e., for reasons of safety the flare is folded inward on itself, as shown. Since bending a tube causes its walls to collapse, the operation requires a special *tube bender*. The most common type is a tightly wound coil spring that is slid over the tube section to be bent (Fig. 13:8).

To prevent vapour lock, i.e., the formation of vapour bubbles, which may interfere with the action of the fuel pump, all fuel lines should be kept away from hot parts, particularly the exhaust manifold.

Tube Fittings

Tube fittings are usually made of brass or steel and are available in many different sizes and styles. The most common types are shown in Fig. 13:9. Because sealing compounds may interfere with the operation of jets, valves, and certain hydraulic devices, many automotive fittings employ a tapered pipe thread of the "dry seal" type, which is, as the name implies, self-sealing.

The system of pipe thread sizes is somewhat confusing. The sizes are said to be nominal, i.e., the size indicated is not really the actual size of the fitting. Fig. 13:10 shows the true sizes of the four most common pipe threads. These diagrams can be used to identify the size of a fitting to be replaced. It should be noted that connectors of a given external thread size may have different "mouth" sizes. For example, 1/8" connectors, while always of the same *external* thread size, may have different *internal* threads to receive nuts for tube diameters of 1/8", 3/16", 1/4" and 5/16". The nuts used on flared brake and fuel lines have a straight thread; i.e., they are without a taper.

Brass fittings are more expensive than steel fittings and are not as strong. On the other hand, they do not corrode or seize up and, being softer, they form a very good seal. Because of the safety hazards involved, especially with brake and fuel systems, the following rules must always be observed:

1. Use only approved replacement parts, and don't substitute one material for another; e.g., do not use brass fittings on brake lines.
2. To prevent the tube or hose from being twisted, don't allow the connector attached to the carburetor, fuel pump, etc., to turn while you tighten or loosen the line nut.
3. Whenever possible use flare nut wrenches (Fig. 1:10). The thin and relatively soft walls of fittings are easily crushed.

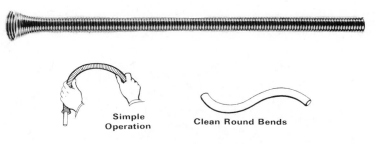

Simple Operation

Clean Round Bends

The Weatherhead Company of Canada, Ltd.

Fig. 13:8   Spring-type Tube Benders

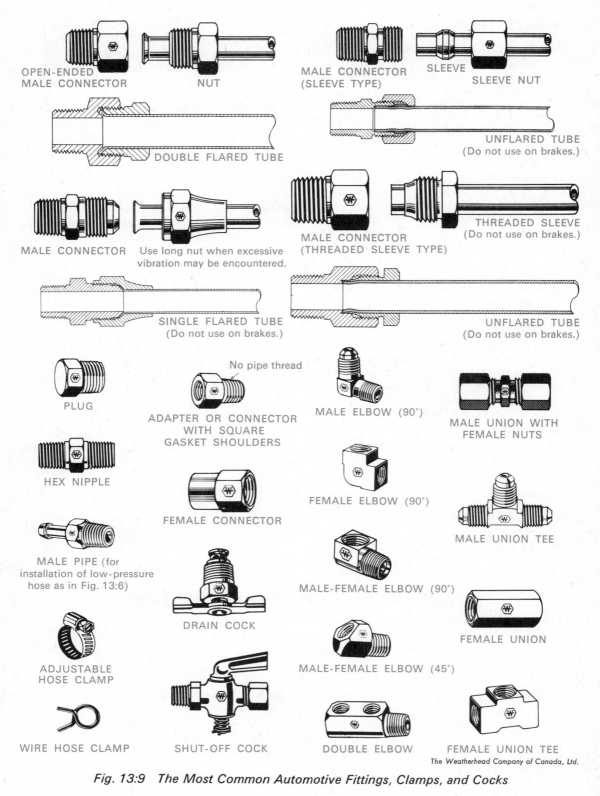

OPEN-ENDED MALE CONNECTOR

NUT

MALE CONNECTOR (SLEEVE TYPE)

SLEEVE

SLEEVE NUT

DOUBLE FLARED TUBE

UNFLARED TUBE
(Do not use on brakes.)

MALE CONNECTOR

Use long nut when excessive vibration may be encountered.

MALE CONNECTOR (THREADED SLEEVE TYPE)

THREADED SLEEVE
(Do not use on brakes.)

SINGLE FLARED TUBE
(Do not use on brakes.)

UNFLARED TUBE
(Do not use on brakes.)

PLUG

No pipe thread

ADAPTER OR CONNECTOR WITH SQUARE GASKET SHOULDERS

MALE ELBOW (90°)

MALE UNION WITH FEMALE NUTS

HEX NIPPLE

FEMALE CONNECTOR

FEMALE ELBOW (90°)

MALE UNION TEE

MALE PIPE (for installation of low-pressure hose as in Fig. 13:6)

DRAIN COCK

MALE-FEMALE ELBOW (90°)

FEMALE UNION

ADJUSTABLE HOSE CLAMP

MALE-FEMALE ELBOW (45°)

WIRE HOSE CLAMP

SHUT-OFF COCK

DOUBLE ELBOW

FEMALE UNION TEE

The Weatherhead Company of Canada, Ltd.

Fig. 13:9   The Most Common Automotive Fittings, Clamps, and Cocks

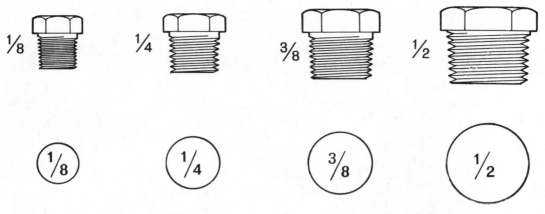

Fig. 13:10   Actual Sizes of Pipe Threads

4. Align the tubes properly, starting the fittings by hand to prevent cross-threading. Fittings with tapered pipe threads are usually tightened 2½ turns beyond "hand tight". Nuts fitted to double flared lines are tightened ⅙ of a turn beyond the point where a solid feeling is encountered.
5. Always check for leaks under operating pressures.

The Fuel Pump

The fuel pump (Fig. 13:11) pumps the fuel from the fuel tank to the carburetor. The mechanical type of fuel pump is driven by an eccentric on the camshaft. The eccentric may rub directly against the rocker arm of the pump or it may activate a push rod, which in turn will work the rocker arm. The location of the pump determines which method is used.

As the high part of the eccentric forces the rocker arm down (Fig. 13:12a), the rocker arm link pulls the diaphragm upwards against the pressure of the diaphragm spring. This causes a low-pressure area in the chamber below the diaphragm. As a result the inlet valve opens and the outlet valve closes. Both valves are essentially one-way check valves, acting like those in a human heart. The two valves are identical except that they are installed to work in opposite directions. The atmospheric pressure on the gasoline in the fuel tank is now greater than the pressure below the diaphragm, causing the gasoline to flow from the tank to the fuel pump. When the low part of the eccentric faces the rocker arm (Fig. 13:12b), the diaphragm

spring forces the diaphragm down, thus creating pressure on the gasoline inside the pump. This closes the inlet valve and the fuel is pumped past the open outlet valve into the fuel line connected to the carburetor float chamber. When the carburetor has received all the fuel it needs, the diaphragm is held in its upper position because the gasoline caught in the chamber below it won't allow the diaphragm spring to expand. At this point the rocker arm, assisted by the rocker arm return spring, is riding on the eccentric without doing any work. The rocker arm can idle in this manner because of the special split-linkage arrangement between the rocker link and the rocker arm. (The design is like an elbow joint that will bend in one direction but not in the other.) As soon as the carburetor needs more fuel, the diaphragm is lowered once again by the diaphragm spring. How far the diaphragm moves downwards from its upper position during each and every stroke depends solely on how much fuel must be supplied to the carburetor at any given moment; and that in turn is determined by the varying fuel requirements of the engine itself. Under normal operating conditions, the diaphragm would merely vibrate in its upper position. The only time the diaphragm would actually go through the full length of its maximum stroke would be when the carburetor was empty (for instance, after repairs, or when the tank runs out of fuel). It is obvious then that fuel pump pressure is governed mainly by the strength of the diaphragm spring.

To maintain a more even fuel flow between strokes, some pumps are equipped with an air

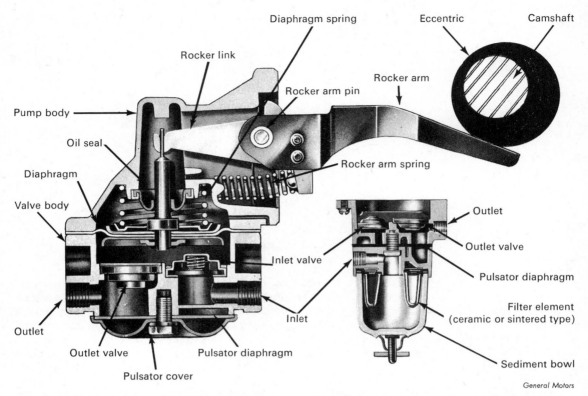

Fig. 13:11 Cross-section of a Mechanical-type Fuel Pump. The filter bowl assembly shown on right can be installed in place of a pulsator cover.

cushion or a pulsator diaphragm connected to their outlet side (Fig. 13:11). When the outlet valve closes, the expanding air cushion (or pulsator diaphragm) maintains the flow in the fuel line joining the pump and the carburetor. Frequently, the pump includes some type of strainer or filter, and a sediment bowl. On many engines the fuel pump is installed with the pulsator cover facing upwards. Some fuel systems employ electrical fuel pumps. Their advantage is that they can be mounted in a cooler place away from the engine or even in the fuel tank itself. They also begin to pump as soon as the ignition key is turned on.

The rebuilding of fuel pumps is no longer a common practice; in fact, many pumps are sealed, non-serviceable units. It is more economical now to install a new pump or a factory-rebuilt unit. The most common causes of fuel pump failure are a worn linkage, a weak or broken diaphragm spring, and leakage through the valves or the diaphragm. Leakage through the diaphragm will cause dilution of the motor oil or even explosions, as it will allow fuel to run directly into the crankcase.

Fuel pumps can be tested for pressure, vacuum, and capacity, i.e., rate of flow.

The Fuel Filter

Some of the passages in the carburetor are so small that even minute particles of rust, metal chips, or dirt may cause interference. The fuel filter removes these particles before the fuel enters the carburetor. The filter may be part of the fuel tank (Fig. 13:2), the fuel pump (Figs. 13:11 and 13:12), or the carburetor (Figs. 13:13 and 13:15), or it may be connected to the fuel line between the pump and the carburetor (Fig. 13:1). Many fuel systems have two or even three fuel filters, each at one of the points mentioned above. Some fuel filters can be

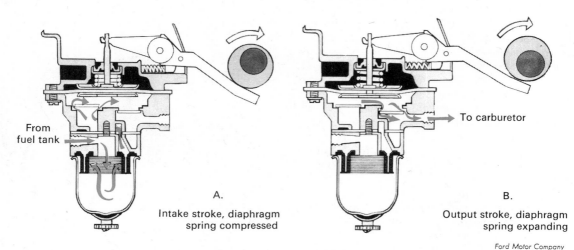

A.	B.
Intake stroke, diaphragm spring compressed	Output stroke, diaphragm spring expanding

From fuel tank

To carburetor

Ford Motor Company

Fig. 13:12 Operation of a Fuel Pump

cleaned; others are non-serviceable replacement items. The filter element itself is made of some type of microporous material, such as synthetic fibre, ceramic, sintered bronze granules, laminated sheet brass, or very fine wire gauze. Unfortunately, very small rust particles suspended in the fuel still manage to get through. Because the sediment formed by these minute particles interferes with the very small passages in the carburetor, one of the fuel filters may incorporate a magnetic trap.

The Carburetor

The carburetor (Fig. 13:13) mixes the air and the fuel in the correct ratio for all driving condi-

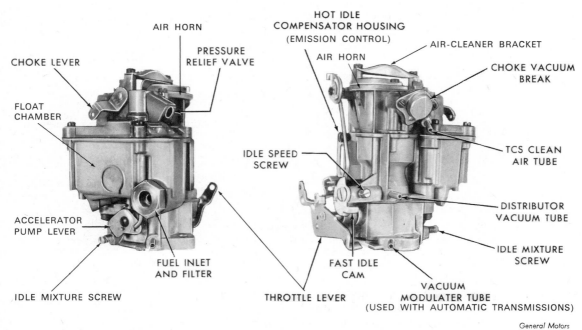

CHOKE LEVER

AIR HORN

PRESSURE RELIEF VALVE

FLOAT CHAMBER

ACCELERATOR PUMP LEVER

FUEL INLET AND FILTER

IDLE MIXTURE SCREW

HOT IDLE COMPENSATOR HOUSING (EMISSION CONTROL)

AIR HORN

AIR-CLEANER BRACKET

CHOKE VACUUM BREAK

IDLE SPEED SCREW

TCS CLEAN AIR TUBE

DISTRIBUTOR VACUUM TUBE

IDLE MIXTURE SCREW

FAST IDLE CAM

THROTTLE LEVER

VACUUM MODULATER TUBE (USED WITH AUTOMATIC TRANSMISSIONS)

General Motors

Fig. 13:13 Single-barrel Carburetor Seen from Two Sides

tions. It supplies this mixture to the cylinders through the intake manifold and the intake ports. The preparation of the mixture involves four basic steps:

1. *metering the fuel* (i.e., controlling the amount of fuel mixed with the air);
2. *breaking up the fuel* into minute particles so that the fuel's surface area in contact with the air is increased (this process, which aids evaporation, is often called "atomization", even though the fuel breaks down at best only into molecules);
3. *vaporization*, i.e., changing these fuel particles into the gaseous or vapour state (fuel droplets wouldn't burn quickly enough). Vaporization, however, is not completed in the carburetor but continues in the intake manifold and ports; and
4. *distribution of the mixture* to the cylinders.

These four steps are illustrated in Fig. 13:14.

In terms of maximum engine efficiency and power output, a mixture of air and gasoline containing by weight fifteen parts of air and one part of gasoline, or 9,000 parts to one part in volume, would do the best job. Modern engines with emission controls generally run on very "lean" mixtures, sometimes beyond 18:1. On the other hand, certain operating conditions, such as cold starts, engine idle, and sudden acceleration, may require "rich" mixtures considerably below 15:1.

Automotive carburetors consist of seven systems or circuits:

1. The float system (Fig. 13:15)
2. The low-speed or idle system (Fig. 13:16)
3. The transition system (Fig. 13:16)
4. The high-speed or main system (Fig. 13:17)
5. The accelerator-pump system (Fig. 13:19)
6. The power system (Fig. 13:17)
7. The choke system (Fig. 13:22)

The Float System

The float system maintains a constant level of gasoline in the float chamber at all times (Fig. 13:15). Fuel entering the carburetor travels through the needle-and-seat valve into the float chamber. As the float rises with the fuel, it reaches a predetermined level at which the float mechanism forces the needle valve against its seat. At this point, fuel delivery from the fuel pump is cut off momentarily, until more fuel is needed. The float thus maintains the

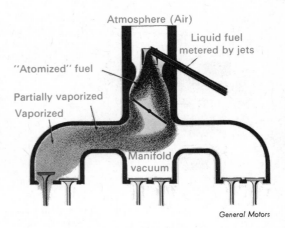

Fig. 13:14 *The Four Functions of Carburetion: Metering, Atomization, Vaporization, and Distribution of the Fuel*

specified fuel level, lowering and rising just enough to satisfy the carburetor's demand for gasoline.[47] Should the gasoline tank run out of fuel, the float must be prevented from dropping to the bottom of the float chamber, as it might cause the needle valve to jam. This condition would result in dangerous flooding when the engine was restarted. A stop tang on the float arm prevents this. Both the float level and the float drop are adjusted to the manufacturer's specifications. Correct float settings are extremely important, as they affect the proper

[47]This action is very similar to the float action in a toilet tank.

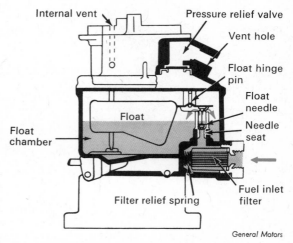

Fig. 13:15 *The Float System*

functioning of all fuel circuits in the carburetor. The float is made of either hollow brass or some synthetic foam material. To prolong life service and to improve sealing, some needle valves have tips made of a resilient plastic. Worn needle-and-seat valves and floats that have lost their buoyancy must be replaced as they cause poor engine performance, high emission, low fuel mileage, flooding, and even fires.

The Low-speed System, or Idle System

The low-speed system, or idle system, supplies the engine with the correct air-fuel mixture at idle and when the engine is under very light loads with the *throttle plate* (also called the throttle valve) almost closed (Fig. 13:16). In this position a relatively low pressure (about 21″ or 533 mm of mercury) is created below the throttle plate. (It's like putting your hand across the suction pipe of a vacuum cleaner.) This "vacuum" causes the fuel in the float chamber, which is under atmospheric pressure, to be pushed through the *main jet*, the *idle tube*, and the *idle passage*, and finally out of the *idle discharge port*. The purpose of the *idle air bleeds* is to premix fuel and air even before the fuel is discharged into the main air stream. The air bleeds also prevent the fuel in the float chamber from being siphoned off through the idle port and into the manifold when the engine is stopped. The spring-loaded *idle mixture screw*, or *idle mixture needle*, allows the mechanic to adjust the proper low-speed mix-

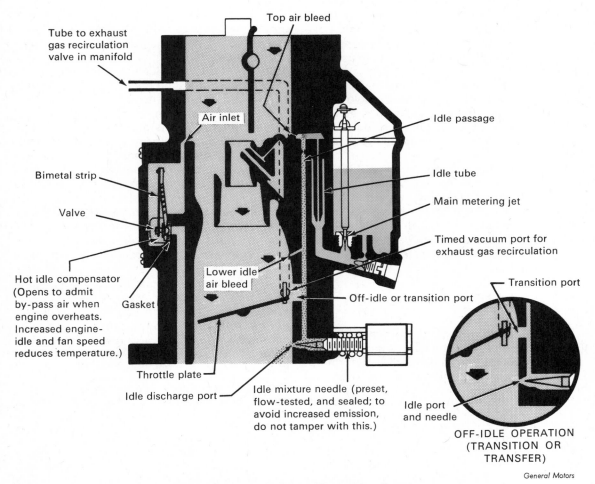

Fig. 13:16   The Idle and Transition System

ture setting.[48] The *idle speed screw*, or *throttle stop screw* (Fig. 13:13), on the other hand, controls the minimum throttle opening, and thus the engine-idle speed, if the foot is removed from the accelerator. On some carburetors the throttle is closed completely at idle and the necessary air is supplied through a by-pass port. In this case, idle speed is adjusted by means of an air screw in the carburetor body.

The Transition System, or Transfer System

This is actually part of the idle system and its function is to provide a smooth change-over or "transfer" from the idle system to the high-speed system (usually somewhere between 25 mph and 40 mph, or 40 km/h and 60 km/h, in high gear and on level ground). When the throttle valve is opened beyond the idle position, the airflow increases, but the pressure below the throttle decreases. This causes less fuel to be drawn out of the idle discharge port. Since higher engine rpm and loads require more fuel, not less, the engine would simply stall at this point if it were not for the transition circuit. Note that at part throttle the transfer port, which was above the throttle valve at idle speed, is now below the raised edge of the throttle plate. The manifold "vacuum" below the throttle plate, while less than before, can now draw fuel from the idle discharge port as well as the transfer port. The proper mixture ratio is thus maintained. With the throttle closed, the transfer port (and there can be more than one) also serves as an additional air bleed for the idle circuit.

The High-speed System, or Main System

The high-speed system, or main system, supplies the engine with the correct mixture as the "vacuum" at the idle and transition ports gradually *decreases*, while the volume and velocity of

the airflow through the venturi *increases*. The term *main circuit* is more appropriate because neither driving speed nor engine speed alone governs its operation. For example, when you are going down a hill with your foot off the accelerator pedal, and with the throttle valve almost closed, both driving speed and engine speed (rpm) may be relatively high, but little or no fuel is discharged through the main system. On the other hand, when the vehicle is being driven up the same hill in first or second gear, the throttle may be wide open. Engine rpm would be high, while driving speed might be only somewhere around 25 mph (40 km/h). Under these conditions, the main circuit would, in fact, supply most of the fuel, as the volume and the velocity of the mixture are near maximum.

As stated earlier, any further opening of the throttle causes a drop in "vacuum" at the idle and transition ports, and eventually, even together, they cannot supply sufficient amounts of fuel; and yet the volume and the velocity of the air moving through the carburetor continue to increase. The ring-shaped *main venturi*, located approximately in the middle of the carburetor throat, restricts the passage of air and thereby causes its velocity to increase. Obviously the air speed is highest at the narrowest point of the venturi. It is here that the main discharge nozzle is located. As shown in Fig. 13:18, "static" pressure measured at right angles to the air stream actually decreases as the velocity and "dynamic" pressure of the moving air column increases. In other words a low-pressure area is created and this causes the discharge of fuel.[49] To improve the break-up of the fuel further and to ensure its thorough mixing with the air, one or two smaller *booster venturis* (Figs. 13:17 and 13:24) may be added to the main venturi. The drop in pressure caused by the venturis also lowers the boiling point of the gasoline and thereby aids in the evaporation of the fuel.

---

[48] *Warning:* Never tamper with sealed mixture screws on units with emission controls. They are flow-tested by the manufacturer to stringent specifications. The idle mixture ratio must be fairly rich (between 11:1 and 12.5:1) because at very low rpm some exhaust gases remain in the cylinder, thereby causing the mixture to be diluted.

[49] If a car window is opened slightly at high speeds, a low-pressure area is created inside the vehicle. You can actually feel it in your ears, and any smoke or dust floating around is pulled outside. In fact, a car heater works much better this way than with the windows completely shut. The slot in the window represents the "jet" and the air rushing by on the outside represents the venturi stream.

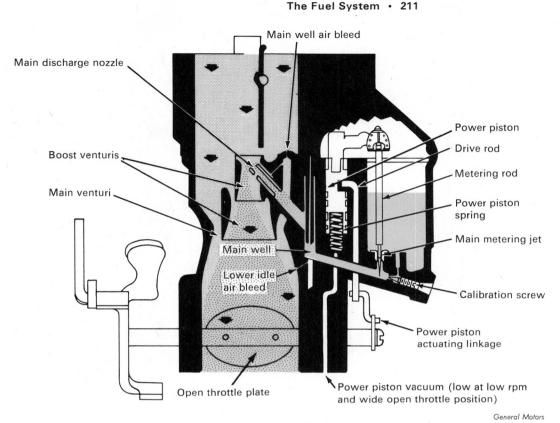

Fig. 13:17   *The Main Metering System and the Power System*

The gasoline is metered as it leaves the float chamber by the *main metering jet* (Fig. 13:17). The main metering jet supplies the fuel not only to the main circuit but also to most of the other circuits as well. Some main systems employ a tapered *metering rod* which, by sliding up and down in the main jet, controls the amount of fuel delivered to the main circuit. The movement of the metering rod is governed by either a mechanical linkage, a vacuum passage, or a combination of both, as is the case in Fig. 13:17. The position of the metering rod thus depends on the throttle position and sometimes on engine loads as well. Note that the main circuit also includes *air bleeds* to premix fuel and air before the fuel is discharged at the main nozzle in the venturi.

The Accelerator-Pump System

The accelerator-pump system (Fig. 13:19) overcomes engine hesitation or "flat spots"

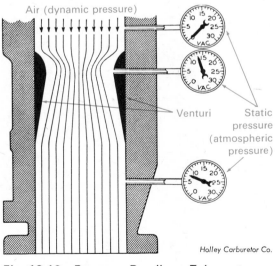

Fig. 13:18   *Pressure Readings Taken at Different Points in Air Passage (Note: Static pressure is lowest where dynamic pressure is highest.)*

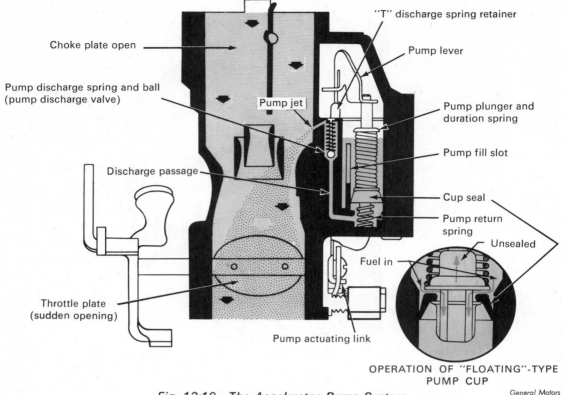

Choke plate open

"T" discharge spring retainer

Pump lever

Pump discharge spring and ball
(pump discharge valve)

Pump jet

Pump plunger and
duration spring

Pump fill slot

Discharge passage

Cup seal

Pump return
spring

Unsealed

Fuel in

Throttle plate
(sudden opening)

Pump actuating link

OPERATION OF "FLOATING"-TYPE
PUMP CUP

General Motors

Fig. 13:19   The Accelerator-Pump System

during rapid acceleration by injecting a small amount of fuel into the air passing through the venturi. The reason why the engine otherwise tends to hesitate or "stumble" is because under sudden, wide-throttle openings, engine rpm does not pick up quickly enough to create a sufficient "suction" either at the idle and transition ports or at the main discharge nozzle. The fuel, being heavier than the air, also has too much inertia to immediately catch up with the increased airflow. The extra fuel injected by the accelerator pump at this critical moment enriches the resulting lean mixture until engine rpm has increased sufficiently to activate the main circuit. In a sense, the accelerator-pump circuit momentarily takes over the function of the transition circuit, which cannot cope satisfactorily with sudden throttle openings.

The accelerator pump may be of the *diaphragm type* or the *plunger type* (Fig. 13:19). In either case the pump mechanism is controlled by the *accelerator linkage*. Linkage pressure is, however, exerted against the accel-

erator pump *duration-spring* rather than against the pump plunger (or diaphragm) directly. Thus, if the driver "tramps" the throttle, the spring is first compressed. It then slowly decompresses as the pump plunger is forced downwards. This causes the fuel to be pushed out of the accelerator discharge nozzle in a continuous spray, lasting roughly one second —just enough time to compensate for the inertia of the fuel flowing through the main jet. Meanwhile the engine also begins to pick up sufficient rpm to draw on the main circuit. When the accelerator pedal is returned to part throttle, the pump return-spring raises the plunger (or diaphragm) and more fuel is admitted into the pump well. The purpose of the inlet and outlet valves is simply to control the fuel flow. In fact, these valves work exactly like those in the fuel pump. The "floating"-type pump cup shown in Fig. 13:19 is unseated when the plunger is raised and thereby also acts as an inlet valve. In addition, it permits trapped vapours to escape the pump well.

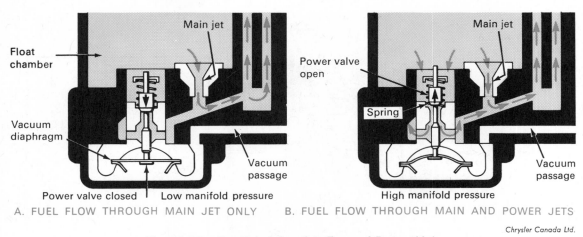

A. FUEL FLOW THROUGH MAIN JET ONLY   B. FUEL FLOW THROUGH MAIN AND POWER JETS

Chrysler Canada Ltd.

Fig. 13:20   Details of Another Type of Power Valve

The Power System

The power system (Figs. 13:17 and 13:20) supplies additional fuel for heavy engine loads, high rpm, or sudden throttle openings, i.e., conditions where manifold pressure is relatively high (8″ or 203 mm of mercury or less). For example, a hill might be steep enough that, even under full throttle, driving speed may not exceed 40 mph (64 km/h) in top gear. Let us assume that engine speed is around 2,000 rpm. Under these conditions (i.e., wide-open throttle and relatively low engine rpm), venturi velocities and "suction" are insufficient for the idle, transition, or main circuits to discharge adequate amounts of fuel. Nor does the accelerator pump operate while the accelerator is held to the floor. This is when the power circuit goes into action. At this point the spring tension of the power valve is stronger than the low-pressure area in the manifold, and the power valve opens to admit additional fuel to the main system (Fig. 13:20a and b). Assume now that the crest of the hill has finally been reached and the driver cuts the throttle back. This causes manifold pressure to decrease and thereby pull the power valve shut against the tension of the spring (Fig. 13:20a and b). The exact design of the power circuit system may vary with different carburetors. Some are activated by a pressure-controlled piston, some by a diaphragm, as is the one in Fig. 13:20. Others (Fig. 13:17) combine the power valve mechanism with the tapered metering rod described on page 211.

The Choke System

The choke system (Figs. 13:21, 13:22, and 13:23) gives a rich mixture for cold starts. This is necessary because at low temperatures only part of the fuel changes into the more combustible gaseous state. In fact, some vapours condense again to liquid gasoline at the cold walls of the manifold and the cylinders. If the choke plate, also called the choke valve, is closed, it restricts the airflow entering through the air horn. This sufficiently reduces the pressure below it to draw additional fuel from the various discharge ports. To prevent overchoking, especially if engine rpm increases, various devices are used. Some manually controlled

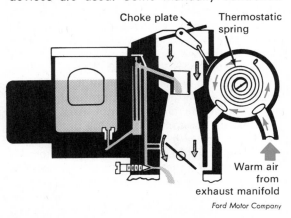

Ford Motor Company

Fig. 13:21   The Choke System (automatic type) Note the heavy fuel discharge due to high vacuum with the choke plate closed.

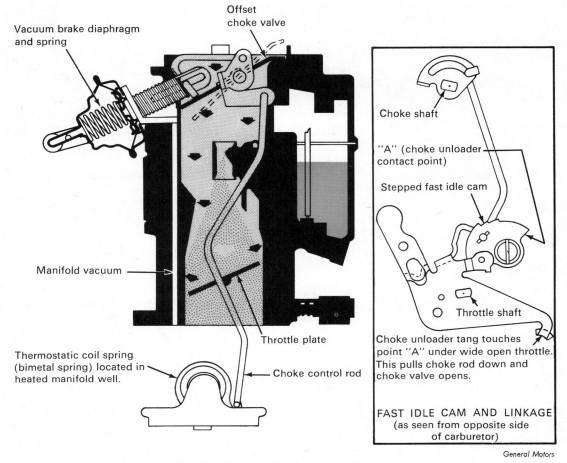

Vacuum brake diaphragm and spring

Offset choke valve

Manifold vacuum

Thermostatic coil spring (bimetal spring) located in heated manifold well.

Throttle plate

Choke control rod

Choke shaft

"A" (choke unloader contact point)

Stepped fast idle cam

Throttle shaft

Choke unloader tang touches point "A" under wide open throttle. This pulls choke rod down and choke valve opens.

FAST IDLE CAM AND LINKAGE
(as seen from opposite side of carburetor)

General Motors

Fig. 13:22   The Choke System

choke plates have a spring-loaded by-pass valve that admits sufficient air if the "suction" is excessive. On modern carburetors the same effect is obtained by means of an offset choke plate as shown in Fig. 13:22. The air rushing through the air horn forces the larger of the two choke-plate wings downwards and thereby admits additional air as rpm increases.

Most carburetors also employ a *choke unloader linkage* (Fig. 13:22). This device permits the "unloading" or forced opening of a closed choke plate. If an engine doesn't start because it is overchoked or "flooded", the accelerator pedal is simply held to the floor until the cylinders begin to fire. With the choke plate and the throttle plate forced wide open, cranking speeds are too low to cause any further discharge of fuel, even through the idle circuit. The rich fuel mixture is thus sufficiently diluted with

fresh air or vented through the exhaust. Pumping the accelerator would naturally do the exact opposite.

On automatic chokes a carefully adjusted bimetal spring closes the choke plate when the engine is cold. In one design (Fig. 13:21) the choke housing is mounted on the side of the carburetor. A special heat tube inside the exhaust manifold itself, or inside the exhaust cross-over passage of the intake manifold, conducts hot air (not exhaust fumes!) to the bimetal spring. Circulation through the choke housing is maintained by a carburetor vacuum connection. This connection may also activate a small vacuum piston inside the choke housing. The piston assists the opening of the choke plate as the coiled bimetal spring is heated up and begins to relax. In other designs, especially those used on engines with emission controls,

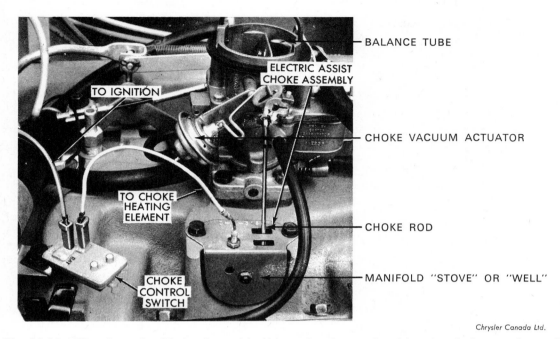

BALANCE TUBE

ELECTRIC ASSIST
CHOKE ASSEMBLY

TO IGNITION

CHOKE VACUUM ACTUATOR

TO CHOKE
HEATING
ELEMENT

CHOKE ROD

CHOKE
CONTROL
SWITCH

MANIFOLD "STOVE" OR "WELL"

Chrysler Canada Ltd.

Fig. 13:23   Electric-assist Choke Assembly (bimetal spring assisted by electric heater element)

the bimetal spring is placed inside a small "stove", which is mounted either directly on the exhaust manifold or inside the intake manifold just above the exhaust cross-over passage (Figs. 13:23 and 14:5). The advantage is that the bimetal spring becomes more responsive to temperature changes. It also eliminates exhaust emission due to overchoking. With this type of choke, which may, in addition, include an electric heater element, the opening of the choke plate is usually assisted by a diaphragm and linkage arrangement attached to the outside of the carburetor (Figs. 13:22 and 13:23). The diaphragm assembly, sometimes called the "vacuum" actuator, or simply the choke brake, also provides smooth acceleration when the engine is still cold. Normally, the manifold "vacuum" acting against the diaphragm is sufficient to pull the choke plate towards the open position against the tension of the diaphragm spring. Under sudden acceleration, however, manifold "vacuum" drops momentarily, thus allowing the spring to partially close the choke plate once again. This enriches the mixture and rpm increases smoothly until both the manifold "vacuum" and the choke offset overcome spring tension and reopen the choke. Naturally, once proper operating temperature is reached

and the bimetal spring is fully relaxed, the choke valve will remain fully open regardless of pressure conditions. There are also chokes employing electric heater coils. On some models both kinds are used in combination (Fig. 13:23).

Starting a Cold Engine

When the engine is cold, the driver usually depresses the accelerator just once before starting the engine. This accomplishes three things:

1. The accelerator pump injects some fuel into the carburetor throat (Fig. 13:19);
2. The choke plate closes (Fig. 13:21);
3. A stepped cam device, called the fast idle cam, raises the idle stop screw[50] to increase rpm to roughly 1,500 as soon as the engine starts to fire (Figs. 13:13 and 13:22).

Both the choke and the fast idle cam return gradually to the normal position as the engine warms up.

Note : To avoid flooding and other starting problems, never pump the accelerator, especi-

---

[50]On many carburetors a separately adjustable screw or tang is employed.

ally when the engine is hot. This bad practice can cause overchoking and hard starting, as well as excessive engine wear, oil dilution, deposits, emission, and even a carburetor fire.

The Balance Tube

The balance tube (Fig. 13:23) interconnects the air horn and the float chamber and thus maintains equal pressure in both, even if the air-cleaner becomes slightly restricted with dirt. Without a balance tube this condition, especially at high rpm, would create a choking effect and thus excessive fuel consumption and emission.

Direction of Carburetor Draft

Most automotive carburetors, as shown in this chapter, are of the down-draft type. This means they are located above the manifold, and the mixture is first drawn down through the carburetor and then, at right angles, into the intake ports. Some high-performance engines use side-draft carburetors; i.e., the mixture moves sidewards directly into the intake manifold. (Up-draft carburetors, once quite common, are no longer used.)

Multi-barrel Carburetors

Large cylinder displacements and high rpm require large carburetor throats to handle enormous volumes of air, in some cases over 3,500 gallons (15 900 litres) per minute. At very low rpm, however, large throats and venturis would result in air velocities insufficient to ensure a thorough mixing and break-up of fuel particles. The answer is to have either several carburetors or a *two-* or *four-barrel carburetor*, i.e., a carburetor in which several throats are fed from one or two float chambers, which they share in common.[51] On a four-barrel carburetor (Fig. 13:24), most of the mixture is supplied by two relatively small-bore throats or barrels. This is known as the *primary stage*. The other two barrels, called the *secondary stage*, open only

---

[51] Some high-performance engines use several multi-barrel carburetors, or even one carburetor for each cylinder. Another common solution is to employ constant velocity carburetors in which the throat of the venturi and the main jet is varied by a vacuum piston equipped with a metering rod.

at high rpm and high intake velocities. To handle large amounts of air and yet provide good atomization at low rpm, the bores of the secondary stage are usually bigger than those of the primary stage.

For further information on carburetors and manifold heat control, refer to pages 79-80 and 226-7.

The Carburetor Air-Cleaner

The carburetor air-cleaner protects the engine against abrasive dust particles drawn in with the air. These materials cause engine deposits, sludge, and excessive wear, especially on pistons, rings, and cylinder walls. In addition, the air-cleaner muffles the sound of the air rushing into the carburetor. In the event that the engine backfires through the carburetor, the air-cleaner also acts as a flame arrester.

There are three types of air-cleaners:
1. The dry-filter type (Fig. 13:25)
2. The oil-bath type (Fig. 13:26)
3. The oil-saturated type (Fig. 13:27)

The dry-filter type has a replaceable filter element made of a special type of microporous paper. The oil-bath filter contains some type of fibre or metallic gauze. Servicing consists of washing the element and the filter housing, as well as replacing the oil in the oil bath (SAE 30 or SAE 40). The oil-saturated type, which is usually made of sponge-like polyurethane, requires periodic cleansing in a mineral-base solvent (kerosene or Varsol). The element is then moistened with a light motor oil (SAE 10 or SAE 20). Like the mucus in the human nose, the oil helps to collect those particles that are too large to be filtered out. Similar types of air-cleaners are widely employed on small engines (lawn mowers, outboard engines, etc.).

Some air-cleaners contain a filter element made of oiled paper that is used either singly or in combination with a polyurethane band. The oiled-paper element must be replaced periodically.

How often a filter should be changed or serviced depends mostly on its appearance. (Under average operating conditions a filter element will last approximately 24,000 miles, or 38 000 km.) Dry, loose dust can be removed from dry-filter elements by a muffled blast of compressed air directed from the inside out, i.e., against normal airflow. Sharp, direct air

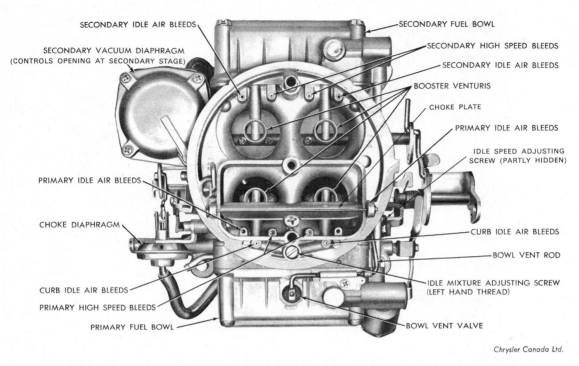

SECONDARY IDLE AIR BLEEDS

SECONDARY VACUUM DIAPHRAGM
(CONTROLS OPENING AT SECONDARY STAGE)

SECONDARY FUEL BOWL

SECONDARY HIGH SPEED BLEEDS

SECONDARY IDLE AIR BLEEDS

BOOSTER VENTURIS

CHOKE PLATE

PRIMARY IDLE AIR BLEEDS

IDLE SPEED ADJUSTING
SCREW (PARTLY HIDDEN)

PRIMARY IDLE AIR BLEEDS

CHOKE DIAPHRAGM

CURB IDLE AIR BLEEDS

BOWL VENT ROD

IDLE MIXTURE ADJUSTING SCREW
(LEFT HAND THREAD)

CURB IDLE AIR BLEEDS

PRIMARY HIGH SPEED BLEEDS

PRIMARY FUEL BOWL

BOWL VENT VALVE

Chrysler Canada Ltd.

Fig. 13:24   Typical Four-barrel Carburetor with Two Side-mounted Float Chambers

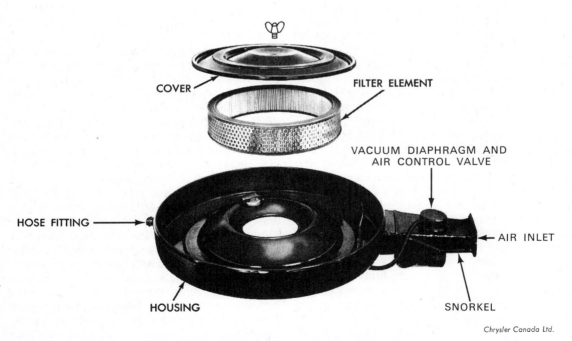

COVER

FILTER ELEMENT

VACUUM DIAPHRAGM AND
AIR CONTROL VALVE

HOSE FITTING

AIR INLET

HOUSING

SNORKEL

Chrysler Canada Ltd.

Fig. 13:25   Dry-filter-type Air-Cleaner

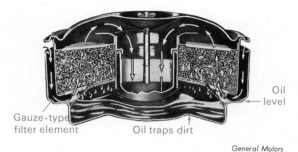

Gauze-type filter element   Oil traps dirt   Oil level

General Motors

Fig. 13:26   Oil-bath-type Air-Cleaner

blasts must be avoided, as this increases the size of the filter pores. A sticky or oily dry-filter element should be replaced.

Other Fuel Systems

Fuel Injection is used on all Diesel engines, and there is an increasing number of gasoline engines employing this system. Although relatively expensive, it is a very precise means of fuel distribution and mixture preparation, thus increasing engine efficiency, while at the same time reducing exhaust emission. There are two basic types—*direct fuel injection* into the cylinders and the so-called *port injection*. In the first case a very fine spray of fuel is injected at extremely high pressure right into the combustion chamber itself. This system is used on all Diesel engines (page 107) but rarely on gasoline engines. Port injection, as used on many gasoline engines, injects the fuel into the intake port, which is usually located just ahead of the intake valve. Both systems require special fuel pumps and injectors. Port injection (Fig. 13:28) is much cheaper than direct injection because it operates at much lower pressures and injector temperatures. The amount and timing of the fuel injected may be controlled mechanically or electronically. A further advantage of fuel injection is that it responds more accurately than port injection to changing operating conditions, such as engine loads, engine temperature, rpm, and climatic conditions. It eliminates fuel condensation in the intake manifold, and there is no problem of uneven fuel distribution to the cylinders. On deceleration the fuel can be cut completely, and thus fuel consumption and emission are reduced.

For information on LPG (Liquefied Propane and Petroleum Gas) engines see page 108.

Wing nut (finger tight)

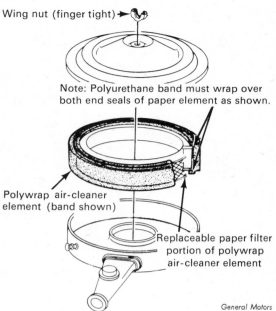

Note: Polyurethane band must wrap over both end seals of paper element as shown.

Polywrap air-cleaner element (band shown)

Replaceable paper filter portion of polywrap air-cleaner element

General Motors

Fig. 13:27   Oil-saturated-type Air-Cleaner Combining Paper Filter and Polyurethane Band (Note: Polyurethane band is cleaned in kerosene or Varsol, squeezed dry, and moistened with light engine oil. Never wring the band!)

Automotive Fuels

Gasoline is by far the most widely used automotive fuel. Although it is usually dyed for brand identification, it is actually colourless. It is also a very volatile liquid; i.e., it evaporates easily. Gasoline boils at less than 100°F, or 38°C, and it has an extremely high energy content. In fact, it contains more heat energy than an equal amount of dynamite! Gasoline, like Diesel fuel, belongs to a group of compounds known as *hydrocarbons;* i.e., its molecules are made up of a "chain" of hydrogen and carbon atoms. Most automotive gasoline is a derivative of crude oil. It can, however, be produced from coal by a special chemical process. If crude oil is heated, it breaks down into separate "fractions" (gasoline, kerosene, lubricating oils, etc.) since each of the various compounds contained in it evaporates at a different temperature. The process is called *fractional distillation* (Figs. 13:29 and 13:30). Crude oils contain only 10 per cent to 30 per cent of "straight run" gasoline suitable for

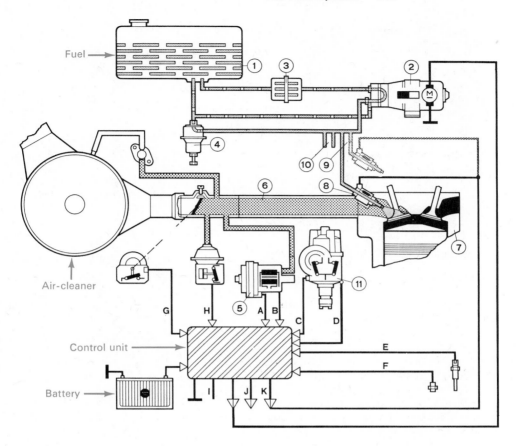

Principle of operation

Key to schematic of system:

① Fuel tank
② Fuel pump
③ Fuel filter
④ Pressure regulator
⑤ Pressure sensor
⑥ Intake air distributor
⑦ Cylinder head
⑧ Fuel injectors
⑨ Fuel distributor pipe, left
⑩ Fuel distributor pipe, right
⑪ Distributor with trigger contacts (Distributor contact I)
(Distributor contact II)

Information for control unit

A + B from pressure sensor (load condition signal)
C + D from distributor contacts
(engine speed and triggering signals)
E from temperature sensor I

F from temperature sensor II
(warming up and cold starting signals)
G from throttle valve switch
(fuel supply cut-off when coasting in gear)
H from pressure switch
(enrichment signal at full throttle)
I from starter solenoid switch, terminal 50 (signal
for enrichening mixture when starting cold engine)
J to the injectors, cylinders 1 and 4
K to the injectors, cylinders 2 and 3

Fuel is drawn from the tank ① via the filter ③ by the fuel pump ②, and forced into the ring main.
The pressure regulator ④, connected to the end of the ring main, limits the pressure of the fuel to 28 psi (2 kg/cm²). The electro-magnetic injectors ⑧ are connected to the ring main via fuel distributor pipes ⑨ and ⑩. From the pressure regulator, surplus fuel can flow through a return line in the frame tunnel back to the tank.

Robert Bosch (Canada) Limited

Fig. 13:28 Schematic Drawing of an Electronically Controlled Fuel Injection System for a Four-cyclinder Engine (Manifold Injection)

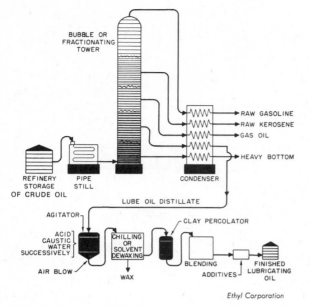

Fig. 13:29   The Processing of Crude Oil

direct use in automotive engines. To increase the yield of gasoline from the crude, a chemical process called *catalytic cracking*[52] is employed. Cracking involves the changing of large molecules, which make up some of the heavier fractions, to smaller, more volatile molecules typical of the lighter gasoline fractions. This process improves the quality of the gasoline, and it may raise the yield to more than 40 per cent of the crude stock.

Further processing and blending gives gasoline certain other desirable qualities. Winter gasoline, for example, contains a percentage of lighter, more volatile fractions to make cold starts easier. If used in the summer, winter gasoline may cause vapour lock, i.e., vapour bubbles are formed that interfere with the action of the fuel pump. Certain hydrocarbons that are too unstable for storage and sulphur, which causes engine corrosion and pollution, are removed. Special additives may be employed to prevent gum deposits, corrosion, combustion residues, and fuel line freeze-ups due to water condensation.

One of the most important qualities of high-grade gasoline is its resistance to *pre-*

[52]A catalyst is a material that, without actually taking part in a chemical reaction, causes the rate of the reaction to speed up.

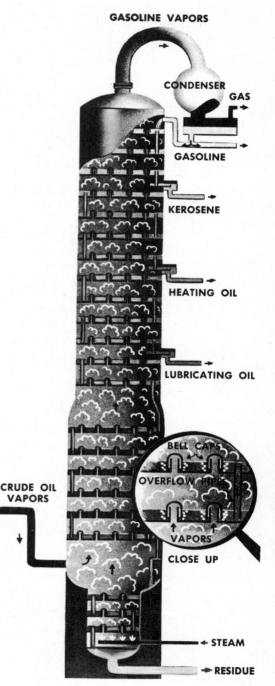

Ethyl Corporation

Fig. 13:30   Fractional Distillation in a Fractionating or "Bubble" Tower

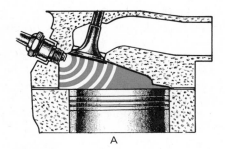

A

Normal flame travel in the combustion chamber (controlled pressure increase)

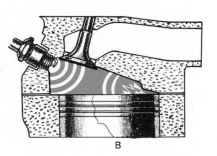

B

Detonation or engine knock, causing engine failure. Note uncontrolled explosion opposite spark plug.

General Motors

Fig. 13:31

ignition (self-ignition) and *detonation* ("engine knock"). Pre-ignition is caused by the high pressure and temperature at the end of the compression stroke, i.e., the fuel simply ignites without a spark as it does in a Diesel engine. Detonation is very similar to pre-ignition, except that the mixture, instead of burning in a controlled way, explodes after, rather than before, spark ignition. Either condition causes poor performance and, in many cases, serious damage to the engine. Improved refining processes and the use of certain additives such as tetraethyl lead, lead manganese, and phosphorus compounds have made it possible to ensure controlled, rather than uncontrolled, combustion under all normal operating conditions (Fig. 13:31).

Octane Ratings

Since such factors as compression ratio and the shape of the combustion chamber determine an engine's tendency to produce pre-ignition and detonation, different grades of gasoline are produced to satisfy particular fuel requirements. For this purpose, gasoline is rated according to its *octane number*. The number is obtained by comparing the behaviour of a fuel sample to a mixture of iso-octane and heptane in a special test engine. Iso-octane is very knock-resistant, while heptane causes very severe engine knock. The test engine is a *Ricardo*-type engine on which the compression ratio can be varied while the engine is running. The compression ratio is increased until engine knock occurs with the fuel sample to be rated. Using the same compression ratio, the engine is then run on a mixture of iso-octane and heptane. The heptane content is increased until the engine knock reappears. If, for example, the engine begins to knock with a mixture of 95 per cent iso-octane and 5 per cent heptane, the fuel sample is assigned an octane number of 95. To test special fuels with octane numbers up to 145, the iso-octane is blended with tetraethyl lead or with other octane-improving compounds.

Note: Since regular fuel contains as much heat energy as premium fuel, neither power nor mileage is gained by using a high-octane fuel in an engine that doesn't require it. On the other hand, if regular fuel is used in an engine designed for premium fuel, mileage and performance will drop noticeably. It also may cause severe damage to such parts as pistons, rings, valves, spark plugs, and the engine bearings, sometimes in a matter of minutes.

Engine knock, which produces a sharp pinging or even a hammering sound, occurs particularly at low to medium rpm and under full throttle. If engine knock persists, even with fuel of the proper octane rating, the cause may be one or several of the following conditions: incorrect ignition-timing, wrong spark-plug heat range (too hot), improper carburetor settings, defective cooling system, incandescent carbon deposits, upshifting at low rpm, and improper parts (incorrect head gasket and pistons, milled cylinder heads, etc.).

Caution: Gasoline must be stored in closed safety containers and away from heat, open flames, and sparks. Never siphon gasoline by mouth. Some additives such as tetraethyl lead are highly toxic and may lead to permanent brain damage.

RECOMMENDED ASSIGNMENTS

1. (a) List the major parts of the fuel system and state the main purpose of each part. (b) Prepare a labelled diagram showing how these parts are connected to one another.
2. Why is it necessary to have a vent in the fuel tank?
3. Name several important precautions to be taken when repairing fuel tanks.
4. Describe the proper shaping of fuel lines.
5. State briefly the purpose of the following fittings: (a) connector, (b) nut, (c) union, (d) sleeve, (e) elbow.
6. List five rules to be followed when installing a hydraulic fitting.
7. Prepare a simple labelled sketch of a fuel pump and state the purpose of each major part.
8. How would the fuel pump diaphragm move under each of the following conditions: (a) engine-idle, (b) heavy engine loads, (c) starting the engine with the float chamber empty?
9. Name four possible causes of low fuel-pump pressure.
10. What determines maximum pressure on a new fuel pump?
11. List three common fuel-pump tests.
12. What is the purpose of the carburetor?
13. List, in proper order, the four main steps involved in mixture preparation.
14. Name the seven carburetor systems and state the main purpose of each.
15. Explain the function of the two float adjustments.
16. What is the function of the air bleeds?
17. Name the two adjustments involved when adjusting engine-idle, and explain their different objectives.
18. What is the purpose of the venturi?
19. Explain the function and operation of a metering rod.
20. How does the accelerator pump extend its discharge even if the accelerator is "tramped"?
21. Describe briefly the operation of the power system.
22. Why do most choke plates have an offset shaft?
23. State, in proper order, the four steps involved when starting a cold engine equipped with an automatic choke. (Include engine warm-up.)
24. Why are overchoking and pumping the accelerator very bad practices?
25. Explain the purpose of the balance tube.
26. How do the intake manifold and the heat-control valve assist carburetion?
27. (a) List the three functions of an air-cleaner. (b) Name the most common types.
28. What is the difference between direct fuel injection and port injection?
29. Explain the terms "fractional distillation" and "cracking".
30. Define the following terms: (a) pre-ignition, (b) detonation, (c) octane number.
31. List eight factors that contribute to engine knock.
32. Discuss briefly the question of safety in the handling and storing of gasoline.

TROUBLE-SHOOTING

1. In each service problem listed below identify the carburetor system most typically involved:
   (a) Poor performance between 25 mph and 40 mph (40 km/h and 60 km/h) in high gear and on a level road.
   (b) Engine doesn't start in cold weather.
   (c) Engine stalls at every stop.
   (d) Engine never reaches high rpm in any gear while under heavy loads.
   (e) Carburetor looks wet; heavy exhaust emission.
   (f) Poor performance between 30 mph and 45 mph (48 km/h and 72 km/h) in high gear on steep hills.
   (g) Sluggish engine response when passing.

14

The Emission-Control System

What Is Pollution?

A forest fire, a dirty smokestack, a volcano, a litterbug, sewage, a dirty river or lake, a freshly paved highway, a garden fire, or the exhaust of automobiles—these are only a few examples of natural and man-made pollution. Because of the vast number of automobiles—well over 100 million in North America alone—automotive emission has been placed under very stringent government legislation and control.

A detailed study of emission control is beyond the scope of this text. This is a relatively new field that is subject to constantly changing legislation and technology, and only a general description of the system is feasible. However, since all current vehicles are required by law to incorporate such a system, you should be familiar with some of the basic principles involved.

Sources and Types of Automotive Emission

Automotive emission is mostly the result of the combustion of hydrocarbon fuels. Emission due to oil consumption, such as that caused by worn piston rings, pistons, cylinders, valve guides, and valve seals, and by leaking intake manifolds (V-8 engines), may be an additional source of pollution. This type of emission is indicated by white-blue smoke leaving the tailpipe. It is easily eliminated by rebuilding the engine to the manufacturer's specifications.

The combustion of hydrocarbons (for example, octane C_8H_{18}) is a chemical reaction that, in combination with air, produces the following compounds: water (H_2O), carbon dioxide (CO_2),[53] carbon monoxide (CO), oxides of nitrogen (NO and NO_2), unburned hydrocarbons, and very small amounts of sulphur oxides. In addition, the exhaust fumes may contain minute particles of ash and lead salts, and other "particulates". The emission of water and carbon dioxide is completely harmless and requires no control. The emission of particulates is so small that most experts don't consider it a health hazard if present levels are maintained. (For example, other lead compounds, especially lead paints, add twice as much lead to the environment as automobile exhaust fumes do.) The reason why low-lead or lead-free gasoline is manufactured is discussed later in this chapter.

The main effort to control emission is therefore directed towards the elimination or reduction of carbon monoxide (see page 229), of unburned hydrocarbons, and of the oxides of nitrogen. If inhaled in a closed room, carbon monoxide is highly toxic and often fatal. But even the highest concentrations found in very dense traffic over an eight-hour period are said to be less than the CO inhaled from two cigarettes. (Cigarettes are also far more harmful because of their nicotine and tar content.)

The unburned hydrocarbons and oxides of nitrogen appear to be no health hazard at present levels. On a sunny, windless day, however, these two compounds undergo chemical changes in the atmosphere and produce the

---

[53]Approximately one gallon (4.5 litres) of water and 1,200 gallons (5455 litres) of carbon dioxide gas are produced by each gallon of gasoline burned in the cylinders.

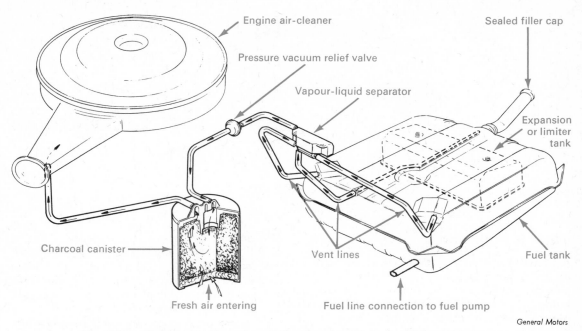

Fig. 14:1   Schematic Drawing of Evaporation Emission-Control System

very objectionable type of smog found in such densely populated areas as Los Angeles and New York. This smog, which irritates both the eyes and the lungs, is called photochemical smog because the chemical reactions involved are triggered by sunlight.[54]

Before the introduction of current emission controls, automobiles contributed to man-made air pollution roughly as follows: 77 per cent of the carbon monoxide, 53 per cent of the un-burned hydrocarbons, 41 per cent of the oxides of nitrogen, 5 per cent of the particulates, and 1 per cent of the sulphur oxides. Thanks to great progress in automotive engineering, the emission caused by automobiles has actually decreased over the years, despite a steady increase in car population.

Methods of Emission Control

On vehicles without emission control, roughly 10 per cent of the unburned hydrocarbons escape from the fuel tank and the carburetor by evaporation; 25 per cent leave through the crankcase, mostly because of blow-by (gas

[54]"Smog" is a contraction of the words "smoke" and "fog".

leakage past the pistons, as shown in Fig. 14:2), and approximately 65 per cent through the exhaust.

Evaporation Emission Controls

The use of special filler caps and vents has practically eliminated fuel evaporation. The filler cap is now similar to the radiator pressure cap in design; i.e., only excessively high vapour pressures are relieved through a relief valve (approximately 1 psi, or 6.89 kPa). The filler cap also has a vacuum valve that permits air to enter the fuel tank. This may occur if the vent lines are restricted and the fuel is being used up, or if the fuel vapours cool down and thus create a partial vacuum. Under normal operating conditions fuel vapours accumulating in the fuel tank are relieved by vent lines leading to the intake side of the engine (Fig. 14:1). To prevent the build-up of fuel vapours in the intake manifold when the engine is shut off, a *vapour-liquid separator* and a *charcoal canister* are connected to the vent lines. The separator returns condensed fuel vapours, i.e., liquid gasoline, to the fuel tank. The charcoal canister is situated close to the engine and collects the more volatile vapours passing through the

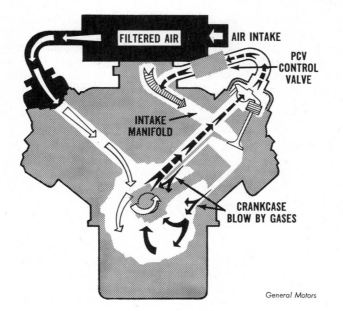

Fig. 14:2   Schematic Drawing of PCV System

separator. The canister contains absorbent (sponge-like) charcoal granules, and when the engine is restarted, the manifold vacuum draws the excess fuel into the cylinders where it is burned.

To prevent the overfilling of the fuel tank, which would interfere with the vent system, a *limiter tank*, or *expansion tank*, may be mounted inside the main tank (Fig. 14:1). If the main tank is filled up to the neck, the fuel level will adjust itself to the desired height by slowly seeping into the small holes provided in the limiter tank.

Crankcase Emission Controls

On engines produced up to the early sixties the crankcase was vented externally by means of a long "road draft tube" attached to the outside of the crankcase. This source of pollution is now controlled by *Positive Crankcase Ventilation* (PCV), which, by utilizing the intake manifold vacuum, recycles the combustible crankcase fumes through the combustion chambers and cylinders (Fig. 14:2). The purpose of the PCV valve is to control the vapour flow between the engine and the intake manifold. Unrestricted flow would, among other things, interfere with normal carburetion. Therefore, at idle the flow

is restricted to roughly 25 per cent (Fig. 14:3). The flow increases with higher rpm. However, under very heavy loads, i.e., normally during low to medium rpm but wide-open throttle operation, cylinder blow-by is relatively high, while intake manifold "vacuum" is low. The low "vacuum" causes the spring inside the PCV valve to push the plunger against the seat of the inlet port and thus into the closed position. This forces the blow-by vapours to travel in a direction *opposite* to that shown in Fig. 14:2 so that they are drawn into the air-cleaner instead. Regardless of the direction in which the vapours flow, whether they enter the intake manifold directly (normal flow) or whether they reverse through the air-cleaner (heavy loads), they combine and burn with the air-fuel mixture.

Fig. 14:3   Valve Position During Idle or Low-speed, Part-throttle Operation

Thus, crankcase emission has been practically eliminated. The burning of combustible crankcase vapours actually produces a slight increase in fuel mileage.

In the event that the engine backfires through the intake ports, the PCV valve shuts completely and, by acting as a flame arrester, it safeguards against any dangerous crankcase explosions.

The PCV system described above is known as a *closed system*. Older, so-called *open systems* do not have the tube connecting the air-cleaner to the rocker cover. In its place a vented oil filler cap or "breather" cap is employed.

Exhaust Emission Controls

Several of the following methods are used in various combinations:

1. A *thermostatically controlled valve* in the air-cleaner regulates the temperature of the intake air (Fig. 14:4). When the engine is warming up, cold air, which hinders the evaporation and combustion of gasoline and thus increases exhaust emission, is preheated by an *exhaust manifold stove*. This also prevents carburetor icing, which usually occurs when humidity is high and air temperatures are between 35°F and 45°F, or 2°C and 7°C.

At a predetermined temperature—somewhere between 85°F and 130°F (29°C and 54°C)—a vacuum diaphragm changes the position of the damper valve in the air-cleaner *snorkel*, and air then enters in the normal fashion (Fig. 14:4b).

2. Carburetors have been redesigned to provide more precise mixture control and leaner mixtures. To compensate for the rough idle caused by these leaner mixtures, idle speeds had to be increased. Wider throttle openings also allow more air into the cylinders. Booster venturis and extra air bleeds have been added to improve the break-up of fuel. Each carburetor is flow-tested by the manufacturer for the leanest possible settings. Intake manifolds are modified to open the choke more quickly and to reduce fuel condensation (Fig. 14:5). The manifold runners and the intake ports are shaped to ensure a more equal mixture distribution. Gently curved humps, especially ahead of the intake valve, are designed to create *induction turbulence* and thus ensure better mixing of the ingoing charge. To stabilize the manifold temperature under all operating conditions, the intake manifold often in-

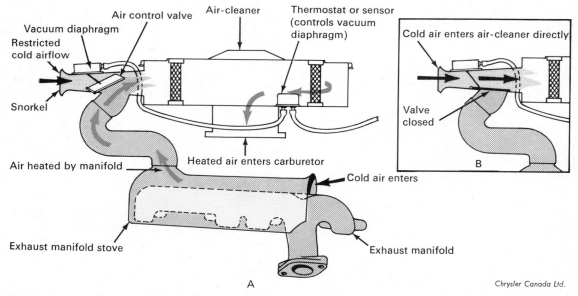

Chrysler Canada Ltd.

Fig. 14:4 (a) *Airflow of Heated Inlet Air System During Engine Warm-up;* (b) *Airflow with Engine at Normal Operating Temperature.*

Stainless steel well, fast heat transfer

Choke coil

No fuel condensation in intake manifold

Pin fins

Exhaust cross-over

Chrysler Canada Ltd.

Fig. 14:5 Redesigned Intake Manifold Exhaust Cross-over Passage for Faster Choke Opening and Improved Fuel Vaporization During Warm-up

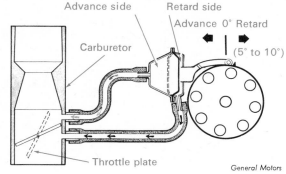

Advance side   Retard side

Advance 0° Retard

(5° to 10°)

Carburetor

Throttle plate

General Motors

Fig. 14:6 Dual-action Vacuum Advance

cludes passages connected to the cooling system. (Also refer to manifold heat-control valves on pages 79-80.) The shape of the combustion chambers has been changed to ensure more complete oxidation of the fuel mixture and to reduce *flame quenching*. The carburetor is usually vented internally rather than externally. At idle, or with the engine shut off, a vent valve permits fuel vapours to escape from the hot float chamber and enter the crankcase. When the engine is restarted, the vapours are drawn off by the PCV system and burnt in the combustion chambers.

3. Ignition-timing and advance have been changed to permit the burning of leaner mixtures. For example, retarding the spark at engine-idle puts an artificial "drag" on the engine. This allows slightly wider throttle openings and thus leaner mixtures as more air is admitted. To retard the spark even beyond the point of initial timing under certain operating conditions, a *dual-action vacuum advance unit* is used on some distributors. As shown in Fig. 14:6, when the throttle is closed at idle, a second port below the throttle plate causes the intake manifold

Vacuum diaphragm choke return

Terminal

Solenoid

Solenoid plunger

Idle adjusting screw

Chrysler Canada Ltd.

Fig. 14:7 Solenoid Throttle Stop

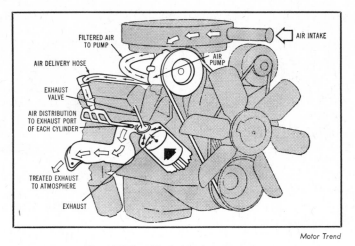

Motor Trend

Fig. 14:8 Air Injection Reactor

"vacuum" to pull the diaphragm and the breaker plate connected to it towards the retarded position. As a result, the timing may be 5° to 10° below the initial setting. Unfortunately, a lean mixture and a late spark increase cylinder temperatures and, combined with wider throttle openings, this often causes the engine to continue running even after the ignition has been turned off. To prevent this condition, known as *self-ignition* or *dieseling*, a special *solenoid-type throttle stop* allows the throttle to be closed almost completely when the engine is shut off (Fig. 14:7).

4. To oxidize unburnt hydrocarbons and to change carbon monoxide (CO) into carbon dioxide (CO_2), some type of *after-burner* or *thermal reactor* is added to the exhaust system. The device is in fact little more than a modified exhaust manifold. In one common design, called an *air injection reactor* (Fig. 14:8), air nozzles reaching into each exhaust port enrich the hot exhaust fumes with fresh air which is supplied by a belt-driven pump. Thus, oxidation (burning) of the pollutants is completed and they are converted into harmless gases (mostly steam and carbon dioxide).

The Control of Oxides of Nitrogen

The control of oxides of nitrogen (NO and NO_2, or simply "NO_x") is the most difficult to accomplish, partly because high temperatures, which lower carbon monoxide and hydrocarbon emission, tend to encourage oxygen and nitrogen to react with one another in the combustion chamber. To control NO_x emission, the following methods have been employed singly or in combination:

1. Lower compression ratios (somewhere around 8:1),[55] less ignition advance, modified valve-timing, and lower operating temperatures and thermostat settings have been used.[56]

Unfortunately, each of the above measures led to losses in engine efficiency; i.e., both engine performance and fuel mileage were reduced. Although this may sound like a contradiction, it actually takes more fuel (in some cases well over 30 per cent more) to burn fuel more completely! Furthermore, some of the above measures, which are designed to lower NO_x emission, actually increase the emission of unburned

---

[55]For best engine performance, compression ratios between 10:1 and 13:1 were used before emission regulations went into effect. Lower compression ratios also permit the use of relatively low octane fuels with reduced or no lead content.

[56]Thermostat opening temperatures were at one time raised to 210°F (99°C) to reduce CO and hydrocarbon emission, and to improve engine efficiency. When NO_x regulations went into effect, thermostats were once again set to open somewhere around 185°F (85°C).

hydrocarbons and carbon monoxide. This is one reason why manifold reactors had to be added: they oxidize these emissions at temperatures somewhere between 1,700°F and 1,800°F (927°C and 982°C), i.e., well below the critical temperature at which NO_x is formed (3,200°F, or 1760°C).

2. A small portion of the exhaust may be admitted into the intake side of the engine by means of a special metering valve or by small jets located in the floor of the intake manifold (Fig. 14:9). The objective of *exhaust recirculation* is to dilute the air-fuel mixture. This lowers combustion temperatures to below the critical point at which No_x is formed. The same effect may be obtained by increasing valve overlap (page 99), which simply causes the fresh mixture to combine with some of the burned gases right inside the combustion chamber.

3. A separate *catalytic converter or reactor* shaped like a muffler may be used to reduce the oxides of nitrogen to nitrogen. The catalyst, usually platinum or some less costly substitute, helps to speed up the chemical reaction taking place in the converter. However, fuel deposits, especially the residues of the anti-knock compound tetraethyl lead (page 221), tend to interfere with the operation of catalytic reactors because of coating and plugging. This is the reason why vehicles with catalytic reactors require fuels of low or no lead content. The lead also forms corrosive materials that very much shorten the life span of the exhaust system. On the other hand, lead is a very good high-temperature lubricant, and its removal requires specially hardened valves and valve seats. To prevent the use of leaded fuels in vehicles designed to operate on unleaded fuels, the fuel tank filler neck incorporates a restrictor that will not accept standard pump nozzles dispensing leaded fuels. The filler cap of these tanks is usually of the threaded type.

Carbon Monoxide: Its Dangers and Its Causes

Carbon monoxide or CO is the result of incomplete combustion of carbon. Since the element carbon is found in many combustible fuels besides gasoline, the danger of carbon monoxide poisoning is by no means confined to the

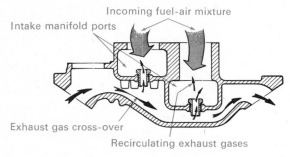

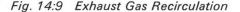

Chrysler Canada Ltd.

Fig. 14:9   Exhaust Gas Recirculation

automotive field. CO is formed by any of the following processes: gas welding; the melting of metal; the burning of coal, wood, or natural gas; and even smoking! Naturally, anything that interferes with the complete oxidation of hydrocarbons also produces CO. Here are some typical examples: rich carburetor settings, carburetor flooding, a dirty air-cleaner, a defective choke, high fuel-pump pressure, faulty ignition, low compression, a defective emission-control system. Obviously, great responsibility is placed on both the motorist and the mechanic. For example, a misfire in just one cylinder on an eight-cylinder engine, caused by a bad spark plug or a faulty high-tension lead, may increase exhaust emission by as much as ten times, and fuel consumption by roughly 7 per cent.

What Is Carbon Monoxide?

Carbon monoxide is a colourless, tasteless, non-irritating, odourless gas. In short, it is a treacherous killer that our senses cannot perceive other than by the effects it has on our bodies. Because the gas is heavier than air, it does not dissipate unless a draft is created.

Effects

As carbon monoxide attaches itself more readily to the red blood cells than oxygen does, a sufficiently high concentration of CO will cause brain tissue to be suffocated. Since brain cells do not regenerate, even a relatively short exposure to CO can cause permanent brain damage. Concentrations as low as .02 per cent CO in the air can have serious effects. (There may be well above 5 per cent CO in the exhaust of a vehicle that is not equipped with an emission-control system or in one that is defective. This is 250 times the critical amount!)

Symptoms

Headache, a feeling of pressure on the temples, weakness in the legs, chilliness, nausea, dizziness, ringing ears, convulsions, and blurred vision are all symptoms of carbon monoxide poisoning. The heartbeat increases to compensate for the oxygen deficiency and the victim usually gets very tired. As a result, the unsuspecting motorist often parks his car "to sleep it off". If he keeps the engine running to keep warm, chances are that he will never wake up again.

First Aid

Bring the victim into the fresh air; keep him warm; don't give him any medication; call the doctor; and do not leave the victim unattended. Watch his breathing. If necessary, give him artificial respiration (see inside back cover).

Prevention

Provide regular maintenance and tune-ups. Check the exhaust system frequently. Be sure there are no holes in the car floor. Do not run the engine in a garage unless there is cross-ventilation, or a *fan-vented* hose is attached to the tailpipe. Close the outside car vents when operating the car inside parking-garages or in dense stop-and-go traffic. Never work in service pits while an engine is running (remember CO is heavier than air!). Don't drive a station wagon with only the tailgate window open; the vortex flow of the air will pull the exhaust inside!

RECOMMENDED ASSIGNMENTS

1. (a) What are the causes and signs of oil consumption? (b) How is this type of pollution controlled?
2. Under two headings list the harmless and the objectionable products of gasoline combustion.
3. Explain why three of the objectionable products of gasoline consumption are considered detrimental to good health.
4. What are the four areas or parts of a vehicle not equipped with emission control from which unburned hydrocarbons can escape?
5. Explain the different functions of the vapour-liquid separator and the charcoal canister.
6. What are the purposes of the PCV valve?
7. How does a thermostatically controlled air-cleaner reduce exhaust emission?
8. What role do the carburetor and the manifold play in emission control?
9. (a) What causes "dieseling" on engines with emission controls? (b) How can this condition be prevented?
10. Explain the function of a thermal reactor.
11. What is the purpose of the air pump?
12. (a) What causes the formation of "NO_x"? (b) Explain various methods employed to reduce "NO_x".
13. What is carbon monoxide?
14. In point form list (a) the causes of carbon monoxide, (b) its effects on man, and (c) the symptoms of CO poisoning.
15. How would you give first aid to a CO victim?
16. How can CO poisoning be prevented?

15

The Power Transmission System (The Drive Train)

The power that the engine develops is transmitted to the wheels by several units varying in arrangement with different designs. The most common arrangement in vehicles with front engines and rear wheel drive is as shown in Fig. 15:1:

1. The Clutch Assembly (on standard transmissions) or Torque Converter or Fluid Coupling (on automatic transmissions)
2. The Transmission
3. The Drive Shaft Assembly
4. The Differential and Rear Axle Assembly

A front wheel drive is illustrated in Fig. 9:8.

The Clutch

The clutch (Fig. 15:2) permits the driver to engage and disengage the flow of power from the engine to the remaining units of the power

transmission system (the drive train). This not only allows the shifting of gears but it also prevents the engine from stalling when moving from a standstill. By raising the engine rpm above idle before engaging the clutch, both torque and power are increased sufficiently to ensure smooth pick-up. This is particularly important when the vehicle is set in motion under heavy loads or on steep hills.

The clutch usually consists of two main members: the *clutch disc*, or driven plate, and the *pressure plate and cover assembly* (Fig. 15:3). The pressure plate and cover assembly is mounted on the smooth, rearward face of the flywheel. In the engaged position the clutch disc is "sandwiched" firmly between the flywheel and the pressure plate by means of very strong springs inside the clutch cover. The clutch disc thus transmits the engine torque to

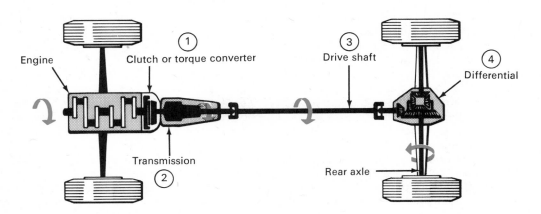

Fig. 15:1   The Drive Train

231

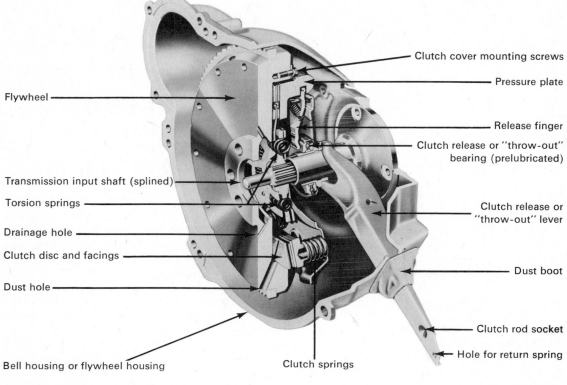

Clutch cover mounting screws

Pressure plate

Release finger

Clutch release or "throw-out"
bearing (prelubricated)

Flywheel

Transmission input shaft (splined)

Torsion springs

Drainage hole

Clutch disc and facings

Dust hole

Clutch release or
"throw-out" lever

Dust boot

Clutch rod socket

Hole for return spring

Bell housing or flywheel housing

Clutch springs

Ford Motor Company

Fig. 15:2   Typical Clutch Assembly and Bell Housing

the *transmission input shaft* (also called the *clutch shaft* or *pilot shaft*) by means of a splined hub and a series of torsional coil springs fitted around it. The *facings*, or *friction linings*, which are riveted to the cushion springs of the clutch disc, are made of tough, metal-reinforced asbestos (Fig. 15:4). The torsion springs and the shape of the cushion springs give a cushioning action to the clutch when it is engaged. The torsion springs also reduce the effects of engine vibration and of road shock, which travel in the opposite direction, from the drive shaft through the transmission.

The clutch is disengaged when the driver pushes the clutch pedal forward. The foot pressure may be transmitted hydraulically or, more commonly, either by a lever and linkage arrangement (Fig. 15:5) or by a cable assembly. If pressure is transmitted hydraulically, the pedal is connected to a hydraulic cylinder. The hydraulic cylinder is, in turn, connected by a

flexible hose to a "slave" cylinder mounted on the bell housing. The advantage of the hydraulic system over mechanical arrangements is two-fold:
1. Less effort is required.
2. Since engine vibration cannot be transmitted through a flexible hose, clutch "chatter" (vibration) is eliminated.

With either system the pedal movement is then relayed through the *clutch release lever* (*throw-out lever* or *throw-out fork*) to the *clutch release bearing* (*throw-out bearing*), as shown in Figs. 15:2 and 15:5. The forward movement of the clutch release bearing, in turn, causes the *release fingers* to be pushed deeper into the clutch cover. As a result, the spring-loaded pressure plate is withdrawn from the flywheel. At this point no power is transmitted, as the clutch disc is released between the holding faces of the flywheel and the **pressure** plate.

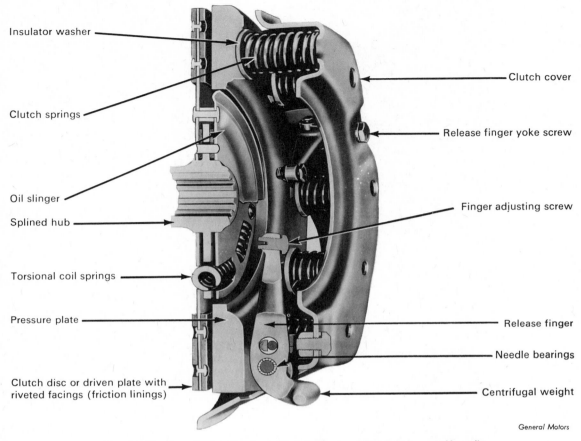

Insulator washer

Clutch springs

Oil slinger

Splined hub

Torsional coil springs

Pressure plate

Clutch disc or driven plate with riveted facings (friction linings)

Clutch cover

Release finger yoke screw

Finger adjusting screw

Release finger

Needle bearings

Centrifugal weight

General Motors

Fig. 15:3 Detail of a Typical Clutch Assembly (semi-centrifugal)

Types of Clutches

Clutches can be classified by the type of springs or by the method used to keep the pressure plate under tension.

The *Coil-Spring-type Clutch* (Figs. 15:2, 15:3, and 15:5), which features the clutch release fingers described above, uses a cluster of several very strong coil springs between the pressure plate and the clutch cover.

The *Diaphragm-type Clutch* (Fig. 15:6) employs, in place of the coil springs, a concave (or "dished") metal disc, known as the *diaphragm*. No separate release fingers are needed as the release bearing works directly against the diaphragm. The centre area of the diaphragm is either slit or folded to form its own pie-shaped fingers. To visualize its operation, you might think of a round, curved lid, which,

when pressed against a flat surface, acts as a spring.

The *Semi-centrifugal-type Clutch* (Fig. 15:3) uses centrifugal weights on the outer ends of the release fingers. As engine rpm (and torque) increase, these weights exert a centrifugal pull that assists the holding tension of the coil springs. This enables the manufacturer to use comparatively light-pressure springs. The result is reduced clutch pedal effort when the driver is shifting at low engine speeds; yet at higher engine speeds the increased holding pressure prevents the disc from slipping. Clutch slippage generates very high temperatures, and this is a very common cause of clutch failure.

The *Dual-Plate-type Clutch* uses two pressure plates and discs stacked one on top of the other but only one common set of coil springs.

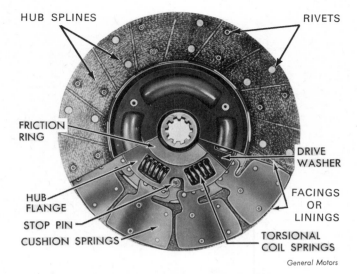

HUB SPLINES

RIVETS

FRICTION RING

DRIVE WASHER

HUB FLANGE

STOP PIN

CUSHION SPRINGS

FACINGS OR LININGS

TORSIONAL COIL SPRINGS

General Motors

Fig. 15:4   Clutch Disc or Driven Plate Assembly

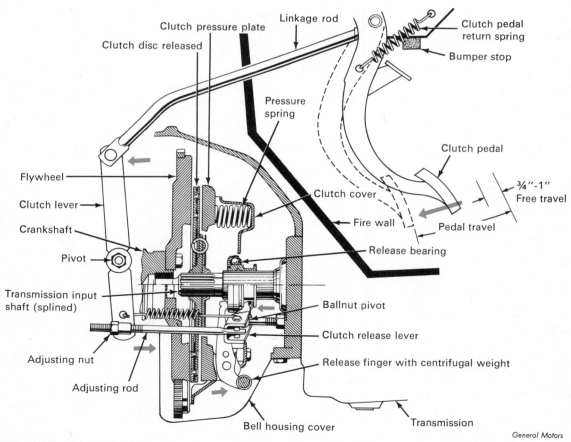

Clutch pressure plate

Linkage rod

Clutch disc released

Clutch pedal return spring

Bumper stop

Pressure spring

Clutch cover

Clutch pedal

Flywheel

Clutch lever

Clutch pedal

¾"–1" Free travel

Crankshaft

Fire wall

Pedal travel

Pivot

Release bearing

Transmission input shaft (splined)

Ballnut pivot

Clutch release lever

Adjusting nut

Release finger with centrifugal weight

Adjusting rod

Bell housing cover

Transmission

General Motors

Fig. 15:5   Clutch Linkage and Movement (pedal partly depressed, clutch disc released)

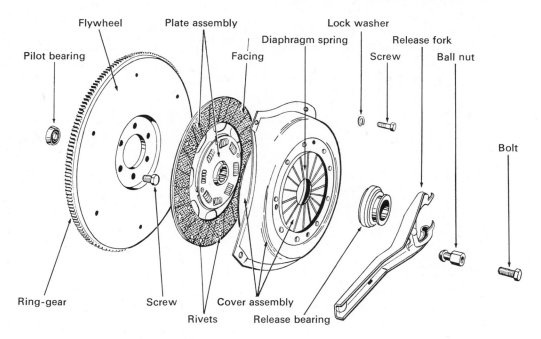

Fig. 15:6 Flywheel and Clutch Assembly (diaphragm type)

This style of clutch is employed on engines producing very high torque.

Clutch Maintenance

Clutch maintenance consists mostly of the adjustment of the free travel of the clutch pedal between its resting position against the bumper stop and the point where clutch release is initiated (Fig. 15:5). This point is reached when the release bearing can be felt touching the clutch release fingers or the diaphragm. The free travel, or *clutch lash*, decreases as the clutch linings begin to wear. If the clutch lash is less than specified, the clutch will slip and burn out, and the service life of the release bearing will be reduced. The release bearing is of the pre-lubricated type and normally requires no service (see page 48). Excessive clutch lash, on the other hand, will result in noisy shifts (*gear clash*) and worn transmission gears because of insufficient clutch release. The lash (usually about ¾" to 1", or 1.9 cm to 2.54 cm)[57] is adjusted by changing the length of the adjusting rod (Fig. 15:5). Worn discs should be replaced before they begin to score

[57]A different procedure applies to hydraulically operated clutches.

the flywheel or the pressure plate. If the whole clutch assembly must be replaced, either a new one or a rebuilt exchange unit is installed. If a rebuilt exchange unit is not properly balanced, or the release fingers are not properly adjusted, vibrations are a probable result.

Gearing and Gear Ratios

The operation of gears is based on the principle of *mechanical advantage*, or leverage (Fig. 15:7. See also page 1). In fact, gears were originally

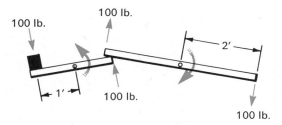

Torque of little lever shaft, 100 lb. × 1' = 100 lb.-ft.
Torque of large lever shaft, 100 lb. × 2' = 200 lb.-ft.

Note: Torque refers to the twisting forces at the pivot shafts and not the forces acting at the lever tips!

Fig. 15:7 The Principle of Levers

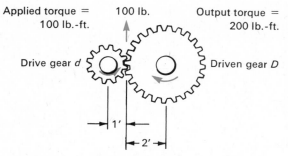

Applied torque = 100 lb.-ft.

100 lb.

Output torque = 200 lb.-ft.

Drive gear *d*

Driven gear *D*

1′

2′

Gear ratio = 2:1, hence, torque of shaft *D* is double that of shaft *d*, while shaft speed is halved.

Fig. 15:8   The Principle of Gears

little more than several levers arranged about a common hub.

For the present purpose we shall call the smaller gear (Fig. 15:8) the *drive gear* (*d*) because we assume it is attached to the clutch and thus to the engine itself. It has only 12 teeth and a leverage of 1 foot. The larger gear engaged with the smaller gear shall be the *driven gear* (*D*). The distance between the centre of gear *d* and the point of tooth contact, called the *pitch point*,[58] is one foot. The applied torque is 100 lb.-ft. Note that gear *D* is exactly twice as large as gear *d*; i.e., it has twice as many teeth (24) and its leverage is 2 feet. What happens to gear *D* and the shaft on which it is mounted?

1. The direction of rotation is reversed.
2. The speed of shaft *D* (rpm) is *reduced* to one-half of that of shaft *d* because the 12 teeth of gear *d* must go around twice to cover the 24 teeth of gear *D*.
3. The torque of shaft *D* is increased to double that of shaft *d* because 100 lb. × 2 feet = 200 lb.-ft. of torque. (Remember: torque is force × leverage!)

Note that when a smaller gear drives a larger one, *torque increases*, while *shaft speed* (*rpm*) *decreases*. This is called an *inverse relationship*.[59] If the gears were of the same size, neither

torque nor speed would change. If gear *D* became the drive gear in Fig. 15:8, then torque would be halved and speed would be doubled. You should note that power remains unchanged in either case. Only if both torque *and* shaft speed were increased at the same time would power be said to have increased as well—but no gearing or any transmission can possibly do this. To accomplish this a more powerful engine would be needed.

For the purpose of calculating torque and speed, we merely need to know the *relative* size of the gears, as expressed in the *gear ratio*. To determine the gear ratio itself, we can count the number of teeth or the number of rotations required by the smaller gear to turn the larger gear through one whole rotation. If we were to deal with pulleys (e.g. crankshaft-, water pump-, or generator-pulleys), we would simply compare their diameters or radii.

Gear ratios express the relationships that exist between two or more gears. The gear ratio in Fig. 15:8 is $\frac{\text{driven gear } D}{\text{drive gear } d}$ or $\frac{24 \text{ teeth}}{12 \text{ teeth}}$ or $\frac{2 \text{ feet}}{1 \text{ foot}}$ or simply 2:1 (read as "two to one"). If gear *D* became the drive gear and *d* the driven gear, the ratio would be .5:1 because $\frac{12}{24} = \frac{1}{2} = \frac{.5}{1}$. In Fig. 15:9 the four gears have a ratio of $\frac{B \times D}{A \times C}$ or $\frac{30 \times 27}{15 \times 18}$ or 3:1. Note that both small gears are *drive gears* and the two large gears are *driven gears*. What happens to torque and speed with a 3:1 gear ratio? Since, in the example chosen, the drive gears are smaller than the driven gears, speed is reduced and torque is increased. (Such a gear train is called a *reduction gear*.)[60] To be exact, for every three revolutions of the power input shaft, the output shaft will make only one revolution. On the other hand, the torque of the output shaft will be increased threefold over that of the input shaft. That is what the gear ratio of 3:1 tells us. You should also note that with an even set of more

[58]The circle joining the pitch points of all teeth is the pitch circle. The radius of the pitch circle of the smaller gear (*d*) is one foot. The pitch is the distance between the teeth.
[59]When a cyclist climbs a hill he changes to a larger rear sprocket (higher torque but lower

speed). On level ground he selects a smaller rear sprocket (lower torque but higher speed).
[60]If the drive gears are larger than the driven gears, the gear train is called an overdrive; i.e., shaft speed increases as torque decreases.

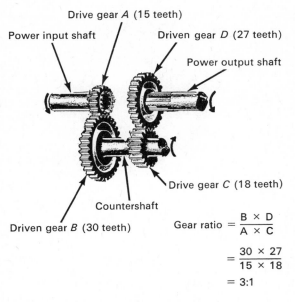

Power input shaft
Drive gear *A* (15 teeth)
Driven gear *D* (27 teeth)
Power output shaft
Drive gear *C* (18 teeth)
Countershaft
Driven gear *B* (30 teeth)

$$\text{Gear ratio} = \frac{B \times D}{A \times C}$$

$$= \frac{30 \times 27}{15 \times 18}$$

$$= 3:1$$

Fig. 15:9 The Gear Ratio of a Simple Gear Train

than two gears, where two gears share a common *countershaft*, the direction of both input and output shafts remains the same. If shaft rotation must be reversed, or if two shafts are too far apart and a chain drive is undesirable, an *idler gear* is inserted (Fig. 15:11d). Note that idler gears, regardless of size, do not change the gear ratio; hence neither torque nor speed is affected.

Types of Gears

The most common types of gears are shown in Fig. 15:10. The advantage of the *helical gear* (Fig. 15:10b) over the straight tooth *spur gear* (Fig. 15:10a) is that the angular tooth design of the helical gear allows more than two teeth to be in contact at all times. The result is quieter and smoother gear operation, as well as greater strength. Helical gears with teeth running in opposite directions (Fig. 15:10b) are used on parallel shafts such as those found in standard transmissions. Those with teeth cut in the same direction (Fig. 15:10c) are employed on shafts operating at right angles to one another (oil pump, distributor, and speedometer drive gears). *Sprockets* (Fig. 15:10d), which require special chains or toothed belts, may be made from

steel, cast iron, aluminum, or even nylon. They are widely used for camshaft drives. *Bevel* and *hypoid gears* (Figs. 15:10f and g) also permit power to be transmitted at right angles. If the bevel gears have curved teeth and their extended centre lines intersect each other, they are called *spiral bevel gears* (not illustrated). *Hypoid gears* are similar to spiral bevel gears except that the centre line of the drive pinion is offset by as much as 25 per cent in relation to that of the *ring*, or *crown*, *gear*. This feature makes them ideal for modern car designs, which require very low drive shafts. Hypoid gears are also stronger, smoother, and quieter in operation than straight bevel gears since they are always in contact with more than one tooth. *Worm gears* are yet another means of transmitting power at right angles, especially where high gear ratios are involved (steering gears, speedometer heads, and some differentials, usually of foreign origin).

Planetary gear trains (Fig. 15:10h) are widely used in automatic transmissions and overdrives.[61] They are very compact and each set provides several gear ratios, including reverse, without any shifting of gears. This is made possible by holding one member stationary with either bands or clutches, driving another, and leaving the third member free to transmit the torque. For example, holding the sun gear and driving the planet carrier would cause the internal gear to revolve in the same direction but at a faster speed and with less torque. On the other hand, driving the sun gear while holding the planet carrier would result in the internal gear being reversed at a lower speed but with higher torque.

General Gear Information

Most mass-produced transmission gears are made from a powdered steel alloy. The powder is pressed into shape under very high forming pressures and temperatures (approximately 100,000 psi and 2,000°F, or 689 000 kPa and 1090°C). This very economical process is called *sintering*.

Most gear failures are due to a lack of lubrication, the wrong type of lubricant, dirt, misalign-

[61]A device that increases drive shaft rpm over crankshaft rpm for the purpose of more economical highway cruising.

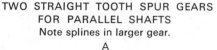

General Motors

TWO STRAIGHT TOOTH SPUR GEARS FOR PARALLEL SHAFTS
Note splines in larger gear.
A

General Motors

TWO HELICAL GEARS FOR PARALLEL SHAFTS
Left-hand (upper) and right-hand (lower)
B

Boston Gear

TWO RIGHT-HAND HELICAL GEARS   **TWO LEFT-HAND HELICAL GEARS**
For shafts at right angles
C

TRW Inc.

CHAIN SPROCKET
Parallel shafts only
D

General Motors

WORM AND WHEEL GEAR
For shafts at right angles
E

General Motors

STRAIGHT TOOTH BEVEL GEAR
For shafts at right angles.
Note splines in larger gear.
F

Fig. 15:10 (A-F)   Common Types of Automotive Gears

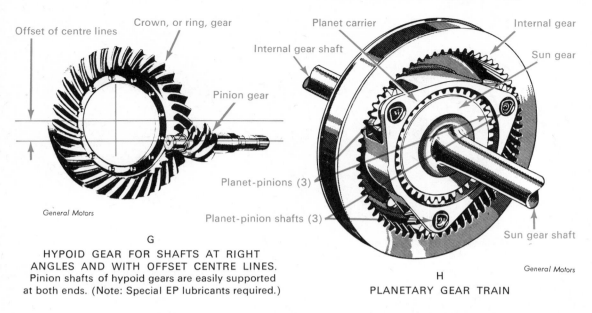

Offset of centre lines

Crown, or ring, gear

Pinion gear

General Motors

G

HYPOID GEAR FOR SHAFTS AT RIGHT
ANGLES AND WITH OFFSET CENTRE LINES.
Pinion shafts of hypoid gears are easily supported
at both ends. (Note: Special EP lubricants required.)

Planet carrier

Internal gear shaft

Internal gear

Sun gear

Planet-pinions (3)

Planet-pinion shafts (3)

Sun gear shaft

General Motors

H

PLANETARY GEAR TRAIN

Fig. 15:10 (G & H)   Common Types of Automotive Gears (continued)

ment, improper installation, high temperatures, and excessive loads. Never touch transmission parts with a magnetic tool! The transmission drain plug often incorporates a magnet to trap metal shavings. The plug should be left in the transmission housing and not mixed with the other parts during overhauls. Noisy gears are either worn or misaligned.

The Transmission

The transmission has six main functions:
1. To transmit the power of the engine from the clutch to the drive shaft.
2. To allow the engine to run in its most efficient rpm range—usually between 1,200 rpm and 5,000 rpm—regardless of the driving speed.
3. To vary the speed and torque of the drive shaft.
4. To better utilize the engine for braking power when driving down hills, or when decelerating.
5. To permit the engine to idle when the vehicle is not moving (i.e., to provide "neutral").
6. To reverse the rotation of the drive shaft, i.e., the direction in which the vehicle travels.

The transmission also includes the speedometer drive gear and supports the rear of the engine by means of the transmission mount, and on automatic transmissions a "parking pawl" locks the drive train for the purpose of parking. There are two basic types of transmissions: (a) manually shifted, or standard, transmissions (Figs. 15:11 and 15:19) and (b) automatic transmissions (Fig. 15:23). While "automatics" are now the most common type, standard transmissions are still widely used. Your study of transmissions should begin with the standard transmission because its basic operating principles apply to all devices employing gears, such as differentials, steering gears, overdrives, starter gears, and even automatics.

Standard Three-speed Transmissions

Standard transmissions have three forward speeds and one reverse gear. Because four- and five-speed transmissions are very similar in design, we do not cover them in this text.

First Gear or Low Gear

When moving a vehicle from a standstill, more torque is required to start it rolling than to keep

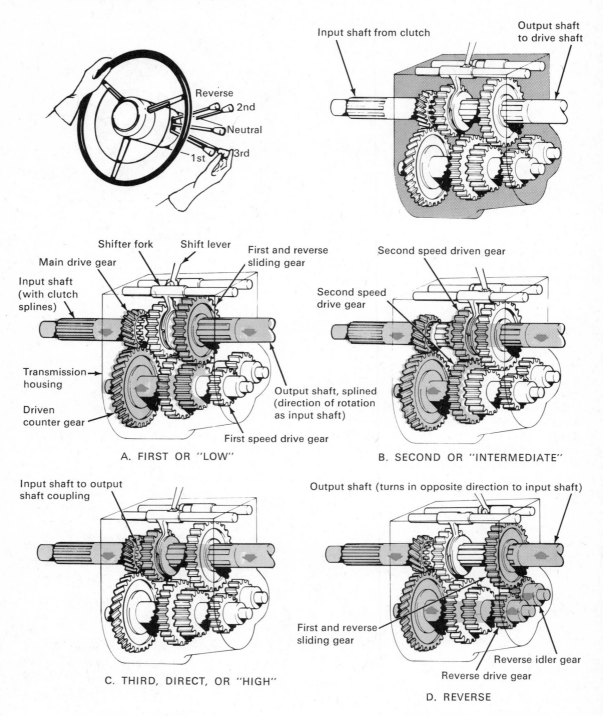

Reverse
2nd
Neutral
1st 3rd

Input shaft from clutch

Output shaft to drive shaft

Shifter fork
Shift lever
Main drive gear
First and reverse sliding gear
Input shaft (with clutch splines)
Transmission housing
Driven counter gear
First speed drive gear
Output shaft, splined (direction of rotation as input shaft)

A. FIRST OR "LOW"

Second speed driven gear
Second speed drive gear

B. SECOND OR "INTERMEDIATE"

Input shaft to output shaft coupling

C. THIRD, DIRECT, OR "HIGH"

Output shaft (turns in opposite direction to input shaft)
First and reverse sliding gear
Reverse idler gear
Reverse drive gear

D. REVERSE

Fig. 15:11   Three-speed Standard Transmission (simplified)

it going after the wheels have begun to revolve. The high gear ratio of first gear is therefore designed to provide a substantial increase in torque at low drive shaft speeds and high engine rpm. The term "first" does not apply here to a particular gear but rather to a combination of four gears with the highest forward gear ratio. As shown in Fig. 15:11a, the power flow is as follows: (Because different names are often given to the same parts, the most common alternative ones are given in brackets.)

1. from the input shaft (clutch shaft) and the main drive gear;
2. to the driven counter gear (driven cluster gear);
3. to the first speed drive gear (low-speed counter gear or low-speed cluster gear);
4. to the first speed driven gear (low-speed driven gear or first and reverse sliding gear); and
5. out through the output shaft (main shaft).

The output shaft in turn transmits the torque to the drive shaft.

The gears on the countershaft form one single cluster, and therefore always rotate in unison when the engine is running. This occurs even in neutral, unless the clutch is disengaged and the input shaft stops turning. The gears on the countershaft are often referred to as the cluster gears.

First gear is also used for slow driving speeds, very heavy loads, and hill-climbing.

Second Gear or Intermediate Gear

Second gear (Fig. 15:11b) is used for intermediate driving speeds and torque requirements. The flow of power through the transmission is, as shown,

1. from the input shaft and the main drive gear;
2. to the driven counter gear;
3. along the cluster gear assembly to the second speed drive (or cluster) gear;
4. to the second speed driven gear, and
5. from the output shaft to the drive shaft.

Note that in second gear the gear ratio is less than it is in first gear. Because the second drive gear and the second driven gear are almost the same size, most of the speed reduction and torque increase is accomplished between the input gear and the driven counter gear.

Third Gear, Direct Drive, or High Gear

Third gear (Fig. 15:11c) is engaged at normal driving speeds and when torque requirements are relatively low. On level roads the lower limit is usually somewhere around 30 mph, or 50 km/h, on a three-speed transmission. At driving speeds slower than this, the engine rpm and the engine torque would be too low. If, under these conditions, the throttle is forced wide open, firing pressures and temperatures would be high enough to cause serious damage to the engine (pistons, rings, bearings, valves, etc.). At higher rpm, however, third gear saves fuel and reduces wear because the crankshaft and piston speeds are lowered. As the name implies, direct drive is obtained by coupling the input shaft directly with the output shaft. The ratio between the engine and drive shaft is therefore 1:1. (The ratios for the other gears vary greatly between different models, as the correct gearing depends on engine design, the gear ratio in the differential, and the size of the wheels.) The point at which a downshift is to be made is a matter of good judgment, as it depends mostly on road conditions (uphill, downhill, level pavement, etc.) and the torque curve of the engine. Excessively high rpm (over-revving, noisy engine) and abnormally low rpm (lugging, heavy engine vibrations) must be avoided at all costs.

Reverse Gear

On some transmissions the first driven gear is used for both low and reverse, hence the term *first and reverse sliding gear*. In this case the power flow (Fig. 15:11d) is as follows:

1. from the input shaft and the main drive gear;
2. to the driven counter gear;
3. along the cluster gear assembly to the reverse drive gear (or reverse cluster gear);
4. to the reverse idler, which is mounted on a separate shaft;
5. to the low and reverse sliding gear; and
6. from the output shaft to the drive shaft.

Reverse gear usually has the highest (i.e., the slowest) gear ratio of all gears. The only function of the idler gear is to reverse the rotation. (As mentioned previously, idler gears have no effect on the gear ratio.)

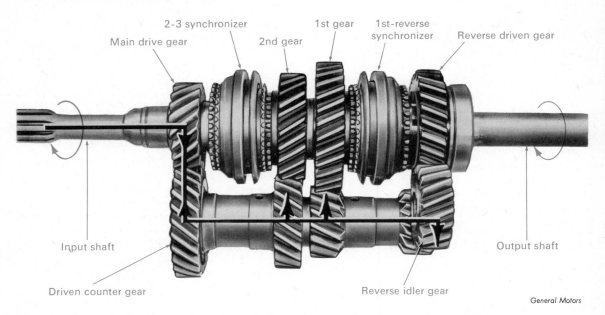

Fig. 15:12 Neutral Power Flow Through a Three-speed Constant Mesh Transmission (fully synchronized)

Neutral Gear

"Neutral" permits the driver to disconnect the flow of power between the input and output shafts while the engine is idling, and also between gear shifts. On older transmissions, neutral was obtained simply by moving the driven gears on the output shaft sideways into a disengaged or neutral position. As Fig. 15:11 shows, the output shaft and the hub of the gears were provided with matching splines to make this possible. A similar method is still used on some first and reverse sliding gears.

The Constant Mesh Transmission

On this type of transmission (Figs. 15:12 to 15:16) the gears always remain engaged with one another. This means that all the gears revolve as soon as the input shaft begins to turn.[62] For example, if the transmission is in high gear, all driven gears on the output shaft revolve at their own speed because each one of them is in constant mesh (engagement) with a different-sized cluster gear. This is made pos-

[62]Some transmissions are only partly constant mesh; i.e., they still use a sliding gear for first and reverse.

sible by allowing the driven gears to freewheel on the output shaft when they are not in use. Since the gears themselves do not have to be engaged or disengaged, shifting is smoother, noise and wear are reduced, and the transmission is less likely to jump out of gear.

Synchromesh Transmissions

The word "synchromesh" means exactly what it says, namely, that two revolving gears or members that are about to mesh are first brought to the same speed, i.e., "synchronized". Obviously, if two members revolve at different speeds, either it will be impossible to join them, or, if they are forced to be joined, the result will be excessive wear and noise (gear clash). A typical synchromesh unit is shown in Figs. 15:17 and 15:20. Since the inner hub splines are keyed to the output shaft, the entire assembly, including sleeve and blocking rings, must always revolve with the output shaft. In the neutral position the sleeve is held in the middle position on the hub by spring-loaded inserts or ball bearings. While synchronization may be used on all gears, let us assume, for the purpose of illustration, that a shift is made from second gear to high gear. The sleeve is pushed forward

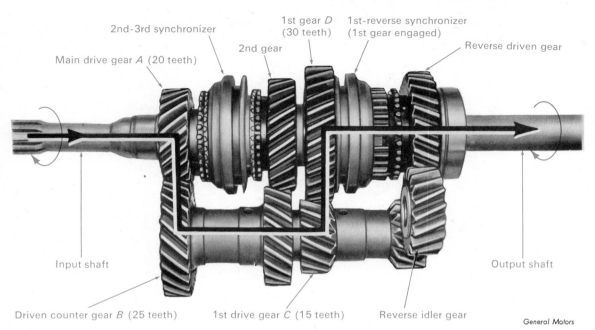

Fig. 15:13 *First Gear Power Flow Through a Three-speed Constant Mesh Transmission (fully synchronized)*

$$Gear\ ratio = \frac{driven\ gears}{drive\ gear}\ or\ \frac{B \times D}{A \times C} = \frac{25 \times 30}{20 \times 15} = \frac{5}{2}\ or\ 2.5{:}1$$

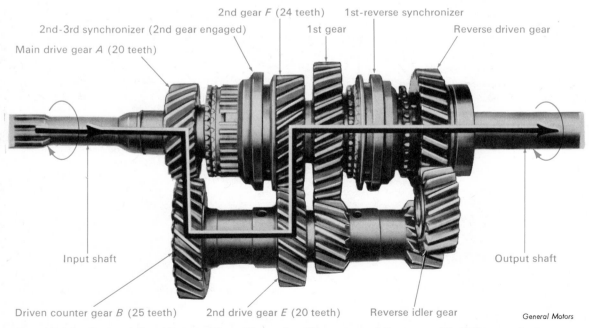

Fig. 15:14 *Second Gear Power Flow Through a Three-speed Constant Mesh Transmission (fully synchronized)*

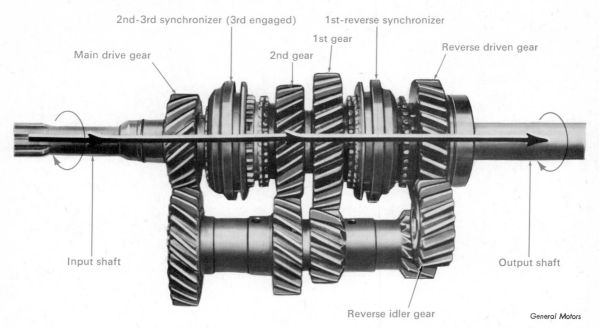

Fig. 15:15   *Third Gear Power Flow Through a Three-speed Constant Mesh Transmission (fully synchronized). Gear ratio 1:1, i.e., "direct drive".*

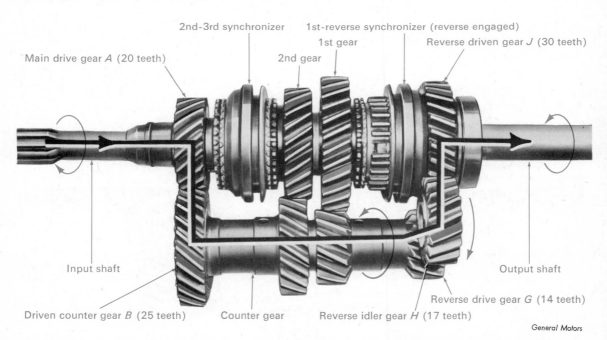

Fig. 15:16   *Reverse Gear Power Flow Through a Three-speed Constant Mesh Transmission (fully synchronized)*

$$Gear\ ratio = \frac{B \times H \times J}{A \times G \times H} = \frac{25 \times 30}{20 \times 14} = \frac{75}{28}\ or\ 2.68$$

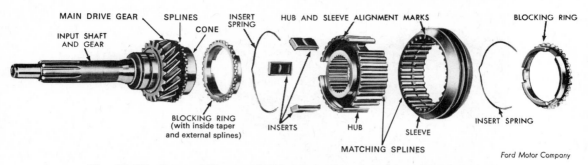

MAIN DRIVE GEAR SPLINES INSERT SPRING HUB AND SLEEVE ALIGNMENT MARKS BLOCKING RING

INPUT SHAFT AND GEAR CONE

BLOCKING RING (with inside taper and external splines) INSERTS HUB SLEEVE INSERT SPRING

MATCHING SPLINES

Ford Motor Company

Fig. 15:17 Second Gear and Third Gear Synchronizer (disassembled)

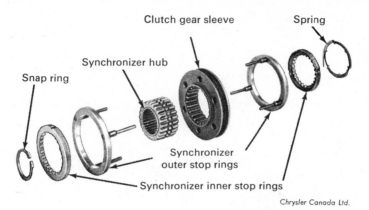

Clutch gear sleeve Spring

Synchronizer hub

Snap ring

Synchronizer outer stop rings

Synchronizer inner stop rings

Chrysler Canada Ltd.

Fig. 15:18 Pin-type Synchronizer

over the blocking ring until the internal splines of the sleeve join together the outer splines of the hub, the blocking ring, and the hub of the main drive gear. Note that the sliding action and the drag of the sleeve and the spring-loaded inserts would first push the loosely fitted blocking ring towards the hub of the main drive gear. The end of this hub is cone-shaped and fits exactly into the inside taper of the blocking ring. It is the friction between this cone and the tapered blocking ring that causes the speed between the input and the output shafts to synchronize *before* the sleeve has moved all the way to couple the two shafts. Thus, the speed of the input shaft is synchronized with that of the output shaft, which, in turn, is determined by the speed of the drive shaft, i.e., vehicle speed. The pin-type synchronizer shown in Fig. 15:18 is also widely used and works on similar principles.

Obviously, improper viscosity of the gear lubricant may interfere with proper synchro-mesh action. The synchronizers can also be damaged by excessively fast shifts, especially when the transmission is cold and the lubricant is still stiff. Another bad habit is that of resting the hand on the gearshift lever, as this will cause the synchronizer to wear out.

Two conventional or *standard* three-speed transmissions are shown in Figs. 15:19 and 15:20.

The Shifter Mechanism

The shifter mechanism has three functions:
1. It engages and disengages the gears selected by the driver.
2. It helps to hold the gears or synchromesh sleeves in the chosen position.
3. It prevents more than one gear speed from being engaged at the same time, which would cause the transmission to lock up.

The gear shift lever may be mounted on the steering column (Fig. 15:21) or on the floor directly above the transmission. The latter type is more commonly known as the *stick shift* or *floor shift*. The column-mounted type requires a fairly complex linkage and lever arrangement,

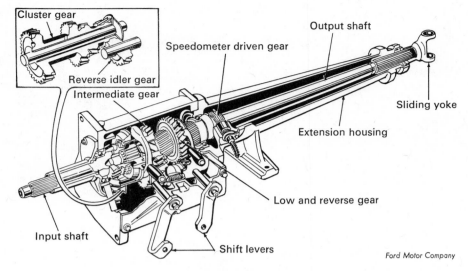

Cluster gear

Reverse idler gear

Intermediate gear

Speedometer driven gear

Output shaft

Sliding yoke

Extension housing

Low and reverse gear

Input shaft

Shift levers

Ford Motor Company

Fig. 15:19   Conventional Three-speed Transmission

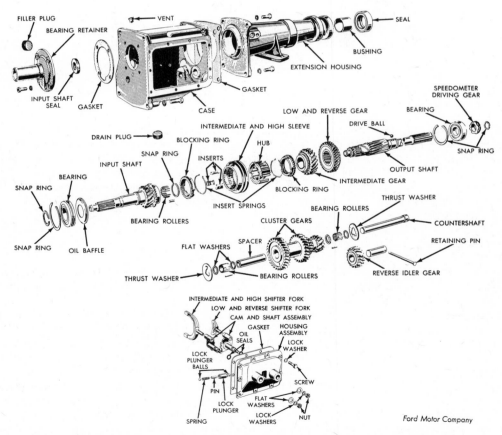

Ford Motor Company

Fig. 15:20   Conventional Three-speed Transmission (disassembled)

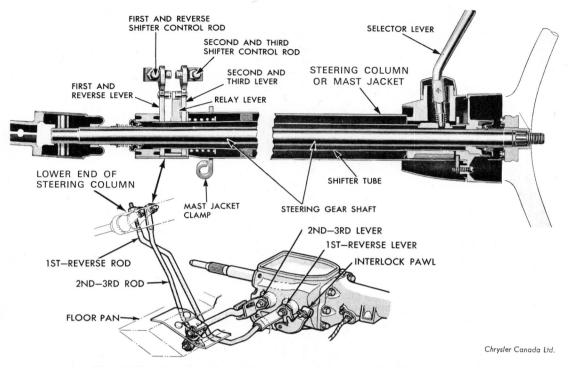

FIRST AND REVERSE
SHIFTER CONTROL ROD

SECOND AND THIRD
SHIFTER CONTROL ROD

SELECTOR LEVER

SECOND AND
THIRD LEVER

FIRST AND
REVERSE LEVER

STEERING COLUMN
OR MAST JACKET

RELAY LEVER

LOWER END OF
STEERING COLUMN

SHIFTER TUBE

MAST JACKET
CLAMP

STEERING GEAR SHAFT

2ND—3RD LEVER

1ST—REVERSE LEVER

INTERLOCK PAWL

1ST—REVERSE ROD

2ND—3RD ROD

FLOOR PAN

Chrysler Canada Ltd.

Fig. 15:21   Typical Gearshift Linkage for a Standard Transmission

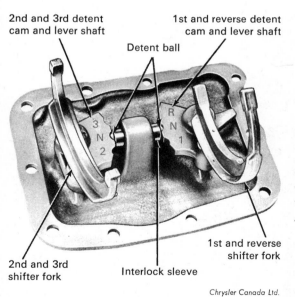

2nd and 3rd detent
cam and lever shaft

1st and reverse detent
cam and lever shaft

Detent ball

2nd and 3rd
shifter fork

Interlock sleeve

1st and reverse
shifter fork

Chrysler Canada Ltd.

Fig. 15:22   Shifter Cover Assembly (inside view)

whose specific design varies with different models.

The actual shifting inside the transmission is accomplished by *shifter forks* that either move the gears themselves (sliding-type gears) or the *synchronizer sleeves* (Figs. 15:19 and 15:20). Both the gears and the synchronizer sleeves are equipped with deep circular grooves for the forks to reach into. One method of holding the forks in the chosen position is illustrated in Fig. 15:22. In this case the position is neutral. The spring-loaded *detent balls* riding on the notched *detent cams* not only prevent the transmission from jumping out of gear but they also help the driver to "feel his way through the gears" as he moves the *selector lever* (gearshift lever).

If two gear speeds were engaged at the same time, the transmission would simply lock up, and neither the output nor the input shaft would be able to turn. A small pin inside the *interlock sleeve* (Fig. 15:20) prevents this. The pin is just short enough for one detent ball to be depressed but too long for both to clear the notches of the detent cams simultaneously.

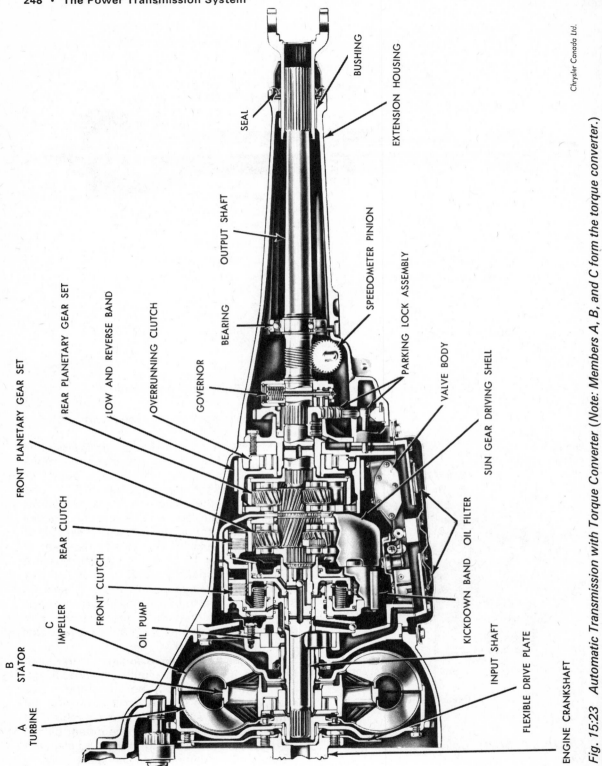

A
TURBINE

B
STATOR

C
IMPELLER

FRONT PLANETARY GEAR SET

REAR PLANETARY GEAR SET

LOW AND REVERSE BAND

OVERRUNNING CLUTCH

GOVERNOR

BEARING   OUTPUT SHAFT

SEAL

BUSHING

EXTENSION HOUSING

SPEEDOMETER PINION

PARKING LOCK ASSEMBLY

VALVE BODY

SUN GEAR DRIVING SHELL

REAR CLUTCH

FRONT CLUTCH

OIL PUMP

KICKDOWN BAND   OIL FILTER

INPUT SHAFT

FLEXIBLE DRIVE PLATE

ENGINE CRANKSHAFT

Chrysler Canada Ltd.

Fig. 15:23 Automatic Transmission with Torque Converter (Note: Members A, B, and C form the torque converter.)

General Transmission Information

It is a good rule to drive down a hill in the gear that would be needed to climb the same hill. Using the engine for braking power in the lower gears results in better vehicle control, and it reduces brake loads and wear.

Automatic Transmissions

Automatic transmissions (Fig. 15:23) fulfil the same basic function as standard transmissions except that they require no shifting by the driver once the shift lever is placed in the desired position, i.e., P (Park), R (Reverse), N (Neutral), D (Drive), or L (Low). The clutch is replaced by either a *fluid coupling* (rarely used on modern vehicles) or a *torque converter*. Both are hydraulic devices that allow a very smooth transmission of engine power. As the name implies, the torque converter has the additional function of changing torque; i.e., it accomplishes hydraulically what gears do mechanically. The drive members and the driven members of fluid couplings and torque converters are often likened to two cooling fans facing each other. If one of the cooling fans (the drive member) is turned on, the airflow causes the second one

(the driven member) to turn on its own. Obviously, the drive members and the driven members of fluid couplings and torque converters are completely enclosed units, filled with transmission fluid rather than air.

The required gear ratios are obtained from planetary gear trains, as described on page 237. These units are controlled by hydraulically activated clutches and bands responding to varying operating conditions, such as driving speed and engine load.

A more detailed description of automatic transmissions can be found in most service manuals or specialized texts.

The Drive Shaft or Propeller Shaft

The drive shaft or propeller shaft (Fig. 15:24) transmits the power from the transmission to the differential and the rear axle shafts. Front-wheel-drive vehicles or those with rear engines do not require a drive shaft.

There are two basic types of drive shaft designs:
1. The *open drive shaft* or *Hotchkiss drive*. It may consist of a single or a "split" drive shaft, i.e., two drive shafts connected in tandem. One advantage of this arrangement

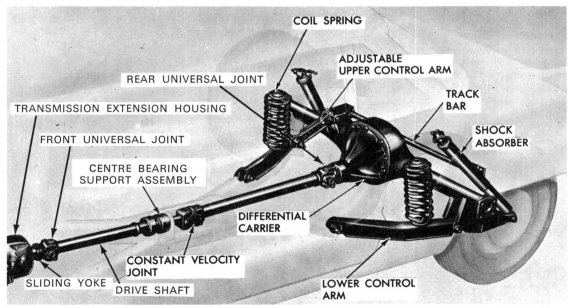

General Motors

Fig. 15:24 Drive Shaft and Rear Axle Assembly (live axle type)

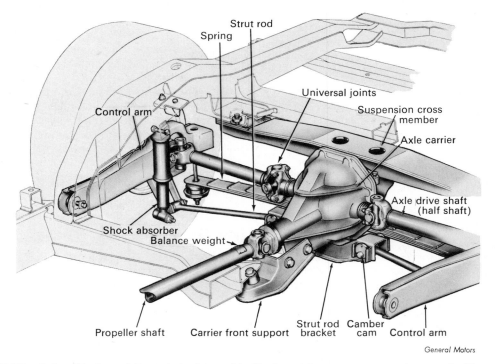

Fig. 15:25   *Drive Shaft and Rear Axle Assembly* (*independent rear suspension type*). *Note single transverse leaf spring.*

is that by using two shorter shafts with a centre support bearing, drive shaft whip and vibrations are reduced.

2. The *torque-tube drive*, which is rarely used in modern vehicles, employs a fully enclosed drive shaft.

The drive shaft usually consists of a strong, but lightweight, steel tube with a forged *drive yoke* welded to each end. The drive yokes and *trunnion assemblies* together form flexible connections known as the *universal joints* (Fig. 15:26). The rear universal joint is bolted to the *companion flange* of the *differential*, and the front universal joint is attached to the *sliding transmission yoke*, or *slip joint* (Fig. 15:27). The internal splines of the slip joint fit over the external splines of the transmission output shaft. The slip joint thus allows the drive shaft to shift back and forth slightly while the rear axle assembly and suspension system move up and down.

Since the drive shaft may reach well over 4,000 rpm in direct drive, it must be carefully balanced. If necessary, balance weights are spot-welded to the drive shaft (Fig. 15:25). However, even if the shaft is perfectly balanced, drive shaft angles of approximately 3° or more will produce undesirable vibrations. Some designs employ *inertia yokes* or *vibration dampers* to overcome this condition. These devices form part of either the front drive shaft yoke or the sliding yoke (Fig. 15:27).

The Universal Joints

The universal joints (Fig. 15:26) permit the rear axle to move in a vertical direction. The *constant velocity* type of universal joint (Fig. 15:24), as the name suggests, eliminates irregular shaft speeds (and thus vibrations) between the transmission output shaft and the companion flange at critical drive shaft angles. There are other types of universal joints, such as the *ball and trunnion* type and those using rubber couplings.

The Rear Axle

The rear axle, sometimes referred to as the *rear end* or *third member*, has four main functions:

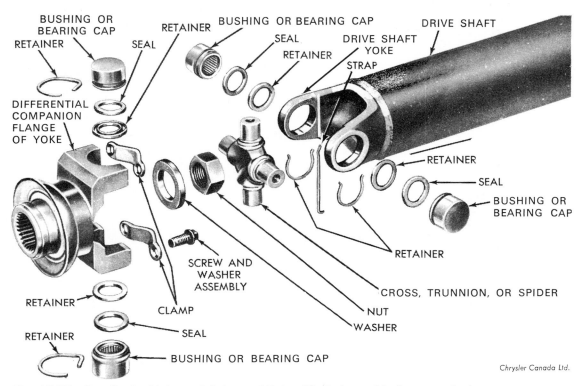

BUSHING OR BEARING CAP RETAINER

RETAINER SEAL

BUSHING OR BEARING CAP SEAL RETAINER

DRIVE SHAFT

DRIVE SHAFT YOKE STRAP

DIFFERENTIAL COMPANION FLANGE OF YOKE

RETAINER SEAL BUSHING OR BEARING CAP

RETAINER

SCREW AND WASHER ASSEMBLY

CROSS, TRUNNION, OR SPIDER

RETAINER CLAMP SEAL

NUT WASHER

RETAINER BUSHING OR BEARING CAP

Chrysler Canada Ltd.

Fig. 15:26 Detail of a Universal Joint and Drive Shaft Assembly (rear section)

1. It turns the power flow at right angles from the drive shaft to the rear axle shafts.
2. It allows one rear wheel to revolve faster than the other when the vehicle is driven through turns.
3. It increases torque but decreases speed between the rear axle shafts and the drive shaft.
4. It supports the vehicle and the rear brake assemblies.

Although there are many different rear axle designs, they usually belong to one of the two following major types:

1. The *Live Axle* (Fig. 15:24) consists of a rigid axle assembly; that is, the entire unit, including the differential, must follow the up-and-down movement of the wheels.
2. The *Independent-Suspension-type Rear Axle* (Fig. 15:25) has axle shafts equipped with flexible joints similar to those used on drive shafts. The differential housing is, with this type, mounted to the frame or some substructure welded to the body. It therefore does not move with the suspension

system as it does with the live axle. This arrangement is very popular with faster cars, and particularly with imported vehicles.

Live axles are usually of the *semi-floating* or

Insulator

Yoke

Internal splines

Damper

General Motors

Fig. 15:27 Sliding Yoke with Vibration Damper

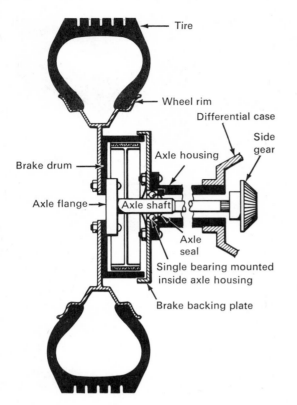

Fig. 15:28 Semi-floating Rear Axle (Axle shaft transmits torque and carries full vehicle load.)

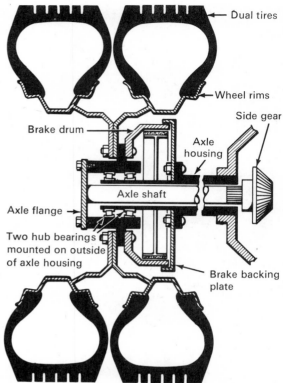

Fig. 15:29 Full-floating Rear Axle (Axle shaft transmits torque only; full vehicle load is carried by axle housing.)

the *full-floating* type.[63] With the semi-floating type (Fig. 15:28) used on most passenger cars, the outer ends of the axles are supported by bearings *inside* the axle housing. This means that the outer ends not only transmit the drive torque but must also bear the weight of the vehicle, as well as the thrust forces generated by cornering. Because the outer ends of the axle shafts are used for support, while the inner ends, which are splined to the differential side gears, are not, the design is said to be of the semi-floating type. The purpose of the *retainer ring* and the *retainer flange* (Fig. 15:30) is to hold the axle bearing and the axle shaft in the axle housing. The retainer ring and the bearing are usually pressed onto the axle shaft by means of a hydraulic press. The oil seal prevents any

[63]A third type, the three-quarter-floating axle, which in a sense is a cross between the two types described above, is now very rarely used.

loss of lubricant past the axle shaft and onto the brakes. On some rear axles, the bearing is a ball bearing of the sealed, prelubricated type and it is mounted on the "dry" side of the rear axle seal, i.e., between the retainer flange and the seal in the axle housing. In another design an "open", or non-sealed, roller bearing or ball bearing exposed to the rear axle lubricant is mounted on the "wet" side behind the seal. In this case the axles are retained by "C" locks located on the ends of the axle shafts inside the differential (Fig. 15:31).

The full-floating axle (Fig. 15:29) is used on trucks and carries no weight. It is bolted to the wheel hub and its sole purpose is to transmit the drive torque. The load is supported by two hub bearings (rather than inner axle bearings) located between the hub and the axle housing. The bearings are held in position by specially secured locking nuts. With this arrangement the axle shafts can be removed without either

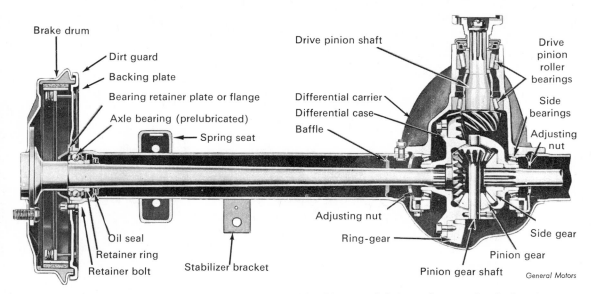

Brake drum
Dirt guard
Backing plate
Bearing retainer plate or flange
Axle bearing (prelubricated)
Spring seat
Oil seal
Retainer ring
Retainer bolt
Stabilizer bracket
Drive pinion shaft
Differential carrier
Differential case
Baffle
Adjusting nut
Ring-gear
Pinion gear shaft
Drive pinion roller bearings
Side bearings
Adjusting nut
Side gear
Pinion gear
General Motors

Fig. 15:30 Sectional View of Rear Axle Assembly. Note prelubricated type of axle bearing mounted on "dry" side of axle seal.

the wheels being taken off or the vehicle being unloaded.

The Differential

The differential, also called the "final drive" (Fig. 15:31), is part of the rear axle and its main functions have already been discussed at the beginning of the previous section.

When making a turn (Fig. 15:32), the outer rear wheel must travel a greater distance than the inner rear wheel.[64] Obviously, if power were applied to a single axle shaft joining both wheels, traction and power would be partly lost, and the tires would wear very rapidly. The differential, however, permits the two wheels, though powered by a common drive pinion, to revolve at different speeds. This is how it works: The drive pinion (Fig. 15:33), which is connected to the drive shaft, transmits the torque to the ring gear and thus to the pinion shaft. While the pinion shaft does not turn about its own axis, it must nevertheless move around with the ring gear, thus carrying the differential pinion with it in an orbital path around the centre line of the differential. When

the vehicle is going straight ahead, it takes equal torque on *both* side gears to turn the wheels at the same speed. The small differential pinion, which is engaged with both side gears, will therefore not rotate, but will act as if it were rigidly connected to the side gears. Thus, the entire assembly, i.e., the ring gear, the pinion shaft, the differential pinion, the side gears, and the axle shafts themselves, will rotate in unison, as if made out of one single part. Let us assume now that the vehicle makes a left-hand turn (Fig. 15:34). Here the left inner wheel slows down, and naturally so does the left axle shaft and the side gear, which is splined to it. Obviously, if the left side gear slows down, it holds the differential pinion back on the left side. This causes the differential pinion, which is fitted loosely to the pinion shaft, to turn about its own axis as it is forced to "walk" around the slower left side gear. It is this rotation of the differential pinion which, when added to the rotation of the right side gear, causes the outer wheel to speed up. Needless to say, the opposite would be true if the vehicle were to make a right-hand turn.[65] (To simplify our explanation we have left out

[64]While this also applies to the front wheels, it poses no problem there, unless the vehicle is equipped with front wheel drive.

[65]The inventor of this rather ingenious device (1827!) was a Frenchman, Onésiphore Pecqueur.

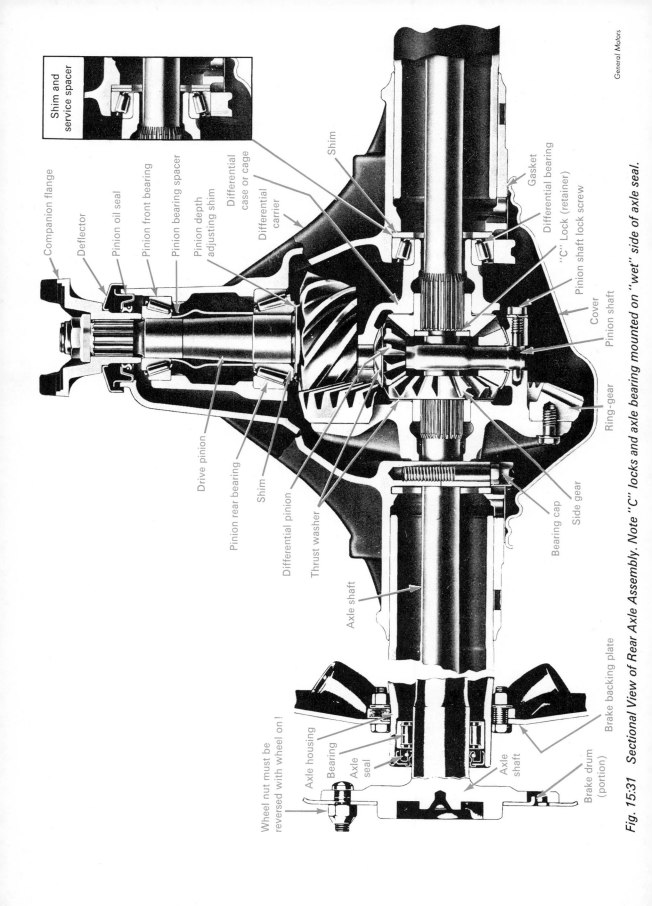

General Motors

Shim and service spacer

Companion flange

Deflector

Pinion oil seal

Pinion front bearing

Pinion bearing spacer

Pinion depth adjusting shim

Differential case or cage

Differential carrier

Shim

Gasket

Differential bearing

"C" Lock (retainer)

Pinion shaft lock screw

Cover

Pinion shaft

Ring-gear

Bearing cap

Side gear

Drive pinion

Pinion rear bearing

Shim

Differential pinion

Thrust washer

Axle shaft

Wheel nut must be reversed with wheel on !

Axle housing

Bearing

Axle seal

Axle shaft

Brake drum (portion)

Brake backing plate

Fig. 15:31 Sectional View of Rear Axle Assembly. Note "C" locks and axle bearing mounted on "wet" side of axle seal.

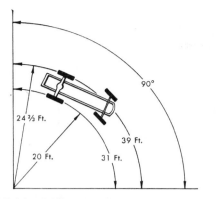

Fig. 15:32 Difference in Wheel Travel as Car Makes a 90° Turn

the second differential pinion, as well as the differential case shown in Fig. 15:31. Some heavy-duty units even employ four differential pinions.)

The standard differential has drawbacks in that it may produce excessive wheel spin of one of the rear wheels under certain road conditions, such as in snow and mud, or on ice, gravel, and wet pavement. Wheel spin is also frequently encountered on the inner rear wheel due to vehicle "roll" in fast, sharp turns. *Limited slip differentials* (Fig. 15:35) are designed to reduce excessive wheel spin of one wheel by means of built-in friction discs, cones, or other devices, while still permitting the wheels to rotate at slightly different speeds when going around turns. These units are more popularly known as "Posi-Traction", "Twin-Traction", "Equa-Lok", and "Sure-Grip" differentials.

General Rear Axle Information

The curved tooth design of hypoid gears results in considerable wiping action between the

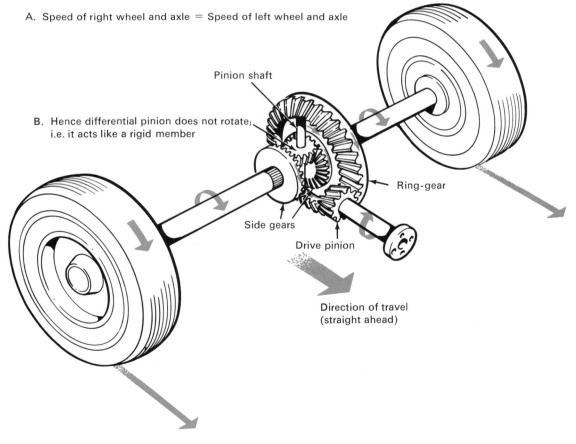

Fig. 15:33 Operating Principles of a Differential

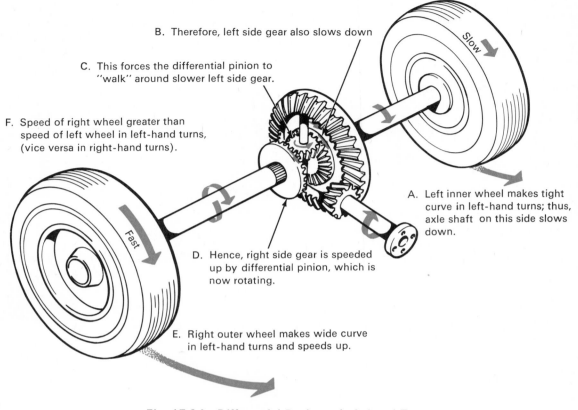

B. Therefore, left side gear also slows down

C. This forces the differential pinion to "walk" around slower left side gear.

F. Speed of right wheel greater than speed of left wheel in left-hand turns, (vice versa in right-hand turns).

A. Left inner wheel makes tight curve in left-hand turns; thus, axle shaft on this side slows down.

D. Hence, right side gear is speeded up by differential pinion, which is now rotating.

E. Right outer wheel makes wide curve in left-hand turns and speeds up.

Slow

Fast

Fig. 15:34   Differential During a Left-hand Turn

gear teeth, which, in addition to the very high tooth contact pressures (up to 400,000 psi, or 2 756 000 kPa), tends to displace the lubricant. It is therefore of utmost importance that only recommended hypoid oils (EP lubricants) of correct viscosity be used in order to prevent gear scuffing. (Limited slip differentials require special lubricants. Refer to page 137.) Even under normal operating conditions the rear axle lubricant will reach fairly high temperatures. Vapour pressures which build up as a result are relieved through a vent, which is usually mounted on top of one of the axle housing tubes. If the vent is plugged, the lubricant will leak out of the pinion or the axle seals. This can be a great safety hazard, as it will foul up the brakes.

Differentials are usually available in different ratios. An increase in the rear axle ratio from 3:1 to 3.5:1, for example, would result in an increase in engine rpm, rear axle torque, and acceleration, but it would also decrease fuel

mileage and top speed. Obviously, decreasing the ratio would do exactly the opposite.

Differential drive pinions and ring gears are sold in matched sets and must always be replaced together. The adjustment of a new or used gear set requires great skill. It involves the adjustment of proper tooth contact and bearing preloads, as well as the checking of gear run-out and backlash (Figs. 15:36 and 1:97). The tooth contact can be checked by applying a special type of paint known as *red lead*.[66] If the gears are then rotated under light load, the contact pattern obtained will give the mechanic an idea of whether or not further adjustments are needed. If they are, the necessary corrections are made by altering the position of the drive pinion with *shims* and that of the ring gear by means of *shims* or *adjusting nuts*

---

[66]*Caution:* Red lead is highly toxic and causes brain damage. Avoid contact with the mouth and open wounds!

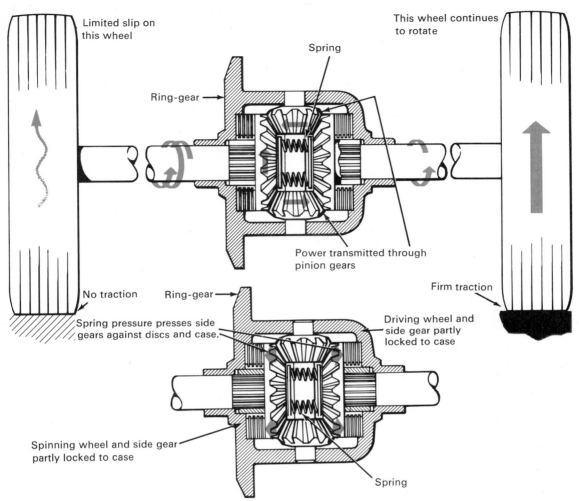

Limited slip on this wheel

Spring

Ring-gear

This wheel continues to rotate

Power transmitted through pinion gears

No traction

Ring-gear

Spring pressure presses side gears against discs and case.

Driving wheel and side gear partly locked to case

Firm traction

Spinning wheel and side gear partly locked to case

Spring

Energized clutches (or cones) cause partly locked differential.

General Motors

Fig. 15:35   Operating Principles of Limited Slip Differential

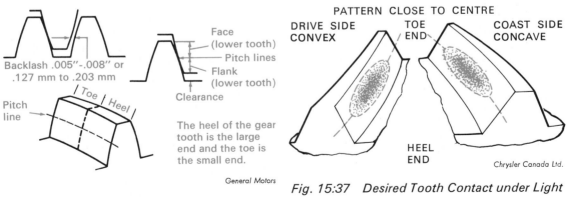

Backlash .005″-.008″ or .127 mm to .203 mm

Face (lower tooth)

Pitch lines

Flank (lower tooth)

Clearance

Pitch line

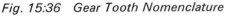

Toe | Heel

The heel of the gear tooth is the large end and the toe is the small end.

General Motors

Fig. 15:36   Gear Tooth Nomenclature

PATTERN CLOSE TO CENTRE

DRIVE SIDE CONVEX

TOE END

COAST SIDE CONCAVE

HEEL END

Chrysler Canada Ltd.

Fig. 15:37   Desired Tooth Contact under Light Load

(Figs. 15:30 and 15:31). A normal contact pattern is shown in Fig. 15:37. Note that the tooth curve of the driving side of the ring gear forms a D (Drive) while the coasting side forms a C (Coasting). This is always true if the gear tooth is assumed to stand on its broad "heel".

Defective differentials and rear axle bearings produce noises very similar to those produced by some tires, especially snow tires. Confusing the two defects can be a costly mistake.

RECOMMENDED ASSIGNMENTS

1. Name, in order, the units that transmit power from the flywheel to the rear wheels.
2. What is the purpose of the clutch?
3. Explain what happens in the clutch as the pedal is depressed and then released. Illustrate your answer.
4. What is the name and function of the coil springs in the clutch disc?
5. Name four types of clutches and describe their main features.
6. What happens to clutch pedal lash as the clutch linings wear down?
7. What will be the result if pedal lash is (a) too little, or (b) too much?
8. What is the result when (a) a large gear drives a small one, and (b) when a small gear drives a large one? (Three factors change in each case.)
9. (a) Gear A has 10 teeth; gear B, which is driven by A, has 40 teeth. What is the gear ratio?
   (b) If shaft A produces 50 lb.-ft. torque at 2,000 rpm, what is the torque and rpm of shaft B?
10. Explain the advantages of a helical gear over a straight spur gear.
11. Why are hypoid gears used in most modern differentials?
12. List the six main functions of an automotive transmission.
13. Name the gears in the order in which power is transmitted through them in (a) first, (b) second, (c) high, and (d) reverse gear.
14. Can a transmission increase power? Discuss.
15. How does the reverse idler affect torque and shaft speed in reverse gear?
16. (a) What is constant mesh? (b) What is its advantage?

17. Explain the purpose and operation of the synchromesh unit.
18. How do the following things interfere with the operation of the synchromesh unit:
    (a) improper viscosity of the gear lubricant,
    (b) excessively fast shifting,
    (c) low temperature,
    (d) resting the hand on the gearshift lever?
19. What are the functions of the detent balls and the shift interlock mechanism?
20. (a) What is the purpose of the universal joints?
    (b) Explain the function of a constant velocity universal joint.
21. What are the four main functions of the rear axle?
22. Comment on the terms "semi-floating rear axle" and "full-floating rear axle".
23. (a) If the drive pinion has 10 teeth and the ring gear 34, what is the rear axle ratio?
    (b) How is the torque affected if we increase the ratio in this way?
    (c) What happens to the axle shaft speed?
24. (a) What is the speed of the ring gear in relation to the axle shafts when the car is travelling straight ahead?
    (b) What would the differential pinions do?
25. What lubricants are needed (a) for standard hypoid differentials and (b) for limited slip differentials?
26. Name the adjustments required when installing a differential assembly.

TROUBLE-SHOOTING

The number of possible reasons appears in brackets.
1. Shortly after a new clutch has been installed, the driver complains about clutch slippage. (3+)
2. Even after the clutch is adjusted it doesn't release properly. (4+)
3. The transmission jumps out of gear in first and reverse. (3+)
4. When the driver shifts from first to reverse, and vice versa, a loud snapping noise is heard from below the floor pan as the clutch is engaged. (2+)
5. The rear axle is noisy, but only when going around corners. (2)

16

The Running Gear

The running gear consists of the wheels, the suspension system, the steering gear and linkage, the brakes, the frame (if used), in short, all those parts that either support the body or control the vehicle.

The safety of the driver, his passengers, and everyone sharing the road with him depends on the components listed above. Their maintenance and repair involve great responsibility.

The Frame

The frame forms the "backbone" to which all the other units of the entire vehicle are attached. To prevent squeaks and rattles and to keep steering and suspension members in alignment, the more rigid a frame can be made, the better it is.[67] Yet, for reasons of performance and cost, the frame must also be as light as possible; it should take up little space and be able to withstand low-speed collisions.

In a heavy collision, the front and the rear ends of a well-designed vehicle absorb most of the energy released at impact; that is to say, they collapse in a controlled way without affecting the centre section of the body and frame.

The most common frame designs are shown in Fig. 16:2. Note that the design illustrated in Fig. 16:3 utilizes the body itself as a structural member. To support the engine, the bumpers, and the suspension system, it is reinforced by frame-like steel stampings, welded into the body. Hence the term *unitized body-frame construction*. Advantages claimed for this design

---

[67]On trucks the frame is designed to flex with the load.

are lower cost, light weight, and fewer rattles and squeaks.

An impact-absorbing bumper system is shown in Fig. 16:4.

The Front Suspension System

All modern passenger vehicles have *independent front wheel suspensions*, while many trucks still employ a rigid front axle.

Independent front suspension has three very important advantages all of which add up to improved wheel traction and thus greater vehicle control:

1. Each wheel is free to respond *independently* to the contour of the road bed, and any disturbance in one wheel leaves the opposite wheel more or less unaffected.

2. It reduces over-all weight and, specifically, the weight of those parts that, like the wheels themselves, are not cushioned by spring action. Generally, the lighter the *unsprung masses* are (tire, rim, wheel spindle, etc.), in relation to the *sprung masses* (frame, body, engine, etc.), the better the ride is. This is the reason why, for example, some advanced designs use inboard-mounted brakes as shown in Fig. 9:8. A light suspension system has much less trouble in following the shape of the road, and there is less "kick-back".

3. The independent front suspension permits lower vehicle designs. This results in a lower centre of gravity, less roll in turns, reduced air drag, and improved visibility and styling.

There is a great variety of front suspension systems, but the *ball-joint type with unequal*

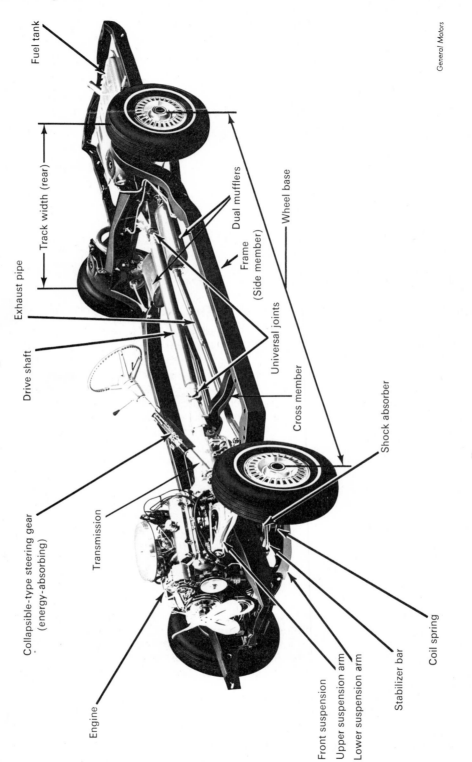

General Motors

Fuel tank

Track width (rear)

Exhaust pipe

Drive shaft

Collapsible-type steering gear
(energy-absorbing)

Transmission

Engine

Dual mufflers

Frame
(Side member)

Universal joints

Cross member

Wheel base

Shock absorber

Front suspension

Upper suspension arm

Lower suspension arm

Stabilizer bar

Coil spring

Fig. 16:1   The Running Gear

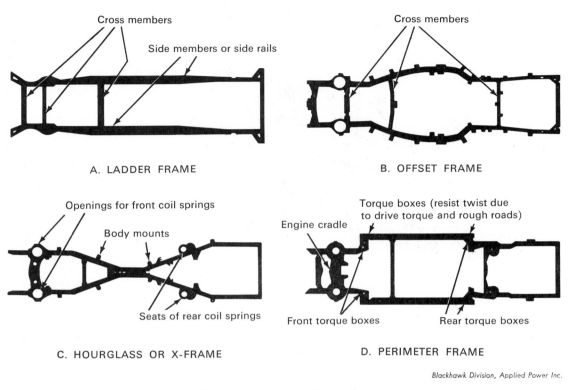

Cross members

Side members or side rails

A. LADDER FRAME

Cross members

B. OFFSET FRAME

Openings for front coil springs

Body mounts

Seats of rear coil springs

C. HOURGLASS OR X-FRAME

Torque boxes (resist twist due to drive torque and rough roads)

Engine cradle

Front torque boxes

Rear torque boxes

D. PERIMETER FRAME

Blackhawk Division, Applied Power Inc.

Fig. 16:2   Common Types of Passenger Car Frames

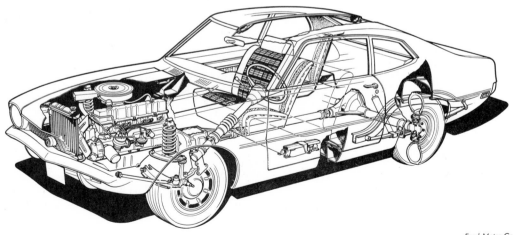

Ford Motor Company

Fig. 16:3   Unitized Body and Frame Design

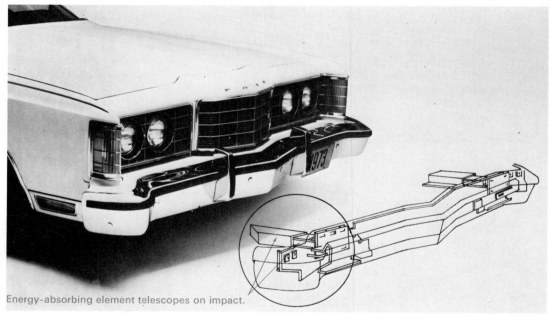

Energy-absorbing element telescopes on impact.

Ford Motor Company

Fig. 16:4   Impact-absorbing Bumper System

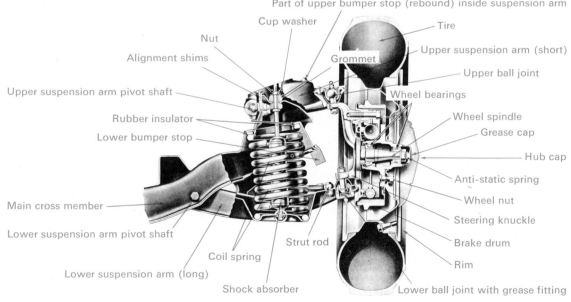

Part of upper bumper stop (rebound) inside suspension arm

Cup washer

Nut

Tire

Alignment shims

Grommet

Upper suspension arm (short)

Upper ball joint

Upper suspension arm pivot shaft

Wheel bearings

Rubber insulator

Wheel spindle

Lower bumper stop

Grease cap

Hub cap

Anti-static spring

Main cross member

Wheel nut

Lower suspension arm pivot shaft

Steering knuckle

Strut rod

Brake drum

Coil spring

Rim

Lower suspension arm (long)

Shock absorber

Lower ball joint with grease fitting

General Motors

Fig. 16:5   Independent Front Suspension with Unequal-length Suspension Arms, Coil Springs, and Ball Joints

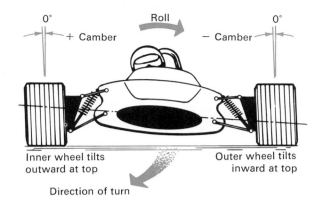

Fig. 16:6 *Unequal arm suspension keeps wheels upright and tire treads flat on pavement in turn despite vehicle roll.*

suspension arms (Fig. 16:5) is the most common. The ball joints permit the wheel both to be steered and to be moved up and down. The main advantage of unequal suspension arms is that track width does not change appreciably at the point where the wheel touches the pavement, regardless of wheel travel or changes in vehicle load. Obviously, if the suspension arms were parallel to one another and of equal length, full track width could only be obtained with the arms in a horizontal position. In either the up (loaded) or down (unloaded) position, the entire wheel on both sides would be pulled inwards like the tips of a bird's wings. Fig. 16:6 shows an unequal arm suspension system in action. It can be seen that the "outer wheel" is subjected to a heavy load. However, the non-parallel and shorter upper suspension arm pulls the wheel inwards only at the top, thus maintaining track width at the bottom. (The outward tilt of the unloaded inner wheel at this point is explained later in the chapter.) Unequal arm suspension also helps to improve wheel traction in sharp turns. Because of the loads imposed on the outer front suspension system during vehicle roll, the outer wheel tilts inwards at the top in relation to the vehicle, and yet in relation to the pavement it remains upright. With today's "flat-footed" wide oval tires the advantage is obvious.

There are two *bumper stops* on each side that limit the wheel travel under extreme impact

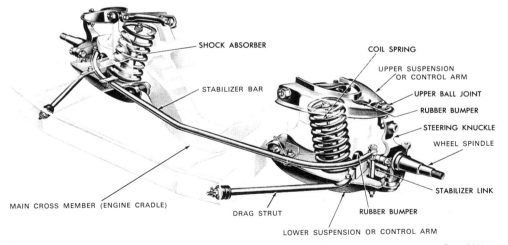

General Motors

Fig. 16:7 *Independent, Unequal Arm Front Suspension with Stabilizer Bar*

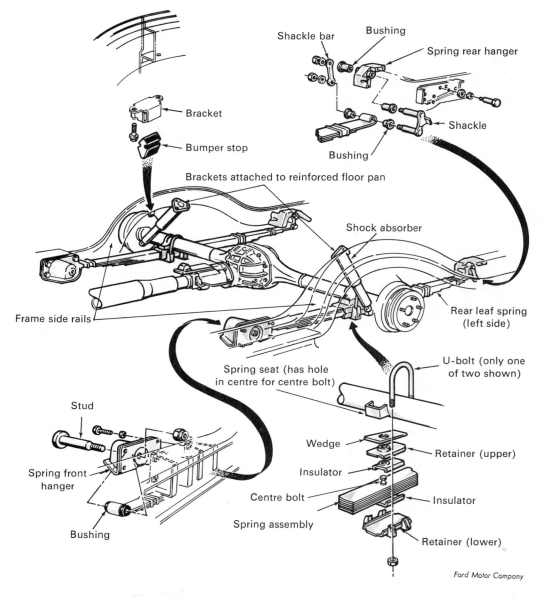

Shackle bar Bushing Spring rear hanger

Bracket

Bumper stop

Shackle

Bushing

Brackets attached to reinforced floor pan

Shock absorber

Frame side rails

Rear leaf spring
(left side)

Spring seat (has hole
in centre for centre bolt)

U-bolt (only one
of two shown)

Stud

Wedge — Retainer (upper)

Insulator

Spring front
hanger

Centre bolt — Insulator

Bushing

Spring assembly

Retainer (lower)

Ford Motor Company

Fig. 16:8   Live Axle with Multiple Leaf Springs

loads. The lower one acts on impact, the upper one on rebound (Fig. 16:5).

The Stabilizer Bar, or Anti-roll Bar

The stabilizer bar, or anti-roll bar (Fig. 16:7), which is mounted to the frame by rubber-insulated brackets, is essentially a torsion bar (see page 265) designed to counteract vehicle

roll in turns. In sharp turns the downward pressure of the relaxed inner spring (Fig. 16:6) and its suspension arm is transmitted through the stabilizer bar to the opposite suspension arm, thus assisting the compressed outer spring to keep the vehicle reasonably level. Some manufacturers use stabilizer bars in both the front and the rear.

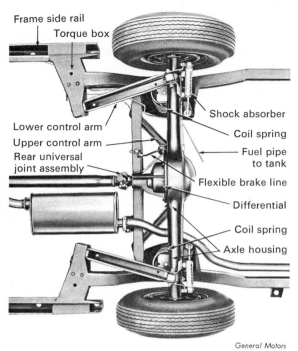

Frame side rail
Torque box
Lower control arm
Upper control arm
Rear universal joint assembly
Shock absorber
Coil spring
Fuel pipe to tank
Flexible brake line
Differential
Coil spring
Axle housing

General Motors

Fig. 16:9   Live Axle with Coil Springs and Control Arms as Seen from Below

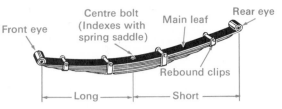

Front eye
Centre bolt (Indexes with spring saddle)
Main leaf
Rear eye
Rebound clips
Long — Short

Fig. 16:10   Multiple Leaf Spring

Rear Suspension

The most common rear suspension systems employ a *live axle*, i.e., a rigid, one-piece axle housing (Fig. 16:8). If coil springs are used, the axle is held in position by some type of locating linkage employing such devices as tracking bars, panhard rods, sway bars, radius rods, and control arms (also known as suspension arms or trailing arms) (Fig. 16:9). These linkages also counteract rear axle wind-up, that is, the drive shaft's tendency, especially under heavy acceleration, to take the rear axle around with it. An example of independent rear suspension is shown in Fig. 15:25.

Springs

The springs are usually of one of three types: (1) *coil spring* (Figs. 16:5 and 16:7), (2) *leaf spring* (Figs. 16:8 and 16:10), or (3) *torsion bar* (Fig. 16:11). The leaf spring can be of either a multi- or a single-leaf design. There are also pneumatic (air) and hydraulic systems,

but they are less common. Many cars use one type of spring in the front and another in the rear. There is no absolute advantage that can be claimed for any particular type of spring. The coil spring is essentially a coiled-up torsion bar, as its springing effect is derived from the twisting of steel. Torsion bars, however, permit spring tension to be adjusted more easily. Because the leaf spring is very rigid horizontally, it also serves as a locating arm for the rear axle.

The *multi-leaf spring* (Fig. 16:10) is made up of a series of specially tempered steel plates separated by friction inserts. The inserts, which are made of various synthetic materials, give some damping action to the spring and eliminate squeaks and rattles. The leaf spring is held together by the *centre bolt* and the *rebound clips*. The term "centre bolt" is a misnomer because it is usually positioned closer to the forward end of the spring. The centre bolt acts as a locating dowel for the spring seat, or saddle, on the axle housing (Fig. 16:8), and it prevents any shifting between the spring leaves themselves. Each spring is clamped to the axle by means of a pair of *U-bolts* and a *mounting plate*. The mounting plate often serves as an anchor for the lower shock absorber pivot. The ends of the main leaf, which are rolled up to

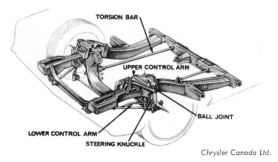

TORSION BAR
UPPER CONTROL ARM
BALL JOINT
LOWER CONTROL ARM
STEERING KNUCKLE

Chrysler Canada Ltd.

Fig. 16:11   Independent Front Suspension with Torsion Bars

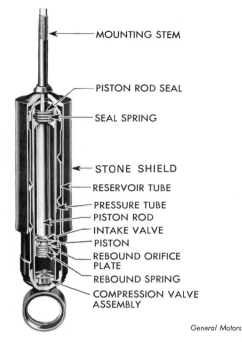

MOUNTING STEM

PISTON ROD SEAL

SEAL SPRING

STONE SHIELD

RESERVOIR TUBE

PRESSURE TUBE

PISTON ROD

INTAKE VALVE

PISTON

REBOUND ORIFICE PLATE

REBOUND SPRING

COMPRESSION VALVE ASSEMBLY

General Motors

Fig. 16:12   Typical Shock Absorber (sectional view)

form an "eye", are connected to the *hangers*. The spring *shackle* at the rear hanger permits the lengthening and shortening of the spring as it flexes. The bolts connecting the spring to the hangers and the shackle are insulated by *rubber bushings*. They require no lubrication; in fact, they would deteriorate quickly if treated with regular lubricants. For ease of installation, a few drops of brake fluid or tire soap can be applied if necessary.

Shock Absorbers

When a spring is compressed under an impact load, caused, for example, by a bump in the road, it rebounds with almost equal force. This cycle repeats itself and thus the oscillations of the spring produce a very "bouncy" ride. If the vehicle strikes another bump at the very moment the spring is on the rebound, the occupants will be badly shaken up. At high speeds, however, the wheels will be completely lifted off the pavement. As a result, traction is lost, and so is vehicle control. If the impact is very severe, the spring and the axle will "hit bottom" —and so will the occupants of the vehicle.

Mechanical damage is likely to follow.

Shock absorbers (Fig. 16:12) prevent these conditions by damping the spring action in the same way as those you have seen used on some doors. The main difference is that modern automobile shock absorbers are hydraulic and double-acting; i.e., they retard spring action on impact as well as on rebound. They are usually designed to offer greater resistance to rebound than to impact; the ratio may be as high as 4:1. The retarding action of the shock absorber is obtained by pumping a hydraulic fluid from one chamber into another through metered passages. Some designs are adjustable to compensate for load changes or wear.

Caution: To maintain the balance of the suspension system, replace worn front or rear shock absorbers only in pairs. Fluid leakage or bouncy spring action are sure signs of bad "shocks". Manual testing is not reliable.

The Steering System
The Steering Gear Assembly

The steering gear assembly (Figs. 16:13-16:15) consists of the steering box, the steering column (mast jacket), the steering shaft, and the steering wheel, which is splined to the steering shaft. The assembly also includes the turn signal switch, the mechanism to sound the horn, and, in many cases, parts of the gearshift linkage, as well as an ignition and steering lock. Modern steering gears are designed to reduce the danger of injury in case of a collision. The steering wheel is dished, or even padded, and the steering column will collapse or telescope under heavy impact (Fig. 16:13). These "energy-absorbing" steering columns are now required by law on all new cars.

Caution: Never hammer the steering column or shaft! This will permanently damage the energy-absorbing parts of the steering gear assembly.

Some steering shafts consist of two or more angled shaft sections connected by universal joints or flexible insulator couplings. This arrangement allows the steering box to be installed in a position that could not be reached by a straight shaft, and, in case of repairs, it greatly simplifies the removal and installation of the steering box. The insulator couplings

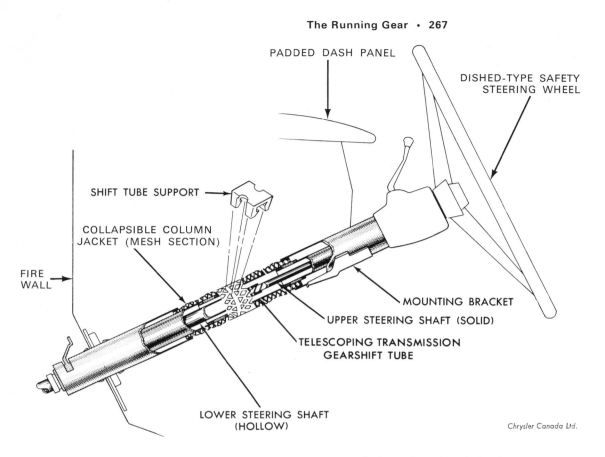

PADDED DASH PANEL

DISHED-TYPE SAFETY STEERING WHEEL

SHIFT TUBE SUPPORT →

COLLAPSIBLE COLUMN JACKET (MESH SECTION)

FIRE WALL →

MOUNTING BRACKET

UPPER STEERING SHAFT (SOLID)

TELESCOPING TRANSMISSION GEARSHIFT TUBE

LOWER STEERING SHAFT (HOLLOW)

Chrysler Canada Ltd.

Fig. 16:13 Energy-absorbing-type Steering Column (sectional view)

also reduce the transmission of wheel shake and other vibrations.

The effort required to turn the steering wheel depends on many factors, such as the speed and the weight of the vehicle, the type of pavement, the tire size, the tire pressure, and the steering gear itself. The mechanical advantage of a steering gear is determined by the size of the steering wheel and the length of the pitman arm, but most of all, by *the steering ratio*. If the ratio is 16:1, for example, the steering wheel has to be turned 16° to move the front wheels 1°. Modern steering gears often have a variable ratio; that is, when the driver is turning the steering wheel through the first quarter-turn, either to the left or to the right, the ratio may be relatively high, e.g., 16:1, while any further rotation may gradually reduce the ratio to 13:1. This means less direct steering while going straight ahead but quick response in sharp, slow turns (street corners, parking, etc.). The

variable ratio is usually obtained by having teeth of unequal length on the sector gear. The shape of the sector and the ball nut also results in less free play in the centre position, called the "high spot". The steering ratio not only reduces steering effort but also the amount of road shock transmitted to the driver's hands.

The most common type of steering gear employs a *worm gear* (Fig. 16:16). Another design, called *rack and pinion steering*, features a toothed rack and a pinion gear (Fig. 16:17). This type is particularly popular on imported automobiles, but it is also found on some domestic models. Its advantage is very positive, precise steering. In sharp turns particularly, there is less free play in the steering wheel. Either kind may be used with hydraulically assisted power steerings.

Worm-gear-type steering gears can be classified as follows:

1. *The Recirculating Ball Type* is shown in

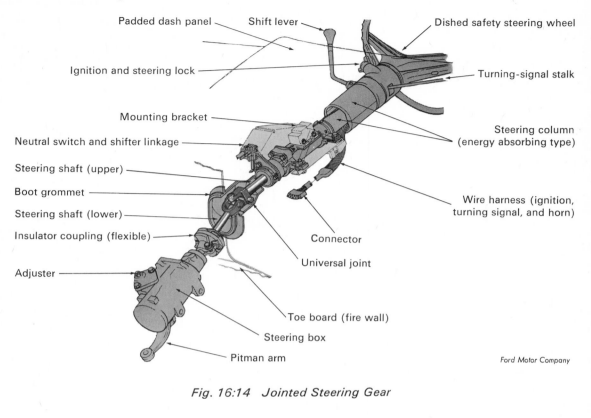

Padded dash panel

Shift lever

Dished safety steering wheel

Ignition and steering lock

Turning-signal stalk

Mounting bracket

Steering column (energy absorbing type)

Neutral switch and shifter linkage

Steering shaft (upper)

Boot grommet

Steering shaft (lower)

Insulator coupling (flexible)

Wire harness (ignition, turning signal, and horn)

Adjuster

Connector

Universal joint

Toe board (fire wall)

Steering box

Pitman arm

Ford Motor Company

Fig. 16:14 Jointed Steering Gear

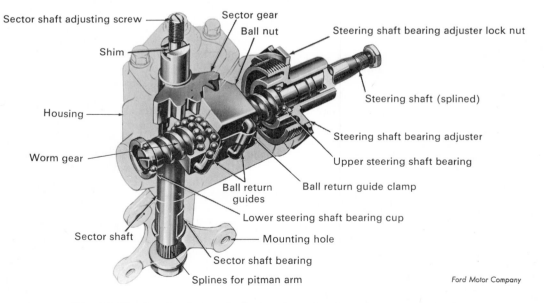

Sector shaft adjusting screw

Sector gear

Ball nut

Steering shaft bearing adjuster lock nut

Shim

Housing

Steering shaft (splined)

Worm gear

Steering shaft bearing adjuster

Upper steering shaft bearing

Ball return guides

Ball return guide clamp

Lower steering shaft bearing cup

Sector shaft

Mounting hole

Sector shaft bearing

Splines for pitman arm

Ford Motor Company

Fig. 16:15 Recirculating-ball-type Steering Gear (phantom view)

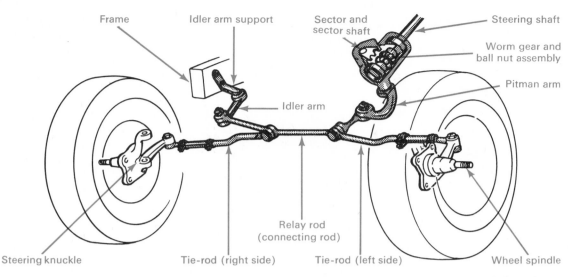

Frame · Idler arm support · Sector and sector shaft · Steering shaft · Worm gear and ball nut assembly · Pitman arm · Idler arm · Steering knuckle · Tie-rod (right side) · Relay rod (connecting rod) · Tie-rod (left side) · Wheel spindle

Fig. 16:16 Conventional Steering System

Ford Motor Company

Fig. 16:16. The steel balls act as ball bearings between the *worm gear* and the *ball nut* and thereby reduce friction and steering effort. The ball nut, as the name implies, is threaded up and down the worm gear as the steering shaft is turned. This movement is transmitted to the *sector gear*, the *sector shaft*, and thus to the *pitman arm* (Fig. 16:16), which is splined to the *sector shaft*.

2. *The Worm and Roller Type* (not shown; now rarely used). The main difference between this type and the recirculating ball type is that this type employs a *toothed roller* mounted on ball bearings instead of a

gear sector. The roller engages directly into the worm gear.

3. *The Cam and Lever Type* (not shown; rarely used) has one or two sliding *studs* or *cams* mounted to the sector shaft head in place of a roller. The sliding studs reach directly into the grooves of a specially designed worm gear.

Steering Gear Service

Servicing of the steering gear consists mostly of checking the steering box for the proper lubricant level and excessive free play. Unless

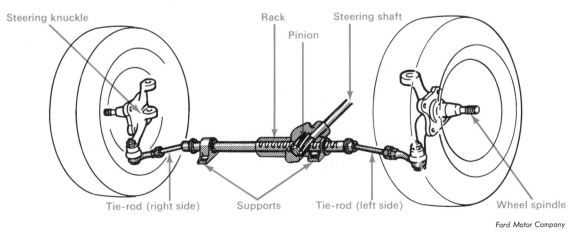

Steering knuckle · Rack · Pinion · Steering shaft · Tie-rod (right side) · Supports · Tie-rod (left side) · Wheel spindle

Ford Motor Company

Fig. 16:17 Rack and Pinion Steering

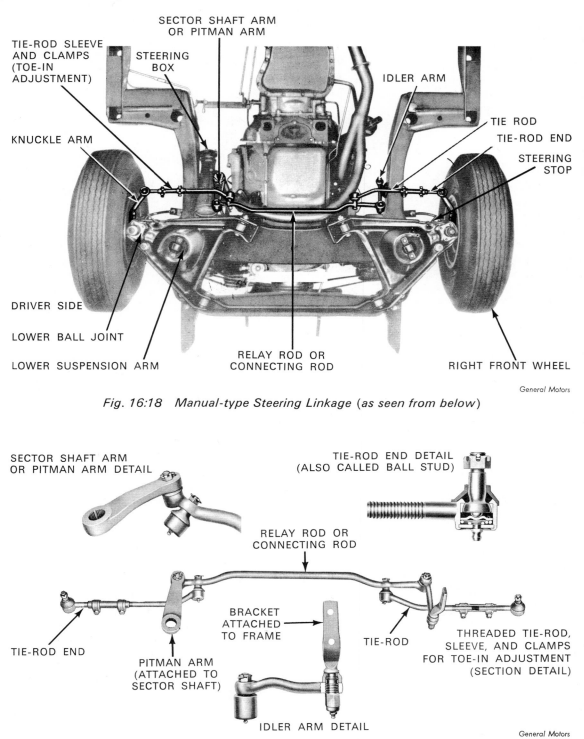

SECTOR SHAFT ARM
OR PITMAN ARM

TIE-ROD SLEEVE
AND CLAMPS
(TOE-IN
ADJUSTMENT)

STEERING
BOX

IDLER ARM

KNUCKLE ARM

TIE ROD
TIE-ROD END

STEERING
STOP

DRIVER SIDE

LOWER BALL JOINT

LOWER SUSPENSION ARM

RELAY ROD OR
CONNECTING ROD

RIGHT FRONT WHEEL

General Motors

Fig. 16:18   Manual-type Steering Linkage (as seen from below)

SECTOR SHAFT ARM
OR PITMAN ARM DETAIL

TIE-ROD END DETAIL
(ALSO CALLED BALL STUD)

RELAY ROD OR
CONNECTING ROD

TIE-ROD END

BRACKET
ATTACHED
TO FRAME

TIE-ROD

THREADED TIE-ROD,
SLEEVE, AND CLAMPS
FOR TOE-IN ADJUSTMENT
(SECTION DETAIL)

PITMAN ARM
(ATTACHED TO
SECTOR SHAFT)

IDLER ARM DETAIL

General Motors

Fig. 16:19   Typical Steering Linkage (in detail)

the steering gear is badly worn, the play can usually be removed by means of the *sector shaft adjusting screw* (Fig. 16:15). (Follow the manufacturer's instructions!) The preload of the steering shaft bearings is also adjustable, either by shims or by threaded adjusters. A loss of lubricant is usually caused by a worn sector shaft seal.

The Steering Linkage

The steering linkage (Figs. 16:18 and 16:19) connects the *steering knuckle arms* of the front wheels to the *pitman arm* of the steering gear. As the pitman arm swings to either one side or the other in response to the turn of the steering wheel, the steering linkage moves the front wheels into the desired direction. Note that the swivel action of the *tie-rod ends* permits movement, not only horizontally but also vertically, to follow suspension travel. The *tie-rod sleeves* have two functions:

1. They allow the outer tie-rod ends to be replaced as separate parts.
2. They provide a means of shortening or lengthening the tie-rods for the purpose of

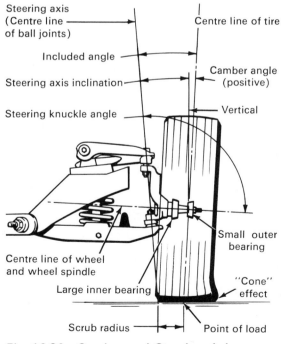

Fig. 16:20 Camber and Steering Axis Inclination

toe-in adjustments (Figs. 16:19 and 16:26).

The tie-rod ends, also called ball studs, are equipped with special seals to prevent the entry of dirt and water. Some are prelubricated; others require periodic lubrication.

The sole function of the *idler arm* is to support the right end of the *relay rod* (also called the steering connecting rod).

Suspension and Steering Geometry

Suspension and steering geometry is the theory related to the design and behaviour of the parts already discussed in this chapter. Whenever two or more of these parts, such as the suspension arms, steering knuckles, tie-rods, etc., are connected together, they must follow certain geometrical laws. What complicates matters is the fact that suspension and steering members constantly change their positions relative to one another. This situation arises when the vehicle is being steered at the same time as the wheels are moving up and down in response to varying load and driving conditions.

While it is the responsibility of the engineer to design the system, it is the responsibility of the mechanic to maintain the proper adjustments, especially after making repairs to the vehicle. This is what the trade commonly calls *wheel alignment*, even though it usually involves the entire suspension system and even the frame itself. A working understanding of the theoretical principles involved is, therefore, essential. It will also help you to determine the causes of certain abnormal conditions associated with misalignment, such as uneven tire wear, hard steering, and pulling to one side.

Camber

Camber (Fig. 16:20) is the outward or inward tilt of the wheel at the top. If tilted outward, it is *positive camber*, and if tilted inward, it is *negative camber*. Positive camber reduces steering effort by placing the road contact point of the wheel more nearly to the point where the *steering axis* intersects the pavement. The distance between these two points is called the *scrub radius* or *rolling radius*. The steering axis is the theoretical line joining the two ball joints, and therefore it is the axis about which the wheel is being steered. Positive camber also puts most of the weight on the larger, inner

All angles are greatly exaggerated to illustrate the principles involved

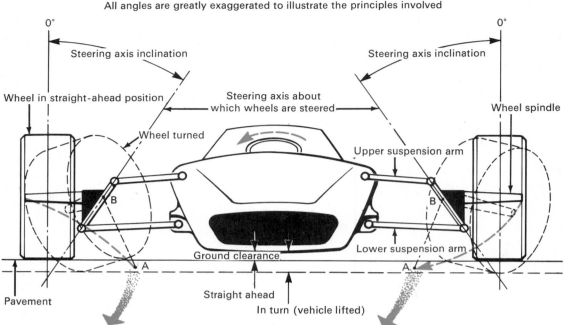

Fig. 16:21   The Self-straightening Action (Steering Return) of Steering Axis Inclination.
If the wheels were removed and the wheel spindles turned until they touched the lower suspension
arms, the spindle tips would move along the downward sloped arc (coloured line) to point A.
The spindles would then be in position A-B. This movement transmitted through the wheels
raises the vehicle.

wheel bearing. Furthermore, since positive camber reduces the scrub radius, it reduces tire wear, and the wheels are less likely to be kicked outwards at the front because of braking forces, rolling friction, and road obstructions.

Steering Axis Inclination

Steering axis inclination, often called *king pin inclination*,[68] is the inward tilt of the steering axis at the top (Fig. 16:20). Like positive camber, steering axis inclination shortens the scrub radius, and thus it also reduces steering effort. The need for positive camber is therefore reduced or even eliminated. Moreover, if the wide treads of modern tires are to be kept flat against the pavement, the less camber the better it is. In addition, steering axis inclination helps the wheels to straighten when the vehicle is coming out of a turn, and there is less front

[68] Many trucks and some older models of cars employ king pins instead of ball joints.

wheel *shimmy* (flutter). As illustrated in Fig. 16:21, the inclination of the steering axis also causes the wheel spindle to raise the vehicle when it is going into the turn. Obviously, if the driver removes his hands from the steering wheel at this point, the weight of the vehicle would cause the wheels to straighten out. This is also one of the reasons why front wheel shimmy is reduced.

The combined angles of steering axis inclination and camber are called the *included angle* (Fig. 16:20).

Caster

Positive caster (Fig. 16:22) is the backward tilt of the steering axis at the top. The slanted front forks of bicycles and motorcycles are typical examples.

The purpose of positive caster is to improve the directional stability of the front wheels (that is, it prevents wheel shimmy) by giving

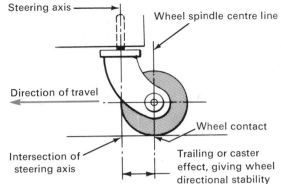

Fig. 16:23 The Furniture Caster

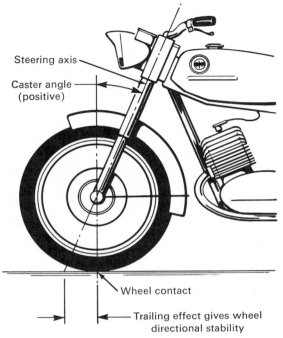

Fig. 16:22 Positive Caster

the wheels a *trailing effect*. The trailing effect can easily be observed when you are pushing a shopping cart with caster-type wheels (Fig. 16:23). These wheels always align themselves according to the direction in which the vehicle is pushed. In Fig. 16:22 it can clearly be seen that the point of wheel contact also trails the point at which the steering axis intersects the pavement.

Fig. 16:24 illustrates how positive caster causes the weight of the vehicle to push the front wheels inwards. This raises two important points:

1. If caster is not exactly the same on both front wheels, the car will pull towards the side with the least caster (because the wheel with the most caster steers more strongly towards the centre line of the vehicle).

2. If a turn is made, the inner wheel, which points *away* from the vehicle's centre line, *raises* the vehicle (Fig. 16:24b). The outer wheel, which points *towards* the centre line, however, *lowers* the vehicle (Fig. 16:24c). Unfortunately, this adds to the problem of vehicle roll in turns, which is caused by

centrifugal forces. If anything, the opposite action is needed.

Negative caster is the forward tilt of the steering axis at the top (Fig. 16:25a). Since negative caster would produce a leading effect (as opposed to the trailing effect with positive caster), it may be necessary to move the entire steering axis forward (Fig. 16:25b). This will restore the trailing effect and thus make the wheel as stable as it is with positive caster. Furniture casters are a typical example of the wheel spindle being made to trail behind the steering axis (Fig. 16:23). If the direction of wheel travel in Fig. 16:24 were assumed to be in the opposite direction, positive caster would become negative caster. Furthermore, the effects of vehicle lift and drop would also become reversed. In other words, negative caster reduces undesirable vehicle roll in turns as it raises the vehicle on the outside, while lowering it on the inside.

What type of caster is used in a given vehicle (positive caster, negative caster, or no caster at all) depends on its over-all design. In fact, the whole concept of suspension and steering geometry is so complex that computers are employed to arrive at the most advantageous settings. This text can deal only with the basic principles involved.

Toe-in

Toe-in is the inward set of the front wheels. In Fig. 16:26 it is the difference between dimensions X and Y. The purpose of toe-in is to compensate for any play in the steering linkage

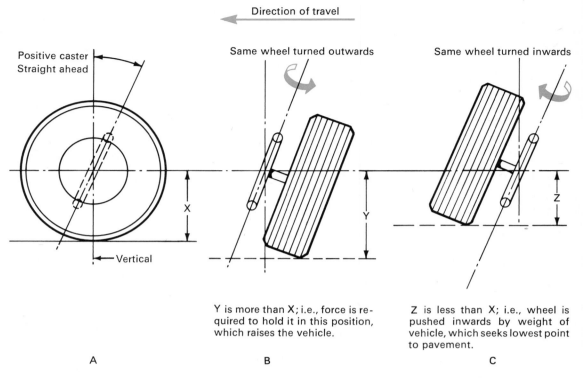

Fig. 16:24   The Effects of Positive Caster on Wheel Pull and Vehicle Height (Study centre diagram first.)

and the front wheels' tendency to toe-out. The outward pull on the wheels may be created by rolling friction, the scrub radius, and the "cone" effect caused by positive camber (Fig. 16:20). In fact, these forces combined reduce toe-in to zero, once the vehicle is in motion.

Toe-out

Toe-out on turns, or *Ackerman's Principle* (Fig. 16:27), allows the inner front wheel to turn more sharply than the outer front wheel when the vehicle rounds a bend or a corner,

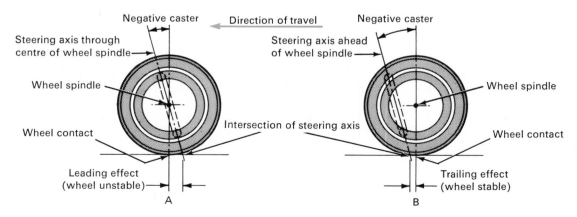

Fig. 16:25   Negative Caster Without Trailing Effect and With Trailing Effect

"Y" IS LESS THAN "X" WHEN WHEELS TOE-IN

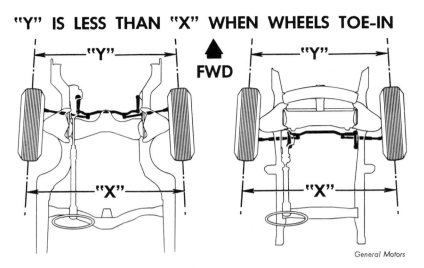

General Motors

Fig. 16:26 Toe-in Settings of Two Vehicles with Different Steering Linkage Arrangements (Toe-in is exaggerated in this illustration.)

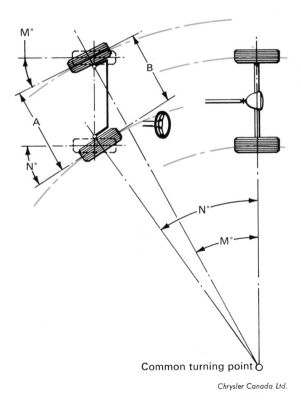

Common turning point

Chrysler Canada Ltd.

Fig. 16:27 Toe-out on Turns Where A Is Wider Than B. Difference between angles M and N is usually 1° to 4°.

thus allowing each wheel to follow its natural path. Toe-out on turns is obtained by reducing the steering knuckle arm angle to less than 90° (Fig. 16:28). Obviously, if there weren't any toe-out in turns, traction, as well as tread rubber, would be lost owing to tire scrubbing. The angles have been greatly exaggerated here for the purpose of illustration. In reality, if the inner wheel turns 23°, for example, the outer one might turn only 20°.

The terms *track width* and *wheel base* are illustrated in Fig. 16:1. The track width for the front wheels is not necessarily the same as that for the rear wheels.

Steering Stops

There are a pair of stop pads, which sometimes are adjustable, on each side of the front suspension system, usually on the steering knuckle and lower suspension arm (Fig. 16:18). They allow the steering wheel to be turned from lock to lock (extreme left to extreme right) without either putting undue strain on the steering gear or causing the tires to scrub the fenders.

Front End Alignment

Caster and camber are adjustable by means of shims (Fig. 16:5), eccentrics, or threaded pivots. The adjustment of toe-in is illustrated in Fig. 16:19. Toe-out on turns and steering axis inclination, as well as wheel run-out (wobble)

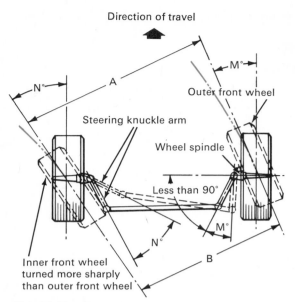

Fig. 16:28 Toe-out on Turns Due to Steering Knuckle Arm Angle Set at Less Than 90° (Note: A is wider than B because wheel-turning angle N is larger than M.)

are non-adjustable. If any one of these three items is not within specifications, the cause is likely to be worn or bent parts (ball joints, steering knuckle, wheel spindle, rim, etc.). Indications of misalignment are hard steering, pulling to one side, wheel shimmy, wandering from side to side, and, particularly, uneven tire wear (Fig. 16:39), since the other signs are often "covered up" by power steering.

Oversteer and Understeer

Oversteer and understeer are widely used terms to describe vehicle behaviour. Simply stated, if a car breaks loose in the rear first, when going into a fast turn, it oversteers; if, on the other hand, the front wheels break traction before the rear ones do, the vehicle understeers. Vehicles that break traction front and rear at the same time are said to have neutral steering. Whether a car oversteers or understeers depends on such factors as general design, weight distribution, tire pressure, and type and condition of tires.

Tires, Rims, Hubs, and Front Wheel Bearings

The wheel of a passenger car consists of the rim and the tire. In the rear, the wheel is attached to the flanges of the axle shafts (Fig. 16:62); in the front it is bolted to the wheel hub (Figs. 16:5 and 16:29). Either the hub is part of the brake drum or the two are separate parts held together by the wheel studs, screws, or rivets. On many makes, brake discs are used instead of brake drums. The wheel bearings are usually tapered roller bearings. (Cup-and-cone-type ball bearings may be employed in some cases.) Regardless of the type, the tapers of the larger inner bearing and of the smaller outer bearing always face each other (Figs. 16:29 and 16:64). Wheel bearings are lubricated with a special type of grease (page 138) and adjusted according to the manufacturer's specifications. A very

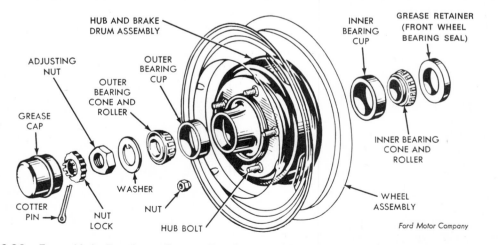

Fig. 16:29 Front Hub, Bearings, Grease Retainer, and Rim (Caution: Chamfered side of wheel nut must face the rim for self-centring and locking action!)

important difference between front wheel bearings of the tapered roller type and those of the ball bearing type is that the tapered roller bearing type is adjusted relatively loosely, while the ball bearing type is torqued to a specified pre-load.

Rims

The rim is made of stamped steel or some light alloy (magnesium or aluminum). The *drop-centre* of the rim (Fig. 16:31) permits one side of the tire (when deflated) to be dropped into this low area, so that the opposite side can be raised over the rim flange during removal or installation of the tire.[69] The bead seats of the rim may be equipped with humps (Fig. 16:64) to prevent the tire from shifting or jumping off the rim during blow-outs. If a tubeless tire is fitted onto the rim, a special valve stem assembly is installed in the valve hole (Fig. 16:30). The length of the valve stem and its diameter must be matched with the old one.

Rim sizes vary both in width and in diameter. The diameter is measured across the rim face and between the bead seats (Fig. 16:35). The most common rim sizes for passenger cars are 13″, 14″, and 15″.

Note: Dirty, rusty, or dented rim flanges and bead seats will cause leakage on tubeless tires.

Tires

In a sense the tires are the most important part of the car. They must support the vehicle, cushion road shock, transmit power, provide friction for braking, absorb forces generated by fast cornering, and maintain traction, even under extreme weather and road conditions. And yet the tires are often the most neglected part of the entire vehicle.

Most modern cars are sold equipped with *tubeless tires*. Advantages claimed for tubeless tires are lower tire temperatures, less danger of sudden blowouts, easier repair and installation, light weight, and lower cost. However, tube tires are still widely used, especially on trucks and heavy equipment. Special tires designed for particular driving conditions are available

---

[69]The tire is removed and installed over the rim flange closest to the drop-centre. This is not always the outer one! In Fig. 16:31 the tire would be removed from the right side.

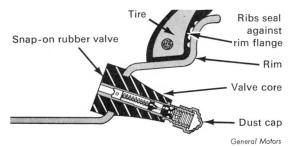

Fig. 16:30 *Detail of Valve Stem Assembly for Tubeless Tires (Note: Stem assembly is available in different lengths to fit various rim and hub cap designs.)*

(snow, rain, racing, etc.). Among many other qualities, a good tire must be well-balanced, give good traction and reasonable tread mileage, have a low noise level, and be able to withstand high speeds and heavy loads. It is very difficult to meet all of these demands in the same tire. For example, a tire with a widely spaced, deeply grooved, thick tread pattern may be ideal for snow, mud, and long service life at low speeds, but it is generally quite unsuitable

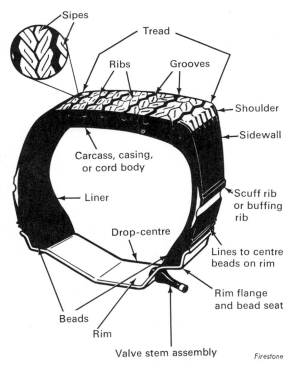

Fig. 16:31 *The Parts of a Tubeless Tire and Rims*

for fast summer driving. Such tires are usually noisy and they give poor traction on hard ice. Generally, the finer the tread pattern, i.e., the more ribs, grooves, "sipes", or "blades" a tire has, the better its performance as a rain tire will be. The edges of the deeply slit sipes (Fig. 16:31) cut through the slippery film of the wet pavement, while the grooves allow the water to escape. Thus, "aquaplaning" or "hydro-planing" of the tires, where they begin to skim over the water film like water skis, is substantially reduced. This dangerous condition may cause sudden and complete loss of vehicle control. Heavy treads are also likely to cause high-speed "chunking" due to overheating; that is, the tread rubber will separate from the plies and be thrown off. The heat is generated by friction and the constant flexing of the tire, especially in the sidewalls (Fig. 16:32). Tire temperatures vary with vehicle load, speed, tire pressure, and road conditions, as well as tire design. Very thick treads and sidewalls generally do not dissipate heat very well and therefore are less suitable for fast driving. Normal tire temperatures during fast highway cruising lie somewhere between 140°F and 175°F (60°C and 80°C). No damage is likely to occur up to 250°F (121°C). The surest way of avoiding critical tire temperatures is to stay within recommended load limits and tire pressures.

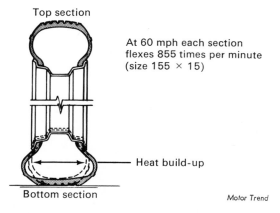

Top section

At 60 mph each section flexes 855 times per minute (size 155 × 15)

Heat build-up

Bottom section

Motor Trend

Fig. 16:32 Two Cross-sections of the Same Tire at the Same Moment. As the tire sidewall flexes under the weight of the car, the friction between the plies can cause extensive heat build-up. Radial-ply construction causes less friction from cord deflection and thus reduces the danger of blowouts and tread separation.

And consider this: tires wear roughly twice as fast at 80 mph (128 km/h) as they do at 50 mph (80 km/h). If, in addition, atmospheric temperature rises from 60°F to 90°F (16°C to 32°C), the tires will wear four times faster!

The main parts of a tubeless tire are shown in Fig. 16:31. Each of the *plies* is coated with rubber, and together they form the tire *carcass* or *casing*. The plies may be made of rayon (regenerated cotton or wood pulp cellulose), nylon, polyester, fibreglass, or fine steel wire, which is used in some tread plies. When the vehicle is parked for long periods, nylon tires have a tendency to take on a "set", i.e., a flat spot, which may cause tire thumping for a short distance. Polyester tires generally don't do this, but they are more sensitive to high temperatures. Low tire temperatures are therefore far more critical with this type of tire. Steel and fibreglass[70] are usually used in combination with other materials. A poly-glass tire, for example, uses both polyester and fibreglass. The *bead core* is made of a stranded, copper-plated steel cable, wrapped and reinforced by *filler cords* (Fig. 16:33b) and moulded into rubber to fit the rim. The side of the bead that faces the rim flange is sometimes ribbed to form a better seal (Fig. 16:30). The rubber is made of a mixture of synthetic and natural rubber, with carbon black, sulphur, and other ingredients added to it. While the *tread* consists of a special wear- and abrasion-resistant compound, a more flexible rubber is used for the *sidewalls*. The soft, rubberized material applied to the inside of the tubeless tire that makes it airtight is called the *liner* (Fig. 16:31).

Types of Ply Construction

Three different types of ply construction are shown in Fig. 16:33:
1. In the bias-ply tire (Fig. 16:33a) the ply cords are laid on the bias; i.e., they are angled to one another.
2. The belted bias-ply tire in Fig. 16:33b employs additional, relatively narrow stabilizer belts below the tread.

[70]Some manufacturers of fibreglass tires recommend that a used fibreglass tire should be so installed that the direction of rotation is not reversed. Reversal may cause internal shredding of the fibreglass plies.

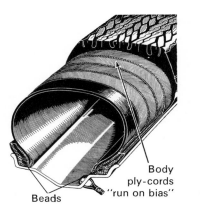

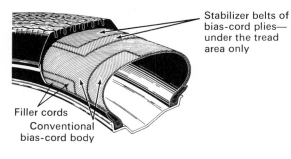

Stabilizer belts of bias-cord plies— under the tread area only

Filler cords
Conventional bias-cord body

B. BELTED BIAS-PLY CONSTRUCTION.
(This is a 2-ply tire.)

Body ply-cords "run on bias"

Beads

A. CONVENTIONAL BIAS-PLY CONSTRUCTION.
(This is a 4-ply tire.)

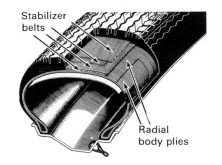

Stabilizer belts

Radial body plies

C. RADIAL-PLY CONSTRUCTION.
(This is a 2-ply tire with four belt plies.)   *Firestone*

Fig. 16:33   Major Types of Ply Construction

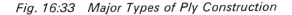

3. The radial-ply tire (Fig. 16:33c) usually has two body plies, with the cords running parallel to one another, extending radially at 90° or slightly less from bead to bead. The tread is always reinforced with stabilizer belts.

While radial tires (usually identified by a letter *R* on the sidewall) produce a somewhat firmer, harsher ride at low speeds, they are smoother at high speeds. Their main advantage is that they produce less tread distortion, especially in fast turns, and when rolling over parallel obstructions such as streetcar tracks and soft shoulders (Fig. 16:34). This means improved directional stability, less tire squeal in turns, shorter braking distances, and much better tread mileage. They also give slightly lower fuel consumption especially above 60 mph (96 km/h) because tread scrubbing, heat build-up, and rolling friction are reduced. The belted bias-ply tire, which is cheaper than the radial tire because it does not require special manufacturing facilities, has a very rigid tread that improves both service life and handling. All belted tires, including the radial tire, are more resistant to punctures and cuts. *Under no circumstances must different ply designs be mounted on the same car.* This will make

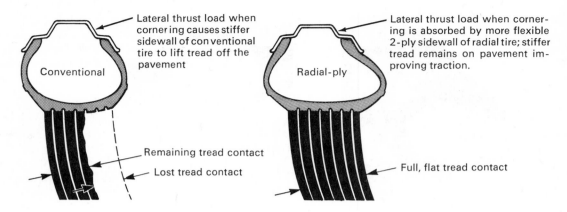

Lateral thrust load when cornering causes stiffer sidewall of conventional tire to lift tread off the pavement

Conventional

Remaining tread contact

Lost tread contact

Lateral thrust load when cornering is absorbed by more flexible 2-ply sidewall of radial tire; stiffer tread remains on pavement improving traction.

Radial-ply

Full, flat tread contact

Fig. 16:34   The Advantage of Radial Tires in Turns

vehicle behaviour unpredictable, and many accidents are attributed to this bad practice.

The Ply Number

The ply number, which is usually inscribed on the sidewall, indicates the number of plies.

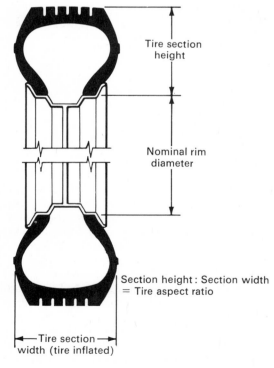

Tire section height

Nominal rim diameter

Section height : Section width = Tire aspect ratio

Tire section width (tire inflated)

Fig. 16:35   Rim Dimensions and Tire Aspect Ratio

Generally, the more plies a tire has, the greater the load it can carry. However, since the *denier*, or thickness, of individual ply-cords may differ between brands, a two-ply tire is often as strong as one with four plies, if not stronger! The number of plies should not be confused with the *ply rating*.

Ply Rating

Ply ratings, such as 2, 4, and 6, give an indication of ply strength. For example, a 2-ply tire may be given a 4-ply rating, a 4-ply tire a 6-ply rating, etc. The advantage claimed for a tire with a 4-ply rating but only 2 body plies is that the sidewall is more flexible and thus runs cooler than a 4-ply tire.

Load Range

The load range, which is indicated in letters from *A* to *J*, is a term now used instead of the ply rating. For example, an *A* tire has a 2-ply rating (rarely used), a *B* tire a 4-ply rating, a *C* tire a 6-ply rating, etc. The letters also identify a tire's load and inflation limits. The maximum inflation pressures are 32 psi for load range *B*, 36 psi for load range *C*, and 40 psi for load range *D*. Obviously, the load limit for a given tire is reduced if the tire is inflated to a pressure lower than maximum.

Tire Size

The size of a tire is determined by the distance between the sidewalls when the tire is inflated (called *section width*) and the diameter of the rim on which it is mounted (Fig. 16:35). For example, a tire with the number *8.25-15* is 8.25″ wide and is mounted on a 15″ rim. Some imported tires list the section width in millimetres and the rim size in inches. The metric equivalent of the above tire size is roughly *205-15*. On many tires, the section width is indicated by a letter rather than a number. For example, the size *8.25-15, 70* series, may be inscribed on the tire as *G70-15*. The approximate size equivalents for some of these letters are: *B* = 6.50, *C* = 7.00, *E* = 7.35, *F* = 7.75, *G* = 8.25, *H* = 8.55, *J* = 8.85. These letters also indicate the load-carrying capacity of the tire. Let us assume a car has a curb weight of 4,000 lb. (1814 kg), that is, including fuel, oil, and water. In addition, the car is to carry 950 lb. (431 kg) in passengers and luggage. The gross weight of the loaded vehicle is therefore 4,950 lb. (2245 kg). This would require *F* tires with a load-carrying capacity of 1,280 lb. (581 kg) at 24 psi because the car's four tires together could then support 4 × 1,280 lb. or 5,120 lb. (2322 kg). Increasing the tire pressure to 28 psi or 30 psi might be advisable, especially for prolonged high-speed driving in the summer. This will increase the load capacity close to the maximum, and the tire temperatures will be less, as sidewall- and tread-flexing is reduced.

Only recommended tire sizes must be used; otherwise the suspension and steering geometry will be altered and therefore the handling of the vehicle will be changed. Unless another speedometer drive gear is installed, the accuracy of the speedometer will also be affected.

Tire Series

The tire series (Fig. 16:36) classifies tires according to the *tire aspect ratio*, i.e., the ratio between the section height and the section width of the tire (Fig. 16:35). For example, the 70 series tire discussed earlier has a section height that measures 70 per cent of the section width. Some common series are 88 (widely used until 1965), 82, 78, 70, and 60.[71] The last two series are typically low-profile or "wide

oval" tires. Low-profile tires, which were first used on racing cars, give better traction because of their relatively wide tread. They also provide improved directional stability, especially under low pressure and during blowouts.

Retreads

Retreads or "recaps" are tires that have been retreaded, i.e., a new tread has been vulcanized

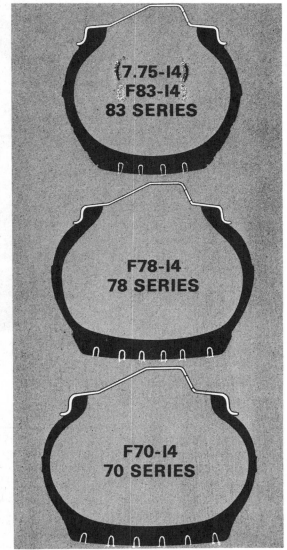

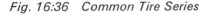
Firestone

Fig. 16:36 Common Tire Series

---

[71]One tire manufacturer has actually gone to a 50 series tire which is mounted on a specially designed rim.

SIZE—In this area may be found the size of the tire. In the example we find it is marked FR70-14.

F = Load-carrying capacity (1,500 lb. at 32 psi maximum pressure).
R = Radial-ply construction.
70 = Series (height to width ratio). The height of the tire = 70 per cent of the width.
14 = Rim size diameter.

CONSTRUCTION TYPE—In this area we find the type of construction when it is a radial tire. In our example, it is readily identified as a radial-ply construction but this is not required for other types of constructions.

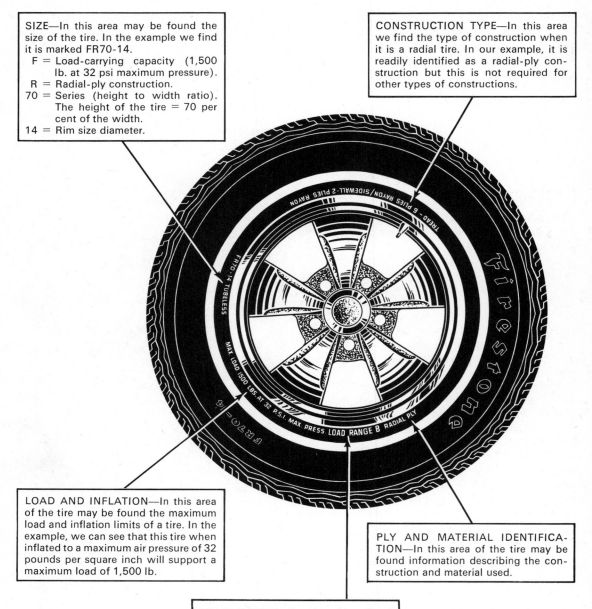

LOAD AND INFLATION—In this area of the tire may be found the maximum load and inflation limits of a tire. In the example, we can see that this tire when inflated to a maximum air pressure of 32 pounds per square inch will support a maximum load of 1,500 lb.

PLY AND MATERIAL IDENTIFICATION—In this area of the tire may be found information describing the construction and material used.

LOAD RANGE—On the sidewall of every tire may be found the words "load range" followed by a letter. Load range letters are used to identify load and inflation limits and replace the former ply rating term. Load range B replaces what was called a 4-ply rating. Load range C = 6-ply rating, and load range D = 8-ply rating.

Firestone

Fig. 16:37   Tire Sidewall Coding

on a used carcass. Properly processed, these tires can give good service as snow tires or even as standard tires if driven at normal speeds.

Life-guard Tires

Life-guard tires are tires that have a tire within a tire. If the outer casing is damaged, causing it to go flat, the car can be driven without loss of control at about 40 mph for up to one hour.

Tire Repairs

Tubeless tire repairs are mostly confined to sealing punctured tires. Special plugs and "hot patches" are available for this purpose. The plugs can be installed from the outside, but hot patching requires the removal of the tire. If the plies are cut or torn, the tire must be replaced. Leakage can occur at the bead, the valve stem hole, or the valve, or through the rim itself and the tire.

Tire Pressure

Tire pressure should be within the manufacturer's specifications and be checked either before the vehicle is driven more than one mile (1.6 km) or after three hours of use. Both under-inflation and over-inflation will cause damage to the tires and the suspension system, as well as alter vehicle behaviour. For example, too little pressure in the front tires may encourage understeer in fast turns; in the rear tires it may lead to oversteer. The advantages of radial tires are also lost with improper inflation. The tire pressure indicated on some tires is not the recommended pressure but rather the rated maximum pressure. Fast driving and heavy loads will generate sufficient heat to increase tire pressure by several psi. This is actually desirable, and no attempt should be made to reduce the tire pressure. Just one psi under-inflation may raise the tire's temperature by 10F° (5.6C°).

Caution: Never inflate a damaged tire. Don't use any other lubricant for installation than water or recommended tire soaps. Avoid parking a car in oil puddles. This will soften the rubber and produce flat spots in the tire. Remove excess chassis grease to prevent it from reaching the sidewalls. And remember: only a fool installs a bald or cracked tire, or drives on one that is partly flat! Do not install tubes in tubeless tires, as the rim may pinch the tube. To prevent the tubes from chafing and sticking, they should be lubricated with talcum powder. Do not seat the beads of a radial tire by hitting the sidewalls with a mallet hammer.

Tire Rotation

Rotating the tires periodically will prolong their life (Fig. 16:38). No general rule applies to all cases, since tire wear is determined by driver habits, road conditions, weight distribution, engine power, front wheel drive, rear wheel drive, etc. Tire wear usually gives some indication which procedure will produce the best

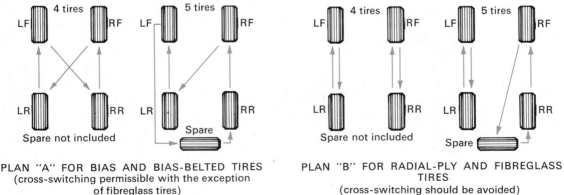

PLAN "A" FOR BIAS AND BIAS-BELTED TIRES
(cross-switching permissible with the exception of fibreglass tires)

PLAN "B" FOR RADIAL-PLY AND FIBREGLASS TIRES
(cross-switching should be avoided)

Fig. 16:38 Recommended Tire Rotation Plans

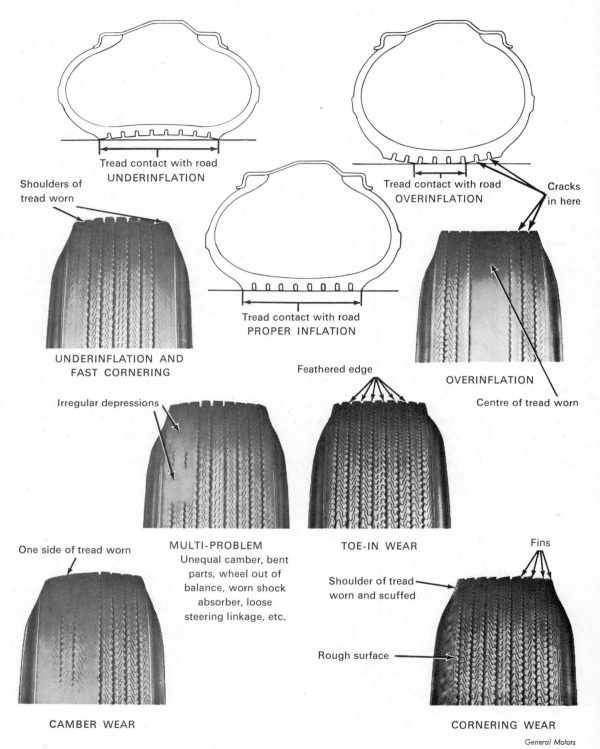

Tread contact with road
UNDERINFLATION

Tread contact with road
OVERINFLATION

Cracks in here

Tread contact with road
PROPER INFLATION

Shoulders of tread worn

UNDERINFLATION AND
FAST CORNERING

OVERINFLATION

Centre of tread worn

Irregular depressions

Feathered edge

MULTI-PROBLEM
Unequal camber, bent
parts, wheel out of
balance, worn shock
absorber, loose
steering linkage, etc.

TOE-IN WEAR

Fins

One side of tread worn

Shoulder of tread
worn and scuffed

Rough surface

CAMBER WEAR

CORNERING WEAR

General Motors

Fig. 16:39   Tire-Wear Diagnosis

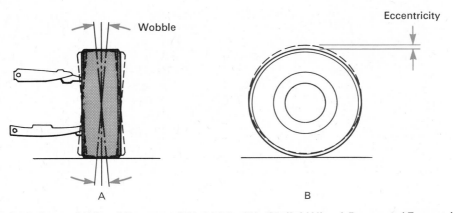

Fig. 16:40 (a) *Lateral Wheel Run-out (Wobble);* (b) *Radial Wheel Run-out (Eccentricity).*

results. Cross-switching of tires, i.e., changing their rotation, is no longer recommended, especially with fibreglass and radial-ply tires. Unusual wear patterns and their causes are shown in Fig. 16:39. A new set of tires should be installed only after the factors listed have been thoroughly checked.

Wheel Balance

Wheels should be checked for *lateral and radial run-out* (wobble and eccentricity), which may be caused by a bent hub, axle, or rim, or by a defective tire (Fig. 16:40). These conditions, if they exist, must be corrected before proceeding with the wheel balancing. The first sign of an unbalanced wheel is usually a vibrating steering wheel. The vibrations typically come and go at certain speeds and persist even on smooth pavement.

Static Wheel Imbalance (Fig. 16:41) means that the wheel would be out of balance even if it were stationary. In severe cases, when the wheel is jacked up, the heavy spot will actually cause the wheel to turn until the heavy spot comes to rest at the bottom. When the vehicle is in motion, static imbalance can lead to severe radially directed vibrations called *wheel tramp*. For example, an imbalance of only one ounce, one foot away from the centre of the wheel, will produce a centrifugal force of close to 15 pounds at 60 mph (7 kg at 96 km/h) and four times as much at double the speed! Furthermore, the heavy spot in the tire must constantly change its speed in relation to the road. When at the top, it must travel not only at the forward

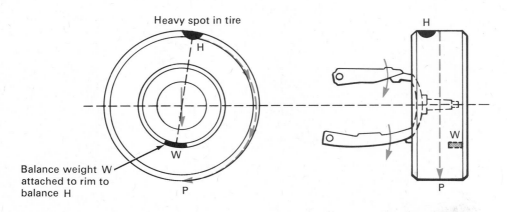

Fig. 16:41 *Static Imbalance (Note: Without the balance weight W, the heavy spot H would push the suspension arms downward as it approached pavement P.)*

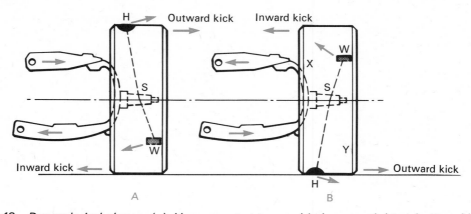

Fig. 16:42 Dynamic Imbalance: (a) Heavy spot at top and balance weight at bottom kick the wheel sidewards. (b) Same wheel half a revolution later with heavy spot at bottom. Note the reversal of sideward kick which results in wheel wobble.

speed of the vehicle, but also at the rotational speed of the wheel itself; thus, at 50 mph (80 km/h) driving speed, the heavy spot must actually travel at 100 mph (160 km/h). Yet, when it meets the road, it momentarily comes to a complete standstill in relation to the pavement before it is once again accelerated in an upward direction to the top. The flexing action of the springs and of the inflated rubber tends to amplify these vibrations.

Dynamic Wheel Imbalance means that even though the wheel might be in balance statically, i.e., in a radial direction, it is still out of balance in a lateral, or sideward, direction. To illustrate the principles involved, let us assume that the dotted lines *HS* and *WS* in Fig. 16:42 are strings holding the masses *H* and *W* in an orbital path around the middle of the wheel spindle *S*. Obviously, they would not only pull outwards but also sidewards in the direction indicated. This sideward pull, however, occurs only with the wheel in motion, hence the term "dynamic imbalance". In Fig. 16:42a the wheel is kicked outward at the top and inward at the bottom. In Fig. 16:42b, after half a revolution, the direction of the disturbing forces is reversed. As a result, the wheel will develop severe wobble, similar to that caused by lateral run-out (Fig. 16:40). Note that in Fig. 16:43 the balance weight is relocated on the same side as the heavy spot *H*. The wheel is therefore in balance both statically and dynamically as the outward kick of *H* is now cancelled out by the forces acting on the balance weight *W*.

But what happens if a wheel is unbalanced only dynamically? Such a condition would exist if *W* in Fig. 16:42b represented a valve stem or another heavy spot in the rim or the tire that could not be moved. In this case, we would attach balance weights *X* and *Y* to the rim exactly opposite *H* and *W* to counteract the side kick of the two heavy spots. As long as we keep the two dynamic balance weights even, the static balance will remain unaffected.

Most well-equipped automotive repair shops have wheel balancers that pinpoint the position of any heavy spots. The balance weights are made of lead and are calibrated in ounces or grams. A small steel clip keeps them securely attached to the rim flange. A special pair of

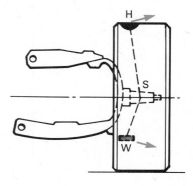

Fig. 16:43 Dynamic Balance. Here the same wheel is dynamically balanced. Note that the balance weight W placed on the same side counteracts the heavy spot H.

pliers is used for the installation or removal of the weights, and also for trimming them in case they are too heavy. Some second-rate tires, as well as those that are unevenly worn or have been driven in an unbalanced condition for too long, cannot be balanced. All new tires should be rebalanced after the first few hundred miles, as a new tire will stretch by one to two per cent. Thereafter, tires should be balanced whenever any vibration is felt in the steering wheel while the vehicle is on smooth pavement. Large wheels are naturally more sensitive to a state of imbalance than smaller ones. Dynamic balance has become particularly critical with modern wide oval tires.

Brakes

As required by law, all modern vehicles are equipped with two brakes, the service, or foot, brake and the emergency brake.

There are many different automotive brake designs, but most employ the same basic principles. The speed of a rotating member mounted to the wheel or the axle shaft is retarded by a stationary member that is pressed against it by levers or hydraulic pistons, or a combination of both. The stationary member is lined with a material chosen for its very high coefficient of friction, usually some heat-resistant compound containing asbestos and metal powder. When the brake lining is applied to the rotating member, the kinetic energy (moving energy) of the wheels and the whole vehicle is, by means of friction, converted to heat energy. The heat generated may reach hundreds of degrees and

the brakes must be carefully designed to dissipate it. Excessive temperatures will produce brake fading or even a total loss of braking power. The hot parts become distorted and the overheated brake linings give off a gas that acts as a lubricant between the lining surface and the revolving member. Brake fading may also be caused by overheating of the brake fluid, which typically occurs after repeated vigorous applications of the brakes. As a result, the stopping distance may increase suddenly and drastically. Many accidents are caused simply because the driver often fails to take this into account. There are, however, some advanced brake designs that produce practically no brake fading at all. Apart from the brake design and the driver's reflexes, the stopping distance depends primarily on the weight and speed of the vehicle, the type and condition of the tires, the pavement, and the temperature.

Hydraulic Brakes

Hydraulic brakes transmit the pedal pressure applied by the driver's foot to the individual wheel brakes by means of a special liquid called *brake fluid*. The operating principle of hydraulic brakes is based on *Pascal's law of hydraulics*. It says that *pressure exerted at any point in a confined liquid is transmitted undiminished in all directions and acts with the same force on all equal areas and in a direction at right angles to them* (Fig. 16:44). By applying this law of hydraulics, you can calculate the output force of a piston by multiplying the pressure in the hydraulic system by the area of

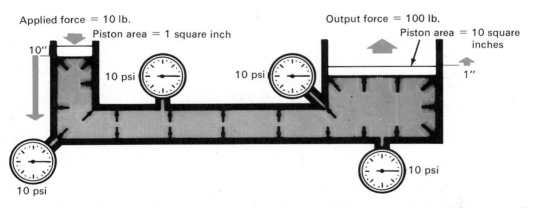

Fig. 16:44 The pressure applied to a confined liquid is transmitted equally in all directions. Note that the output force equals the pressure in the system times the area of the output piston.

the piston head. In the system illustrated in Fig. 16:44, it is 10 psi times 10 square inches, or 100 lb. This increase in output force, however, doesn't come about by some act of magic. Note that while the force of the larger piston increases over that of the smaller one, the distance over which the larger piston moves is reduced by the same ratio. In the case illustrated, the ratio is 10:1.

This principle allows the engineer to get any desired force at each of the wheel brakes by increasing or decreasing the relative sizes of the master cylinder and wheel cylinder pistons. The advantage is twofold:
1. Braking effort on the part of the driver is greatly reduced.
2. By using different sizes of wheel cylinder pistons in front and rear, the brake system can be so balanced that rear wheel lock-up is less likely to occur.

Regarding the second advantage, you should realize that when the brakes are applied, there is a weight transfer from the rear to the front wheels.[72] As a result, the rear wheels, with less weight pressing them against the pavement, tend to lock up. This causes a loss of tread

rubber, and since traction is reduced, the braking distance increases considerably. The maximum braking effect can only be obtained when the wheels are still turning, that is, when there is little or no sliding between the treads of the tires and the surface of the pavement. Friction is then mostly "static", good traction is maintained, and the brake can be applied with great effect. If the wheels lock up, however, they will skid over the pavement. This results in "kinetic" friction, which produces much lower braking forces.[73] By dimensioning the wheel cylinder pistons accordingly (Fig. 16:53), it is possible to distribute the front and rear braking forces as needed, just as a skilled cyclist applies his front brakes with greater force than the rear ones. A locked wheel also loses all directional stability; it skids sidewards just as easily as it does forwards or backwards.

Hydraulic brakes have several other important advantages over mechanically activated brakes. Since fluids produce little friction and because they are practically incompressible, the system is very efficient. The pressure with which the brakes are applied on opposite

---

[72]The "nose dive" of the car and the forward thrust of the occupants' bodies during sudden stops are visible signs of this weight transfer.

[73]Pumping the brake pedal on ice produces shorter stopping distances because the driver is less likely to misjudge the pedal pressure needed to keep the wheels moving and to maintain traction.

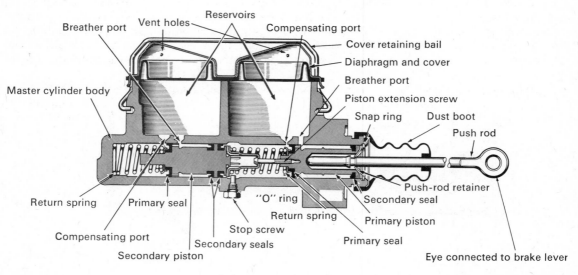

Breather port — Vent holes — Reservoirs — Compensating port
Cover retaining bail
Diaphragm and cover
Breather port
Master cylinder body
Piston extension screw
Snap ring — Dust boot
Push rod
Push-rod retainer
Return spring — Primary seal — "O" ring — Secondary seal
Return spring — Primary piston
Compensating port — Stop screw — Primary seal
Secondary seals
Secondary piston — Eye connected to brake lever

*Fig. 16:45 Tandem or Dual Master Cylinder (**cross-sectional view**)*

wheels is always the same, and hydraulic brakes are therefore much less prone to cause pulling to one side. Furthermore, there is no complex linkage requiring frequent adjustments and lubrication.

The Brake Master Cylinder

The brake master cylinder (Figs. 16:45 and 16:46) converts the driver's foot pressure to hydraulic pressure and acts as a reservoir for the brake fluid. While older models used single-piston-type master cylinders, current models are required by law to employ *tandem*, or *dual*, *master cylinders*. The latter type consists of a long, single cylinder using two pistons and usually has two separate fluid reservoirs. The primary piston, which is the one at the open

end of the cylinder, and which is activated directly by the brake pedal linkage, supplies hydraulic pressure to one set of wheel cylinders (Fig. 16:48). The secondary piston at the closed end of the cylinder serves the other two wheel cylinders and is normally activated by hydraulic pressure created by the primary piston. Which of these two circuits is connected to the front brakes and which one to the rear brakes depends on the model and make of the vehicle. Some circuits, though less common, are connected diagonally; i.e., one circuit serves the left front and the right rear brakes, while the other serves the right front and the left rear brakes. Yet another design is so arranged that one of the two separate hydraulic circuits supplies hydraulic pressure to all four wheels (Fig. 16:47). The advantage of "split" systems

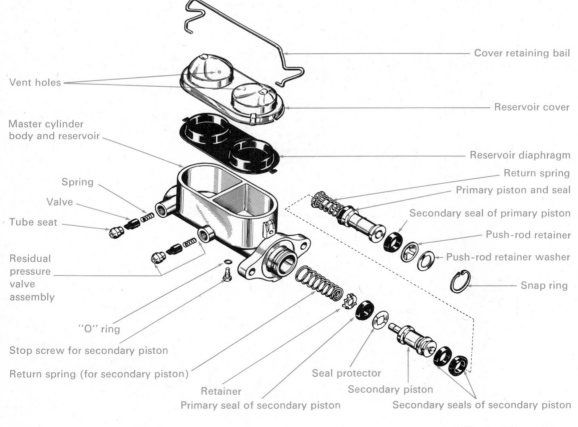

Vent holes

Cover retaining bail

Reservoir cover

Master cylinder body and reservoir

Reservoir diaphragm

Return spring

Primary piston and seal

Spring

Valve

Secondary seal of primary piston

Tube seat

Push-rod retainer

Push-rod retainer washer

Residual pressure valve assembly

Snap ring

"O" ring

Stop screw for secondary piston

Return spring (for secondary piston)

Seal protector

Secondary piston

Retainer

Secondary seals of secondary piston

Primary seal of secondary piston

International Harvester Company

Fig. 16:46 Tandem or Dual Master Cylinder (exploded view)

is increased safety. Even with a complete loss of pressure in one of the two hydraulic circuits, the vehicle can still be brought to a safe stop.

Operating Principles

The leverage of the brake pedal lever multiplies the foot pressure exerted against the brake pedal (Fig. 16:48). For example, a 6:1 ratio lever would increase a pressure of 80 pounds applied at the pedal to 480 pounds at the master cylinder piston. If the area of the piston is one square inch, then, according to Pascal's law, the hydraulic pressure throughout the system is 480 psi.

Let us now see what happens in the master

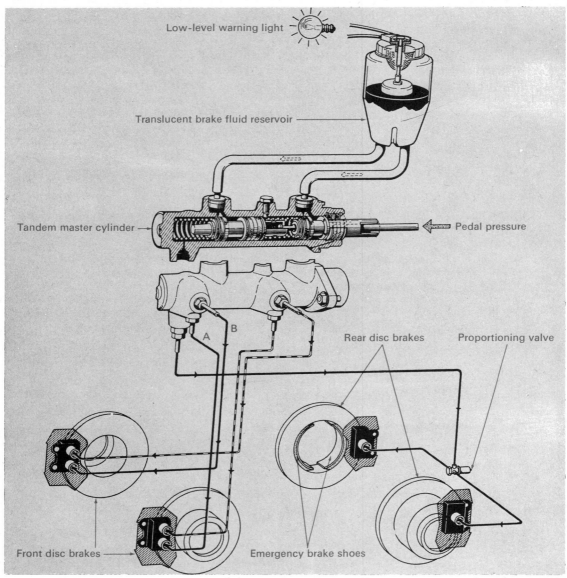

Low-level warning light

Translucent brake fluid reservoir

Tandem master cylinder

Pedal pressure

A   B

Rear disc brakes

Proportioning valve

Front disc brakes

Emergency brake shoes

Bayerische Motoren Werke

Fig. 16:47 *Complete Hydraulic Brake Circuit for Four-wheel Disc Brakes* (*schematic drawing*). *Note that in this design the secondary circuit serves both front and rear brakes. On more conventional designs the lines A and B are eliminated.*

cylinder as the brake pedal is depressed. Both the *primary* and the *secondary pistons* are pushed forward, thus sealing off the two very small *compensating ports*. This pushes the brake fluid out through the *outlet ports* connected to the *wheel cylinders* by means of hydraulic *brake lines*. Note that the secondary piston is pushed forward by the brake fluid trapped between the two pistons, and not by the piston extension screw. The principle is known as "slave action" and the secondary piston is therefore sometimes called a *slave piston*. (The return spring of the primary piston is relatively weak and therefore has little effect on the pressure applied to the secondary piston.) When the brake pedal is released, the pressure in the brake lines and the tension of the piston return springs push the two pistons towards the pedal. The primary piston comes to rest against the lock ring, and the secondary piston against the stop screw (provided the brake pedal linkage is properly adjusted to maintain the necessary free play between the push rod and the piston). While the *residual pressure valves* (Fig. 16:46) located in the

outlet ports of the master cylinder allow a more or less unrestricted flow of brake fluid into the wheel cylinders, their springs are so calibrated that they will close when the flow *returning* from the *wheel cylinders* drops to approximately 6 psi to 18 psi (41 kPa to 124 kPa). However, this pressure, called residual pressure, is not high enough to hold back the very strong return springs that retract the brake shoes when the driver removes his foot from the brake pedal.

The purpose of residual pressure is twofold:
1. It keeps the hydraulic seals, or *wheel cylinder cups*, in the wheel cylinder firmly seated so that they do not collapse. It thus prevents brake fluid leakage and the entry of air. Since air is a compressible medium, its entry would cause either partial or complete loss of brake action.
2. By maintaining a sufficient amount of brake fluid in the wheel cylinders, it reduces brake pedal travel.

For reasons that will be given later, brake master cylinders connected to disc brakes usually have no residual pressure valves. Master cylinders used with mixed brake systems em-

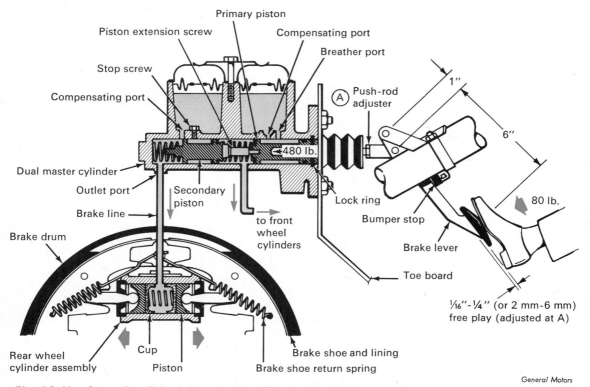

General Motors

Fig. 16:48   Operating Principles of a Hydraulic Brake System

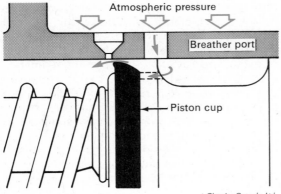

Fig. 16:49 Breather ports provide fluid to pump up pedal.

ploy a residual pressure valve for the rear drum brakes but not for the front disc brakes.

The *breather port* (Fig. 16:49) allows brake fluid to by-pass the primary seal and flow through the holes in the piston when the brake pedal is suddenly released. In this case the piston return springs push the pistons against their respective stops faster than the reverse flow of fluid from the wheel cylinders can follow them. The low pressure created in the master cylinder as a result would cause air to be drawn past the secondary seal of the primary piston at the open end of the cylinder. The relatively large breather ports prevent this dangerous condition by allowing an unobstructed transfer of fluid between the cylinder and the reservoirs. The breather ports, together with the residual pressure valve, also permit the hydraulic system to be pumped up in case of brake failure, which may be caused by the

entry of air, a partly collapsed seal, a low brake-fluid level, or incorrect brake adjustment. Under these conditions, the rapid pumping of the brake pedal admits more fluid through the breather ports than what is returned from the wheel cylinders past the residual pressure valve. This usually raises the brake pedal sufficiently to restore at least some pressure.

The main function of the *compensating ports* (Fig. 16:50) is to keep the pressure from building up in the master cylinder and thus prevent the brakes from dragging when the pedal is released. This condition could result from repeated pumping of the brake pedal or from fluid expansion caused by the heat generated during braking. When the liquid cools off and contracts, the compensating ports "compensate" by admitting more brake fluid into the system.

The *rubber diaphragm* under the vented reservoir cover (Fig. 16:46) permits atmospheric pressure to be maintained in the reservoir regardless of brake fluid movement or temperature changes. In older master cylinders the fluid in the reservoir was vented directly into the atmosphere. This led to evaporation, fluid oxidation, and condensation (brake fluid attracts moisture). The latter two conditions caused sludge formation and plugged ports.

A Question of Safety

What happens if one of the two circuits connected to the front or rear brakes fails, as a result of the rupture of a brake line, for example? If the pressure loss occurs in the secondary brake circuit, the secondary piston will simply "hit bottom" and the primary piston will operate

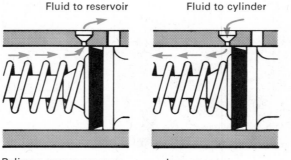

Fig. 16:50 Compensating ports prevent brake drag and leakage in hydraulics.

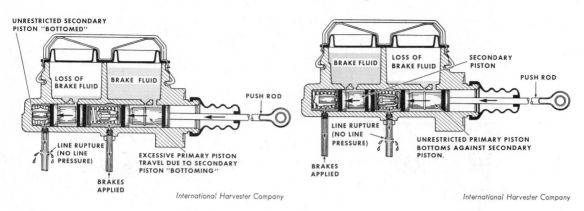

UNRESTRICTED SECONDARY PISTON "BOTTOMED"

LOSS OF BRAKE FLUID

BRAKE FLUID

PUSH ROD

LINE RUPTURE (NO LINE PRESSURE)

BRAKES APPLIED

EXCESSIVE PRIMARY PISTON TRAVEL DUE TO SECONDARY PISTON "BOTTOMING"

International Harvester Company

BRAKE FLUID

LOSS OF BRAKE FLUID

SECONDARY PISTON

PUSH ROD

LINE RUPTURE (NO LINE PRESSURE)

UNRESTRICTED PRIMARY PISTON BOTTOMS AGAINST SECONDARY PISTON.

BRAKES APPLIED

International Harvester Company

Fig. 16:51   Failure of the Secondary System   *Fig. 16:52   Failure of the Primary System*

as usual (Fig. 16:51). In case the pressure loss occurs in the primary circuit, it is the head of the piston extension screw that will contact the secondary piston (Fig. 16:52). The roles are now reversed and it is the secondary piston that continues to work in the normal fashion. Under these conditions, the forward movement of the secondary piston is caused by mechanical, rather than by hydraulic, pressure, since the piston extension screw, the primary piston, and the push rod are acting now as a single solid

part. In either case the vehicle should be considered unsafe, requiring brake service to eliminate the cause.

Caution: With improperly adjusted brakes or entry of air into the hydraulic system, both pistons may hit bottom if pressure is lost in only one hydraulic circuit.

The *wheel cylinders* shown in Fig. 16:53 are simple in design and require little comment. Because the braking pressures needed at the front brakes· are greater than those needed at

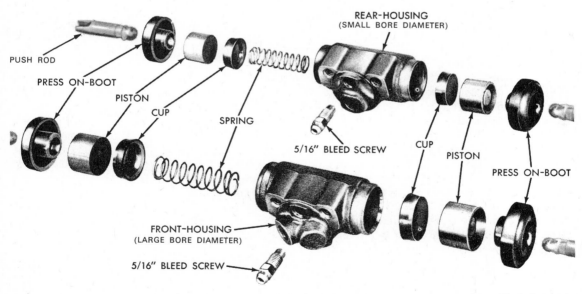

PUSH ROD

PRESS ON-BOOT

PISTON

CUP

SPRING

REAR-HOUSING (SMALL BORE DIAMETER)

5/16" BLEED SCREW

CUP

PISTON

PRESS ON-BOOT

FRONT-HOUSING (LARGE BORE DIAMETER)

5/16" BLEED SCREW

Chrysler Canada Ltd.

Fig. 16:53   Front and Rear Wheel Cylinders. Note the difference in size.

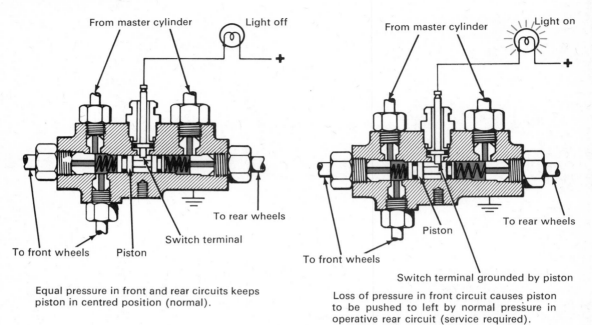

Equal pressure in front and rear circuits keeps piston in centred position (normal).

Loss of pressure in front circuit causes piston to be pushed to left by normal pressure in operative rear circuit (service required).

Fig. 16:54 Hydraulic System Safety Switch

General Motors

the rear, the front wheel cylinders are usually larger in diameter. The *bleed screw* permits the removal of air that may have entered the hydraulic system during repairs. Air in the brake fluid will result either in a ''spongy'' brake pedal or in no brakes at all.

The Hydraulic System Safety Switch

The hydraulic system safety switch (Fig. 16:54), which is usually located in the vicinity of the master cylinder, is triggered when pressure is lost in one of the hydraulic brake circuits as the result of a ruptured line, a leaking seal, a low reservoir level, or a plugged port.[74] The two springs that hold the piston in a centred position are very stiff and they are calibrated to allow the piston to move only if the pressure difference between the front and the rear circuits is at least 100 psi (689 kPa). The safety switch is connected to a warning light at the dash. The light tells the driver when a serious failure has occurred in one of the hydraulic circuits. On some makes the same light also

[74]Once triggered, the safety switch must be reset according to the manufacturer's instructions.

indicates that the emergency brake is still engaged or that the brake fluid level is dangerously low (Fig. 16:47). Even if the light fails, a loss of pressure in one of the hydraulic circuits is easily spotted, as both the travel of the brake pedal and the effort required to push it will increase considerably.

The Proportioning Valve

The proportioning valve (Fig. 16:55) often forms part of the hydraulic safety switch. It limits the hydraulic pressure applied to the rear brakes to prevent the rear wheels from locking during *hard stops*. When a certain pressure is reached, for example, 300 psi (2067 kPa), the pressure serving the rear brakes may be reduced by roughly 50 per cent. The valve often includes a by-pass that ensures full line pressure should the front circuit fail.

The Metering Valve

The metering valve (Fig. 16:55) is often combined with the devices mentioned above. It directs hydraulic pressure to the rear brakes before applying the front brakes. This accomplishes two things:

HYDRAULIC SAFETY SWITCH TERMINAL

FRONT MASTER CYLINDER
INLET PORT

REAR MASTER CYLINDER
INLET PORT

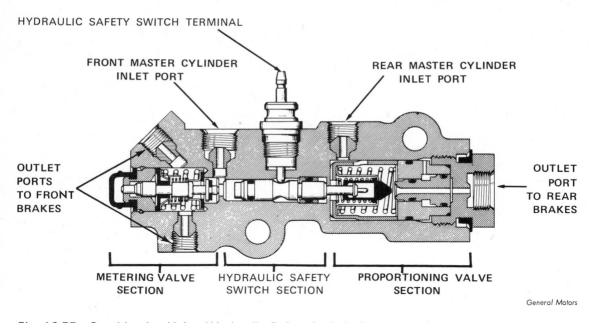

OUTLET
PORTS
TO FRONT
BRAKES

OUTLET
PORT
TO REAR
BRAKES

METERING VALVE
SECTION

HYDRAULIC SAFETY
SWITCH SECTION

PROPORTIONING VALVE
SECTION

General Motors

Fig. 16:55 Combination Valve (Hydraulic Safety Switch, Proportioning Valve, and Metering Valve)

1. On mixed brakes (disc brakes in the front and drum brakes in the rear), it first overcomes the pull of the retracting springs of the rear brake shoes so that the shoes touch the brake drum before the front pads are applied.
2. The metering valve may be used on any type of brake to prevent front wheel lock-up or skidding during light braking on icy or slippery roads. It is usually set to cut off front line pressure until 110 psi to 150 psi (758 kPa to 1034 kPa) is reached. Beyond this point, some designs permit equal pressure in the front and rear circuits; others partially restrict the rear line pressure up to 440 psi to 750 psi (3032 kPa to 5168 kPa) and only then allow pressures to be equalized. With the former design the opening of the metering valve can be felt by the foot as a slight bump when the pedal is depressed approximately one inch.

The Stop-light Switch

The stop-light switch is attached either to the master cylinder itself or to some fitting very close to it. When the brakes are applied, a set of breaker points, in response to either hydraulic or mechanical pressure, closes an electric circuit and the stop lights go on.

Types of Brakes

There are two basic types of brakes employed in modern passenger cars: the *drum brake* and the *disc brake*. Some vehicles use disc brakes in the front and drum brakes in the rear. There may be several reasons for this: drum brakes are cheaper and more suitable as an emergency brake, and the rear brakes do not need to be as powerful as the front brakes.

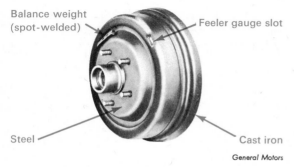

Balance weight
(spot-welded)

Feeler gauge slot

Steel

Cast iron

General Motors

Fig. 16:56 Standard Drum Brake

Drum Brakes

The drum brake (Fig. 16:56) is still widely used. The rim of the drum is usually of a special cast iron that is fused to a steel disc. The disc is held firmly in position by the wheel studs, or it may be screwed or riveted to the hub. To improve the dissipation of heat, some brake drums are equipped with cooling fins; others, also finned, are made of aluminum with cast-iron liners on the inside. Drums are often belted with long coil springs to dampen high-frequency vibrations, commonly referred to as *brake squeal*. The stationary members of the brake assembly are mounted on the brake backing plate, which, in turn, is usually bolted either to the rear axle housing or to the steering knuckle in the front.

While there are a great variety of drum brakes, most current styles are similar to the Bendix-type brake shown in Fig. 16:57. Note that when the brakes are applied, the *forward*, or *primary, shoe* is pushed into the brake drum in the same direction as the rotation of the wheel. Because the rotation of the drum tends to pull the primary shoe even tighter into the drum, brake pedal effort is reduced. This principle, called *self-energizing action*, can easily be

demonstrated by resting the rubber tip of a pencil at an angle on a piece of paper. The slanted pencil and rubber represent the brake shoe and the paper represents the drum. When the paper is pulled against the extended rubber tip, braking friction is high, owing to the self-energizing action; when it is pulled the other way, however, there is little friction.

What about the *secondary shoe*? This shoe is linked to the primary shoe by the *brake adjuster assembly* at the bottom; i.e., both shoes form, in a sense, one long, continuous brake shoe, flexibly jointed in the middle. Only the *anchor pin* at the top prevents the two shoes from turning around with the brake drum. When the vehicle is moving forward, it must shoulder the end thrust of the *secondary brake shoe*. Obviously, then, the secondary shoe is also self-energizing, but, in addition, it is assisted by the *primary shoe*, which would like to turn with the drum. The secondary shoe, therefore, is pushed into the brake drum not only by the wheel cylinder piston at the top, but also by the torque action of the primary shoe at the bottom. (The roles of the two shoes are reversed when the vehicle moves backwards.) Since the primary shoe serves the secondary

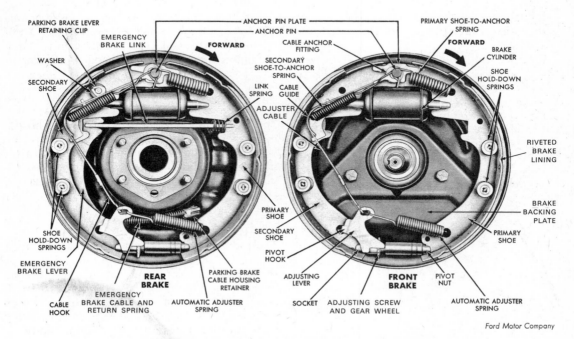

Ford Motor Company

Fig. 16:57 The Bendix-type Brake (self-adjusting)

shoe, the principle is called *servo-action*. This increases the braking power of the secondary shoe to almost twice that of the primary shoe, and thus pedal effort is reduced considerably. The high servo-pressure acting on the secondary shoe requires a longer and harder brake lining than the lining used on the primary shoe.

In each of the rear brake assemblies the lower end of the *emergency brake lever* is hooked to one of the two ends of the *emergency brake cable* (Figs. 16:57 and 16:58). When the emergency brake is applied, the lever, which is hinged to the secondary shoe, is pushed against the *emergency brake link*. This causes both shoes to move outward and thereby to lock the drum. The *equalizer* between the front and the rear cable equalizes the braking forces between the rear wheels.

The *adjusting screw* and *pivot nut assembly* allow the brake shoes to be brought nearer to the drum to compensate for wear on the brake linings. Most brakes are self-adjusting, but some are manually adjusted through a small window in the brake backing plate (or sometimes in the brake drum) by means of a special adjusting tool. The window is covered by a removable plug that must always be replaced to prevent the entry of dirt and water. The self-adjusting brake, as shown in Figs. 16:57 and 16:59, employs a cable-controlled adjusting lever. This turns the star wheel, or gear wheel, of the adjusting screw in a ratchet-like manner whenever the clearance between the worn linings and the brake drum becomes excessive. The automatic adjustment usually takes place only when the brakes are applied while the vehicle is moving backwards. This causes the secondary shoe to shift away from the anchor pin and pull on the adjuster cable. Thus, the adjusting lever is raised sufficiently to climb one tooth on the gear wheel. If the car is then moved forward, the adjuster spring forces the adjusting lever down and the adjuster screw is tightened by one notch. The whole sequence can only occur if the linings are sufficiently worn to permit the secondary shoe to shift away from the anchor pin. Over-adjusting of the brakes is therefore impossible under normal conditions. Sometimes it becomes necessary, however, to back off the automatic adjuster in order to remove the brake drum. It may also have to be done after a new

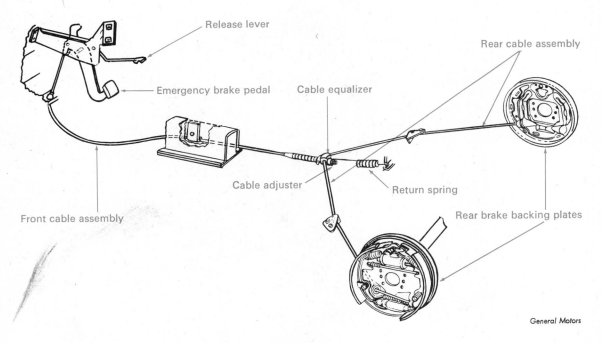

General Motors

Fig. 16:58   Schematic Diagram of an Emergency Brake

set of brake shoes has been installed and the brakes have to be preset. In this case a screwdriver or welding rod can be inserted into the backing plate window (sometimes there are two windows) to release the adjusting lever (Fig. 16:59). The star wheel of the adjusting screw can then be turned in the usual manner.

The *anchor springs* (return, retracting, or pull-back springs) retract the brake shoes and the wheel cylinder pistons when the brake is released; this also causes the brake fluid to return to the master cylinder.

Disc Brakes

One of the oldest types of disc brake is the caliper-type rim brake used on many bicycles. The advantages of automotive disc brakes (Figs. 16:47 and 16:60 to 16:64) over conventional drum brakes of comparable size are that they are more powerful and they are less prone to brake fading (see page 287). This is partly due to the fact that the brake pads or shoes on

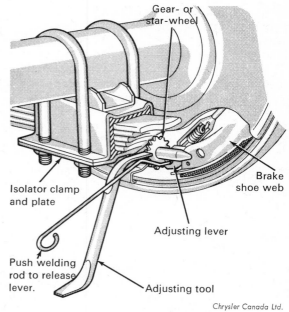

Chrysler Canada Ltd.

Fig. 16:59 Manual Adjustment of a Self-adjusting Brake

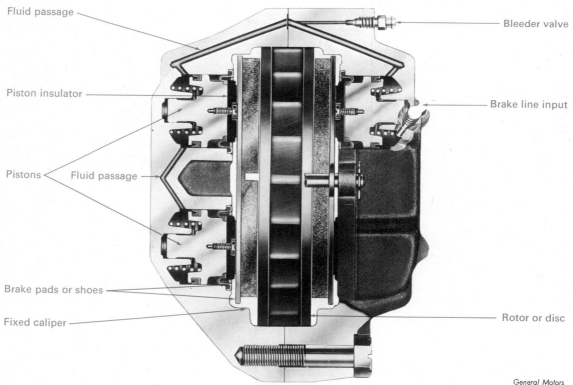

General Motors

Fig. 16:60 Disc Brake Assembly—Fixed Caliper with Four Pistons

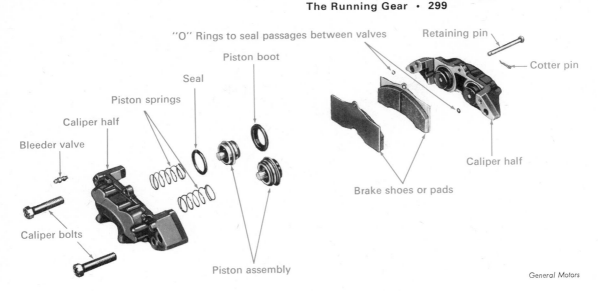

Fig. 16:61   Exploded View of Fixed Caliper

disc brakes apply pressure against *both sides* of the rotating member, as they do on bicycles. The rotating member is called the *rotor*, or, with reference to its shape, the *brake disc*. Typically, disc brakes use small lining areas under very

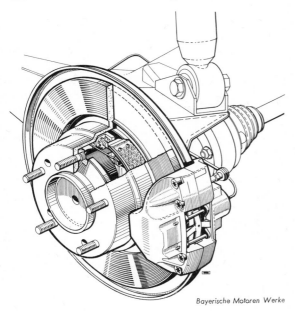

Fig. 16:62   Sectional View of a Rear Disc Brake—Non-vented, Two-piston, Fixed Caliper Type. Note emergency brake in centre and independent suspension.

high pressures, while drum brakes employ relatively large lining areas under lower pressures. Another advantage of disc brakes is that they are self-adjusting without the need of added devices; they rarely pull to one side because there is no self-energizing action or servo-action, and water and dirt are thrown off the rotor faces owing to centrifugal forces.

The reason that disc brakes require no adjustments to compensate for lining wear lies in the fact that the brake pads have no retracting springs. The design and elasticity of the caliper seals is such that they have some retracting action of their own. The pads must always remain in very light contact with the discs.[75] With the large hydraulic pistons used, the slightest clearance between the pads and the rotor would otherwise drastically increase the travel of the brake pedal. Some pads have a small metal tab that touches the disc when the linings are worn thin. This produces a scraping sound that warns the driver to replace the brake pads. Other disc brake systems may even set off a warning light.

There are two basic disc brake designs: the *fixed caliper type* and the *floating caliper type*. With the fixed caliper type, each brake pad is activated independently, as they are on some bicycles. The cross-section in Fig. 16:60 illus-

---

[75]The clearance is roughly 0.005" (0.13 mm).

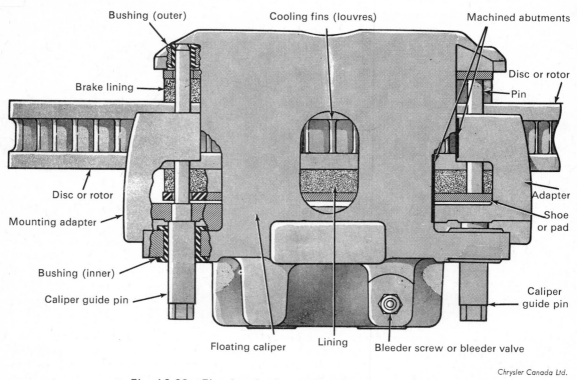

Bushing (outer)

Cooling fins (louvres)

Machined abutments

Brake lining

Disc or rotor

Pin

Disc or rotor

Mounting adapter

Adapter

Shoe or pad

Bushing (inner)

Caliper guide pin

Caliper guide pin

Floating caliper

Lining

Bleeder screw or bleeder valve

Chrysler Canada Ltd.

Fig. 16:63 Floating Caliper Assembly (sectional view)

trates clearly how the inner and outer brake pads are pushed against the rotor by four hydraulic pistons mounted in a fixed caliper. The caliper that straddles the disc is bolted rigidly to the steering knuckle or to the rear axle housing. Where independent suspension is used, the caliper may be attached to the differential assembly housing (Fig. 9:8, inboard disc brake) or to the suspension system (Fig. 16:62, outboard disc brake). Note that the hub of the rear disc in Fig. 16:62 forms a small brake drum for the emergency brake shoes. A fixed caliper is shown fully dismantled in Fig. 16:61.

The *floating-caliper-type disc brake* (Figs. 16:63 and 16:64) could be compared to a C-clamp. The workpiece represents the rotor, and the clamp represents the floating caliper. Even though only one side of the C-clamp is movable in relation to the clamp frame, the workpiece gets squeezed from both sides. The same principle also applies to floating-caliper disc brakes, as they require only one or two hydraulic pistons on the inboard side of the

caliper (Fig. 16:64). The floating action of the caliper is made possible by the two *caliper guide pins* (Fig. 16:63). So-called *sliding calipers* have slide rails machined into them that allow them to move sidewards without the use of guide pins. The advantages of the floating, or sliding, calipers are obvious: the design is simple, there is more room for the wheel rim, and the brake is not quite as sensitive to lateral run-out of the rotor.

While the disc brake illustrated in Fig. 16:62 is of the *non-vented* type, those shown in Figs. 16:63 and 16:64 are equipped with *vented rotors* to dissipate the heat generated during braking. (Disc brakes can actually get red hot!) The louvres of these rotors are essentially fan blades that draw fresh air from the hub area between the rotor cheeks and then throw the hot air outwards as the wheel spins around (Fig. 16:64). The impeller action of a water pump is very similar. Vented rotors also seem to be less prone to brake squeal, a real problem with earlier designs. This squeal is caused by a high-frequency vibration in the disc. The piston

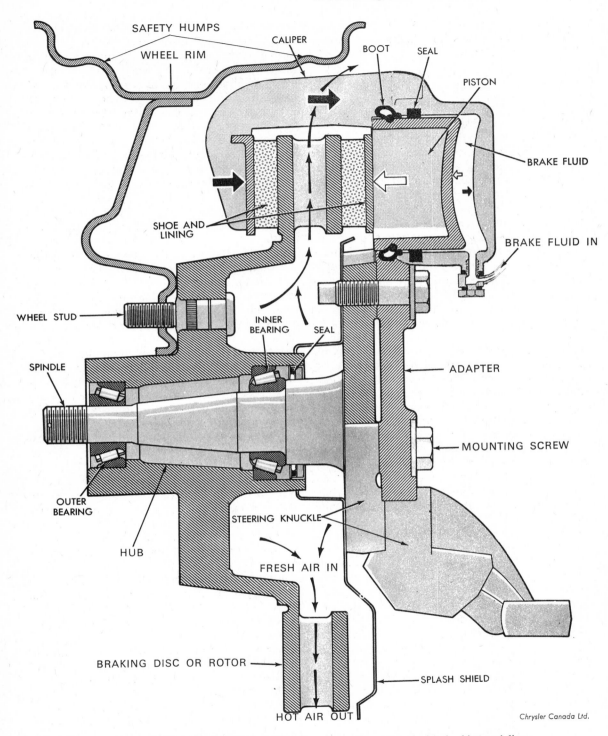

SAFETY HUMPS

WHEEL RIM

CALIPER

BOOT

SEAL

PISTON

BRAKE FLUID

BRAKE FLUID IN

SHOE AND LINING

WHEEL STUD

INNER BEARING

SEAL

ADAPTER

SPINDLE

MOUNTING SCREW

OUTER BEARING

STEERING KNUCKLE

HUB

FRESH AIR IN

BRAKING DISC OR ROTOR

SPLASH SHIELD

HOT AIR OUT

Chrysler Canada Ltd.

Fig. 16:64 Front Disc Brake Assembly—Floating Type (sectional view). Note airflow between the rotor cheeks.

insulator (Fig. 16:60) not only keeps the heat away from the brake fluid, but also dampens these vibrations.

General Brake Information

Brake linings used on drum brakes are either riveted or bonded to the brake shoe by a special process. Most service centres replace worn linings by installing a complete front and/or rear set of factory-reconditioned brake shoes. The replacement of single shoes is considered bad practice, as it often causes the brakes to pull to one side. Disc brake pads are replaced with new ones. Scored or warped drums or discs can be refinished on a lathe or with a special sander, but the amount of material removed must be within specifications. If one drum or disc is refinished, the one on the opposite side, even if in good condition, should be refinished as well to prevent brake pull to one side.

Because of the very high pressures involved, defective brake lines must be replaced with specified steel lines. They are tinned to prevent corrosion. The lines should be kept away from hot parts, especially the exhaust system, to prevent the formation of compressible vapour bubbles. Only steel fittings and double flares (page 203) are to be used. Flexible brake lines made of a very tough, nylon-reinforced rubber are employed between the frame and the moving suspension members (Fig. 16:9). While flexible brake lines are designed to move, they will fail if stretched. The full suspension and steering travel must therefore be considered when installing a new line!

A low but firm pedal is usually the result of improper brake shoe adjustment, excessive free play, or a defect in one of the hydraulic circuits. A spongy brake pedal indicates air in the hydraulic system and distorted or badly fitting parts. A brake pedal that goes slowly down to the floor is a sign of a leak (defective seals, fittings, brake lines, worn master cylinder or wheel cylinders, etc.). A vibrating pedal is typical of warped brake drums or discs.

If the vehicle pulls to one side when the brakes are applied, the cause may be one or more of many reasons. Only the most common reasons can be mentioned: worn or fouled linings (dirt, oil, grease, brake fluid, water, condensation, etc.); scored or newly machined drums; improper installation of parts (reversed primary and secondary brake shoes); seized wheel cylinder pistons; and excessive braking, causing fading. If either the front or the rear wheels lock up, the proportioning valve should be checked; if they stay locked up, there is probably insufficient free play in the brake pedal. This prevents the master cylinder pistons from clearing the compensating ports. To obtain the correct clearance, the master cylinder push rod should be adjusted. The push rod is either threaded for this purpose (Fig. 16:48), or the pivot connecting it to the brake lever is an adjustable eccentric.

None of the hydraulic members, especially the seals and rubber cups, should be exposed to ordinary cleaning fluids. Only brake fluid or recommended solvents should be used for cleaning. Hydraulic brake fluids are special liquids with a high boiling point (above 370°F, or 188°C) that are formulated to preserve and lubricate the parts of the hydraulic system. Special silicone-type brake fluid must not be mixed with the regular type. Silicone fluids have less affinity for moisture, they possess good lubricity, and they have an even higher boiling point than the regular type.

When replacing master cylinders, care must be taken to install the proper type. For example, master cylinders on drum brakes use two residual pressure valves; those on mixed brake systems use only one for the rear; and those on disc brakes use none at all, since they employ different seals and are not equipped with retracting springs. Disc brakes require master cylinder reservoirs of increased capacity, as wear on the pad linings causes the larger pistons to draw considerably more fluid.

The repair or replacement of any part in the hydraulic system requires "bleeding", that is, the removal of trapped air through the bleeder valves.

Because of the safety hazards involved, the repair and service of brake systems must be carried out under the close supervision of qualified persons only.

The discussion of vacuum-assisted power brakes is beyond the scope of this text. Well-illustrated descriptions of these systems are given in most service manuals.

RECOMMENDED ASSIGNMENTS

1. (a) What is independent front suspension?
   (b) What advantages are claimed for it?
2. Give two reasons why the front suspension arms are of unequal length.
3. Explain the purpose and operation of the stabilizer bar.
4. (a) What is the function of the centre bolt?
   (b) Why is the term misleading?
5. Name and describe briefly three common types of automotive springs.
6. Explain the function of the shock absorber.
7. A shock absorber has a 3:1 ratio. What does this mean?
8. (a) What is steering ratio?
   (b) What are its two purposes?
9. Name four types of steering gears and describe the differences between them.
10. List two important steering gear checks.
11. Explain the purposes of (a) the tie-rod ends and (b) the tie-rod sleeves.
12. Define the terms (a) steering axis and (b) scrub radius.
13. Explain both the meaning and the purpose of the following: (a) camber, (b) steering axis inclination, (c) positive caster, (d) negative caster, (e) toe-in, (f) toe-out on turns, and (g) steering stops.
14. What are the following: (a) track width, (b) wheel base, (c) oversteer, and (d) understeer?
15. What are the most common signs of improper wheel alignment?
16. Explain the purpose of (a) the drop-centre and (b) the rim humps.
17. What factors affect tire temperatures?
18. (a) Explain, by means of simple sketches if necessary, three types of ply structures.
    (b) What are the advantages of two of these designs?
19. Why should tires of different ply designs never be installed on the same vehicle?
20. (a) What is the difference between the ply number and the ply rating?
    (b) What does the term "load range" signify?
21. Explain the following tire specifications: (a) 8.25 × 15, 78 series, and (b) GR 70-15.
22. List five possible areas where air leakage may cause a loss of tire pressure.
23. Name six important precautions related to the maintenance and repair of tires.
24. What conditions may be indicated by abnormal tread patterns?
25. List and explain four conditions that should be checked during a wheel balance.
26. What causes brake fading?
27. Why should the locking of wheels be avoided when applying the brakes?
28. Explain why modern hydraulic brake systems are of the "split" type.
29. The brake pedal lever ratio is 5:1; the bore of the master cylinder is 1"; the caliper piston is 2" in diameter; and the applied foot pressure is 100 lb. Calculate the following: (a) the lever force applied to the master cylinder piston, (b) the hydraulic pressure in the brake system, and (c) the output force of the caliper piston.
30. What is the function of each of the following: (a) the compensating ports, (b) the breather ports, (c) the small holes in the master cylinder pistons, (d) the residual pressure valves, and (e) the reservoir diaphragm?
31. (a) How would a ruptured front or rear brake line affect the operation of the brake master cylinder?
    (b) Name four signs that would indicate such a failure.
32. What is the purpose of the bleeder valves on wheel cylinders, calipers, and some master cylinders?
33. List the functions of (a) the hydraulic system safety switch, (b) the proportioning valve, and (c) the metering valve.
34. Explain the difference between self-energizing action and servo-action.
35. How do disc brakes compensate for lining wear?
36. Explain why caliper pistons have larger head areas than wheel cylinder pistons.
37. Name two important differences between a master cylinder used for drum brakes and one used for disc brakes.
38. Why must the disc pads remain in light contact with the rotors even with the brake pedal released?
39. What are the main differences between a fixed-caliper and a floating-caliper disc brake?
40. What precautions apply when (a) replacing brake shoes, (b) replacing brake lines,

and (c) cleaning hydraulic parts?

41. (a) What is the purpose of the free play in the brake pedal?

(b) How much should it be?

(c) How is it adjusted?

(d) What are the effects of insufficient free play in the brake pedal?

42. (a) How could air enter the hydraulic system?

(b) What effects would it have?

TROUBLE-SHOOTING

The number of possible causes is given in brackets.

1. The outer tread ribs of the front tires are badly worn. (2)

2. Without the brakes being applied, a car pulls badly towards one side. (several possibilities)

3. After the brakes are applied several times in succession, they no longer release, and the stop light stays on. (2)

4. A motorist replaces the brake linings on his car. During a road test he applies the brakes and the vehicle pulls sharply to one side. (several possibilities)

5. Under light to medium foot pressure, the brake pedal goes slowly right down to the toe board; yet under heavy pressure it holds up well. (2)

6. After two very good tires of correct size have been installed and the tire pressure in all four wheels has been checked, the car feels as if it is being driven on a slippery road. (1)

7. Even though only the hydraulic circuit in the front has been ruptured, the brake pedal goes right down to the toe board. (several possibilities)

Appendices

Weights and Measures

English Measure		Metric Equivalents

Length

1 inch (in.)	=	25.40 millimetres (mm) or 2.54 centimetres (cm)
12 inches = 1 foot (ft.)	=	30.48 centimetres (cm)
3 feet = 1 yard (yd.)	=	0.914 metre (m)
5,280 feet = 1 mile (mi.)	=	1.6093 kilometres (km)

Volume (Liquid)

1 imperial ounce (oz.)	=	28.4 cubic centimetres (cm³) or 28.4 millilitres (ml)
20 imperial ounces = 1 imperial pint (pt.)	=	0.57 litre (ℓ)
2 imperial pints = 1 imperial quart (qt.)	=	1.14 litres
4 imperial quarts = 1 imperial gallon (gal.)	=	4.55 litres
26.34 imperial gallons = 1 barrel	=	120 litres
1 U.S. ounce	=	29.57 cubic centimetres or 29.57 millilitres
16 U.S. ounces = 1 U.S. pint	=	0.47 litre
2 U.S. pints = 1 U.S. quart	=	0.95 litre
4 U.S. quarts = 1 U.S. gallon	=	3.97 litres

Note: The correct symbol for cubic centimetre(s) is now cm³, although the symbols cc and ccm are still used in some publications.

Weight

1 ounce (oz.)	=	28.35 grams (g)
16 ounces = 1 pound (lb.)	=	453.6 grams or 0.4536 kilogram (kg)
2,000 pounds = 1 short ton	=	907 kilograms
2,240 pounds = 1 long ton	=	1016 kilograms

Temperature

1 degree Fahrenheit (°F)	=	$\frac{5}{9}$ degree Celsius (°C)
freezing point of water =	32°F =	0°C
boiling point of water =	212°F =	100°C

To convert a Fahrenheit temperature to Celsius, subtract 32 and multiply the remainder by $\frac{5}{9}$.

Pressure

Atmospheric pressure at sea level = 14.7 pounds per square inch (psi)
= 100 kilopascals (kPa) (approximately)
= 1.03 kilograms per square centimetre (kg/cm³)

Note: The correct SI metric unit is the kilopascal. 1 kPa = 6.89 psi
The unit kilograms per square centimetre (kg/cm²) will no longer be used.
A vacuum of 1 Hg (one inch of mercury) = 0.5 psi or 3.39 kPa below atmospheric pressure.

Torque

1 pound-inch (lb.-in.) = .083 pound-foot (lb.-ft.) = 1.356 newton metres (N·m)
= 0.138 kilogram metre (kg·m)
12 pound-inches = 1 pound-foot = 16.27 newton metres
= 1.56 kilogram metres

Note: The units pound-inch and pound-foot are often written as inch-pound (in.-lb.) and
foot-pound (ft.-lb.), even though, strictly speaking, the latter terms should only be used
to express work and power (see below).
The correct SI metric unit is the newton metre (N·m).

Power

1 horsepower (hp) = 550 foot-pounds (ft.-lb.) per second or 33,000 foot-pounds per minute =
0.746 kilowatt (kW)
1 watt = 1 volt (V) × 1 ampere (A)

Metric Measure   English Equivalents

Linear

1 millimetre (mm)	= 0.0394 inches (in.)
10 millimetres = 1 centimetre (cm)	= 0.3937 inches
100 centimetres = 1 metre (m)	= 39.37 inches or 3.281 feet (ft.) or 1.0936 yards (yd.)
1000 metres = 1 kilometre (km)	= 3,281 feet or 0.62137 miles (mi.)

Volume

1 millilitre (ml)   = 0.0352 imperial ounce (oz.) = 0.0338 U.S. fluid ounces (fl. oz.)

1000 millilitres = 1 litre (ℓ) = 1.760 imperial pints (1 pt.) = 0.880 imperial quarts (qt.)
                                                                     = 0.220 imperial gallons (gal.)
                              = 2.114 U.S. pints = 1.057 U.S. quarts = 0.264 U.S. gallons
1 cubic centimetre (cm³) = 0.61 cubic inches (cu. in.)
1000 cubic centimetres = 1 litre = 61.025 cubic inches

Mass (Weight)

1 gram (g)	= 0.353 ounce (oz.)
1000 grams = 1 kilogram (kg)	= 2.205 pounds (lb.)
1000 kilograms	= 1 tonne (t) = 2205 pounds = 1.10 short tons

Note : The mass of 1 cm³ of water at 4°C is 1 g. The mass of a substance compared with the mass of an equal volume of water at the same temperature is called its relative density (or specific gravity). For example, an electrolyte sample of 1.270 is that many times heavier than water.

Temperature

1° Celsius (°C)   = 1.8° Fahrenheit (°F)
freezing point of water =   0°C =   32°F
boiling point of water = 100°C = 212°F

To convert a Celsius temperature to Fahrenheit degrees, multiply by ⁹/₅ and add 32.

Pressure

1 kilopascal (kPa) = 0.145 pound per square inch (psi)
                           = 0.295 inches of mercury (Hg)

Torque

1 newton metre (N·m) = 0.1024 kilogram metre (kg·m) = 0.7375621 pound-foot (lb.-ft.)
1 kilogram metre   = 9.762 newton metres   = 7.235 pound-feet

Note : The newton metre (N·m) is the SI unit to be used for torque.

Power

1 watt (W) = 1 volt (V) × 1 ampere (A)
1000 watts   = 1 kilowatt (kW)
1 kilowatt   = 1.34 horsepower (hp)

Decimal Equivalents

1/64	.015625	33/64	.515625
1/32	.03125	17/32	.53125
3/64	.046875	35/64	.546875
1/16	.0625	9/16	.5625
5/64	.078125	37/64	.578125
3/32	.09375	19/32	.59375
7/64	.109375	39/64	.609375
1/8	.125	5/8	.625
9/64	.140625	41/64	.640625
5/32	.15625	21/32	.65625
11/64	.171875	43/64	.671875
3/16	.1875	11/16	.6875
13/64	.203125	45/64	.703125
7/32	.21875	23/32	.71875
15/64	.234375	47/64	.734375
1/4	.25	3/4	.75
17/64	.265625	49/64	.765625
9/32	.28125	25/32	.78125
19/64	.296875	51/64	.796875
5/16	.3125	13/16	.8125
21/64	.328125	53/64	.828125
11/32	.34375	27/32	.84375
23/64	.359375	55/64	.859375
3/8	.375	7/8	.875
25/64	.390625	57/64	.890625
23/32	.40625	29/32	.90625
27/64	.421875	59/64	.921875
7/16	.4375	15/16	.9375
29/64	.453125	61/64	.953125
15/32	.46875	31/32	.96875
31/64	.484375	63/64	.984375
1/2	.5	1	

Index

57 67 77 87 97 08 18 28 38 BP 9 8 7 6 5 4 3 2 1

FIRST AID CHART

First Aid is the immediate and temporary care given to the victim of an accident or sudden illness. Its purpose is to preserve life, assist recovery, and prevent aggravation of the condition, until the services of a doctor can be obtained.

ARTIFICIAL RESPIRATION

Casualties who have stopped breathing from drowning, electric shock, poisons, etc., should be given mouth-to-mouth resuscitation. Make sure the mouth and throat are free of obstruction. Lift the neck, tilt the head, and blow into the victim's mouth about every five seconds. If head injuries make this impossible, use the Revised Sylvester Method.

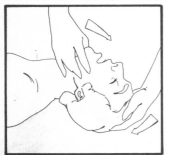

MOUTH-TO-MOUTH RESUSCITATION

REVISED SYLVESTER

POISON

Inhaling carbon monoxide fumes released by the exhaust pipe of an automobile can be fatal. Never leave a car engine running in a closed garage. If your car breaks down in cold weather, don't sit with the engine running unless one car window is open.

If a poisonous substance has been swallowed, get the casualty to hospital IMMEDIATELY. Casualties who have stopped breathing from inhaling poisonous gases must be given mouth-to-mouth resuscitation AT ONCE. First, if the accident occurs inside, open doors and windows to let in fresh air or take the casualty outside. Lift the neck, tilt the head, and blow into the victim's mouth about every five seconds. If head injuries make this impossible, use the Revised Sylvester Method.